The thought of the period 1780–1830 was dominated by the issues of foreign wars and social change more completely than ever before in English history. It is quite wrong to suppose that the Romantics were "beautiful and ineffectual angels beating in the void their luminous wings in vain". They were deeply concerned with social and political questions, and above all with the problems of liberty, and their comments on political and social questions were often acute and statesmanlike. The issues of democracy and "Jacobinism" were faced for the first time since the seventeenth century, and the principles of political liberty formulated anew. A review of the thoughts of such men as Blake, Wordsworth, Coleridge, Southey, Shelley, Keats and Byron makes it easy to see why England escaped revolution in these years. Yet none of them was a mere reactionary. It is significant that Wordsworth rejected the landscaping of the age of Capability Brown, not on aesthetic but on social grounds, that it gave a false importance to the landed aristocracy. Romanticism was a complex movement involving a new view of society, a new attitude to history and a new aesthetic experience in what has been called the Age of the Picturesque, and it is the theme of this book to explore its nature.

This volume is part of a new series, *History and Literature*, of which the author is the General Editor.

Romanticism and
the Social Order 1780-1830

Romanticism and the Social Order 1780-1830

R. W. HARRIS

*Head of the History Department
and Master of Studies in the
King's School, Canterbury*

BARNES AND NOBLE INC.
PUBLISHERS, BOOKSELLERS
SINCE 1873

First published 1969

© Blandford Press Ltd

Published in the United States by Barnes & Noble, Inc.

Printed in Great Britain

Contents

ACKNOWLEDGEMENTS

Acknowledgement is due to the following for their kind permission to reproduce photographs:

Nos. 6 and 7 reproduced by gracious permission of H.M. the Queen
British Museum, Nos. 19, 20, 22, 23, 24
Country Life Ltd., Nos. 16, 18
Crown Copyright, reproduced by permission of the Rt. Hon. Mr. Speaker, No. 3
National Galleries of Scotland, No. 5
National Portrait Gallery, London, Nos. 1, 2, 21, 25
Radio Times Hulton Picture Library, No. 15
Royal Institute of British Architects, No. 17
The Royal Pavilion, Brighton, Nos. 13, 14
The Tate Gallery, London, No. 10
Victoria and Albert Museum, Nos. 4, 8, 9, 11, 12

List of Illustrations

1 : Introduction : The Age of Romanticism

In the period 1780–1830 there was much in English life and thought which was simply a continuation of the earlier eighteenth century. Beau Brummel would not have found it difficult to have adapted himself to the age of Beau Nash, the patrons of Henry Holland to the architecture of William Kent and the Palladians, or Francis Jeffrey to the world of Addison and Pope. Yet there were changes of thought and attitude after 1780 which were both crucial and fundamental, and it is clear that they were intimately connected with the political and social changes of the time.

The loss of the American colonies, and still more the defeat by France in 1783, were shocks to national pride, and within a decade Britain was again embarked on a war with France which was to last for virtually twenty-two years. Both the American and the French Wars began in some sense as wars of ideas, and during their course not only was national existence at times at stake, but political values were questioned or defended with a new determination and clarity. Political issues again became fundamental as they had not been since 1714, with the assertion of radicalism on the one hand, and the defence of conservatism on the other. It was not simply that England came under the influence of foreign revolutionary ideas, but that with the rapid growth of population, urbanisation, trade disloaticons and periodic famines, social misery was such as to breed discontent and revolt, while among the governing classes there was a mixture of fear, misgivings and social conscience. The magnitude of the problem was so enormous that it would be fair to say that no contemporary either fully understood it, or had an adequate solution for it, but at least there was no lack of attempts at both, and there were few writers of the period who were not touched by it, for the seriousness of the problem burnt itself upon the minds of all who thought about it.

On the one hand there was the emergence of radical and socialist thought which, although often drawing sustenance from the American and French Revolutions, was primarily a native product. Its first manifestations were demands for parliamentary reform. 'Parliamentary reform' might mean many things; it might mean the end of royal patronage, or the increase of the representation of country gentlemen in parliament, or the abolition of rotten boroughs, or it might mean votes for all adult men, but there was always the underlying idea that it would end the corruption and inefficiencies of government revealed during the American War. The reformers were divided among themselves, and many were cured of their desire for change by the onset of the French Revolution. As for the extremists, Tom Paine was their mentor, and British Jacobinism became a considerable force in the seventeen-nineties. Radicalism also included those Dissenters and Roman Catholics (the latter chiefly in Ireland) who demanded the end of religious disabilities; and socialists like Thomas Spence and Robert Owen, who advocated the end of either land-ownership or capitalism, or both. William Cobbett, as we shall see, was a radical of a special kind, seeking by means of a parliamentary democracy to save the individuality of workers and peasants threatened by the three-fold Leviathan of government, enclosures and capitalism. Specific radical achievements in the period were few, but the general effect, after a period of reaction, was to produce a working-class consciousness and an atmosphere favourable to the reforms of the eighteen-twenties, and the great Reform Act of 1832.

Equally in reaction to the social problems of the time, a great seriousness swept over an important part of the nation, a deep concern for morality, an acute sense of guilt and sin, on both a personal and a national level, requiring a re-examination of personal and social morality, and accompanied by an urgent sense of the need for a return to religion. The Evangelicals made a deep imprint upon the thought of the period, and indeed did much to shape the character of Victorian England. Opposed as they were to most of the ideas of the radicals, they nonetheless were passionately desirous of such reforms as would encourage social morality, and thus Evangelicalism was a powerful influence in education, factory reform, and the abolition of the slave trade. Evangelicals for the most part rejected the principles of individualism which underlay radical thought, and were thus entirely opposed to parliamentary reform. They feared any attack upon the social structure, but wished to replace the selfish instincts which underlay *laissez-faire* principles by a new code of social morality based upon a more personal Christianity. To many radicals such talk appeared mere humbug, yet in some respects the instincts of the Evangelicals were wise, for they were more likely to carry reforms which did not seem to threaten the social order than those which did.

Closely connected with a renewed sense of social cohesion, and consequently new view of the nature of society, was a new sense of the importance of history and of organic growth. The Neo-Platonic tradition of European thought had been inimical to the study of history, and eighteenth-century rationalists had found it easy to dismiss the whole historical process as falling into a simple three-fold pattern: (1) the classical age of Greece and Rome; (2) mediaeval darkness and superstition; and, finally, (3) the coming of the Enlightenment. But with the retreat from the worship of Reason, which was a marked feature of eighteenth-century English thought, there was a greater disposition to study the past for its own sake, and to see it as an organic process. David Hume pointed the way,[1] Edmund Burke provided the philosophical accompaniment, and Sir Walter Scott provided the romantic nostalgia. It is perhaps curious that England between the time of Hume and Gibbon on the one hand, and Macaulay, Carlyle and Stubbs on the other, did not produce a first-class historian. Perhaps the writing of history flourishes best in more settled times than those of 1780–1830; but Burke and the influence of German philosophy did much to bring about a greater sense of continuity and of the evolutionary nature of a society and nation, and this in turn had profound influence on the formation of political consciousness. Wordsworth, for instance, after 1808 was greatly influenced by a new sense of history.

Before we turn to the nature of Romanticism, we might illustrate some of the characteristics of the period already mentioned from the writings of George Crabbe who, in 1783, a year after he had been appointed chaplain to the Duke of Rutland (through the influence of Edmund Burke), published his poem *The Village*. Crabbe's sombre view of society was part of that great wave of seriousness and manifestation of social conscience of which we have spoken, and which was most clearly seen in the life and works of William Wilberforce and the Evangelicals. In other respects Crabbe was fully in the eighteenth-century tradition. His interest in the life of the lower classes was reminiscent of Defoe, and his real compassion for poverty came nearest to that of Dr. Johnson. He had a strict religious and moral code, although he disliked religious enthusiasm. He was a lover of the countryside, a student of botany and natural history; but above all he was a student of human nature. He was not a social reformer, and he had no political axe to grind. He did not rail against enclosures, or blame the landowners, and seemed scarcely aware of the existence of an industrial revolution. Want and hardship were facts of nature, and must be borne; life did have occasional pleasures, but they were only temporary relief from pain:

> For what is Pleasure, that we toil to gain?
> 'Tis but a slow or rapid flight from Pain.

He in no way shared the Romantic attitude to nature; to him it was not a subject for mysticism, but merely a relentless repetition against which men played out their lives. Where however he differed from much of eighteenth-century writing was that, as his art matured, he was more interested in individuals and idio-syncrasies than in social or moral types, and his art was thus closer to that of the novelist than to that of Pope. However, in his compassion for the sufferings of rustic life he was clearly close to Wordsworth.

Devoted as he was to the poetry of Pope, Crabbe had"seen too much of the harsh realities of rustic life to tolerate the idyllic themes of shepherds and shepherdesses in pastoral poetry:

> Yes, thus the Muses sing of happy swains,
> Because the Muses never knew their pains.

Crabbe knew better; he had seen too much of poverty to idealise it:

> By such examples taught, I paint the Cot,
> As Truth will paint it, and as Bards will not.

Poetry was poor compensation for cold and hunger when poets failed to recognise that famine was a frequent experience in the lives of country-folk:

> . . . these are scenes where Nature's niggard hand
> Gave a spare portion to the famish'd land;
> Hers is the fault, if here mankind complain
> Of fruitless toil and labour spent in vain;
> But yet in other scenes more fair to view,
> When Plenty smiles—alas! she smiles for few—
> And those who taste not, yet behold her store,
> Are as the slaves that dig the golden ore—
> The wealth around them makes them doubly poor.

Country life was not a story of rustic contentment, but of an endless routine of labour from dawn to dark, in heat and cold, until age and sickness reduced men and women to penury, the poor-house and the grave.

> No longer truth, though shown in verse, disdain,
> But own the Village Life a life of pain.

Crabbe made a deep impact upon contemporaries. Jeffrey praised him highly: 'Mr. Crabbe exhibits the common people of England pretty much as they are, and as they must appear to every one who will take the trouble of examining into their condition. . . . He shows us something which we have all seen, or may see, in real life; and draws from it such feelings and such reflections as every human being must acknowledge that it is calculated to excite.' The *Edinburgh Review* in 1807 declared: 'There is a truth and a force in these descriptions of rural life, which is calculated to

sink deep into the memory; and, being confirmed by daily observation, they are recalled upon innumerable occasions when the
ideal pictures of more fanciful authors have lost all their interest.'
To the 'vulgar impression' that Crabbe was a gloomy poet, the
Quarterly Review in 1834 replied that this was because of the deep
impression made by 'that exquisitely-finished, but heart-sickening
description' of the Poor-house in *The Village*. As this passage was
the forerunner of so many similar descriptions in nineteenth-
century literature it is worth quoting, at least in part.

> Theirs is yon House that holds the parish poor,
> Whose walls of mud scarce bear the broken door;
> There, where the putrid vapours, flagging, play
> And the dull wheel hums doleful through the day;
> There children dwell who know no parents' care;
> Parents, who knew no children's love, dwell there!
> Heart-broken matrons on their joyless bed,
> Forsaken wives, and mothers never wed;
> Dejected widows with unheeded tears,
> And crippled age with more than childhood fears;
> The lame, the blind, and, far the happiest they!
> The moping idiot, and the madman gay.

It was a grim picture, and one which touched the conscience of
the age. It was to be echoed in a long succession of writers from
Coleridge and Cobbett to Carlyle and the Chartists; but unlike
them Crabbe called for no specific social remedies. All he asked
was for great human compassion from those whose lot in life was
happier. As he wrote in his Preface to *The Borough*: 'It has always
been held as a salutary exercise of the mind, to contemplate the
evils and miseries of our nature: ... It ties and binds us to all
mankind by sensations common to us all, and in some degree
connects us, without degradation, even to the most miserable and
guilty of our fellow-men.'

Hazlitt did not enjoy Crabbe's poetry: 'His song is one sad
reality, one unraised, unvaried note of unavailing woe.' Yet he had
to admit that 'Mr. Crabbe is one of the most popular and admired
of our living authors. That he is so can be accounted for on no

other principle than the strong ties that bind us to the world about us, and our involuntary yearnings after whatever in any manner powerfully and directly reminds us of it.' (*The Spirit of the Age*.) Hazlitt dated a change of taste from the last years of Dr. Johnson's life, about the date of Crabbe's first poem. 'We cannot help thinking that a taste for the sort of poetry which leans for support on the truth and fidelity of its imitations of nature, began to display itself much about that time, and, in a good measure, in consequence of the direction of the public taste to the subject of painting.' Instead of the ideal world of the classical scholar, there was now a taste for the existing world. 'Thus an admirer of Teniers or Hobbima might think little of the pastoral sketches of Pope or Goldsmith; even Thomson described not so much the naked object as what he sees in his mind's eye, surrounded and glowing with the mild, bland, genial vapours of his brain; but the adept in Dutch interiors, hovels, and pigsties must find in Mr. Crabbe a man after his own heart. . . . Pope describes what is striking, Crabbe would have described merely what was there.' Crabbe regarded his poetry in the same light, and as directly comparable with painting. He accepted Sir Joshua Reynolds' view that 'the artist who takes an accurate likeness of individuals, or a faithful representation, may not rank so high in the public estimation as one who paints an historical event, or an heroic action; but he is nevertheless a painter, and his accuracy is so far from diminishing his reputation, that it procures for him in general both fame and emolument: nor is it perhaps with strict justice determined that the credit and reputation of those verses which strongly and faithfully delineate character and manners, should be lessened in the opinion of the public by the very accuracy which gives value and distinction to the productions of the pencil'. (Preface to *Tales*.) Crabbe regarded his art of story-telling as strictly in the tradition of Chaucer. In 1816 Mary Leadbeater wrote to ask him whether his characters were 'really existing creatures'. Crabbe replied: 'There is not one of whom I had not in my mind the original. . . . Indeed, I do not know that I could paint merely from my own fancy; and there is no cause why we should. Is there not diversity sufficient in society? and who can go, even but a little, into the assemblies of our fellow-wanderers from the way of perfect rectitude, and not find characters so varied and so pointed, that he need not call upon his imagination?' (*Life and Poems*, 1834, I, p. 234.) The result was often a vivid picture of contemporary life.

Like Crabbe, the young Wordsworth and Coleridge were acutely aware of the hardships suffered by the poor. Wordsworth, who had had to fight a difficult legal case to gain possession of his small patrimony from the hands of the first Earl of Lonsdale, was very much aware of the oppressive weight of the aristocracy upon the countryside, and of the sufferings of the poor in times of unemployment and famine. For a time, as we shall see, they toyed with Jacobin and Godwinian ideas. But when they met some of the republican leaders of the time, men like Thelwall and Horne Tooke, they were soon cured of their republicanism. Coleridge wrote in 1801: 'The professed Democrats, who on an occasion of uproar would press forward to be the Leaders, are without knowledge, talents or morals. I have conversed with the most celebrated among them; more gross, ignorant, and perverted men I never wish to see again!—O it would have made you, my friend! "a sadder and a wiser man" if you had been with me at one of Horne Tooke's public Dinners! I could never discover by any train of Questions that any of these Lovers of Liberty had either a distinct *object* for their Wishes, or distinct views of the *means*.' The transition in the thought of Wordsworth and Coleridge will be the theme of later chapters, and is part of the evolution of Romanticism, and it is with the nature of Romanticism that we shall be concerned in the remainder of this chapter.

The word 'romantic' seems first to have come into use in England about the middle of the seventeenth century, when it meant 'having the wild or exciting qualities of mediaeval romances'. In the eighteenth century it might be used as a term of abuse, implying what was irrational, as when Dr. Johnson wrote of 'romantic absurdities', but it was also sometimes used to describe a scene, such as a moonlit landscape, which aroused pleasurable sensations of mystery and loneliness. Rousseau used it in this latter sense. It was the Germans who first used 'romantic' as an opposite of 'classical'. They rejected the philosophy of the

Enlightenment, with its assumption that this was a rational universe in which all problems had a rational answer, and they sought to explore the irrational, to discover a meaning on a deeper level than was explored by science. They found a deeper significance in history, and they explored the irrational forces which governed human actions. In England the conflict between the romantic and the classical was less marked, because the fundamentals of classical thought had been eroded more thoroughly by the empiricism of the eighteenth century. Yet in England, too, Wordsworth accompanied his poetical experiments with an attack upon Pope, and Burke jeered at the philosophy of Bolingbroke with his rhetorical question, 'Who now reads Bolingbroke?'

The Romantic poets sought to give new dimensions both to nature and the human mind. Coleridge suggested that there was a two-fold approach to the problem. Commenting on the composition of the *Lyrical Ballads*, he wrote: 'It was agreed that my efforts should be directed to persons and characters supernatural, or at least romantic, yet so as to transfer from our inward nature a human interest and a semblance of truth sufficient to procure for these shadows of imagination that willing suspension of disbelief for the moment which constitutes poetic faith. Mr. Wordsworth, on the other hand, was to propose to himself as his object to give the charm of novelty to things of every day, and to excite a feeling analogous to the supernatural, by awakening the mind's attention from the lethargy of custom and directing it to the loveliness and the wonders of the world before us: an inexhaustible treasure, but for which, in consequence of the film of familiarity and selfish solicitude, we have eyes yet see not, ears that hear not, and hearts that neither feel nor understand.' These were not however two separate operations, but different aspects of the same exploration of the 'inward nature' of which Coleridge wrote. In a sense however Coleridge's attitude was the more completely 'romantic' because he was dealing more directly with the faculty of the imagination. De Quincey noted this when in his *Lake Reminiscences* he commented:

Coleridge himself most beautifully insists upon and illustrates the truth that all which we find in nature must be created by ourselves: and that alike whether nature is so gorgeous in her beauty as to seem apparelled in her wedding-garment, or so powerless and extinct as to seem palled in her shroud:

> 'O Lady, we receive but what we give
> And in *our* life alone does nature live . . .
> I may not hope from *outward* forms to win
> The passion and the life whose fountains are *within*.'

Wordsworth on the other hand was more conscious of the existence of a spirit in wild nature which existed independent of men's minds, but which reflected the same stirrings as moved humanity; it was the idea of the mind being in accord with the spirit of nature which so inspired him. This was why Blake regarded Wordsworth with some suspicion, for the idea to him smacked too much of naturalism. There were, he thought, two Wordsworths, one at war with the other: 'the Natural Man rising up against the Spiritual Man continually, and then he is No Poet but a Heathen Philosopher at Enmity against all true Poetry or Inspiration'. For to Blake it was not Nature, but the spirit of man which was important. Wordsworth, for his part, thought Blake mad, although he added that 'there is something in the madness of this man which interests me more than the sanity of Lord Byron and Walter Scott'.

The attitude of the Romantics to nature might be esoteric, sublime, and difficult to comprehend, but in their simple appreciation of wild scenery they were interpreting a general opinion. Even so prosaic a journal as the *Edinburgh Review* assumed that this was so when in May 1811 it asked what was so attractive about mountain scenery, and answered its own question: 'There is the sublime impression of the Mighty Power which piled the massive cliffs upon each other, and rent the mountains asunder, and scattered their giant fragments at their base;—and all the images connected with the monuments of ancient magnificence and extinguished hostility,—the feuds and the combats, and the triumphs of its wild and primitive inhabitants, contrasted with the stillness and desolation of the scenes where they lie interred;—

and the romantic ideas attached to their ancient traditions, and the peculiarities of the actual life of their descendants,—their wild and enthusiastic poetry,—their gloomy superstitions,—their attachments to their chiefs,—the dangers and the hardships and enjoyments of their lonely huntings and fishings—their pastoral shielings on the mountains in summer—and the tales and the sports that amuse the little groups that are frozen into their vast and trackless valleys in the winter. Add to all this the traces of vast and obscure antiquity that are impressed on the language and the habits of the people, and on the cliffs and caves and gulfy torrents of the land; and the solemn and touching reflection perpetually recurring, of the weakness and insignificance of perishable man, whose generations thus pass away into oblivion, with all their toils and ambition; while nature holds on her un-varying course, and pours out her streams, and renews her forests, with undecaying activity, regardless of the fate of her proud and perishable sovereign.' This passage does not specifically express romanticism, but rather a generally accepted view of 1811. Yet it does underline some important constituents of romanticism, a new sense of history, of people retaining their ancient traditions through long periods of time, and expressing them in poetry and song on long winter evenings, and all this taking place against a background of nature, not yet evolutionary, but pursuing its 'unvarying course' regardless of man's fate.

The Romantic poet and philosopher started from the assumption that empirical science and philosophy were inadequate as a means of answering all the most important questions concerning human life. The argument is clearly put in Shelley's *A Defence of Poetry*, and may be summarised as follows. Locke and his followers operated upon a certain level of thought which was limited by the confines of empiricism. So far as they went they did much good. Had Locke, Hume and Voltaire never lived, 'a little more non-sense would have been talked for a century or two; and perhaps a few more men, women and children burnt as heretics. We might not at this moment have been congratulating each other on the abolition of the Inquisition in Spain'. But that was all. The thought of Locke and his followers led directly to utilitarianism.

Now utility might be thought of as operating upon two different levels, the one 'transitory and particular', the other 'durable, universal and permanent', and the utilitarians concerned themselves with the former and disregarded the latter. They regarded the selfish and transitory interests of man as alone of significance. But these led directly to the principles of *laissez-faire*, which Shelley regarded merely as the philosophy of selfishness. 'They have exemplified the saying, "To him that hath, more shall be given; and from him that hath not, the little that he hath shall be taken away." The rich have become richer, and the poor have become poorer; and the vessel of the state is driven between Scylla and Charybdis of anarchy and despotism. Such are the effects which must ever flow from an unmitigated exercise of the calculating faculty.' What was needed therefore was to transfer the argument to the higher level of reality, that of the permanent and the universal. This was why Shelley placed poets above what he called 'reasoners and mechanists', and imagination above reason. 'A man, to be greatly good, must imagine intensely and comprehensively; he must put himself in the place of another and of many others; the pains and pleasures of his species must become his own. The great instrument of moral good is the imagination; and poetry administers to the effect by acting upon the cause.' There was no want of moral, political, historical and economic knowledge at man's disposal. What was needed was 'the creative faculty to imagine that which we know; we want the generous impulse to act that which we imagine; we want the poetry of life: our calculations have outrun conception; we have eaten more than we can digest'.

Shelley therefore called upon the arts of music, poetry, architecture and painting to restore imagination to its rightful place in human affairs. He described them as 'the teachers who draw into a certain propinquity with the beautiful and the true, that partial apprehension of the agencies of the invisible world which is called religion'. The idea is essentially Platonic; the poet apprehends a harmony which exists in the universe beneath the conflicting fragments and transitory details of daily life. 'Man is an instrument over which a series of external and internal impressions are driven, like the alternations of an ever-changing wind over an Aeolian lyre, which move it by their motion to ever-changing melody. But there is a principle within the human being, and perhaps within all sentient beings, which acts otherwise than in the lyre, and produces not melody alone, but harmony, by an internal adjustment of the sounds or motions thus excited to the impressions which excite them. It is as if the lyre could accommodate its chords to the motions of that which strikes them, in a determined proportion of sound; even as a musician can accommodate his voice to the sound of the lyre.'

This is a most remarkable passage, stating clearly, as it does, the romantic attitude in complete contrast to that of the Augustan age which preceded it. To the age of Locke the mind was a kind of mirror reflecting and recording the external world, and since that world was a rational world governed by ascertainable laws, all that was needed for its comprehension was knowledge and the power of judgment. To the Romantic it was different; there *was* a material world, but it was transcended by an ideal world of the mind. As Shelley wrote, there was in the human being, perhaps in all sentient beings, a 'principle' which *created* harmony. The winds played over the strings of the lyre, but it was the lyre which *created* the harmony, created by the power of imagination, and thus, as Shelley wrote, 'a poet participates in the eternal, the infinite, and the one'. In emphasising the importance of the imagination the poet laid himself open to the accusation that he was merely creating a world of his own, which had no necessary connection with anyone else's world. Shelley clearly believed that this was not so. He was 'participating in the eternal'. His universe was as 'real' as that of Locke; the difference was that it was apprehended in a different way. It was an ideal world, not a materialistic one. Coleridge spoke of the mind as being created in God's image, and in his philosophy came near to holding that the spiritual world was the only real one. The danger was that Romantics might come to think of themselves as Gods, creating their own moral standards, and Byron was certainly not free from this mortal sin. Wordsworth was more humble, and sought patiently for the spirit of the universe as expressed in Nature. Shelley thought he had found it in the spirit of love, and Blake saw the imagination as 'the Divine Vision'. In any case the Romantic poets did not consider themselves as living in ivory towers remote from reality, but in a sense as men of action. Wordsworth wished above all to be considered a teacher. Shelley declared that all the great authors of revolutions in the world's history were poets. 'The most unfailing herald, companion, and follower of the awakening of a great people to work a beneficial change in opinions or institutions is poetry', and he regarded this as particularly true of the poets of his own day. 'It is impossible to read the compositions of the most celebrated writers of the present day without being startled with the electric life which burns within their words. They measure the circumference and sound the depths of human nature with a comprehensive and all-penetrating spirit, and they are themselves perhaps the most sincerely astonished at its manifestations: for it is less their spirit than the spirit of the age. . . . Poets are the unacknowledged legislators of the world.'

The Romantics, then, regarded the nature and function of the poet and artist as altogether different from those which the Augustans had accepted. To the latter poets and artists were interpreters, to the former creators. The difference is clearly seen if we compare two passages, one from Sir Joshua Reynolds, the other from William Blake. Reynolds, in his Discourse of 10 December 1778, declared: 'We cannot . . . recommend an indeterminate manner, or vague ideas of any kind, in a complete and finished picture. This notion, therefore, of leaving anything to the imagination, opposes a very fixed and indispensable rule in our art—that everything shall be carefully and distinctly expressed, as if the painter knew, with correctness and precision, the exact form and character of whatever is introduced into the picture. This is what with us is called Science and Learning; which must not be sacrificed and given up for an uncertain and doubtful beauty.' Blake on the other hand in 1799 was commissioned to illustrate Dr. John Trusler's *Hogarth Moralised*, but Trusler was dissatisfied with the result and said that the illustrations needed interpretation. Blake retorted angrily: 'I had hoped your plan comprehended All Species of this Art, & Especially that you would not regret that Species which gives Existence to every other, namely, visions of Eternity. You say that I want somebody to Elucidate my Ideas. But you ought to know that what is Grand is necessarily obscure to weak men. That which can be made Explicit to the Idiot is not worth my care. The wisest of the Ancients consider'd what is not too explicit as the fittest for instruction, because it rouzes the faculties to act' (*Letters*, 1038–9). In short, Trusler was little better than an idiot for wanting explicit interpretation of Blake's pictures, such as Reynolds had declared every picture should contain.

In general the Romantic poet was aware of an ideal world, often more real than the material world; but it was also a world of imponderable forces which he could never fully understand. The imagination could create it in part, but there was always something which eluded the poet's grasp; he was always aware of a gap between the ideal and the attainment. Nor could it be stated in some form of generalisation, like a philosophical proposition, but could be apprehended only through a particular situation presented by the poet's imagination. Thus, in the *Ancient Mariner*, one of the greatest of romantic poems, Coleridge adopted a story of the supernatural which enabled him to suggest the imponderable forces at work in the universe. It was a tale of wonder and horror, and with Coleridge's vivid pictorial style it is often sufficient to enjoy the poem on that level without seeking a deeper meaning. Nothing could be more horrific than the picture of the becalmed ship:

> The very deep did rot: O Christ!
> That ever this should be!
> Yea, slimy things did crawl with legs
> Upon the slimy sea.

The power of such a picture depends upon the economy of words which thus leaves so much to the imagination. Yet with all the poem's pictorial power, the reader is irresistibly drawn to seek a deeper meaning, and at that point he realises that it is not susceptible of receiving a merely rational interpretation. Is the shooting of a bird really so very important a matter? Why should the crew, who had not participated in the shooting of the albatross, all suffer death, while the mariner alone survives? Such questions do not reveal a weakness in the story, but enhance the sense of mystery as the reader contemplates with wonder the forces at work in nature. The ancient story of the Flying Dutchman, condemned to sail the world for ever in expiation of his sin, is a fascinating one which had a particular appeal to the romantic mind, and here it is combined with the theme that the worst of crimes is the negation of love, and that there is an essential communion between man and all living things. It was a re-discovery of the power of love which released the mariner from the spell of Life-in-Death, and at that moment the albatross fell from his neck.

> O happy living things! no tongue
> Their beauty might declare:
> A spring of love gushed from my heart,
> And I blessed them unaware:
> Sure my kind saint took pity on me,
> And I blessed them unaware.
>
> The self-same moment I could pray;
> And from my neck so free
> The Albatross fell off, and sank
> Like lead into the sea.

The life of the albatross, and indeed the whole of nature, was governed by spirits, and the mariner, although he had been reprieved, must spend the rest of his life recounting his story as an awful warning to mankind. Coleridge intended to write a dissertation on the supernatural as an accompaniment to the poem, in which no doubt he would have expounded the Platonic ideas on the subject, but the essay was never written.

Interest in the supernatural was often accompanied by a revival of interest in mediaeval history and romance. There was to hand a great fund of legend and story in folk tales, and in the collections of seventeenth-century antiquarians, and all that was needed was the desire to break away from classical forms and stories for these to give rise to a new literary form. Horace Walpole pointed the way in his *The Castle of Otranto* (1764).

The Castle of Otranto was, as Sir Walter Scott wrote, 'remarkable not only for the wild interest of the story, but as the first modern attempt to found a tale of amusing fiction upon the basis of the ancient romances of chivalry'. Horace Walpole's deep interest in Gothic architecture, with its darkness, its clanging halls, winding passages and hanging tapestries, led him to reconstruct a fantastic story of the supernatural which contained most of the elements of Romantic mediaevalism, a wicked tyrant, a damsel in distress, a noble hero whose birth for long remains in doubt, a harassed monk, dungeons, secret passages, and a spirit world which intervenes in human affairs. A typical passage will indicate the style:

At these words he seized the cold hand of Isabella, who was half dead with fright and horror. She shrieked, and started from him. Manfred rose to pursue her; when the moon, which was now up, and gleamed in at the opposite casement, presented to his sight the plumes of the fatal helmet, which rose to the height of the windows, waving backwards and forwards in a tempestuous manner, and accompanied with a hollow and rustling sound. Isabella, who gathered courage from her situation, and who dreaded nothing so much as Manfred's pursuit of his declaration, cried, 'Look! my lord! See! Heaven itself declares against your impious intentions!' 'Heaven nor hell shall impede my designs!' said Manfred, advancing again to seize the Princess. At that instant, the portrait of his grandfather, which hung over the bench where they had been sitting, uttered a deep sigh, and heaved its breast. Isabella, whose back was turned to the picture, saw not the motion, nor whence the sound came; but started, and said 'Hark, my lord! What sound was that?' and at the same time, made towards the door. Manfred, distracted between the flight of Isabella, who had now reached the stairs, and yet unable to keep his eyes from the picture, which began to move, had, however, advanced some steps after her, still looking backwards on the portrait, when he saw it quit its panel, and descend on the floor, with a grave and melancholy air. 'Do I dream?' cried Manfred, returning: 'or are the devils themselves in league against me?' (Chap. 1.)

Most dramatic moments in the novel took place at night, and invariably the scene was illuminated by moonlight. Even in the secret passage by which Isabella fled to the convent from her pursuer, the moon came to her assistance: 'as she uttered these words, a ray of moonshine, streaming through a cranny of the ruin above, shone directly on the lock they sought'. Often the most romantic scenes are set among ruins, or in the midst of a craggy desolation which mirrors the mood of the characters: 'Arriving there, he sought the gloomiest shades, as best suited to the pleasing melancholy that reigned in his mind. In this mood he roved insensibly to the caves which had formerly served as a retreat to hermits, and were now reported round the country to be haunted by evil spirits.' (Chap. III.)

Fully in the Neo-Platonic tradition, Nature not only reflected men's mood, but participated in their actions:

In the middle of the court they were met by Manfred, who, distracted with his own thoughts, and anxious once more to behold his daughter, was advancing to the chamber where she lay. As the moon was now at its height, he read in the countenances of this unhappy company, the event he dreaded. 'What? Is she dead?' cried he, in wild confusion—a clap of thunder, at that instant, shook the castle to its foundations: the earth rocked, and the clank of more than mortal armour was heard behind. Frederic and Jerome thought the last day was at hand. The latter, forcing Theodore along with them, rushed into the court. The moment Theodore appeared, the walls of the castle behind Manfred were thrown down with a mighty force, and the form of Alfonso, dilated to an immense magnitude, appeared in the centre of the ruins. (Chap. V.)

In some respects *The Castle of Otranto* is merely transitional to the romantic literature of mystery and horror, for instance in the character of the tyrant Manfred. Manfred as a romantic villain is a lamentable failure. Instead of being the incarnation of evil, he is merely a petty criminal. Walpole delineates him in moderate terms: 'Manfred was not one of those savage tyrants, who wanton in cruelty unprovoked. The circumstances of his fortune had given an asperity to his temper, which was naturally humane; and his virtues were always ready to operate, when his passions did not obscure his reason.' Later we are told that 'ashamed of his inhuman treatment of a princess, who returned every injury with new marks of tenderness and duty: he felt returning love forcing itself into his eyes—but not less ashamed of feeling remorse towards one, against whom he was inwardly meditating a yet more bitter outrage, he curbed the yearnings of his heart, and did not dare to lean even towards pity. The next transition of his soul was an exquisite villainy.' (Chap. I.) This was perhaps as far as the mid-eighteenth century was prepared to go in the psychology of villainy. Manfred pursues Isabella, but is not driven on by the passion of lust, but with the sober intention of divorcing his wife and marrying Isabella in order to procreate sons to secure the succession to Otranto. It appears likely that Walpole was influenced in his choice of story by Shakespeare's *Measure for Measure*, and when he attempts bucolic humour with clowns in the first chapter he is certainly drawing on Shakespearean memories; yet he shies away coyly from the theme of lust in portraying his villain. Manfred was a villain, but one who had rational motives for his villainy.

A further step in the evolution of the romantic novel is seen in the works of Ann Radcliffe (1764–1823). Her second novel, *A Sicilian Romance*, appeared in 1790, *The Mysteries of Udolpho* in 1794, and *The Italian* in 1797, after which she lived mainly in retirement when her health had given way. Since *Udolpho* particularly interested Jane Austen, we may take that work as illustrative of her art. Mrs. Radcliffe specialised in the use of mystery and the art of exciting terror. In a novel of three hundred thousand words, much too long for modern taste, she traces the adventures and sufferings of Emily St. Aubert, who must be the most lachrymose heroine in English literature. Sorely tried as she is, tears flow on almost every page, and she swoons more frequently than is good for any young lady. Mrs. Radcliffe did not have the power of skilfully creating character, nor of permitting character development under the stress of incident. Her characters are elemental types, and she relied for effect upon abundant incident and the use of suspense. Her story is set in France and Italy because these countries allowed a more exotic story, but her knowledge of them was slight, and she makes numerous minor errors of customs and topography. Her story for some reason was made to take place in 1584, but her characters were entirely of the eighteenth century. Regardless of date, Emily was taken to the opera in Venice (and came away feeling 'how infinitely inferior all the splendour of art is to the sublimity of nature'). Mrs. Radcliffe had the impression that French and Italian peasants subsisted mainly on fruit and cream. But such lapses no doubt did not greatly concern her contemporaries, and moreover the book was translated into French and had wide circulation on the continent.

Mrs. Radcliffe is often romantic in the treatment of nature and the poetry of her natural description. She frequently asserts that life among the simplicities of nature is infinitely preferable to the gaudiness and falsity of cities. M. St. Aubert has retired from the world 'more in pity than in anger, to scenes of simple nature'. There he and his wife 'wandered away among the most romantic and magnificent scenes, nor suffered the charms of Nature's lowly children to abstract them from the observance of her stupendous works'. It was among Emily's earliest pleasures 'to ramble among the scenes of nature; nor was it in the soft and glowing landscape that she most delighted; she loved more the mountain's stupendous recesses, where the silence and grandeur of solitude impressed a sacred awe upon her heart, and lifted her thoughts to the GOD OF HEAVEN AND EARTH'. Over Emily and her father, as with Wordsworth, natural scenery 'breathed perpetual benediction'. Mrs. Radcliffe was rarely concerned with the full light of day, she preferred the shadows of evening, or, less often, the first light of dawn.

Before them extended the valley they had quitted: its rocks and woods to the left, just silvered by the rays, formed a contrast to the deep shadow that involved the opposite cliffs, whose fringed summits only were tipped with light; while the distant perspective of the valley was lost in the yellow mist of moonlight. The travellers sat for some time wrapt in the complacency which such scenes inspire.

'These scenes', said Valancourt, at length, 'soften the heart like the notes of sweet music, and inspire that delicious melancholy which no person, who had felt it once, would resign for the gayest pleasures. They waken our best and purest feelings; disposing us to benevolence, pity and friend-ship. Those whom I love, I always seem to love more in such an hour as this.' (Chap. IV.)

No wonder that Valancourt was a man after St. Aubert's own heart, and that his comment upon him was: 'this young man has never been to Paris'. St. Aubert perceived that Valancourt's 'opinions were formed, rather than imbibed—were more the result of thought than of learning: of the world he seemed to know nothing, for he believed well of all mankind: and this opinion gave him the reflected image of his own heart'. Later however, Valancourt falls into evil company in Paris, and when he again meets Emily he is overcome by remorse made all the more intense by a renewal of the power of nature. Emily is speaking:

'You used to be a great admirer of landscape; and I have heard you say that the faculty of deriving consolation under misfortune, from the sublime prospects which neither op-pression nor poverty withholds from us, was the peculiar blessing of the innocent.' Valancourt was deeply affected. 'Yes', he replied; 'I had once a taste for innocent and elegant delights—I had once an uncorrupted heart.' (Chap. XXXVIII.)

The poetry of nature was a frequent theme with St. Aubert:

'The evening gloom of woods was always delightful to me. . . . I remember that in my youth this gloom used to call forth to my fancy a thousand fairy visions and romantic images; and I own I am not yet wholly insensible of that high

enthusiasm which wakes the poet's dream: I can linger with
solemn steps under the deep shades, send forward a trans-
forming eye into the distant obscurity, and listen with
thrilling delight to the mystic murmuring of the woods.'
(Chap. I.)

All the sympathetic characters of the book are touched by the
influences of nature, while the unsympathetic characters remain
quite unaffected; indeed this is often the first indication the
reader has of into which category he is supposed to place a
character. Thus when Count de Villefort and his lady arrive at
their castle, the Countess is annoyed at being so far from Paris:

'There are windows, my lord, but they neither admit
entertainment nor light; they show only a scene of savage
nature.'
'I am at a loss, madame,' said the count, 'to conjecture what
you mean by savage nature.' (Chap. XXXV.)

and we know at once how to interpret their characters.

At times Mrs. Radcliffe's descriptions of rustic life seem to
follow the traditional eighteenth-century pattern, rather than
express a new attitude. In the classical tradition of idyllic life,
she writes:

The peasants of this gay climate were often seen on an
evening, when the day's labour was done, dancing in groups
on the margin of the river. Their sprightly melodies, *débonnaire*
steps, the fanciful figures of their dances, with the tasteful
and capricious manner in which the girls adjusted their
simple dress, gave a character to the scene entirely French.
(Chap. I.)

But at other times she is more realistic. As the St. Auberts
travel through Roussillon they meet with a young woman in
tears, surrounded by her children, and hear a story similar to those
told by Hannah More, in which the shepherd has been ruined by
having his flocks carried off by gipsies; and Valancourt at once
determines to give the woman his few remaining louis, thus by his

generosity restoring a whole family to happiness. St. Aubert makes certain that the moral of the story is appreciated: 'What pity that the wealthy who can command such sunshine should ever pass their days in gloom—in the cold shade of selfishness! For you, my young friend, may the sun always shine as brightly as at this moment! may your own conduct always give you the sunshine of benevolence and reason united!'

To contemporaries, however, it was not the descriptions of nature, but the gothic mysteries which gave the book its peculiar attraction. Mrs. Radcliffe delighted in vaulted halls, winding passages and windswept corridors, in mysterious music heard at night, in legends of ghosts, in shadowy figures disappearing into the dusk, and untold horrors concealed behind a black veil. Here is her description of Emily's first glimpse of the Castle of Udolpho:

> Emily gazed with melancholy awe upon the castle, . . . for, though it was now lighted by the setting sun, the Gothic greatness of its features, and its mouldering walls of dark grey stone, rendered it a gloomy and sublime object. As she gazed, the light died away on its walls, leaving a melancholy purple tint, which spread deeper and deeper as the thin vapour crept up the mountain, while the battlements above were still tipped with splendour. From those, too, the rays soon faded, and the whole edifice was invested with the solemn duskiness of evening. Silent, lonely and sublime, it seemed to stand the sovereign of the scene, and to frown defiance on all who dared to invade its solitary reign. As the twilight deepened, its features became more awful in obscurity; and Emily continued to gaze, till its clustering towers were alone seen rising over the tops of the woods. (Chap. XVIII.)

In such a castle any terror might be encountered. Mrs. Radcliffe's favourite device is the use of suspense, and it is not always successfully used. Emily has been instructed by her father to burn a bundle of letters without reading them. This she does, but she cannot help seeing one sentence 'of dreadful import', but as the reader is not told what the sentence is, the incident is merely annoying. Similarly, when Emily at last looks behind the dreaded veil she at once falls into a faint without the reader being told what she saw; nor does he learn the truth for another four hundred pages. In both cases the reader is entitled to know what Emily herself knows, and the interest in the story would be increased by his knowing. Still, there are exciting moments spent in dark chambers on wind-swept nights, and one of the most effective is the occasion on which Ludovico offers to test the belief that a certain chamber is haunted, settles down there for the night, and in the morning has disappeared. In general however the reader is too much aware that the effects intended are merely the result of the sleight of hand of the novelist, that she is playing for effect, and not exploring the world of the supernatural with any 'willing suspension of disbelief' on her part.

For the truth was that Mrs. Radcliffe remained primarily a child of the eighteenth century. Every supposed supernatural event is in the end given a natural explanation. Emily, as the heroine, must not be supposed for an instant to be credulous. If music is heard at night, she will not accept the common belief that it is supernatural.

> I perceive that all old mansions are haunted; I am lately
> come from a place of wonders; but unluckily since I left it,
> I have heard almost all of them explained. (Chap. XXXVII.)

Mrs. Radcliffe writes disapprovingly of 'that love, so natural to the human mind, of whatever is able to distend its faculties with wonder and astonishment'. It is true that elsewhere she writes that 'human reason cannot establish her laws on subjects lost in the obscurity of imagination, any more than the eye can ascertain the form of objects that only glimmer through the darkness of night' (Ch. XXIV). But where the novelist so often reminds him that romantic fears are foolish, the reader may be forgiven for not entering fully into the romantic aspects of her tale. Nor has she the power to create a truly romantic villain, for Montoni at no point seizes the reader's imagination. He is a contemptible tyrant, but no more than that. Shelley or Emily Brontë would have known how to make him a real object of terror. It is for these reasons that we cannot regard Mrs. Radcliffe as more than standing on the threshold of Romanticism, except in her treatment of nature.

However the novel was enormously popular with contemporaries, and it certainly appealed to the imagination of Jane Austen, who chose to satirise it in *Northanger Abbey*. Catherine Morland, it will be remembered, had been reading *The Mysteries of Udolpho* all the morning:

> 'Yes, I have been reading it ever since I woke; and I am got to the black veil.'
>
> 'Are you indeed? How delightful! Oh, I would not tell you what is behind the black veil for the world! Are you not wild to know?'
>
> 'Oh! yes, quite; what can it be? But do not tell me. I would not be told upon any account. I know it must be a skeleton; I am sure it is Laurintina's skeleton. Oh, I am delighted with the book!'

Catherine, with her head full of such mysteries, was ready to see romantic adventure even in Gloucestershire. At the mere mention of Blaize Castle, near Bristol, she was imagining its towers and galleries, and 'the happiness of a progress through a long suite of lofty rooms exhibiting the remains of magnificent furniture, though now for many years deserted—the happiness of being stopped in their way along narrow, winding vaults, by a low, grated door; or even of having their lamp, their only lamp, extinguished by a sudden gust of wind, and of being left in total darkness'. Even the superior Henry Tilney had read *Udolpho*: 'When he had once begun it, he could not lay it down again.' As for Catherine, 'her passion for ancient edifices was next in degree to her passion for Henry Tilney, and castles and abbeys made usually the charm of those reveries which his image did not fill'. Tilney teased her by describing all the romantic horrors which would befall her, according to the Radcliffe formula, once she reached Northanger Abbey; and surely enough her first night there was stormy. 'Catherine, as she crossed the hall, listened to the tempest with sensations of awe; and ... felt for the first time that she was really in an abbey.' What more natural therefore than to suppose that General Tilney was an English edition of Montoni,

C

that he had imprisoned his wife and driven her to her death?
But it was all a mistake.

> Charming as were all Mrs. Radcliffe's works, and charming
> even as were the works of all her imitators, it was not in them
> perhaps that human nature, at least in the midland counties
> of England, was to be looked for. (Chap. XXV.)

So Jane Austen brings both Catherine and the reader back to a
more sober world of genteel England. It was part of her object
to create a higher status for the novel than it had so far acquired,
and she wrote caustically about those who referred to a book as
'only a novel'!

> It is only 'Cecilia', or 'Camilla', or 'Belinda' or, in short,
> only some work in which the greatest powers of the mind are
> displayed, in which the most thorough knowledge of human
> nature, the happiest delineation of its varieties, the liveliest
> effusions of wit and humour, are conveyed to the world in
> best-chosen language. (Chap. V.)

And if this was the test of a novel, it must be admitted that
Mrs. Radcliffe fell far short of the highest.

Superficially *The Mysteries of Udolpho* had romantic characteristics, and yet in essentials remained merely on the threshold
of Romanticism. Romanticism glorified the individual, and
delighted in the theme of the man of action pursuing some deep
and passionate purpose against enormous odds. It might be a
moral purpose, in which case he would be a good man, but also a
dull one; and the Romantics often preferred to contemplate the
awful consequences of the pursuit of evil for its own sake. If we
want a complete romantic villain we turn, not to Walpole's
Manfred, nor to Mrs. Radcliffe's Montoni, but to Shelley's Count
Francesco Cenci, in his play *The Cenci*:

> All men delight in sensual luxury,
> All men enjoy revenge; and most exult
> Over the tortures they can never feel—
> Flattering their secret peace with others' pain.

But I delight in nothing else. I love
The sight of agony, and the sense of joy,
When this shall be another's, and that mine.
And I have no remorse and little fear,
Which are, I think, the checks of other men. (I, i.)

Count Cenci was an old man and the lusts of the flesh no longer
burned within him; there remained only the pleasure of seeing
others suffer, and thus he planned incest as the only horror he had
not yet experienced:

True, I was happier than I am, while yet
Manhood remained to act the thing I thought;
While lust was sweeter than revenge; and now
Invention palls: Ay, we must all grow old—
And but that there yet remains a deed to act
Whose horror might make sharp an appetite
Duller than mine—I'd do—I know not what. (I, i.)

Shelley believed that the complexity of human nature was such
that audiences must necessarily have much greater interest in, and
sympathy for such characters than they were ever willing to admit.
He discussed the question in his *Defence of Poetry* in connection
with the interpretation of the character of Satan in Milton's
Paradise Lost.

Milton's poem contains within itself a philosophical refuta-
tion of that system, of which, by a strange and natural antithesis, it has been a chief popular support. Nothing can
exceed the energy and magnificence of the character of Satan
as expressed in *Paradise Lost*. It is a mistake to suppose that
he could ever have been intended for the popular personification of evil. Implacable hate, patient cunning, and a
sleepless refinement of device to inflict the extremest anguish
on an enemy, these things are evil; and, although venial in a
slave, are not to be forgiven in a tyrant; although redeemed
by much that ennobles his defeat in one subdued, are marked
by all that dishonours his conquest in the victor. Milton's
Devil as a moral being is as far superior to his God, as one

who perseveres in some purpose which he has conceived to
be excellent in spite of adversity and torture, is to one who in
the cold security of undoubted triumph inflicts the most
horrible revenge upon his enemy, not from any mistaken
notion of inducing him to repent of a perseverance in enmity,
but with the alleged design of exasperating him to deserve
new torments.

In short, Satan is a great and noble character because he is
'one who perseveres in some purpose which he has conceived to
be excellent in spite of adversity and torture', while God appears
as a vindictive tyrant cruelly determined to bend Satan to his will.
Shelley was not criticising Milton as an artist; he thought that
the poem was all the greater because he had 'mingled the elements
of human nature as colours upon a single pallet, and arranged
them in the composition of his great picture according to the laws
of epic truth; that is, according to the laws of that principle by
which a series of actions of the external universe and of intelligent
and ethical beings is calculated to excite the sympathy of succeeding generations of mankind'. His criticism was not of Milton
as a poet, but of the theology he was purporting to expound.
The wilful disregard of God's moral order, which to Milton was
the sin which condemned Satan to outer darkness, became to
Shelley the assertion of individualism against the decrees of a
tyrant, and as such worthy of human admiration.

Under the influence of Romanticism Satan became a hero, and
it was in this role that Byron cast himself, namely as the great
and lonely figure, brooding over deep but unstated thoughts, and
wrestling against powerful 'enemies, scorning the world, and
sharing with the elements great powers and passions. Early in life
he cast himself as one who had suffered fearful wrongs, and who
in consequence sought to avenge himself upon all whom he hated.
Hence the enjoyment with which he suggested to his wife that he
practised incest with his sister, for incest was the ultimate in crime
to the romantic mind, and a theme which fascinated Romantic
writers in England and France for a century.

It is sometimes suggested that the Romantics were social

misfits, weak and vapid in their idealism, beautiful and ineffectual angels, beating in the void their luminous wings in vain. Superficially there might appear to be some truth in the assessment, for Keats, Shelley and Byron, all died young; Shelley was a rebel, Byron a social outcast, Blake a mystic, Coleridge a drug addict, and only Wordsworth lived on with changed views, to enjoy a respectable if drab old age. Yet it remains both an inaccurate and an uncharitable judgment. For all were major poets, and by general consent Wordsworth's poetic achievement ranks third only to that of Shakespeare and Milton. Moreover, it is wrong to suppose that they were solely or indeed mainly concerned with daffodils and daisies, skylarks and belles dames. Except for Byron, all were deeply concerned with the philosophical significance of life, and wrote poetry, as Keats said, to ease 'the burden of the mystery'. They were all agreed in making the highest possible claims for the importance of poetry, resting their claims upon the importance of the human heart, and the faculty of imagination in the pursuit of truth. All were deeply interested in the political problems of their day, and so far from being ineffectual idealists and revolutionaries, Wordsworth, Coleridge and Shelley all showed considerable political acumen and made each in his particular way an independent contribution to the political thought of their time.

These are all aspects which we shall consider in later chapters.

NOTE

[1] See *Reason and Nature in the Eighteenth Century*, Ch. 16.

2 : The Political Protagonists
I : Burke and the Whigs

In 1756 the young Edmund Burke, turning away from a legal career and towards literature, published *A Vindication of Natural Society*. As yet with no personal experience of politics, he simply repeated, although with particular skill, the conventional whig views of the time on the nature of political power. *Natural society* was that which arose from the nature of man and was symbolised in the family. It was quite different from *political society*, which was artificial, amoral and imposed upon man by superior force. Political society was set up in opposition to the state of nature, and it derived its power by trampling upon the law of nature. 'All writers on the science of policy are agreed, and they agree with experience, that all governments must frequently infringe the rules of justice to support themselves; that truth must give way to dissimulation; honesty to convenience; and humanity itself to the reigning interest. The whole of this mystery of iniquity is called reason of state.' Wherever political power existed it rested upon engines of force. 'Let us take a review of the dungeons, whips, chains, racks, gibbets, with which every society is abundantly stored by which hundreds of victims are annually offered up to support a dozen or two in pride and madness, and millions in an abject servitude and dependence. . . . It is a misfortune that in no part of the globe natural liberty and natural religion are to be found pure, and free from the mixture of political adulterations.'

Burke surveyed the three traditional forms of government, and found them all bad. As for monarchy, 'many of the greatest tyrants on the records of history have begun their reigns in the fairest manner. But the truth is, this unnatural power corrupts both the heart and the understanding'. There never was a prince who did not have a favourite, by which means 'the tyranny is doubled'. Indeed Burke solemnly declared that 'by sure and uncontested principles, the greatest part of the governments on earth must be concluded tyrannies, impostures, violations of the natural rights of mankind, and worse than the most disorderly anarchies'. And if despotism was bad, government by aristocracy was even worse; for whereas a tyrant died, and was sometimes succeeded by a better man, government by aristocracy was unchangeable. 'Never was it known that an aristocracy, which was haughty and tyrannical in one century, became easy and mild in the next.' Burke was particularly scathing about the government of the Venetian Republic: 'here you see a people deprived of all rational freedom, and tyrannized over by about two thousand men; and yet this body of two thousand are so far from enjoying any liberty by the subjection of the rest, that they are in an infinitely severer state of slavery'.

Burke's experience of democracy was confined to his reading of Greek history, but from this he deduced that democracy was usually a short-lived preliminary to tyranny, that democracy hated special merit, and that in a democracy people 'entered into wars rashly and wantonly'. In short, each form of government seemed worse than the other, and hence Burke asked the question why men submitted themselves to government at all: 'what slave so passive, what bigot so blind, what enthusiast so headlong, what politician so hardened, as to stand up in defence of a system calculated for a curse to mankind? a curse under which they smart and groan to this hour.' 'Kings are ambitious; the nobility haughty; and the populace tumultuous and ungovernable. Parties in a State reveal enough of each other's faults to make a reasonable man cautious of either.' 'It is of no consequence what the principles of any party, or what their pretensions are; the spirit which actuates all parties is the same; the spirit of ambition, of self-interests, of oppression and treachery.' The whigs, he said, had promoted popular sedition in one reign, and had been 'a patron of tyranny' in the next. 'I could show that they have all of them betrayed the public safety at all times, and have very frequently with equal

perfidy made a market of their own cause, and their own associates.' 'In vain you tell me that artificial government is good, but
that I fall out only with the abuse. The thing! the thing itself is
the abuse!'

Political society was based upon injustice. 'The whole business
of the poor is to administer to the idleness, folly, and luxury of the
rich; and that of the rich, in return, is to find the best methods
of confirming the slavery and increasing the burdens of the poor.
In a state of nature, it is an invariable law, that a man's acquisitions
are in proportion to his labours. In a state of artificial society, it is
a law as constant and as invariable, that those who labour most
enjoy the fewest things; and that those who labour not at all have
the greatest number of enjoyments.' In short, political society was
based on injustice, it was responsible for devastating wars throughout history, and no one form of government was better than
another, for all were a negation of natural reason upon which
alone men should rely.

So Burke wrote in 1756, and it would not have been necessary
to give so much space to so early a work, but for the fact that in his
later philosophy he was to deny the truth of almost everything he
had written in 1756. Indeed much of *A Vindication of Natural
Society* reads like an extract from the works of William Godwin.
In his later writings the concept of 'natural society' disappeared
altogether as Burke discovered the necessity for civil society. So
too did the sense of injustice at the prospect of thousands of
workers in mines and factories living in poverty and misery. So
far from regarding aristocratic government as one of the worst
of governments, Burke became of all philosophers the one who
most ardently defended it as the best of governments, at least for
Britain. So far from being cynical about the character of party
government, Burke was to provide the classic justification for its
existence. For over thirty years, it is true, he maintained his
whiggish suspicions of the power of monarchy, yet in his last years
he was to write an impassioned defence of the monarchy of
Louis XVI; and when Tom Paine advocated the principles of the
French Revolution as being in conformity with natural rights,
Burke denied that he knew what 'natural rights' meant.

So remarkable a transformation of ideas might, with some cynicism, be explained in terms of Burke's political career. From 1759 onwards, when he began to write the *Political Register*, he was able to observe the political scene more closely. In 1765 he became secretary to the Marquis of Rockingham, who was about to form an administration, and who was one of the greatest aristocrats of the time. Thereafter he became virtually party manager and resident philosopher to the Rockingham whigs. The Rockingham government was weak, lacking political support in the Commons, or popular support outside it, but Burke chose to believe that it was overthrown by the hostility of 'placemen and pensioners' in spite of enjoying 'the confidence of the nation'. (See *A Short Account of a Late Administration*.) Thereafter he came quickly to the conclusion that 'Party divisions, whether on the whole operating for good or evil, are things inseparable from free government.' (*Observations on The Present State of the Nation*.) Still smarting under the sense of failure of the Rockingham Administration, he published in 1770 his famous *Thoughts on the Cause of the Present Discontents*, in which he painted a vivid picture of the growth of royal influence, and its threat to parliamentary liberties: 'The power of the crown, almost dead and rotten as Prerogative, has grown up anew, with much more strength, and far less odium, under the name of Influence.' His theory was that there had grown up a Court party, or *King's Friends*, who took their orders from the Court, and who were ready to overthrow any Ministry in whom the King had lost confidence. It was a jaundiced and inaccurate view, but one which Rockingham endorsed, and henceforth it became a leading tenet of the Rockingham whigs. Burke still professed that he was 'no friend to aristocracy', but he was beginning to see the great whig families as the guardians of the 'Principles of 1688', the constitutional liberties of the nation. When the American Revolution gave Burke and the Rockingham whigs a national cause, he refused to argue the American case upon the basis of 'natural law' of which he had been so sure in 1756. It was sufficient to argue it from the premise of the constitutional rights of British subjects, no matter where they lived. Indeed, with the growing instincts of a statesman, Burke was disposed to argue the American cause, not from philosophical generalities, but from a recognition of the inevitability of conflict unless the British government made concessions: 'The temper and character which prevail in our colonies are, I am afraid, un-alterable by any human art. We cannot, I fear, falsify the pedigree of this fierce people, and persuade them that they are not sprung from a nation in whose veins the blood of freedom circulates. The language in which they would hear you tell them this tale would detect the imposition; your speech would betray you. An English-man is the unfittest person on earth to argue another Englishman into slavery.' (*Speech on Conciliation with America*, March 1775.) Later when Burke was attacked for his inconsistency in supporting the American, yet condemning the French Revolution, it was easy for him to argue that the two Revolutions were quite different, that the American Revolution was in defence of the 'Principles of 1688', and that in such matters circumstances were everything. In fact Burke, in defending the Americans, never endorsed the principles of Tom Paine; his prime concern was not that the British government should win a philosophical argument, but that it should avoid any occasion for conflict.

Burke's unalterable hostility to the French Revolution as set out in the *Reflections on the Revolution in France* (1790) and other works, sprang from his fear of the unbridled power of a people once released from the restraints and conventions of civil society. 'Liberty, when men act in bodies, is *power*.' He was convinced that the people, once released from their 'natural' leaders, would soon fall victims to tyrants and usurpers unrestrained by considerations of morality or justice. Since 1756 Burke had come to reverence society as a complex structure which had grown up over great periods of time, held together by institutions, custom, laws, conventions and human affections. Destroy this organism, and there would remain nothing but the 'moleculae of a disbanded people', ripe for the destruction of what remained. 'When the fence from the gallantry of preceptors is broken down, and your families are no longer protected by decent pride, and salutary domestic prejudice, there is but one step to a frightful corruption.' (*Letter to a Member of The National Assembly*, 1791.) Burke painted a lurid picture of an egalitarian society, in which Jack was as good as his master, and political power was vested in the hands of mob orators and self-seekers. He had come to believe in 'the wisdom of the ages', the slow building up of laws and traditions, the destruction of which would release the worst passions of men. Once tradition was overthrown, he doubted the power of reason to rebuild anew. Tradition was needed 'to fortify the fallible and feeble contrivances of our reason'; 'the idea of a liberal descent inspires us with a sense of habitual dignity'.

Burke did not deny the need for gradual reform, indeed, he declared, 'a state without the means of some change is without the means of its conservation'. It must however be achieved within the context of the traditional social and political structure; it must not attempt to 'dissolve the whole fabric'. To the French he declared: 'Your constitution was suspended before it was perfected; but you had the elements of a constitution very nearly as good as could be wished.' In his *Letter* of 1791 he wrote: 'I am constantly of opinion that your states, in three orders, on the footing on which they stood in 1614, were capable of being brought into a proper and harmonious combination with royal authority. This constitution by estates was the natural and only just representation of France.' In 1614 the States-General in France had met for the last time before 1789, before royal despotism was consolidated by Richelieu, and Burke proposed that the French should return to the constitution they had known. His use of the word 'natural' in the phrase 'natural and only just representation of France' is interesting. It is the same word as in 'natural law', but it is clear that Burke meant something quite different; now it meant 'traditional', 'in accordance with history and custom', and if the institution fulfilled that qualification, it followed that it was also 'just'.

Here we are near the heart of Burke's political philosophy. He rejected the doctrine of natural rights of men in society because he denied that it was possible to formulate rights which were applicable to all men at all times and in all places. Natural rights therefore could only exist when men were in a state of nature. Once they entered society they acquired civil rights, and these were most secure when they were guaranteed by some 'fundamental law' or traditional constitution. Hence his suspicion of the National Assembly in France: 'That Assembly, since the destruction of the orders, has no fundamental law. . . . Nothing in heaven or upon earth can serve as a control on them.' And in the *Letter* of 1791 he wrote: 'I doubt much, very much, indeed, whether France is at all ripe for liberty on any standard. Men are qualified for civil liberty in exact proportion to their disposition to put moral chains upon their own appetites. . . . Society cannot exist unless a controlling power upon will and appetite be placed somewhere, and the less of it there is within, the more there must be without. It is ordained in the eternal constitution of things, that men of intemperate minds cannot be free. Their passions forge their fetters.' Burke's view of society was that of a complex of loyalties and affections, of families, villages, classes and interests, linked together by traditional loyalties. 'To be attached to the subdivision, to love the little platoon we belong to in society, is the first principle (the germ as it were) of public affection.' In contrast, the France of the Revolution seemed to him to have become simply a population of twenty-four millions dominated by an assembly of five hundred. 'At present, you seem in everything to have strayed out of the high road of nature.' Again the word was 'nature', but what he meant was 'history'.

Burke clearly defined his own attitude to liberty. He wrote to M. Dupont in October 1789: 'You have kindly said, that you began to love freedom from your intercourse with me. Permit me then to continue our conversation, and to tell you what the freedom is that I love, and that to which I think all men entitled. This is the more necessary because, of all the loose terms in the world, liberty is the most indefinite. It is not solitary, unconnected, individual, selfish liberty, as if every man was to regulate the whole of his conduct by his own will. The liberty I mean is *social* freedom. It is that state of things in which liberty is secured by the equality of restraint. A constitution of things in which the liberty of no one man, and no body of men, and no number of men, can find means to trespass on the liberty of any person, or any description of persons, in the society. This kind of liberty is, indeed, but another name for justice; ascertained by wise laws, and secured by well-constructed institutions. I am sure that liberty, so incorporated, and in a manner identified with justice, must be infinitely dear to every one who is capable of conceiving what it is. But whenever a separation is made between liberty and justice, neither is, in my opinion, safe.'

Burke did not deny that men had rights in society. 'If civil society be made for the advantage of man, all the advantages for which it is made become his right'; but he denied that a share in government was one of them. 'Government is not made in virtue of natural rights. . . . Government is a contrivance of human wisdom to provide for human *wants*.' The 'rights of man', however, seemed to him to be an empty phrase. He wrote to M. Dupont in October 1789: 'You have theories enough concerning the rights of men;—it may not be amiss to add a small degree of attention to their nature and disposition. It is with man in the concrete;—it is with common human life, and human actions, you are to be concerned. . . . Never wholly separate in your mind the merits of any political question from the men who are concerned in it.' As Burke disliked abstract rights, so he was suspicious of blueprints for a new constitution, because, as he wrote, 'there is, by the essential fundamental constitution of things, a radical infirmity in all human contrivances'. That constitution was best, therefore, which had best stood the test of time. Events in France seemed to justify his worst fears. He wrote of the revolutionaries in a letter to a fellow-member of parliament (31 January 1792): 'They began (the destruction of government) by subverting, under pretexts of rights of man, the foundations of civil society itself. They trampled upon the religion of their country, and upon all religion;—they systematically gave the rein to every crime and every vice. They destroyed the trade and manufactures of their country. They rooted up its finances. They caused the greatest accumulation of coin probably ever collected amongst any people, totally to disappear as by magic; and they filled up the void by a fraudulent, compulsory paper-currency, and a coinage of the bells from their churches. . . . The means by which all this was done leaves an example in Europe never to be effaced, and which no thinking man,

I imagine, can present to his mind without consternation.' Finally, when England and France went to war a year later, Burke regarded it as a just war: 'We are at war with a *principle*, and with an example, which there is no shutting out by Fortresses, or excluding by territorial limits. No lines of demarcation can bound the Jacobin empire. It must be extirpated in the place of its origin, or it will not be confined to that place.' (*Letter to the Comte de Mercy*, August 1793.) Burke had broken with his old ally, Charles James Fox, and in the following year the Duke of Portland and his followers broke away from the whigs and went over to the support of Pitt. Burke had never been a popular politician, but the bulk of the governing classes had come round to his way of thinking about the French Revolution. In parliament Fox's followers shrank to a handful.

Burke had come a long way since 1756; in the interval something like a transformation had taken place in his thinking. In 1756 he had readily accepted the conventional view of suspicion of and hostility to government; the central problem of political theory was how to preserve, once man had entered society, the 'natural rights' of man, namely those which existed in the state of nature, since society existed solely in order to maintain law and order. By 1790 the idea of the state of nature had disappeared. Burke had discovered a fuller and richer purpose in society so that man could no longer be thought of except as part of a society. Moreover, society grew up through long periods of time; there was a wisdom of the ages which men would disregard at their peril. In the process of change Burke had discovered a sense of history, and although it was never highly developed in himself, it was a marked characteristic of his followers in the nineteenth century. Under its influence natural rights became historical rights, and Burke came to fear breaches in customs and traditions which were likely to destroy the fabric of society. He thus denied the right of rebellion except in defence of traditional rights. 'Neither the few nor the many have a right to act merely by their will, in any matter connected with duty, trust, engagement or obligation. The constitution of a country being once settled upon some compact, tacit or expressed, there is no power existing of force to alter it, without the breach of the covenant, or the consent of all the parties. Such is the nature of the compact.' (*Appeal from the New to the Old Whigs*, 1791.) It was not a convincing argument, and Burke would have done better to have dispensed altogether with the idea of compact, and to have based his argument entirely on history and expediency; but it was an argument which suited the mood of the time. Elsewhere he discarded the traditional view entirely, and declared that 'Nothing universal can be rationally affirmed on any moral, or political subject. Pure metaphysical abstraction does not belong to these matters. The lines of morality are not like ideal lines of mathematics. They are broad and deep as well as long. They admit of exceptions; they demand modifications. These exceptions and modifications are not made by the process of logic, but by the rules of prudence. Prudence is not only the first in rank of the virtues political and moral, but she is the director, the regulator, the standard of them all.' (ibid.) In short, before men risked the evils of change, they ought to be very certain of the good they were seeking to achieve. In this Burke became the spokesman for his age, and the philosopher of nineteenth-century conservatism.

·   ·   ·   ·   ·   ·

When Burke condemned the French Revolution and all its works, he carried the bulk of the governing classes with him. Charles James Fox for the remainder of his life continued to defend the Revolution as being essentially concerned with liberty, however misguided the French had been in proceeding to excesses, but his followers shrank to a small and select group, and after his death they took up a moderate and restrained position which was not always very different from that of many tories in the Pittite tradition. Between the extreme tories and the radicals they occupied a kind of middle position. They rejected the extreme conclusions which could be drawn from Burke's *Reflections*, and the views of the tory reactionaries; they were unmoved by what they thought of as sentimental philanthropy on the part of the tory Evangelicals, yet they detested the demagogic doctrines of Tom Paine and the Jacobins. Whig political thought can be seen clearly in the pages of the *Edinburgh Review*, a powerful journal founded in 1802, to which the chief contributors were Francis Horner (who died young), Francis Jeffrey and Sydney Smith. Indeed in the fifth number Jeffrey provided a remarkable portrait of a typical whig in describing John Millar, a Glasgow professor: 'There never was any mind, perhaps, less accessible to the illusions of that sentimental and ridiculous philanthropy which has led so many to the adoption of popular principles. He took a very cool and practical view of the conditions of society; and neither wept over the imaginary miseries of the lower orders, nor shuddered at the imputed vices of the higher. . . . He laughed at the dreams of perfectibility and looked with profound contempt upon all these puerile schemes of equality that threatened to subvert the distinctions of property, or to degrade the natural aristocracy of virtues and of talents. At the same time, he was certainly jealous, to an excess, of the encroachments of the regal power; and fancied that, in this country, the liberty of the subject was exposed to perpetual danger, from that patronising influence which seemed likely to increase with the riches and importance of the nation.'

Whig political theory rested upon the doctrine of the need for constitutional balance. On the one hand there was the danger of despotism arising from 'the tremendous patronage of the government', and on the other the danger of destructive revolution. Jeffrey expounded the theory in an article in July 1808. 'Liberty, like love, is as hard to keep as to win. . . . Whenever there is power, we may be sure that there is, or will be, a disposition to increase it; and if there be not a constant spirit of jealousy and of resistance on the part of the people, every monarchy will gradually harden into despotism.' With the growth of national wealth there had increased a complexity of government. 'Government has the disposal of nearly twenty millions per annum, and the power of nominating to two or three hundred thousand posts or places of emolument.' Since the population in 1808 amounted to about five million adult men, of whom the great mass were poor, it followed that 'beyond the rank of mere labourers there is scarcely one man out of three who does not hold or hope for some appointment or promotion from government, and is not consequently disposed to go all *honest* lengths in recommending him to its favour. This is a situation which justifies some alarm for the liberties of the people'.

Jeffrey argued that the nation had been very naturally alarmed at the course of the French Revolution. 'This alarm, in so far as it related to this country, was always excessive, and in a great degree unreasonable, but it was impossible altogether to escape it; and the consequences have been incalculably injurious to the interests of practical liberty.' Under the fear of Jacobinism 'a sort of tacit convention was entered into, to say nothing, for a while, of the follies and vices of princes, the tyranny of courts, or the rights of the people'. By 1808 he believed that the time had come to restrain these fears, and to look once again more steadily at the political situation.

Jeffrey believed that it was whig policy to advocate moderate reform, so long as the safeguards remained adequate. His view of society was essentially that of Burke: 'Human society is not like a piece of mechanism which may be safely taken to pieces, and put together by the hands of an ordinary artist. It is the work of Nature, and not of man; and has received, from the hands of its Author, an organisation that cannot be destroyed without danger to its existence, and certain properties and powers that cannot be altered or suspended by those who may have been entrusted with its management.' (*Edinburgh Review*, April 1805.) Reform must be gradual, like that of a gardener tending his plants. When Jeffrey talked of liberty, it is clear that he meant above all the liberty of private property, and thus he was certain that political power must remain in the hands of the propertied classes. 'No representative legislature, it appears to us, can ever be respectable or secure, unless it contain within itself a great proportion of those who form the natural aristocracy of the country, and are able, as individuals, to influence the conduct and opinions of the greater part of its inhabitants. Unless the power and weight and authority of the assembly, in short, be really made up of the power and weight and authority of the individuals who compose it, the factitious dignity they may derive from their situation can never be of long endurance.' He was thus proud of the fact that in the House of Commons 'the most certain and the most permanent

D

influence is that of rank and of riches'. Laws are respected all the more because people know that they have been enacted by 'their natural superiors'. There could never be a perfect legislature, but Jeffrey made it plain that he thought that the House of Commons came as near perfection as possible. 'The natural representative is the individual whose example and authority can influence the opinions of the greater part of those in whose behalf he is delegated. This is the natural aristocracy of a civilized nation: and its legislature is then upon the best possible footing, when it is in the hands of those who answer to that description.' In February 1811 he wrote in defence of the 'natural influence of property'. 'There could be no security either for property, or for anything else, in a country where the possession of property did not bestow some political influence.' This however did not extend to 'unnatural' influence, and Jeffrey was opposed to the buying and selling of seats.

In a curious sentence in an article of November 1812 Jeffrey wrote: 'the *balance* of the constitution, in so far as it has any real existence, will be found to subsist almost entirely in the House of Commons, which possesses exclusively both the power of impeachment, and the power of granting supplies: and has besides, the most natural and immediate communication with that great body of the Nation, in whom the power of control over all the branches of the Legislature is ultimately vested. The Executive therefore has its chief Ministers in that House, and exerts in that place all the influence which is attached to its situation'. The constitutional historian might make two comments upon this, first that if the statement was true, it would be a sign of imbalance rather than balance, and second, that it under-estimated the power which still then remained with the House of Lords. What he meant was that the political centre of gravity was already located in the House of Commons, and his theme in this article was not the powers of the Legislature, but those of the Executive. As a good whig he was well aware of Burke's arguments against the powers of the Crown set out in the *Thoughts on the Cause of the Present Discontents*, but he was aware also of how far the pendulum had swung back since 1769. Monarchy, he wrote, was indeed but a human institution, yet it was 'highly beneficial'. It had a double justification. A hereditary monarchy prevented a perpetual struggle for the first place in the nation. Its powers must be limited, but 'we must give enough of real power and distinction and prerogative to make it truly and substantially the first place in the State, and also to make it impossible for the occupiers of inferior places to endanger the general peace by *their* contentions'. It was necessary to give the Crown just enough power to provide political stability, but not so much as to endanger liberty. 'It is in the reconciling of these two conditions that the whole difficulty of the theory of a perfect monarchy consists. If you do not control your sovereign, he will be in danger of becoming a despot; and if you do control him, there is a danger that you create power that is uncontrolled and uncontrollable.' If the power of the King is reduced until he becomes a mere tool in the hands of a ministerial majority, then the nation will have made for itself a new master. Jeffrey's solution of the problem was that the power of the King and of his Ministers should be a counter-balance to each other. The chief power of the King lay in the fact that he could appoint Ministers, although it did not extend to 'the power of maintaining them in their offices against the sense of the nation—but the power of *trying the experiment*, and putting it on the country to take the painful and difficult step of insisting on their removal'. Moreover, the King, as a 'Perpetual Minister', might use his experience and authority powerfully to influence policy.

On the subject of parties, Jeffrey followed the teaching of Burke, 'Parties are necessary in all free governments—and are indeed the characteristics by which such governments may be known. . . . When bad men combine, good men must unite:—and it would not be less hopeless for a crowd of worthy citizens to take the field without leaders or discipline, against a regular army, than for individual patriots to think of opposing the influence of the Sovereign by their separate and uncombined exertions.' (January 1810.)

In politics Jeffrey stood for the middle way. He complained that 'the great body of the nation appears to us to be divided into two violent and most pernicious factions:—the courtiers, who are almost for arbitrary power,—and the democrats, who are almost for revolution and republicanism. Between these stand a small, but most respectable band—friends of liberty and of order, the Old Constitutional Whigs of England, with the best talents and best intentions, but without present power or popularity'. The number of dangerous democrats was increasing, as the popularity of Cobbett's *Political Register* showed, and Jeffrey was convinced that the whigs had no alternative but to trust the people. 'In the present crisis, we have no hesitation in saying, that it is to the popular side that the friends of the constitution must turn themselves; and that, if the Whig leaders do not first conciliate, and then restrain the people,—if they do not save them from the leaders they are already choosing in their own body, and become themselves their leaders by becoming their patrons, and their cordial, though authoritative advisers; they will in no long time sweep away the Constitution itself, the Monarchy of England, and the Whig aristocracy by which that Monarchy is controlled and confirmed and exalted above all other forms of polity.' To the whigs arbitrary and demagogic power were equally obnoxious. Jeffrey concluded his January 1810 article: 'We, in short, are for the monarchy and the aristocracy of England, as the only sure supports of a permanent and regulated freedom; but we do not see how either is now to be preserved, except by surrounding them with the affection of the people. . . . The true friends of the constitution must now bring it back: and must reconcile the people of the old monarchy and the old Parliament of their land, by restraining the prerogative within its legitimate bounds, and bringing back Parliament to its natural habits of sympathy and concord with its constituents. The people therefore, though it may be deluded, must be reclaimed by gentleness, and treated with respect and indulgence. All indications and all feelings of jealousy or contempt must be abjured.'

There was in Jeffrey's writing little evidence that he was aware of the economic and social problems which were aggravating the situation. He saw it simply in terms of political ideas and of the dangers of Jacobin influence. But within these limits, and considering that he was writing during a great war, his thought was moderate and refreshing. He was far from understanding the extent of the problems of his age, yet it took courage to write in 1810: 'the first and the greatest outrages will probably proceed from the people themselves; but a deeper curse will fall on the corrupt and supercilious government that provoked them.' In the following year England experienced the Luddite riots.

.   .   .   .   .   .

Sydney Smith was a great exponent of common sense and toleration at a time when the laws of England still imposed penal disabilities upon Roman Catholics and dissenters. One of the original authors of the *Edinburgh Review*, a Yorkshire parson, and later Canon of St. Paul's, he was a brilliant stylist and wit, and one of the most valiant exponents of the whig cause from 1802 until his death in 1845. True to the teachings of John Locke, he asked: 'What right has any government to dictate to a man who shall guide him to heaven, any more than it has to persecute the religious tenets by which he hopes to arrive there?' His *Peter Plymley Letters* (1807–8) were a splendid plea for toleration for Catholics and for a new era of justice for Ireland.

He was wholly opposed to the spirit of intolerance. 'I love the Church as well as you do; but you totally mistake the nature of an establishment when you contend that it ought to be connected with the military and civil career of every individual in the state. It is quite right that there should be one clergyman to every parish interpreting the Scriptures after a particular manner, ruled by a regular hierarchy, and paid with a rich proportion of haycocks and wheatsheafs. When I have laid this foundation for a rational religion in the state—when I have placed ten thousand well-educated men in different parts of the kingdom to preach it up, and compelled everybody to pay them, whether they hear them or not—I have taken such measures as I know must always procure an immense majority in favour of the Established Church; but I can go no further. I cannot set up a civil inquisition, and say to one, you shall not be a butcher because you are not orthodox; and prohibit another from brewing, and a third from administering the law, and a fourth from defending the country. If common justice did not prohibit me from such a conduct, common sense would.' He felt deeply the injustice suffered by the Catholics of Ireland, and feared the legacy of bitterness which was being provoked. He pointed out that the Government spent only thirteen thousand pounds on the education of four million Catholic Irish while it spent a hundred times that sum on one-eighth the number of Protestants. He argued the futility of retaining the Test and Corporation Acts on the statute book although they had not been enforced for sixty-four years. 'I never met a parson in my life who did not consider the Corporation and Test Acts as the great bulwarks of the Church; and yet it is now just sixty-four years since bills of indemnity to destroy their penal effects (were passed) . . . These bulwarks, without which no clergyman thinks he could sleep with his accustomed soundness, have actually not been in existence since any man now living has taken holy orders.' No wonder, he commented, 'the longer we live, the more we are convinced of the justice of the old saying, that an ounce of mother wit is worth a pound of clergy.'

To the old tory cry of 'the Church in danger', he replied: 'I believe the Church to be in no danger at all; but if it is, that danger is not from the Catholics but from the Methodists, and from that patent Christianity which has been for some time manufacturing at Clapham, to the prejudice of the old and admirable article prepared by the Church. I would counsel my lords the bishops to keep eyes on that holy village and hallowed vicinity: they will find there a zeal in making converts far superior to anything which exists among the Catholics; a contempt for the great mass of English clergy, much more rooted and profound; and a regular fund to purchase livings for those groaning and garrulous gentlemen whom they denominate (by a standing sarcasm against the regular Church) gospel preachers and vital clergymen.'[1]

Sydney Smith's opposition to penal legislation in matters of belief, like his opposition to the Game Laws and the use of spring traps, arose in part from his conviction that any law, to be effective, must carry with it a considerable measure of public support. Public opinion he declared, would never be in favour of a law which allowed a man to be hanged, or to have his legs broken, for poaching. 'The efficient maximum of punishment is not what the Legislature chooses to enact, *but what the great mass of mankind think the maximum ought to be.* The moment the punishment passes this Rubicon it becomes less and less instead of greater and greater. Juries and Magistrates will not commit—informers are afraid of public indignation—poachers will not submit to be sent to Botany Bay without a battle—blood is shed for pheasants—the public attention is called to this preposterous state of the law —and even ministers (whom nothing pesters so much as the interests of humanity) are at last compelled to come forward and do what is right.'

Sydney Smith demanded no revolutionary reform, subscribed to no demagogy. He believed in the Lockeian principles of liberty and in the application of common sense and common humanity to social problems. He was a religious man who had not been frightened by the French Revolution into becoming a reactionary. His 'remedies against nervousness' which he once subscribed to a friend, were 'Resolution, Camphor, Cold Bathing, Exercise in the Open Air, Abstinence from tea and coffee, and from all distant views of human life except when religious duties call on you to take them.' He believed in education for the masses and he advocated a recognition of full rights for women. 'Why are we necessarily to doom a girl, whatever her taste or her capacity, to one unvaried line of petty and frivolous occupation? If she is full of strong sense and elevated curiosity, can there be any reason why she should be diluted and enfeebled down to a mere culler of simples and fancier of birds?' The same cool common sense infused all his thinking.

NOTE

[1] For Sydney Smith's hostility to the Evangelicals see p. 141.

3 : The Political Protagonists
II : The Radicals

RADICALISM, which momentarily captivated so many young literary men in the early days of the French Revolution, did not persist with them, once the consequences became more apparent. It was however strong and persistent, although almost entirely unorganised, among great numbers of artisans in London and the Midland and Northern industrial centres. In the formation of radical thought in England in the period 1790–1830 three names stood out in pre-eminence, namely those of Tom Paine, William Cobbett and Robert Owen, two Radicals and a Socialist, and it is with them that this chapter is concerned. Before however we consider them further, mention must be made of one noted 'Jacobin' among the literary men, William Hazlitt, a complete individualist and brilliant stylist, who never departed far from his original radical opinions.

Hazlitt was born in 1778, the son of a Unitarian Minister. In 1798 Coleridge came to preach in the elder Hazlitt's chapel at Wem; he had that marvellous power wherever he went of inspiring those with whom he talked, and the young Hazlitt took fire. Coleridge invited him to spend three wonderful weeks at Nether-Stowey, and it was from that visit that Hazlitt dated his passion for literature. After an unsuccessful period as a painter, he settled down to earn his living by his pen, and for the rest of his life he was a prolific journalist and critic. A turbulent character, often bitter and disillusioned, he was a brilliant essayist and a most perceptive observer. From the first he took up a political position from which he never shifted, and he remained the most forthright Jacobin long after Wordsworth and Coleridge had deserted their youthful enthusiasms.

I am no politician, and still less can I be said to be a party-man: but I have a hatred of tyranny, and a contempt for its tools; and this feeling I have expressed as often and as strongly as I could. I cannot sit quietly down under the claims of barefaced power, and I have tried to expose the little arts of sophistry by which they are defended. I have no mind to have my person made a property of, nor my understanding made a dupe of. I deny that liberty and slavery are convertible terms, that right and wrong, truth and falsehood, plenty and famine, the comforts or wretchedness of a people, are matters of perfect indifference. That is all I know of the matter; but on these points I am likely to remain incorrigible, in spite of any arguments that I have seen used to the contrary.

Thus he wrote in 1819, the year of the Peterloo Massacre, in the Preface to his *Political Essays*. His argument was simple and direct. The English had achieved liberty in the seventeenth century by means of revolution; the French had done the same in 1789. Britain could no more logically defend the principle of legitimacy in France than they could in their own constitution. 'An Englishman has no distinguishing virtue but honesty: he has and can have no privilege or advantage over other nations but liberty. . . . This is the only politics I know; the only patriotism I feel.' The French Revolution was a blow for liberty, but liberty came near to being overwhelmed by the monarchs of Europe. It was rescued by Napoleon, who thus became for Hazlitt the supreme hero. 'He put his foot upon the neck of kings, who would have put their yoke upon the necks of the people: he scattered before him with fiery execution, millions of hired slaves, who came at the bidding of their masters to deny the right of others to be free. The monument of greatness and of glory he erected, was raised on ground forfeited again and again to humanity—it reared its majestic front on the ruins of the shattered hopes and broken faith of the common enemies of mankind. If he could not secure the freedom, peace, and happiness of his country, he made her a terror to those who by sowing civil dissension and exciting foreign wars, would not let her enjoy those blessings.' To the monarchs of Europe Napoleon was 'the child and champion of Jacobinism', and so he was to Hazlitt. 'Passion speaks truer than reason. If Bonaparte was a conqueror, he conquered the grand conspiracy of kings against the abstract right of the human race to be free; and I, as a man, could not be indifferent which side to take.'

Hazlitt took no sides in party conflicts in England. He was contemptuous of the Radicals as mere dreamers after a Utopia which could never be. As for the main parties, 'A Tory is one who is governed by sense and habit alone. He considers not what is possible, but what is real; he gives might the preference over right. He cries Long Life to the conqueror, and is ever strong upon the stronger side—the side of corruption and prerogative.' As for the whigs, 'A modern Whig is but the fag-end of a Tory.' In the seventeenth century they had been Jacobins, but in face of the French Revolution they had become indistinguishable from the governing party. 'So I cannot find out the different drift, so far as politics are concerned, of the Quarterly and Edinburgh Reviews, which remind one of Opposition coaches, that raise a great dust or spatter one another with mud, but both travel the same road and arrive at the same destination.'

Hazlitt bitterly opposed the war against France, and was as scathing as Cobbett against sinecures, political corruption and the heavy taxation which oppressed the poor. Sinecurists he called 'State-paupers who had their hands in every man's dish', and he attacked courtiers who 'would make the throne everything, and the people nothing, to be yourself less than nothing, a very slave, a reptile, a creeping, cringing sycophant, a court favourite, a pander to Legitimacy that detestable fiction, which would make you and me and all mankind its slaves or victims'. (*What is the People?* March 1818.) In this he was doing little more than repeating the argument which Burke had formulated; but he went further. With Hazlitt there was the recurrent theme that political power was evil and inimical to personal liberty. Only the people knew what was good for them, and therefore the only true government was one based on the will of all. Hazlitt rejected the claims of both heredity and privilege. For him the central problem of political science was simple, namely 'with how little expense of liberty and property the Government can keep the peace'; in short he envisaged the function of government as extending little beyond that of maintaining law and order. He did not probe far into the social problems of his time, although he wrote an extensive *Reply to Malthus*, in which he declared that 'Mr. Malthus's reputation may, I fear, prove fatal to the poor of this country'.

To the historian some of Hazlitt's most effective writing is to be found in his *Spirit of the Age*, in which some of the principal figures of his time are assessed with great perception. Jeremy Bentham 'has lived for the last forty years in a house in West-minster, overlooking the Park, like an anchoret in his cell, reducing law to a system, and the mind of man to a machine'. Coleridge's mind Hazlitt found *tangential*: 'there is no subject on which he has not touched, none on which he has rested'. Sir Walter Scott he found too little a creative writer, but 'a learned, a literal, a matter-of-fact expounder of truth or fable'. Byron he found 'a solitary peak, all access to which is cut off not more by elevation than distance'. Southey he could not forgive for having at first embraced the cause of liberty and then abandoned it. 'He wooed Liberty as a youthful lover, but it was perhaps more as a mistress than a bride; and he has since wedded with an elderly and not very respectable lady, called Legitimacy.' Wordsworth's genius he found 'a pure emanation of the Spirit of the Age ... he sees nothing loftier than human hopes; nothing deeper than the human heart'. His old enemy William Gifford he described as without 'pretensions to be thought a man of genius, of taste, or even of general knowledge'. To Francis Jeffrey of the *Edinburgh Review* he was kinder, because he regarded that journal as 'eminently characteristic of the Spirit of the Age; as it is the express object of the *Quarterly Review* to discountenance and extinguish that spirit, both in theory and practice'. Cobbett he described as 'a kind of *fourth estate* in the politics of the country ... not only unquestion-ably the most powerful political writer of the present day, but one of the best writers in the language'. And so the pageant continued, fully revealing Hazlitt's own prejudices, but also critical powers of the first order. Hazlitt continued all his life the member of no party, enjoying no powerful patronage and few friends, the only true 'Jacobin' among the literary men of his day.

.   .   .   .   .   .

One of the most remarkable features of the period 1780–1830 was in the growth and proliferation of the press as a factor in the formation of public opinion in England. Englishmen in the eighteenth century always accounted a free Press as one of the basic English liberties. There was no censorship after 1695, not even during the French Wars, and by the end of the American War of Independence London had nine daily newspapers, selling over twelve million copies a year. This represented an enormous increase since the days of Addison, and a more than corresponding increase in influence, and if to this we add the great number of cheap tracts circulating among the lower classes, the figures give some indication of the power of the Press. The magnitude of the events of the time, and the consequent demand for news and comment had much to do with the increase, which is all the more remarkable because there was still widespread illiteracy, and newspapers were expensive. Sydney Smith for instance said that there were four times as many readers after the Napoleonic Wars as before 1789. Fox's Libel Act (1792) transferred the question of guilt in libel actions from judges to juries, and this gave popular opinion greater influence in attempts to muzzle the press.

None the less the tory governments, and the governing classes in general, were shaken and alarmed at the sudden growth of a popular press and its power to whip up discontent. The *Anti-Jacobin Review* declared in 1801: 'We have long considered the establishment of newspapers in this country as a misfortune to be regretted; but, since their influence has become predominant by the universality of their circulation, we regard it as a calamity most deeply to be deplored.' (Quoted Aspinall: *Politics and the Press* (1949), p. 9.) Pitt's government took the same view, but even at the height of their fears of Jacobinism they did not dare to resort to censorship (although in fact many papers would have preferred it to the uncertainty which they were forced to endure), but instead relied on other means of controlling the flood. First, they could stretch the laws against sedition to their limits. Second, they could increase the newspaper tax, so that by 1797 a paper cost $4\frac{1}{2}d$. Third, they could subsidise loyal newspapers from the Secret Service funds. *The Diary*, for instance, owned by William Woodfall, received £400 a year from 1789 until it collapsed in 1793. The *London Evening Post* received £200 a year for some years after 1784. John Walter of *The Times* in 1789 went over to the support of the government in return for a subsidy of three hundred pounds a year, which continued until 1799. It was not always simply a matter of bribery; a proprietor might decide to support the Government through conviction, and receive a subsidy in compensation for a resultant loss of revenues, either from circulation or advertisements, or both. It must be remembered that in the eighteenth century advertisements were often considered more important than news. *The Times* continued to give general support to the tory government until the time of Peterloo, when it went over to the popular side and attacked the Six Acts. It was also very favourable to Queen Caroline during the Queen's Affair, in the teeth, as one would suppose, of the evidence to the contrary. How powerful the Press was thought to be is shown by the interesting instance of the *Morning Post* in 1788, which began publishing such damaging revelations about the Prince of Wales and Mrs. Fitzherbert that Carlton House decided to buy out the interest of the lessee, John Benjafield, for a thousand guineas and an annuity of £350 for the remaining five years his lease had to run. Henceforth the paper became a supporter of the whigs.

· · · · · ·

Tom Paine was born 1737, the son of a Quaker stay-maker at Thetford, Norfolk. For a time he followed his father's occupation, then became an exciseman at Lewes, was dismissed for negligence, turned his hand to schoolmastering, and eventually in 1774 emigrated to America, where he found his true vocation. Fired by the cause of the American revolution, he became a prolific journalist. His *Common Sense* (1776) and numerous pamphlets and articles did much to encourage American resistance and he became a powerful force on the side of liberty and independence.

In 1787 he returned to England. He had always been passionately interested in science, and he spent much time on several inventions, the most important of which was the construction of the first iron bridge at Wearmouth. The French Revolution again called him to political action. The *Rights of Man* was written in answer to Burke's *Reflections* in 1791, and in spite of proscription by the government, it did so well that Paine could give £1,000 from its profits to the London Corresponding Society. Elected a member of the Convention in France, he was in favour of ending the monarchy, but not of executing the King. He spent ten months in prison, and narrowly escaped the guillotine himself. In his *Age of Reason* he set out the typical religious views of an eighteenth-century Deist. An outlaw in England, and soon out of sympathy with the course of events in France, he returned to America in 1802, and died there a neglected figure in 1809.

Tom Paine, unlike Burke, thought of the science of government as a kind of geometry, to be reduced to a series of propositions. 'There is not', he wrote, 'a problem in Euclid more mathematically true than that hereditary government has not a right to exist.' A political principle, if right, was right for all times and places. 'Time with respect to principles is an eternal NOW: it has no operation upon them: it changes nothing of their nature and qualities.' Natural rights were eternal and immutable; they belonged to man as man, and could not be modified or limited by any government. In order to establish this principle, Paine drew a clear distinction between society and the government. 'Society was a blessing, since no man could arrive at a degree of civilisation without co-operation with his fellow-men: and, if all were equally good there would be no need for government at all. For government was made necessary by 'the inability of moral virtue to govern the world'. Since society preceded the foundation of a government it followed that it was superior to it, and men would not be so foolish as to establish a government which left them worse off than before. But in the course of time kings and aristocracy had usurped powers and privileges by force, and thus the British constitution had emerged, full of false and anachronistic principles. He admitted that 'every nation *for the time being*, has a right to govern itself as it pleases', but what it did not have was the right to bind its successors to a form of government contrary to the principles of the rights of man.

The real point at issue between Burke and Paine was whether 'the people of England had the right to choose their rulers, to cashier them for misconduct, and to adopt a new form of government in its place'. Burke feared the endless change and wholesale proscription which would follow the acceptance of any such principle. Paine took his stand on what he regarded as man's inalienable rights, and on the absurdities and anachronisms which he thought existed in the British constitution of the time. What had happened in 1688 could happen again, for 'that which a whole nation chooses to do, it has a right to do'. He regarded the principle of liberty to be so unanswerable and beneficent that once it was embraced by the people it would be irresistible. Burke, on the other hand, saw it as a terrible power, for 'liberty, when men act in bodies, is *power*'. Since, Paine retorted, that 'it is power, and not principles, that Mr. Burke venerates', it is clear that they were talking of different manifestations of power. Paine exalted the French Declaration of the Rights of Man, and asked whether Burke denied that man had any rights. Burke declared that he knew very well what were the rights of *Englishmen*, but that they did not extend to tearing down the constitution. To Burke a constitution was the result of slow evolution through long periods of history. Paine on the other hand defined it as 'a thing *antecedent* to a government, and a government is only the creature of a constitution. The constitution of a country is not the act of its government, but of the people constituting its government. . . . A constitution therefore is to a government what the laws made afterwards by that government are to a court of judicature'. By such a definition England had never had a constitution, or if it had, it had been lost before the Norman Conquest, and the only peoples who could claim to have one were the Americans and the French after 1791. To Paine all English government since the Norman Conquest was the result of usurpation, since the only legitimate basis for a constitution was the declared will of the people. (At this point he found it convenient to ignore 1688.)

Both Burke and Paine exalted society above the government, but for opposite reasons. To Burke society was a historical concept, and he sought to preserve its ancient framework; to Paine it was a numerical concept, and he sought to use it as a basis for the destruction of as much of the ancient framework as appeared to be inconsistent with reason.

Paine was able to make effective debating points against a country which, in order to uphold the monarchical principle, had had to import a monarch from Hanover, and against the government which had resulted. 'It is very easy to conceive that a band of interested men, such as placemen, pensioners, lords of the bedchamber, lords of the kitchen, lords of the necessary-house, and the Lord knows what besides, can find as many reasons for monarchy as their salaries, paid at the expense of the country, amount to; but I ask the farmer, the manufacturer, the merchant, the tradesman, and down through all the occupations of life to the common labourer, what service monarchy is to him? He can give me no answer.' But in all this the British government was no better or worse than others, for 'all hereditary government is in its nature tyranny'. All through history the natural tendencies of society were 'disturbed or destroyed by the operations of government'. Burke declared the Rights of Man a great process of 'levelling', but Paine asked wherein men were more effectively levelled than in a hereditary monarchy? The hereditary principle of government entailed a perversion of the law in order to maintain the oligarchy in power, and thus 'from the want of a constitution in England to restrain and regulate the wild impulse of power, many of the laws are irrational and tyrannical, and the administration of them vague and problematical'.

In place of the hereditary principle of government Paine advocated 'government by election and representation'. 'Mankind', he wrote, 'are not now to be told they shall not think or they shall not read; and publications that go no further than to investigate principles of government, to invite men to reason and to reflect and to shew the errors and excellencies of different systems, have a right to appear.' This was reasonable enough, but Paine went on to make contemporaries' flesh creep when he added:

'I do not believe that monarchy and aristocracy will continue seven years longer in any of the enlightened countries of Europe.' He painted a terrible picture of the social problem in England: 'When, in countries that are called civilized, we see age going to the workhouse and youth to the gallows, something must be wrong in the system of government. It would seem, by the exterior appearance of such countries, that all was happiness; but there lies hidden from the eye of common observation, a mass of wretchedness that has scarcely any other chance, than to expire in poverty or infamy. . . . Why is it that scarcely any are executed but the poor? The fact is a proof, among other things, of a wretchedness in their condition. Bred up without morals and cast upon the world without a prospect, they are the exposed sacrifice of vice and legal barbarity.' This in fact was little more than Defoe had said seventy years before about poverty in London. The difference was that Paine was advocating a solution of the problem by revolutionary action. He did not indeed preach a social egalitarianism. 'That property will ever be unequal is certain', for men's industry and superiority of talents would see to that. But he argued that taxation favoured the landed gentry, that 'the aristocracy are not the farmers who work the land and raise the produce, but are the mere consumers of rent'; and that 'the Duke of Richmond alone takes away as much for himself as would maintain two thousand poor and aged persons'. He attacked the large annual war expenditure, and advocated the abolition of the armed forces (which, he argued, the French Revolution had made unnecessary), the abolition of the poor rates, and a wholesale reduction of taxation to the relief of the poor. He went further, and proposed the foundation of a Welfare State.

In this respect there was a curious contradiction in Paine's argument. He began by fully accepting the eighteenth-century view of the unimportance of government in a healthy society. 'Government', he wrote, 'is no farther necessary than to supply the few cases to which society and civilization are not conveniently competent'; and again, 'It is but few general laws that civilized life requires.' But in the concluding chapters of the *Rights of Man* his Welfare State presents a very different picture. He proposed the

E

abolition of the poor-rates, State relief for two hundred and fifty thousand poor families, free education for over a million children, family allowances of four pounds a year for every child under the age of fourteen, compulsory elementary education, and the payment of maternity benefits, old age pensions and funeral allowances. In addition he proposed State employment for all the casual poor of London, and the provision of public workshops in order to prevent young people from falling into evil ways through poverty, the money to be raised by a tax on coals. 'The hearts of the humane will not be shocked by ragged and hungry children, and persons of seventy and eighty years of age begging for bread. The dying poor will not be dragged from place to place to breathe their last, as a reprisal of parish upon parish. Widows will have a maintenance for their children, and not be carted away, on the death of their husbands, like culprits and criminals; and children will no longer be considered as increasing the distresses of their parents. . . . Ye who sit in ease, and solace yourselves in plenty—and such there are in Turkey and Russia, as well as in England—and who say to yourselves, 'Are we not well off?' have ye thought of these things? When ye do, ye will cease to speak and feel for yourselves alone.' To pay for his social experiment Paine was relying on the substantial savings from the abolition of the armed forces, and also upon a graduated income tax which reached twenty shillings in the pound on incomes over £22,000 a year. The test of a civilised society, he declared, was one which could say 'My poor are happy'. There was no limit to what could be achieved: 'The present age will hereafter merit to be called the Age of Reason, and the present generation will appear to the future as the Adam of a new world.' Tom Paine was an optimist, with a genuine love of humanity. 'In stating these matters, I speak in open and disinterested language dictated by no passion but that of humanity. To me, who have not only refused offers because I thought them improper, but have declined rewards I might with reputation have accepted, it is no wonder that meanness and imposition appear disgustful. Independence is my happiness, and I view things as they are, without regard to place or person; my country is the world, and my religion is to do good.' This was a fair comment, for he was a warm-hearted man who would rather suffer imprisonment in France than agree to the execution of Louis XVI once he had been deposed. In England *The Rights of Man* became the bible of the extreme radicals, while to the great mass of the governing classes Paine's name was hated and feared as a devil incarnate. His books were proscribed, and booksellers who distributed them were imprisoned.

What was the real significance of Paine's book? The answer lies in the fact that he advocated political power for all men, irrespective of wealth or property. It was this which separated him from the numerous leaders of County Associations and Reform societies which had emerged since 1768, and it was this which branded him as a dangerous man, for it was assumed that manhood suffrage would be merely a preliminary to a general assault upon property. Not since Bunyan's *Pilgrim's Progress* had a book made such an impact on the masses. It was from Paine's *Rights of Man* (the first part of which was published in 1791, the second in 1792) that the masses first learnt the principles of the French Revolution. To the question whether those principles fell on fertile soil in England the answer is a complicated one. In one sense Dissent provided fruitful soil. Dr. Price and Joseph Priestley at once raised the cry of complete religious freedom as the first stage towards liberty. The dissenting attitude often inculcated an independence of mind, a belief in the millennium, and an Old Testament style of speaking which often made political and social reform appear to be a simple matter of Christian justice. In Huddersfield the Methodist New Connection after 1797 were known as the 'Tom Paine Methodists'.[1] Tom Paine himself had a Quaker background, and the great majority of radical leaders up to the time of the Chartists can be shown either to be Dissenters of one kind or another, or to have come from Dissenting homes. Halévy's famous statement that Methodism saved England from revolution has long been shown to have been a considerable over-statement, for there were only eighty thousand Methodists in England, and they could not themselves have withstood a rising tide of revolution. On the other hand, the so-called Church-and-King riots in Birmingham in 1791 against Priestley and the

Dissenters have been now shown to be misnamed[2] for the numbers involved were few, and it is by no means certain whether the attacks were launched on men who were Dissenters, or on men who were rich. In either case the incident cannot be taken as representing the attitude of the masses at the time. The famous treason trials of Thomas Hardy and his friends in 1794 were followed with breathless interest, and there was widespread rejoicing at their acquittal. On the other hand the severe penalties attached to the circulation of Tom Paine's book certainly acted as a powerful deterrent. The eighteenth century may be said to have had a tradition of rioting, as the Porteous Riots and the Gordon Riots, as well as numerous small-town grain riots make clear, and the Gordon Riots had left an indelible mark on the fears of the governing classes. Popular agitation was certainly curbed by repressive legislation, but the partiality of the crowd shown to Radical candidates, such as Sir Francis Burdett and Admiral Cochrane at Westminster in 1807 is a good indication of where sympathies lay.

There was always likely to be a turbulent and riotous aspect to an eighteenth-century crowd, but in a deeper sense the masses were immune from revolutionary instincts. There was a deep-seated belief in the rights of a free-born Englishman, and although this could lead to strong protests against practical grievances, such as the operation of the press-gangs, it did not encourage a desire to overthrow society. The *Rights of Man* was undoubtedly a challenge to authority, but Paine gave no indication how he thought the changes he advocated should be brought about, and he nowhere proposed violence and bloodshed. What he did do was to provide, in a brilliantly effective journalistic style, a clear assertion of the obligations of society to all its members. He did not attack capitalism or the rights of property, but he did emphasise the obligation of society to the poor.

Burke's *Reflections* sold thirty thousand copies during the first two years, Paine's *Rights of Man* two hundred thousand copies. Corresponding and Constitutional Societies sprang up during 1792, particularly in Sheffield, Norwich, Derby, Stockport, Manchester and in Scotland. But with the execution of Louis XVI, and the onset of war, there was a change of attitude. A proclamation was issued against seditious writings, it became dangerous to quote Tom Paine, and in some towns he was hanged in effigy. In the Scottish Trials of 1793–4 Muir, Palmer, Margarot and Gerrald received savage sentences of transportation for attending a Convention at Edinburgh. In England in 1794 the Government swooped on the leaders of the Constitutional and Corresponding Societies, had them arrested, and staged their trial for treason. Public sympathy however was with the accused, and juries acquitted Thomas Hardy, Horne Tooke and John Thelwall, after which the other trials were dropped. In 1795 the window of the King's coach was struck by a stone during a hostile demonstration, and Pitt hurried through the Two Acts, making it a treasonable offence to speak against the King, government or constitution, and prohibiting public meetings. There were few prosecutions under these Acts, and no one suffered execution; the threat was enough. Two years later the government had to deal with mutiny in the fleet, followed by the conspiracies of the United Irishmen and United Englishmen, and rebellion in Ireland, in all of which there was undoubtedly Jacobin influence. By 1798 the great mass of moderate opinion in the country was behind the government, equating reform with revolution, and in these circumstances the threat of revolution receded.

Yet E. P. Thompson (op. cit., Chap. V) has shown the great importance of the years 1791–6 in the formation of a working-class consciousness in England. Deprived almost entirely of middle-class support, the working classes were thrust back upon themselves. Jacobin (that is to say, egalitarian) views persisted, and Mr. Thompson writes: 'Throughout the war years there were Thomas Hardys in every town and in many villages throughout England, with a kist or shelf full of Radical books, biding their time, putting in a word at the tavern, the chapel, the smithy, the shoemaker's shop, waiting for the movement to revive. And the movement for which they waited did not belong to gentlemen, manufacturers, or rate-payers; it was *their own*.' (op. cit., p. 183.)

If they were reading Tom Paine in 1794, twenty years later they were certainly reading Cobbett. William Cobbett was born in 1763 in Farnham, Surrey, the son of a small farmer and inn-keeper. Failing to run away to sea, he eventually went to London and became a lawyer's clerk. He hated the life, joined the army, and was sent to Canada, where he became a sergeant-major. On his discharge he attempted to reveal the peculation of which officers were guilty, and failing in this he fled to France, and thence to the United States, where he became a teacher of English to French immigrants. He had done much private study when in the army; he even wrote an English grammar, and never tired of urging young men to follow his example and educate themselves as the first condition for success in life. A strong patriot, he denounced the French Revolution, Jacobinism, Tom Paine and all Radicalism, and returned to England in 1800 to find himself flattered by the government as a valuable anti-Jacobin propagandist. In 1802 he started *The Political Register*, which he continued until his death in 1835. He soon ceased to support the government, as he became more and more dissatisfied with everything he saw around him. By 1805 he was convinced that England was dominated by a tyranny of fund-holders and borough mongers, what he called 'the System'; that the old England he had known as a boy was being undermined by tax-gatherers, contractors, jobbers and courtiers. As he moved over to the side of the Radicals, the influence of his paper grew. In 1810 he was sent to prison for two years, and heavily fined for opposing flogging in the army. In the grim years of social unrest after 1815 he became a power in the land. With the heavy stamp duty imposed by the government, the *Political Register* cost $12\frac{1}{2}d.$, and was thus far beyond the reach of small farmers, craftsmen and labourers, for whom it was intended. In 1816, however, Cobbett hit upon a way of avoiding the stamp duty, by circulating certain articles as pamphlets, which were sold at $2d.$ Circulation then reached many thousands, and Cobbett worked out an elaborate system of distribution, making it worth while for hawkers to offer them throughout the countryside. The government was alarmed. Lord Sidmouth, the Home Secretary, said that the newspaper Press was 'a most malignant and for-

midable enemy of the Constitution to which it owed its freedom';
and he called the *Political Register* 'trade in sedition'. Effective
pressure was brought on publicans to ban it in their houses. In
1817 the magistrates of Shropshire had two men flogged for
distributing it (Aspinall: *Politics and the Press*, p. 46). An Act was
hurried through plugging the loop-hole Cobbett had found with his
'Twopenny Trash', and for a time he had to flee to the United
States. He continued however to publish his paper, and much else
besides. He was elected member of parliament for Oldham as a
Radical in 1832, but made little mark there, although he spoke
well for the Factory Act of 1833 and he bitterly opposed the Poor
Law Amendment Act of 1834. He died in the following year.

Cobbett was accounted a dangerous Radical, but it was a
radicalism which sprang from his innate toryism. It owed nothing
to Tom Paine and little to anyone else, although Jonathan Swift
was a constant source of inspiration and quotation. He was
enormously proud of being an Englishman, and of the soil from
which he sprang. He loved to idealise the English character, and the
sights and sounds of the countryside he knew so well. He was
convinced that the Englishman worked three times as hard as
foreigners; he loved the signs of prosperity. He wrote, 'Next after a
foxhunt, the finest sight in England is a stage-coach just ready to
start. A great sheep or cattle fair is a beautiful sight; but, in a
stage-coach you see more of what man is capable of performing.
The vehicle itself, the harness, all so complete and so neatly
arranged; so strong and clean and good. The beautiful horses
impatient to be off. The inside full and the outside covered, in
every part, with men, women, children, boxes, bags, bundles. The
coachman taking his reins in one hand and his whip in the other,
gives a signal with his foot, and away go, at the rate of seven miles
an hour, the population and the property of a hamlet.' (*P.R.*,
23 March 1816.) Such things, he argued, could be obtained only by
'incessant labour, which is continually creating things, which give
strength to a country'.

He loved his vision of Merrie England: 'In the whole world
there was not so happy a country as England was. In the reading
of our books and in the hearing of verbal descriptions of cottages

in England; of the industry, the neatness, the order and the regularity of those dwellings of our labourers, the people of other countries think they are listeners to romances. . . . Brass and pewter were seen everywhere. It was a disgrace not to have window curtains, bed-curtains and feather beds. The labourers were happy. Each had his little home. He had things about him worth possessing and worth preserving. . . .' (*P.R.*, 26 July 1817.)

It was because it seemed to him that these things were slipping away that he became a Radical. The war, war taxation and the growth of industrialism seemed to him to be destroying the virtue of old England. Cobbett had a formidable list of hatreds. He hated 'upstarts of trade', loan-jobbers, contractors, nabobs, insurance brokers, usurers, slave-owners, the 'paper-aristocracy' (that is to say, the *rentiers* who thought investment in government stock more desirable than landed property), the Wen (London), and borough-mongers (who dominated parliament), the whole amounting in his parlance to 'the System'. London he called 'this monstrous Wen now sucking up the vitals of the country'. He hated to see the decay of the old landed gentry, and their replacement by the upstart rich, those who had sprung, as he said, 'from the dunghill to a chariot'.

He always proclaimed his loyalty to the monarchy, but the King, he declared, had become a prisoner of the borough-mongers; the royal family had even had to try to bribe the Press in order to offset the calumnies of their enemies. And what kind of government did England have? 'What name to give such a government it is difficult to say. It is like nothing that ever was heard of before. It is neither a monarchy, an aristocracy, nor a democracy; it is a band of great nobles who, by sham elections, and by the means of all sorts of bribery and corruption, have obtained an absolute sway in the country, having under them, for the purposes of *show* and of execution, a thing they call a *king*, sharp and unprincipled fellows whom they call *Ministers*, a mummery which they call a *Church*, experienced and well-tried and steel-hearted men whom they call *Judges*, a company of false money makers, whom they call a *Bank*, numerous bands of brave and needy persons whom they call *soldiers* and *sailors*; and a talking, corrupt, and impudent set, whom they call a *House of Commons*. Such is the government of England.' (*P.R.*, 8 June 1816.)

He hated the Napoleonic Wars, not only for their consequences for the people of England, but also because he was not certain of their purpose. Was it in order to overthrow the military power of France, or was it to suppress the principles of the French Revolution? If the latter, they were bound to fail, for those principles were spreading steadily throughout Europe. He did not flinch from being called a Jacobin, or an advocate of *French principles*; for 'what are these principles? That governments were made for the people, and not the people for governments.—That sovereigns reign legally only by virtue of the people's choice.—That birth without merit ought not to command merit without birth.—That all men ought to be equal in the eye of the law.—That no man ought to be taxed or punished by any law to which he has not given his assent by himself or by his representative.—That taxation and representation ought to go hand in hand.—That every man ought to be judged by his peers, or equals.—That the press ought to be free.' (*P.R.*, 29 April 1815.) If this was Jacobinism, Cobbett did not object to being called a Jacobin.

Yet Cobbett was no revolutionary. He tried hard to understand the causes of the misery and discontent he saw around him, and he pressed for reform, but when violence occurred he was shocked and saddened. His regret was that these things happened in the country whose praises he had been accustomed to sing in America. 'Perhaps you think, by this time, as I do, that we were a set of very ignorant though honest fellows, who confounded admiration of men in power with love of country.' The misery was real enough. He argued in 1806 that six millions a year were spent in parish relief, and that a million people were in receipt of it; that poor relief was humiliating and degrading, and that even when a labourer was fully employed, his wages were likely to be no more than twelve shillings a week at a time when a quartern loaf was eleven pence or more, and that this was not a living wage. The blame he placed on war taxation. 'Back then we still return to the old point; the taxes, the taxes, the taxes! while we are loaded with them as we are now nothing can retard the progress of pauperism and of crimes.' (*P.R.*, 15 May 1816.) In 1823 he wrote that England actually produced a surplus of food, yet men were starving; and this was the 'joyous country, smiling in plenty' of which politicians spoke! When the Luddite riots broke out in 1811, he wrote that they were the result of the Continental System, and could not be blamed on the government. In 1816 he wrote that the Luddites should not blame machinery for their misery; machinery, by reducing prices, ought to increase production, and this must be to the benefit of workers. He probed all the facts and figures at his command, and urged the rioters to place the blame, not on employers or the use of machinery, but on the burdens of taxation. 'It is the sum taken from those who labour to be given to those who do not labour, which has produced our present misery. . . . You pay a tax on your shoes, soap, candles, salt, sugar, coffee, malt, beer, bricks, tiles, tobacco, drugs, spirits, and indeed on almost every thing you use in any way whatever. And, it is a monstrous cheat in the corrupt writers to attempt to persuade you, that *you* pay *no taxes*, and upon that ground to pretend that you have no right to vote for Members of Parliament.' 'Thus, then, my fellow-countrymen, it is not *machinery*; it is not the grinding disposition of your employers; it is not improvements in Machinery, it is not extortions on the part of Bakers and Butchers and Millers and Farmers and Corn-Dealers and Cheese and Butter Sellers. It is not to any causes of this sort that you ought to attribute your present great and cruel sufferings; but wholly and solely to the great burden of taxes, co-operating with the bubble of paper-money.' (*P.R.*, 30 November 1816.)

Cobbett was bitterly hostile to the new Political Economy which formulated the principles of *laissez-faire*. To Malthus he addressed an open letter (8 May 1819): 'Parson, I have, during my life, detested many men; but never any one so much as you.' He was infuriated that Malthus should suggest that parish relief be cut off from children born after a certain date. He detested his talk of the laws of nature: 'the law of nature bids a man *not starve* in a land of plenty, and forbids his being punished for taking food wherever he can find it. Your law of nature is sitting at Westminster, to make the labourer pay taxes, to make him fight for the safety of the land, to bind him in allegiance, and when he is poor and hungry, to cast him off to starve, or to hang him if he takes food to save his life!' Cobbett came to believe that all the governing classes were ranged against the interests of the poor. He did not forget that Malthus was a parson, and that parsons were prominent on the bench when savage penalties were inflicted for breaches of the Game Laws; that Wilberforce had supported Pitt's repressive legislation, and that the Methodists were opposed to social reform (*P.R.*, 5 June 1813). It was for this reason that he was so suspicious of the attempts of the upper classes to 'educate' the poor. Hannah More, 'that prime old prelate in petticoats, that choice tool of the borough-mongers' was a particular butt of his irony, for teaching the poor to be thankful for their lot while they were dying of starvation. The Society for the Diffusion of Useful Knowledge and the activities of Brougham and Lord Althorp pleased him no more. 'This, like all the rest of the "education" schemes, is a combination for the purpose of *amusing* the working classes, and *diverting their attention from the cause of their poverty and misery.* The methodist parsons are the most *efficient* tools in this way. They flatly assert that when a man's dinner is taken away by the taxgatherer, it is *for his good* and that he ought to bless God for it.' (*P.R.*, 29 May 1830.)[3]

Cobbett came to the conclusion therefore that the only real solution to the social problem was parliamentary reform, with annual parliaments, manhood suffrage, the abolition of all property qualifications, and secret ballot. But would this really give the labourer a cow or a pig, bread and cheese and beer? Would it give him back his self-respect, and prevent degrading exploitation? 'The enemies of reform jeeringly ask us, whether reform would do these things for us; and I answer distinctly that IT WOULD DO THEM ALL!' He defended the rioters in the agricultural risings of 1830, on the grounds that they would not have caused disturbances if their conditions had not been desperate. At any rate, he argued, their actions brought parliamentary reform nearer. The Act of 1832 fell far short of his demands, and was in every respect a great disappointment to him.

Cobbett came to regard the nation as divided into two classes, idlers, who lived on the proceeds of taxes, and producers, who were taxed to maintain the idlers. For this reason he was ready to support any move which was aimed at raising the status of the worker. He approved of the early trade unions: 'we are now to see whether a working people will continue to live upon potatoes and salt, while so large a part of their earnings is taken from them to be given to pensioners, sinecure people, men and women, half-pay people, retired-allowance people, military-academy people, and to bands of usurers.' (7 Dec. 1833.) He bitterly attacked the injustice meted out to the Tolpuddle Martyrs in 1834, when seven agricultural labourers were sentenced to seven years' transportation for taking an oath which they did not know to be illegal. He bitterly opposed the appointment of the Poor Law Commission, and still more the Poor Law Amendment Act of 1834, declaring that its purpose was to establish a centralised tyranny in England, to 'reduce the people of England to the state of the people of Ireland; to make them live upon potatoes at best' (potatoes to Cobbett were always a sign of the degradation of the peasants); and finally that the Act would provoke revolution. Cobbett was preparing to organise a nation-wide resistance to the measure when he died in 1835.

Throughout Cobbett's thought there ran the hostility to the growth of governmental power and the encroachment of centralisation, as being inimical to the freedoms of the people. This was what was at the root of his hostility to *The Thing*, as a gigantic conspiracy to deprive producers of their earnings in the form of taxation. Nor did this make him a friend to *laissez-faire*, for he bitterly opposed the teachings of Malthus and Ricardo, and what he called 'Scotch feelosofy', and he was equally opposed to the Utilitarianism which lay at the root of the thinking on Poor Law reform. He usually wrote in kindly terms of Tom Paine, but he was essentially not a Painite radical. In many ways he was a reactionary, looking back nostalgically to an ideal rural England before the days of an Industrial and Agricultural Revolution. He was an acute and warm-hearted observer of the rural scene, though he often misinterpreted the causes of the phenomena he observed. His *Political Register* had immense influence in forming political opinion among the lower classes, and there were many in the government who believed that it had much to do with stirring up the agricultural risings of 1830. A farmer himself, he loved the land, but he resented the tendency of farmers to become *gentlemen*, while their labourers sank into misery and degradation. He could speak with equal effect to the urban workers of the north, for their problems were similar, and their roots not yet entirely severed from the soil. On the whole his influence was not revolutionary; he was concerned to form a powerful public opinion in favour of reform to be achieved by parliamentary means. After 1807 Cobbett, Sir Francis Burdett, Major Cartwright, Orator Hunt and Francis Place were the leading Radicals, and none of them was a revolutionary. Their way out of the perplexing difficulties of the time lay through parliamentary reform. Cobbett certainly had little idea of how to organise to produce such a result; he relied on his pen and on the force of mass opinion, and in this he had considerable success. Samuel Bamford (*Early Days*, p. 11) declared that Cobbett's writings 'were read on nearly every cottage hearth in the manufacturing districts of South Lancashire, in those of Leicester, Derby and Nottingham; also in many of the Scottish manufacturing towns'. Bamford continued that by directing readers to 'the true cause of their sufferings—misgovernment, and to its proper corrective—parliamentary reform', Cobbett turned the working classes away from rioting and towards discussion and organisation. Almost all that the working classes knew of the problems of the time they had learnt from Cobbett. Perhaps the greatest thing which he gave them was a renewed sense of human dignity. He himself however remained suspicious and chary of organisations for the achievement of radical reform: 'I advise my countrymen to have nothing to do with any Political Clubs, and secret Cabals, any Correspondencies; but to trust to individual exertions and open meetings.' He certainly feared government reprisals, and indeed in 1817 he himself took refuge in America. His influence however continued unchecked. He was an intense individualist, with a style capable of seizing the imaginations of the masses. He was able therefore to forge a widespread radical spirit based on democratic principles. Among his contemporaries only Tom Paine and Robert Owen had a comparable influence.

.   .   .   .   .

If a Radical is defined as one primarily concerned with sweeping parliamentary reform, then Robert Owen was not a Radical, for to him parliamentary reform was a matter of complete indifference. His prime concern was to ameliorate the social consequences of the Industrial Revolution, and few of his contemporaries saw more clearly what those consequences were. He recognised that whereas nearly nine hundred thousand families were chiefly employed in agriculture, nearly one million one hundred and thirty thousand families were engaged chiefly in trade and manufactures, and that the disparity was increasing rapidly. 'The manufacturing system has already so far extended its influence over the British Empire, as to effect an essential change in the general character of the mass of the people. This alteration is still in rapid progress; and ere long the comparatively happy simplicity of the agricultural peasant will be wholly lost amongst us. It is even now scarcely anywhere to be found without a mixture of those habits which are the offspring of trade, manufactures and commerce.' (*Observations on the Effect of the Manufacturing System.*) With industrialisation had come the relentless pursuit of profits; 'All are sedulously trained to buy cheap and to sell dear; and to succeed in this art, the parties must be taught to acquire strong powers of deception; and thus a spirit is generated through every class of traders, destructive of that open, honest, sincerity, without which man cannot make others happy, nor enjoy happiness himself.' Meanwhile, long hours in factories were destructive of health, and employment had become merely a cash relationship regardless of moral responsibility.

Born in Newtown, Montgomeryshire, Robert Owen was first employed as an errand-boy, went to London at the early age of ten, was employed in the drapery business, first in Stamford, Lincolnshire and then in London. He rose to a partnership in a business in Manchester, and then, at the turn of the century, became partner and manager of the New Lanark Mills, in Scotland, and for eighteen years conducted his famous experiments to combine industrial capitalism with social reform. His most notable book,

A New View of Society, was published as essays between 1813 and 1818, and was primarily a plea for a national system of education. As a Benthamite Utilitarian, he was convinced that the human character could be moulded to any shape according to experiences to which it was subjected, especially in early life. If, then, the labouring classes were ignorant, brutalised and criminal, the fault was not theirs but the society's which had corrupted them. The problem was a frightening one in its dimensions, for Owen calculated that the class exceeded fifteen millions of persons, and was nearly three-quarters of the population. 'The characters of these persons are now permitted to be very generally formed without proper guidance or direction, and, in many cases, under circumstances which directly impel them to a course of extreme vice and misery; thus rendering them the worst and most dangerous subjects in the empire.' On the other hand, Owen was an optimist in his proposals for dealing with the problem, since he argued that 'children can be trained to acquire any language, sentiments, belief, or any bodily habits and manners, not contrary to human nature'. All that was needed was that children should be taught the principles of happiness, both for themselves and the community. His plan was therefore for the training of children from earliest infancy in principles of rational humanity. And if this, he declared, should be thought visionary, his age was reminded that it spent millions a year on the detection and punishment of crime, and in Poor Relief, which could be eliminated in a happier society.

Robert Owen could claim practical experience of the subject. The Lanark cotton mills had been founded by a man named Dale in 1784, and when Owen took charge fifteen years later he found the most deplorable conditions. 'The population lived in idleness, in poverty, in almost every kind of crime; consequently in debt, in poverty, out of health and in misery. Theft and the receipt of stolen goods was their trade, idleness and drunkenness their habit, falsehood and deception their garb, dissensions, civil and religious their daily practice; they united only in a zealous systematic opposition to their employers.' Children, obtained from workhouses and charities in Edinburgh, worked from six in the morning until seven in the evening, and as a consequence 'many of them became dwarfs in body and mind, and some of them were deformed'. Owen did not blame his predecessor; he was in fact a kind and considerate man; the fault lay with the system which employed children at so early an age. Owen determined upon a reformation. By a system of rewards and punishments he discouraged falsehoods, thefts and drunkenness, and encouraged sobriety and good work. He refused to employ pauper children, or any children under the age of ten; he established a village school where children from the age of five to ten were taught to read and write and to enjoy themselves. He built good houses, paved the streets, planted trees, provided gardens and established an honest village shop. The success of the experiment was startling, not only in the character and happiness of his workers, but also in the improved quality of the output of his mills and the size of his profits. 'Drunkenness is not seen in their streets; and the children are taught and trained in the institution for forming their character without any punishment. The community exhibits the general appearance of industry, temperance, comfort, health and happiness.' The purpose therefore of Owen's *New View of Society* was to propose a national system of education and reform, since 'the experiment cannot fail to prove the certain means of renovating the moral and religious principles of the world, by showing whence arise the various opinions, manners, vices and virtues of mankind, and how the best or the worst of them may, with mathematical precision, be taught to the rising generation'.

Owen's plan therefore was three-fold. First, to provide free schooling for all children between the ages of five and ten. Owen was a hundred years ahead of his time in advocating the importance of happiness and activity as a necessary part of learning. In the importance he attached to education Owen was fully in accord with the spirit of the Enlightenment. 'The history of humanity shows it to be an undeviating law of nature, that man shall not prematurely break the shell of ignorance; that he must patiently wait until the principle of knowledge has pervaded the whole mass of the interior, to give it life and strength sufficient to bear the light of day.' A break-through however had come with the realisation of the truth that men did not form their own individual characters, but that they were formed for them by the influence of society; that society 'may train the young to become effeminate, deceitful, ignorantly selfish, intemperate, revengeful, murderous, ignorant, irrational, and miserable; or to be manly, just, generous, temperate, active, kind and benevolent, that is, intelligent, rational and happy'. Education was therefore the most important factor in the making of national character, for men had no power at all over their own opinions, but were always the creatures of their environment. At Lanark Owen provided an Institute for evening lectures for those who wished to continue their studies after they had left school.

How could such a system of education be achieved? Not, Owen was convinced, by relying upon the selfish instincts of employers. Nor by a reliance upon private charities, for Owen was hostile to the routine methods of education employed by Joseph Lancaster and Andrew Bell, and equally hostile to the religious sects.[4] The answer lay in the intervention of the state. 'Every state, to be well-governed, ought to direct its chief attention to the formation of character, and thus the best-governed state will be that which shall possess the best national system of education.' The way to proceed therefore was by legislation.

Robert Owen was one of the first practical economists to regard unemployment as a form of economic waste. Malthus had pointed to the dangers involved in an increasing population outstripping its food supply. Owen replied that there was no knowing how far science, intelligence and industry together were capable of increasing production. 'For man knows not the limit to his power of creating food. How much has this power been latterly increased in these islands! And in them such knowledge is in its infancy. Yet compare even this power of raising food with the efforts of the Bosgemens or other savages, and it will be found, perhaps, as one to a thousand. . . . Nor is it yet for man to say to what this knowledge may lead, or where it may end.' It is not entirely clear why Owen should have supposed that a national system of education would lead to conditions of full employment, but in the interim he proposed national works of road-, canal- and harbour-building. But it was not simply a matter of economics; Owen was deeply moved by the sight of the sufferings among the labouring class in times of unemployment, when men would come begging for work even at starvation wages.

The second of Owen's proposals was for the enactment of Factory Acts to limit the hours of labour in the mills and factories to twelve a day, and to prohibit the employment of children under the age of ten. He was the principal initiator of the Factory Act of 1819, although he finally disowned it as not going far enough. In March 1818 he addressed an impassioned appeal to Lord Liverpool, the prime minister, for his support for the Bill: 'surely the working man and his family have a fair and just claim for some aid and protection from the legislature of their country'. And again: 'We are unacquainted with any nation, ancient or modern, that has suffered its hundreds of thousands of children of seven to twelve years of age to work incessantly for fifteen hours per day in an overheated unhealthy atmosphere, allowing them only forty minutes out of that time for dinner and change of air, which they breathe often in damp cellars or in garrets, in narrow streets or dirty lanes.' The choice, Owen declared, was a simple one between the claims of materialism and the principles of humanity, and he knew how hard the manufacturers would fight in defence of the former. 'It is the creed of this class that no effort or expense should be spared to improve these trifling baubles and luxuries which when perfected are of no intrinsic value whatever, which cannot add a particle of strength or comfort to the empire (no real advantage has occurred from enabling our fashionable females to purchase fine lace and muslins at one-fourth of the former prices; but, to produce them at this price, many thousands of our population have existed amidst disease and wretchedness, and have been carried prematurely to their graves); while any attempts to ameliorate the condition of human beings are decried as unnecessary and visionary, as travelling out of the proper business of life, which to them is solely and exclusively to accumulate wealth— wealth which is not only acquired at the expense of everything that is truly great or valuable in the character of the nation, but which, when acquired, is useless, nay, in the highest degree injurious, to themselves and others.' (*On the Employment of*

Children in Manufactories: To the Right Honourable the Earl of Liverpool, March 1818.) This was a theme upon which Owen, Cobbett and the Romantic poets could agree, and indeed Coleridge was a powerful ally in the attempts to secure a Factory Act in 1819.

Owen's third proposal was for a national system of relief for the poor, for the establishment of co-operative villages, which would be entirely self-sustaining in food and manufactures. Each would number about twelve hundred persons, and would possess a thousand to fifteen hundred acres. Great attention would be paid to the education of children. Although the initial cost would be great, amounting to about ninety-six thousand pounds each, yet thereafter the village would be self-supporting, and thus the capital outlay could be set against the decreasing poor rates. In 1817, when the governing classes were seriously concerned at the extent of social unrest, the idea found favour with distinguished gentlemen such as the Archbishop of Canterbury and the Home Secretary, Lord Sidmouth. It appealed also to some of the labouring classes, among whom there still lingered the idea that all the land had once belonged to the peasants, until they had been dispossessed by the gentry. Thomas Spence who died in 1814, had taught that all landlordship was wrong, and that there should be a common ownership by the people, and the Society of Spencean Philanthropists, founded in 1816 continued propaganda on the same lines. To many radicals however Owen's plan savoured too much of charity and a glorified workhouse system, and Cobbett denounced Villages of Co-operation as 'parallelograms of pauperism'. At first Owen, as a rich industrialist, had ready access to the houses of the great, and his *New View of Society* at first carried dedications to the Prince Regent and William Wilberforce. But when it was discovered that Owen was opposed to religion, he was dropped by the influential as quickly as he had been taken up. One or two experiments in establishing his villages were attempted, one of them at Orbiston. From 1824–9 Owen was in America, where he lost a great deal of money in founding New Harmony, but the whole idea was a failure, and Owen soon turned to other ideas.

The central object of Owenism was to give back a human dignity to the labouring classes, and for this purpose he was an enthusiastic advocate of trade unionism. The idea had a strong appeal to artisans and craftsmen who were in danger of extinction by the growth of the factory system. Owen taught them to see capitalism as an inherently evil system, and in the eighteen-twenties Owenite communities emerged in London, Birmingham, Sheffield and Norwich, in which craftsmen produced their wares and by-passed capitalist employers. When Owen returned from America in 1829 he found himself a leader of a mass movement. John Doherty was organising the 'Operative Spinners of England, Ireland and Scotland' into a mass union, and in 1830 he founded the National Association for the Protection of Labour in an attempt to unite a wide range of industries, such as textiles, pottery, mines and building into a federation. Owen established Labour Exchanges, in which craftsmen could exchange their products for labour notes which could then be exchanged for other goods, thus again by-passing the capitalist and middle men. They failed because of the difficulty in obtaining any real currency for the labour notes, but by 1832, according to E. P. Thompson, there were 'perhaps five hundred co-operative societies in the whole country, with at least twenty thousand members' (p. 793). In 1834 Owen founded the Grand National Consolidated Trades Union, in which he intended to combine all the trades in the country preparatory to a general assault upon the continuance of the capitalist system, but it collapsed in the following year amidst a welter of unsuccessful strikes. Owen was no organiser, but a visionary, and most of his projects ended in failure. But Owenism continued as a powerful force in the creation of a working-class consciousness, in the early trade union movement, and as a contributory stimulus to Chartism. To the political aspirations of Chartism Owen turned a blind eye, yet many of the Chartists were Owenites. Owen was too fond of promising the masses the millennium, and of publicising the promise in endless lectures and tracts, but Owenite socialism was the first attempt to organise an alternative to capitalism on a nation-wide scale. For this Engels was grateful, and he paid Owen a generous tribute in 1878, when he wrote of him as 'a man of almost sublimely child-like simplicity of character, and at the same time a born leader of men'.

NOTES

[1] For a full treatment of the whole subject see E. P. Thompson: *The Making of the English Working Class* (1963).

[2] R. B. Rose: 'The Priestley Riots', *Past and Present*, Nov. 1960.

[3] Methodism at this time was no friend to radicalism and reform. Cobbett wrote: 'There are, I know, persons who look upon the Methodists, for instance, as *friends of freedom*. It is impossible they should be. They are either fools or tricksters, or so nearly allied thereto, as to be worthy of no consideration. Their heavenly gifts, their calls, their inspirations, their feelings of grace at work within them, and the rest of their canting gibberish, are a gross and outrageous insult to common sense, and a great scandal to the country. It is in vain that we boast of our *enlightened state*, while a sect like this is increasing daily.' (*P.R.*, 12 June 1813.) Blake, Leigh Hunt and Hazlitt took much the same view.

[4] Owen was hostile to the influence of the competing religious sects or 'systems'. 'Let us openly declare to the Church, that a national unexclusive plan of education for the poor will, without the shadow of doubt, destroy all the errors which are attached to the various systems; and that, when this plan shall be fully established, not one of the tenets which is in opposition to facts can long be upheld.'

4 : The Political Economy of Malthus and Ricardo

ADAM SMITH, Robert Malthus and David Ricardo were the three philosophers who attempted to reduce thinking about political economy to a system. They sought to discover the principles which governed the new world of capitalism. Adam Smith, in the *Wealth of Nations*, a massive work of shrewd observation and wisdom, suggested considerations and tendencies without postulating laws.[1] Ricardo attempted to go farther and formulate the laws governing economic affairs. Malthus thought that Ricardo had gone too far, and preferred the more moral approach of Adam Smith. The age however preferred Ricardo to Malthus. James Mill, in his *Elements of Political Economy* (1821), showed himself a convinced Ricardian, and the so-called Classical System of Political Economy held sway until John Stuart Mill published his *Political Economy* in 1848.

The Rev. Thomas Robert Malthus (1766–1834) was the son of Daniel Malthus, an intellectually-minded country gentleman who had once been a friend of Hume and was later a follower of Godwin. In 1798 Robert published his *Essay on the principle of population as it affects the future improvement of society*, in which he rejected the optimistic view of life which his father had imbibed from the *philosophes*. Instead he postulated three main propositions: first that, given mankind's sexual proclivities, the growth of population was necessarily limited by the means of subsistence; second, that when the means of subsistence increased, population increased also; and third, that the only checks on the growth of population must be either moral restraint, or else disease, starvation, misery and vice. Malthus did not think highly of man's ability to exercise moral restraint, and so was led to affirm that the most important checks upon excessive population remained what they had always been throughout history, namely famines, plagues, wars and disease. He was thus opposed to the system of Poor Relief, as an encouragement to early marriage and improvidence, and he warned against the good-natured belief that much good could be done by charity in relieving the lot of the poor. To Cobbett, Southey and the tory reformers this seemed a heartless and cruel doctrine, all the worse because it emanated from a clergyman of the Anglican Church. To others it appeared that Malthus was merely stating one of the facts of life, one of the 'iron laws of economics' which sentiment or sympathy could not explain away, and which provided a powerful argument in favour of *laissez-faire*.

Malthus did not, of course, say that a population could never rise without an increase in attendant misery. The population of England had risen steadily during the eighteenth century, and had been accompanied by a general improvement in the standard of living. But in such a situation there operated the law of diminishing returns; the land would not continue indefinitely to yield an increase of output in proportion to the amount of effort and capital expended upon it, and eventually the forces of restraint of which he spoke would come into operation. In Ireland, he declared, they had operated throughout the eighteenth century: 'Ireland is an instance where increasing produce has occasioned a rapid increase of population, without improving the condition of the people' (*Principles of Political Economy* (1820), Sect. III).

Malthus did not suppose that the general tendency of the time towards capitalist enterprise and expansion could be reversed or halted, but he was no unqualified defender of the Industrial Revolution, in the way that his great opponent Ricardo was. David Ricardo (1772–1823) was a wealthy stockbroker of Jewish extraction, who published his most important work, *The Principles of Political Economy and Taxation*, in 1817. Ricardo attempted to apply a rigorously deductive method to political economy, to reduce economic man to a series of carefully-defined laws. All progress depended upon man's ability to take forethought and forego present pleasures of consumption for the sake of future increased production and profits. When he employed labour it was necessary to ensure that the value created by labour was greater than that paid in wages. This argument was later to be the basis of Marx's theory of exploitation, but Ricardo drew no such conclusion. Rents, wages and prices were determined by the operation of economic laws, and ought not to be interfered with by artificial means such as legislation. Taxation, for instance, which unduly restricted the purchasing power of people, or which limited their power to set aside capital resources, was bad, and governments were enjoined 'never to lay such taxes as will inevitably fall on capital; since by so doing, they impair the funds for the maintenance of labour, and thereby diminish the future production of the country' (*Principles*, Chap. VIII). Prices could not in the long run be artificially manipulated. Although the profits of some specially-favoured producer might appear to be unduly large, prices were in fact determined by the conditions of the least-favoured producer. The same principle held with respect to interest rates. Interest rates were determined by the minimal profits which might be expected by the least-favoured borrower. It seemed to Ricardo that the Bank of England had done more harm than good by lending money during the first twenty years of the century at less than the market rate of interest. Always it was the market price for wages, prices and interest, determined by the forces of supply and demand, which must be left to operate freely in a healthy economy.

It followed, Ricardo argued, that there could never be too great an accumulation of capital, nor a general over-production, for men would not continue to set aside capital when it had ceased to be profitable, and what was not set aside as capital must be spent on consumer goods, or in a rise in the wages of employees, both to the advantage of the consumer market. The accumulation of capital could never be harmful to a society, for if it was employed in creating wages, lowering prices, or simply in increasing the availability of consumer goods, the general benefit to society was equally evident. Whether a man chose to save less and spend more, or the reverse, would depend upon the state of the market for capital and consumer goods, and in either case the process was self-regulating. Ricardo's theory therefore fully endorsed the rapid capitalist expansion of his day and endowed capitalists with the comfortable conviction that in serving their own interests they were serving also the interests of the community.

Malthus was less sure of this. He did not regard political economy, as Ricardo did, as a matter of rigid scientific laws. 'The science of political economy resembles more the sciences of morals and politics than the science of mathematics.' (*Principles*: Introd.) Some of the conclusions of the followers of Adam Smith he regarded as 'crude and premature theories', and some of Ricardo's principles 'erroneous'. He did not believe that the forces working within the economic system were self-adjusting; the severe economic depression following the Napoleonic Wars seemed to prove the contrary. 'The stagnation which has been so generally felt and complained of since the war appears to me inexplicable upon the principles of those who think that the power of production is the only element of wealth, and who consequently infer that if the powers of production be increased, wealth will certainly increase in proportion. Now it is unquestionable that the powers of production were increased by the cessation of war, and that more people and more capital were ready to be employed in productive labour; but notwithstanding this obvious increase in the powers of production, we hear everywhere of difficulties and distresses, instead of ease and plenty' (VII, X). Where, he asked, were the understocked employments waiting to absorb the redundant capital which glutted the market? Among the remedies he proposed were the reduction of the national debt, a cautious increase in the freedom of commerce, and extended public works such as road building and agricultural improvements. Malthus was anxious to retain the prosperity of land-owners and the middle class, not simply as capital-producers, but as consumers upon which agricultural and industrial prosperity greatly depended. He did not think lavish expenditure immoral, since it was such an effective stimulus to production and employment. To Malthus it seemed possible that a nation might well save too much; in any case saving should not be erected, as in Ricardo's theory, to a binding law upon society. 'Saving is, in numerous instances, a most sacred private duty. How far a just sense of this duty, together with the desire of bettering our condition so strongly implanted in the human breast, may sometimes, and in some states of society, occasion a greater tendency to parsimony than is consistent with the most effective encouragement of the growth of public wealth, it is difficult to say; but whether this tendency, if let alone, be ever too great or not, no one could think of interfering with it, even in its caprices. There is no reason, however, for giving an additional sanction to it, by calling it a public duty. The market for national capital will be supplied, like other markets, without the aid of patriotism. And in leaving the whole question of saving to the uninfluenced operation of individual interest and individual feelings, we shall best conform to that great principle of political economy laid down by Adam Smith, which teaches us a general maxim, liable to very few exceptions, that the wealth of nations is best secured by allowing every person, as long as he adheres to the rules of justice, to pursue his own interest in his own way' (VII, X).

Ricardo and Malthus differed in the importance they attached to capital accumulation in a society. Ricardo was more directly concerned with the development of industrial capitalism, Malthus with the preservation of the social structure as it then existed. Ricardo sought to reduce political economy to a science, while Malthus was more concerned with social and moral principles. But both in the main supported the principles of *laissez-faire*, and in so far as they differed on other matters, the future of nineteenth-century political economy in England lay with Ricardo rather than Malthus.

NOTE

[1] On Adam Smith see Chap. 17, *Reason and Nature in the 18th Century*.

5 : William Godwin: Philosopher of Anarchism

WILLIAM GODWIN, almost unread today, and for the latter half of his life almost equally neglected by contemporaries, exercised for a brief spell an extraordinary influence upon the young poets of his day. He did not deserve the adulation they accorded him, but on the other hand, he does not deserve so complete a subsequent neglect. His thought was a culmination, and indeed a kind of dissolution, of an important strand of eighteenth-century thought, and for this reason it deserves consideration. He represented the end of a chain of thought, not a beginning, and this explains why it was that his age so quickly turned away from him. He was the philosopher of anarchism, often saying no more than Burke himself had said as a young man, yet saying it in the far more dangerous era of the seventeen nineties. He raised the whole question of the relationship between the individual and society, and he re-stated the deep suspicions of the eighteenth century about government. His novel *Caleb Williams* raised interesting moral problems, and contained some features of the later romantic novel. If his thought was revolutionary in character, he specifically eschewed revolution as a political and social weapon, and this no doubt explains why he escaped prosecution. In any case his books were expensive, his popular influence was slight, and for the last thirty years of his life (he died in 1836) he was largely a forgotten figure.

Godwin's theories were formed under the influence of the American and French Revolutions, and from reading Locke and Swift, Rousseau, Helvetius and Tom Paine. The theory he adopted in his *Enquiry Concerning Political Justice* was a mild anarchism. The argument ran: the noblest expression of the human mind was individualism; men must ask questions and seek solutions to them by means of their own reason. But society constantly thwarted this process: 'government by its very nature counteracts the improvement of individual intellect' (Preface viii. All references are to the edition of 1798) by providing answers which suited the needs of the ruler rather than accorded with truth. 'Government, as it was forced upon mankind by their vices, so has it commonly been the creature of their ignorance and mistake' (I, p. xxiv). This was the inevitable result of the exercise of power, and the result was that 'the grand moral evils that exist in the world, the calamities by which we are so grievously oppressed, are to be traced to political institutions as their source' (I, p. 5). This was not really surprising when it was remembered that political society grew out of wars and conquests. Politics should be 'the proper vehicle of a liberal morality', but instead it was the means to oppression and violence: 'A numerous class of mankind are held down in a state of abject penury. . . . Whips, axes and gibbets, dungeons, chains and racks are the most approved and established methods of persuading men to obedience, and impressing upon their minds the lessons of reason.' (I, p. 12.) Nine-tenths of mankind were under a form of despotism. Laws were designed to perpetuate the powers of rulers, and always favoured the rich against the poor. (I, p. 21.) In 1798 this appeared a revolutionary thing to say, but it will be noticed that Godwin had borrowed not only the idea, but the very words, from Burke himself. (See p. 40.) But what any conventional philosopher might say in 1756 without causing a stir, had become dangerous subversion in 1798.

Like Burke in 1756, Godwin saw politics in the world around him concerned only with power. But the true end of politics was morality, and morality he defined as 'that system of conduct which is determined by a consideration of the greatest general good' (II, p. 121). The best form of government was therefore that which best gave guarantees of the moral life. On the subject of human nature Godwin was an optimist. Once man was in a position freely to acquire knowledge and exercise his volition, there were no limits to the heights to which he could ascend. 'Nothing can be more unreasonable than to argue from men as we now find them, to men as they may hereafter be made' (II, 120). Man was perfectible, not in the sense that he could ever achieve perfection, but in that he was capable of indefinite improvement (I, 92). Godwin repeatedly urged that the essential idea was that of progress; there must be constant change because there must be development with the expansion of knowledge, and thus a law or institution which might be acceptable at one stage of history would speedily become outmoded.

Godwin was accustomed to apply the utilitarian test to social and political institutions, and this was easily reconciled to this evolutionary view of human history. But at other times he repeated the old Neo-Platonic view of reason without observing any conflict between it and utilitarianism. Thus on one occasion he revived the Chain of Being to support his view that the whole universe was linked in a single rational pattern: 'This view of things presents us with an idea of the universe as of a body of events in systematical arrangement, nothing in the boundless progress of things interrupting this system, or breaking in upon the experienced succession of antecedents and consequents. In the life of every human being there is a chain of events, generated in the lapse of ages which preceded his birth, and going on in regular procession through the whole period of his existence, in consequence of which it was impossible for him to act in any instance otherwise than he has acted.' (IV, p. 384.) This, he declared, was 'a doctrine of moral necessity sufficiently established', and it was men's failure to understand this which was the cause of all the errors throughout history. Now if this was true, Godwin would appear to be formulating a doctrine of moral determinism from which neither government nor any other institution would be exempt, and it would be difficult to reconcile this with his view that all government and most institutions were bad. But Godwin was no systematic philosopher, but rather dependent upon his often-conflicting sources for the foundations of his theories, and his explanation of the apparent conflict would be that usual to the philosophy of anarchism, namely that all government had entailed a perversion of man from his natural course of development. The first condition of progress therefore was for men to break out of this constricting and oppressive prison. 'He who regards all things past, present, and to come, as links of an indissoluble chain, will, as often as he recollects this comprehensive view, find himself assisted to reflect upon the moral concerns of mankind with the same clearness of perception, the same firmness of judgment, and the same constancy of temper, as we are accustomed to do upon the truths of geometry.' (IV, viii, p. 396.) Plato had seen the golden age of man to lie in the past; Godwin and the radicals saw it lying in the future, when ignorance and oppression had been superseded.

Godwin always drew a clear distinction between government and society. Government was the root of all evil. 'Multitudes will never exert the energy necessary to extraordinary success, till they shall dismiss the prejudices that fetter them, get rid of the chilling system of occult and inexplicable causes (he meant religion), and consider the human mind as an intelligent agent.' (I, iv, 44). If men held false views it was because they had been systematically misled. 'Remove the causes and the effects will cease.' The progress of knowledge would not allow men to remain much longer in tutelage. 'The human understanding has so powerful a tendency to improvement, that it is more than probable that, in many instances, the argument which once appeared to us sufficient would upon re-examination appear inadequate and futile. We should therefore subject them to perpetual revival. In our speculative opinions and our practical principles we should never consider the book of enquiry as shut.' (I, v, 69.) Men were essentially equal, and the inequalities which existed were the creations of the unjust society in which men lived. But if equality was to be enforced it might be supposed that there must be some effective authority in society for its enforcement. This however Godwin utterly rejected, 'Society is nothing more than an aggregate of individuals. Its claims and duties must be the aggregate of their claims and duties, the one no more precarious and arbitrary than the other.' (II, ii, 136.) Godwin was opposed to coercion, for 'all men are fallible: no man can be justified in setting up his judgment as a standard for others. . . . We have no infallible judge of controversies' (II, v, 167). As man was a rational being, society must be governed by public opinion, not by force.

Government should concern itself no further than to provide security for individuals; it should never impinge upon the sanctity of private life: 'to give each man a voice in the public concerns comes nearest to that fundamental purpose of which we should never lose sight, the uncontrolled exercise of private judgment'. (III, iv, 215.) 'The uncontrolled exercise of private judgment' was the central idea of Godwin's theory, the object to which society and government should be dedicated. He rejected any theory of the Social Contract as being unreal and unnecessary, for promises and compacts were irrelevant in that they could not change the moral needs of the individual. That every man should have the vote, however, accorded with his needs, and that was the only test needed.

Man being a rational creature, and virtue being a form of knowledge, it followed that the only test needed for an institution was that of utility. By such a test Godwin rejected both monarchy and aristocracy as forms of government. At the outset he declared that ever since 1779 he had been convinced that 'monarchy was a species of government essentially corrupt' (Preface), and the course of the French Revolution had confirmed him in the opinion. In Book V he argued that princes were never educated in the truth, but lived lives of dissipation and ignorance, and that Courts were necessarily corrupt. He rejected arguments in favour of enlightened despotism, because, as with any other despotism, it deprived subjects of active participation in affairs. In a democracy on the other hand every citizen was regarded as equal. He listed the usual objections to democracy, for instance that 'democracy is a monstrous and unwieldy vessel, launched upon the sea of human passions, without ballast' (V, xiv, 117). But no evils, he replied, could be worse than those already experienced in existing governments, and 'the thing most necessary is to remove all those restraints which prevent the human mind from attaining its genuine strength. Implicit faith, blind submission to authority, timid fear, a distrust of our powers, an inattention to our own importance and the good purposes we are able to effect, these are the chief obstacles to human improvement. Democracy restores to man a consciousness of his value, teaches him . . . to listen only to the suggestions of reason, gives him confidence . . .' (ibid.) It was a misfortune that democracy would have to be exercised through representation. It was an imperfect system, and 'not a remedy so excellent or complete as should authorise us to rest in it as the highest improvement of which the social order is capable', but for the time being it must needs be accepted.

Once the old corruption was eliminated, and democracy established, what would society be like? Godwin argued that as men approached perfection, legislation would cease, because men would be guided by their reason, and that would be sufficient to instruct them in the paths of virtue. As legislation ceased, administration would become everything, and it is clear that Godwin, like Marx later, believed that the State would 'wither away'. 'Legislation, that is, the authoritative enunciation of abstract or general propositions, is a function of equivocal nature, and will never be exercised in a pure state of society, or a state approaching to purity, but with great caution and unwillingness. It is the most absolute of the functions of government, and government itself is a remedy that inevitably brings its own evils along with it. Administration, on the other hand, is the principle of perpetual application. So long as men shall see reason to act in a corporate capacity, they will always have occasions of temporary emergency for which to provide. In proportion as they advance in social improvement, executive power will, comparatively speaking, become everything, and legislation nothing.' (V, xxi, 189.) Legislation was authoritarian, and as such had little place in a rational society. The only functions of government would be to prevent injustices between individuals, and to provide defence against foreign invasion. The former, he thought, could be best achieved by judge and jury, and in any case injustices would soon cease, partly because the motives for offences would become weaker, and partly because the pressure of public opinion would become so great that it alone would act as a deterrent. Gradually the need for a national assembly would disappear. Godwin had a poor opinion of assemblies such as was then meeting in France, because they deprived the people of their just voice, encouraged the growth of parties, and enabled groups to impose their will in the name of the people. 'The acts which go under the name of the society are really the acts now of one single person, and now of another.' (VI, i, 217.)

Godwin had a poor opinion of what could be achieved by laws, for, 'if laws were a sufficient means for the reformation of error and vice, it is not to be believed but that the world, long ere this, would have become the feat of every virtue'. When a people were corrupt, laws made things worse, and when they lived in virtuous harmony, they were unnecessary (VI, i, 219). His contempt for law arose from his belief that in general it was the means by which some political master enslaved his subjects. In any case, the field of action of a government should be strictly limited: 'All that we should require on the part of government in behalf of morality and virtue, seems to be, a clear stage upon which for them (the people) to exert their own energies, and perhaps some restraint, for the present, upon the violent disturbers of the peace of society.' (VI, i, 225.) Note the phrase 'for the present'. Once men had attained the full stature of moral liberty, such imposed restraints would be unnecessary. In a state of freedom truth would triumph, for 'who ever saw an instance in which error, unallied to power, was victorious over truth?' He did not exclude the possibility that some social good could be achieved by legislation, but there was a better way to achieve social amelioration: 'The legitimate instrument of affecting political reformation is knowledge. Let truth be incessantly studied, illustrated and propagated, and the effect is inevitable. Let us not vainly endeavour, by laws and regulations, to anticipate the future dictates of the general mind, but calmly wait till the harvest of opinion is ripe. Let no new practice in politics be introduced, and no old one anxiously superseded, till the alteration is called for by the public voice. The task which, for the present, should occupy the first rank in the thoughts of the friend of man, is enquiry, communication, discussion.' Godwin therefore was a democrat, but no advocate of violent revolution; all would come right by peaceful means with the diffusion of knowledge and opinion. Believing that all government was bad, he was not anxious to replace one form of government by another. The object was not the reform of government, but its entire supersession. For, 'the just conclusion is ... that government is little capable of affording

G

benefit of the first importance to mankind. . . . It incites us to look
for the moral improvement of the species, not in the multiplying of
regulations, but in their repeal. It teaches us that truth and virtue,
like commerce, will then flourish most when least subjected to the
mistaken guardianship of authority and laws' (ibid., p. 232). Laws
relieve men of the trouble of thinking for themselves, and in
consequence lead to 'torpor and imbecility'.

For the same reason he was opposed to a country receiving a
fixed constitution, and he was not at all impressed by the work of
constitution-making which was going on in France. Men needed
the principles of equality and justice, but beyond that a fixed
constitution tended to perpetuate a given social situation and thus
prevent progress. 'The language of reason on this subject is: "Give
us equality and justice, but no constitution. Suffer us to follow
without restraint the dictates of our own judgment, and to change
our forms of social order as fast as we improve in understanding
and knowledge." ' (VI, vii, 288.) Laws imposed from above were
useless as instruments in furthering the moral life, and only
impeded men in their pursuit of it. For the same reason he was
opposed to a national system of education, which again would tend
to perpetuate a given social system. The teaching in universities,
he argued, was always a century behind the advanced stages of
knowledge, and 'public education has always expended its energies
in the support of prejudice; it teaches its pupils, not the fortitude
that shall bring every proposition to the test of examination, but
the art of vindicating such tenets as may chance to be established. . . . Even in the petty institution of Sunday Schools, the
chief lessons that are taught are a superstitious veneration for the
church of England, and to bow to every man in a handsome coat.
All this is directly contrary to the true interests of mankind.'
(VI, viii, 299.) For, Godwin declared, the moment men ceased
enquiry and accepted the rule of authority, that was 'the instant
of his intellectual decease'. Godwin believed that a national system
of education could become a powerful instrument of despotism,
by forming opinions according to a mould, and 'stifling for ever
the voice of truth' (VI, viii, 303).

The subject of private property presented Godwin with a

problem he did not know how to solve. He had an instinctive hostility to hereditary wealth, which he felt must be inherently wicked, but he did not relish the idea of a general dispossession in the interests of equality. Moreover, there was no doubt that the great mass of the people approved of private property, which certainly provided a spur to individual effort. He concluded therefore that until there was a general change of opinion, property should be respected as one aspect of 'the sacred and indefeasible right of private judgment', and as providing security which was 'indispensibly necessary to every species of excellence' (VIII, ii, 449). The alternative would be some form of violent dispossession, and Godwin shrank from violence as leading to 'dreadful calamities'. It was to be doubted, he declared 'whether the genuine cause of reform ever demands that, in its name, we should sentence whole classes of men to wretchedness'; and 'the doctrine of rights has no rational or legitimate connection with the practice of tumult.'

We began by saying that Godwin was a 'mild anarchist'. In his innate suspicion of all government, and his belief in the perfectibility of man once he was released from its shackles, he certainly embraced anarchism. Anarchy, however, which is a different thing, he thought preferable to despotism, but still to be avoided if possible. 'Anarchy awakens thought, and diffuses energy and enterprise through the community, though it does not effect this in the best manner. . . . But in despotism, mind is trampled into an equality of the most odious sort.' Better than anarchy, however, was a peaceful consensus of opinion. 'The more anarchy can be held at bay, the more fortunate will it be for mankind.' (VII, v, 371.) For Godwin was fearful of the results of violence, and moreover, at the time at which he wrote, fearful of the long arm of the law in England. He therefore advocated change only by discussion and public opinion. He declared that he was a republican, but that this did not mean that 'I shall enter into a desperate faction to invade the public tranquillity. . . . Every community of men as well as every individual, must govern itself according to its ideas of justice.' (VIII, x, 539.) In the end, what Godwin stood for most clearly was the spirit of free enquiry as the most desirable dissolving influence upon much that was corrupt and oppressive in his day. His conclusion was: 'we wander in the midst of appearances; and plausible appearances are to be found on all sides. The wisest men perhaps have generally proved the most confirmed sceptics'. Through this scepticism there lay the vision of the perfectibility of man. It was this vision which gave Godwin his short-lived influence upon the young poets of his day.[1]

Godwin illustrated his social theories with his *Caleb Williams*, a novel now little read, but in his day an influential work. Its theme was to expose the injustices of the legal system of the time, the rottenness of society and of the power which went inevitably along with wealth and rank. Caleb Williams was the servant of Mr. Falkland, a squire of wealth and learning who won golden opinions upon all sides with his generosity and sense of honour. Whenever Falkland heard of injustice or oppression he would intervene on the side of right, and thus he was in complete contrast to his neighbour, Barnabus Tyrrel, a brutal squire obsessed with his sense of power over all who chose to stand in his way. Tyrrel imprisoned his sister when she refused to marry a local boorish farmer, and eventually drove her to her death. When one of his tenants, Hawkins, dared to thwart him, Tyrrel hounded him to ruin. It was useless, Godwin commented, for a tenant to have right on his side when he was opposed by wealth and influence. Tyrrel, on his side, declared that 'it would be the disgrace of a civilized country, if a gentleman, when insolently attacked in law by the scum of the earth, could not convert the cause into a question of the longest purse, and stick in the skirts of his adversary till he had reduced him to beggary'.

Mr. Falkland remonstrated with Tyrrel at his conduct, and thus earned his bitter hatred. Eventually at a public assembly Tyrrel humiliated Falkland by beating him in full view of the company. So far Falkland has been portrayed as an ideal man, but beneath his beneficient exterior there was a proud nature, and the humiliation was too much for him. Tyrrel was found murdered, and the son of the tenant Hawkins was hanged for the crime. Falkland however became a changed man, a recluse, suspicious and soured. 'He who had lived beyond any man upon the grand and animating reveries of the imagination, seemed now to have no visions but of anguish and despair.' In 'some future period of human improvement' Godwin commented, such things could not happen, but society was based on false ideals of honour and rank, and it was Falkland's pride which turned him into a bitter spirit. Literature and a cultivated mind was no protection against the evils which an unjust society inculcated. Falkland himself realised this: 'why do you suppose, sir, that learning and ingenuity do not often serve people rather to hide their crimes than to restrain them from committing them? History tells us strange things in that respect.' The only remedy for mankind was to overthrow all the traditional standards of honour, justice and virtue, and start afresh with the simple dictates of the heart.

It was not long before Williams was convinced that Falkland was himself the murderer of Tyrrel, and eventually Falkland confessed as much, at the same time binding Williams to secrecy, and telling him that Williams must now remain for ever bound to him as his slave as the only possessor of his guilty secret. The murder of Tyrrel indeed raised an interesting problem for a utilitarian, for his life was utterly worthless, and the world was undoubtedly a better place without him. For one moment Godwin plays with this idea, when Williams wrote: 'I conceived it to be in the highest degree absurd and iniquitous, to cut off a man qualified for the most essential and extensive utility, merely out of retrospect to an act which, whatever were its merits, could not be retrieved.' But Falkland thought otherwise; the thought of the murder was ever with him; it sprang from his foolish ideas of being a man of honour. 'I was the fool of fame. My virtue, my honesty, my everlasting peace of mind, were cheap sacrifices to be made at the shrine of this divinity. But, what is worse, there is nothing that has happened that has in any degree contributed to my cure. I am as much the fool of fame as ever. I cling to it to my last breath. Though I be the blackest of villains, I will leave behind me a spotless and illustrious name.' Such were the false standards of contemporary society. Tyrrel sacrificed the Hawkins family because they thwarted his sense of power. Falkland killed Tyrrel because he could not bear a public humiliation. Williams must remain his prisoner because the secret must be safeguarded; and yet the fear would always remain that a man 'equally passionate and unrelenting will sooner or later make me his victim'. Godwin commented that nine-tenths of mankind's abhorrence of vice sprang from the knowledge of their own guilty secrets. And yet, if Falkland could but think otherwise of his crime, he might put away his guilty conscience. 'It is the thinking ourselves vicious that principally contributes to make us vicious.'

Eventually Williams could stand his imprisonment no longer, and he fled from Falkland's house. Then began a long series of disasters for him. Try as he would, he could never escape from the long arm of Falkland's vengeance. Falkland had him brought back and accused of theft. He was thrown into prison, and there he experienced all the horrors of the common gaol. 'It is impossible to describe the sort of squalidness and filth with which these mansions are distinguished. I have seen dirty faces in dirty apartments, which have nevertheless borne the impression of health, and spoke carelessness and levity rather than distress. But the dirt of a prison speaks sadness to the heart, and appears to be already in a state of putridity and infection.' There in misery and squalor innocent men, or those who had not been brought to trial, were incarcerated for months on end. Some of Godwin's examples were drawn from the records of Newgate, or the writings of John Howard. Once a poor man was accused of a crime, how difficult it was for him to establish his innocence. ' "Thank God", exclaims the Englishman, "we have no Bastille! Thank God, with us no man can be punished without a crime!" Un-thinking wretch! Is that a country of liberty, where thousands languish in dungeons and fetters? Go, go, ignorant fool! and visit the scenes of our prisons! witness their unwholesomeness, their filth, the tyranny of their governors, the misery of their inmates! After that, show me the man shameless enough to triumph, and say, England has no Bastille!'

Godwin commented that one of the worst aspects of the judicial system was that, once a man had committed a crime, no amount of repentance would enable him ever to free himself from its onus, and thus he was often driven to further crime in order to maintain himself. 'If they discover at a distance of fourteen or of forty years an action for which the law ordains that his life shall be forfeit, though the interval should have been spent with the purity of a saint and the devotedness of a patriot, they disdain to enquire into it.'

With great difficulty and suffering, Williams managed to escape from prison, and took refuge with a gang of highwaymen. On leaving them, he sought to lose himself, first by escaping to Ireland, then in London, then in a Welsh village, and finally by escaping abroad. But wherever he went, the vengeance of Falkland pursued him. At one point Falkland begged him to sign a paper declaring his former employer's innocence of murder, but he refused, and the persecution continued. Hounded by Falkland's agents, Williams became an outcast, and finally, driven to desperation, he had Falkland summoned before a magistrate to accuse him openly of the crime which was haunting them both. Falkland appeared, but at once Williams was overcome with contrition at the sight of the sufferings which his master was undergoing. Instead of the deposition, Williams praised the nobility of Falkland, and now it was the turn of the latter to be overcome with remorse. The two were reconciled, and Falkland admitted his guilt, shortly before his death. Williams was left triumphant, but now it was his turn to be crushed at the thought of the suffering he had inflicted upon Falkland.

The conclusion was that 'a nobler spirit than Falkland lived not among the sons of men. Thy intellectual powers were truly sublime, and thy bosom burned with a godlike ambition. But of what use are talents and sentiments in the corrupt wilderness of human society? It is a rank and rotten soil, from which every finer shrub draws poison as it grows. All that, in a happier field and a purer air, would expand into virtue and germinate into usefulness, is thus converted into henbane and deadly nightshade'. Falkland was a noble nature corrupted by 'the poison of chivalry'.

Godwin's theme of the nobility of man corrupted by society was in the full tradition of Rousseau. In prison Williams commented on how few and simple were the wants of man to make himself happy, but 'How different from the man of artificial society! Palaces are built for his reception, a thousand vehicles provided for his exercise, provinces are ransacked for the gratification of his appetite, and the whole world traversed to supply him with apparel and furniture. Thus vast is his expenditure, and the purchase slavery'. But, Godwin repeatedly declared, the mind of man was unconquerable, and could never be permanently subdued. The gang of robbers were romanticised. They were rebels against society, but for that very reason displayed an energy which in a just society would be put to social uses. 'Energy is perhaps of all qualities the most valuable; and a just political system would possess the means of extracting from it, thus circumstanced, its beneficial qualities, instead of consigning it, as now, to indiscriminate destruction.' In the Welsh village Williams found a simple life infinitely preferable to that of the city. 'Among people thus remote from the bustle of human life there is an open spirit of confidence, by means of which a stranger easily finds access to their benevolence and good-will. My manners had never been greatly debauched from the simplicity of rural life by the scenes through which I had passed.'

It is clear that there is much that is ridiculous in Godwin's story. The first half of the book, which was treated fully in the realistic tradition of the eighteenth century, and owes much to Fielding, is much more successful than the second half, in which the mysterious and unseen powers of Falkland require the new romantic treatment. Much of the story is clearly a vehicle for Godwin to explore the injustices of the judicial system, and the story would have been artistically more satisfactory if he had been able to explore more effectively the personal duel of suspicions between Falkland and Williams. Godwin's conclusion, presumably, is that Williams' duty was that of compassion towards a man who was genuinely repentant for his crime, rather than to society to expose the murder. By either test, Williams failed, and the novel ended therefore with his shouldering all the misery and remorse that Falkland had formerly endured. The most effective parts of the novel are the account of Tyrrel's tyranny, and the descriptions of the prison scenes, and these were the subjects in which Godwin's propagandist purpose was most apparent. The final conclusion was that in the corrupt state of contemporary society, no man could be accounted good.

NOTE

[1] Godwin's best-known idea, that marriage should be abolished as an institution inimical to individuality, occupies a single chapter, and is the silliest in his book.

6 : William Cowper: An Eighteenth-Century Evangelical

In seventeen-eighty William Cowper was shaking himself free from a prolonged bout of insanity. He had come through a dark tunnel of despair in which he had been convinced that he must be eternally damned by God. It would not be true to say that it was religion which had made him mad, for the first signs of insanity had appeared when a young man, before he had experienced Evangelical influence,[1] but his innate fears were worsened when for a time he lived in the house of John Newton, the fiery Evangelical curate of Olney. Something of his spiritual agony may be discerned in his *Olney Hymns*, composed during the seventeen-seventies:

> My former hopes are fled,
> My terror now begins;
> I feel, alas! that I am dead
> In trespasses and sins.

> Ah, whither shall I fly?
> I hear the thunder roar;
> The Law proclaims destruction nigh,
> And Vengeance at the door.

Tortured by doubts and fears, he was slowly nursed back to health by Mrs. Unwin, and when Newton moved to a London parish in 1780, Cowper was released from his disturbing presence.

He found a new contentment in gardening, long walks in the country, his pet hares, and pleasant conversation. Henceforth he abandoned religious practices, and showed little interest in any church. In the *Olney Hymns* he was convinced of his own unworthiness:

> My God, how perfect are thy ways!
> But mine polluted are;
> Sin twines itself about my praise,
> And slides into my prayer.
>
> When I would speak what thou hast done
> To save me from my sin,
> I cannot make thy mercies known,
> But self-applause creeps in.
>
> This heart, a fountain of vile thoughts,
> How does it overflow,
> While self upon the surface floats,
> Still bubbling from below.

When taxed about his ceasing to pray, he always afterwards gave the same answer, that he was utterly unworthy. 'Prove to me that I have a right to pray, and I will pray without ceasing. . . . But let me add, there is no encouragement in the Scripture so comprehensive as to include my case, nor any consolation so effectual as to reach it. . . . I have not even asked a blessing upon my food these ten years, nor do I expect that I shall ever ask it again.' (Letter, 28 Oct. 1782.) This was the excuse he gave to the Rev. William Bull, but in truth he knew that it was the only way in which he could preserve his sanity. He retained his absolute belief in God, and an equal conviction of his own unworthiness, but, having paid lip-service to the latter, he was content now to find happiness in the transitory things of life. As an aid to his recovery, he took to writing poetry, and when in 1781 he met Lady Austen, there began the happiest and most fruitful period of his life. It was upon a suggestion from her that he began to write *The Task*, his most considerable poem, and upon its publication in 1785 he awoke to find himself famous. It was a discursive, reflective poem, containing the thoughts of a man in his early fifties on the ideas of his age. Strictly as poetry it was not of the first order, but Cowper's style was easy and graceful, and no other poet since Pope had managed to reflect so much of his age in a single poem. It had generally a favourable reception by the public, and there is no doubt that to a remarkable degree it was able to touch off 'the spirit of the age'. It is therefore of particular interest to the student of the period. There is however one aspect of it which is often forgotten. It was written, not as Wordsworth's *Prelude* was written, as a deep and searching statement of the poet's innermost feelings and philosophy, but as a literary exercise, almost as a therapeutic treatment, which gave the poet great pleasure. It tells the truth, but not the whole truth about the poet's mind. Even more delightful reading than *The Task* is Cowper's letters, and these tell the truth, almost the whole truth. Sometimes the letters contradict the sentiment of the poem, and in such cases it is the letters which must be believed.

There is an important example of this dating from June 1783. Cowper always affected to be little interested in political affairs, but in fact he followed them with great excitement. He was saddened by the loss of the American colonies, and much more by the English defeat at the hands of France. During the summer of 1783 he witnessed an unusual shower of meteors, fogs which blotted out the sun, while the moon appeared hot and red through night mists, and his superstitious nature was aroused. In *The Task* he turned the phenomena to full effect by using them to point the moral: God was angry with so sinful a nation, which must expect divine vengeance:

> Fires from beneath, and meteors from above,
> Portentous, unexampled, unexplain'd,
> Have kindled beacons in the skies . . .
> Is it a time to wrangle, when the props
> And pillars of our planet seem to fail,
> And nature, with a dim and sickly eye,
> To wait the close of all? (Bk. II.)

It was an effective point such as might have been made in many an

Evangelical sermon, but did Cowper really believe it? That they at first touched off his old irrational fears is likely enough, but for his more considered opinion we must turn to his letters. 'I am, and always have been, a great observer of natural appearances, but I think not a superstitious one. The fallibility of those speculations which lead men of fanciful minds to interpret Scripture by the contingencies of the day, is evident from this consideration, that *what the God of the Scriptures has seen fit to conceal, he will not as the God of Nature publish.* He is one and the same in both capacities, and consistent with himself; and his purpose, if he designs a secret, impenetrable, in whatever way we attempt to open it.' The phenomena, he added, were indeed curious, but no more than that. Still, he went on, 'as a poet, nevertheless, I claim, if any wonderful event should follow, a right to apply all and every such post-prognostic, to the purposes of the tragic muse' (Letter of 13 June 1783). In short, if a miracle was an event which increased faith, then he was content to treat the phenomena as a miracle. This illustration reveals the chief weakness of *The Task*, that it is too often a sermon on an evangelical theme, and the didactic purpose is sometimes more in evidence than the inspiration.

Yet, even with this warning in mind, we must recognise that it is a genuinely religious, and at times a deeply personal, poem:

> I was a stricken deer, that left the herd
> Long since: with many an arrow deep infix'd
> My panting side was charged, when I withdrew,
> To seek a tranquil death in distant shades.
> There was I found by one who had himself
> Been hurt by the archers. In his side he bore,
> And in his hands and feet, the cruel scars. (Bk. III.)

As a poet he derived his inspiration from Milton. He described his earliest poetic experiences: as a child

> My very dreams were rural; rural too
> The firstborn efforts of my youthful muse . . .
> No bard could please me but whose lyre was tuned
> To nature's praises . . .

> Then Milton had indeed a poet's charms:
> New to my taste, his Paradise surpass'd
> The struggling efforts of my boyish tongue
> To speak its excellence. I danced for joy. (Bk. IV.)

Time and time again in his poem Cowper returned to Milton's vision of Paradise, with all its peace and security, when

> The various seasons woven into one,
> And that one season an eternal spring,
> The garden fears no blight, and needs no fence.
> For there is none to covet, all are full.
> The lion and the libbard, and the bear
> Graze with the fearless flocks.

Cowper's vision lacks the poetic magnificence of Milton's, but is deeply sincere.

> And fear as yet was not, nor cause for fear.
> But sin marr'd all . . .
> Thus harmony and family accord
> Were driven from Paradise; and in that hour
> The seeds of cruelty, that since have swell'd
> To such gigantic and enormous growth,
> Were sown in human nature's fruitful soil.

Domestic peace was something which Cowper valued very highly, and of all the cruelties of man, the one which affected him most was cruelty towards animals. He was indeed the stricken deer who suffered with every animal which was hunted and killed:

> Earth growns beneath the burden of a war
> Waged with defenceless innocence.

His view of man in Paradise harked back to Milton, but there was a significant difference: man was more the Lord of Creation, more a product of the Age of Reason than Milton's:

> Man scarce had risen, obedient to his call,
> Who form'd him from the dust, his future grave,

When he was crowned as never king was since.
God set the diadem upon his head,
And angel choirs attended. . . .
Vast his empire, absolute his power,
Or bounded only by a law whose force
'Twas his sublimest privilege to feel
And own—the law of universal love.

From such a theme he was led on naturally to consider the attitude of the eighteenth-century philosophers to the universe. To them the subject of miracles had seemed of enormous importance for upon their existence or not seemed to depend the credibility of Christianity. To Cowper it was otherwise: the whole universe was a miracle. He recognised what the philosophers called the laws of nature, but these to him were proof of the existence of God. He was more impressed by the regularity of nature than by any deviations from the norm.

Constant rotation of the unwearied wheel
That nature rides upon maintains her wealth,
Her beauty, her fertility . . .
. . . oceans, rivers, lakes and streams,
All feel the freshening impulse, and are cleansed
By restless undulation: e'en the oak
Thrives by the rude concussion of the storm.

Men did not need the intervention of the miraculous to be convinced of God's presence:

Should God again,
As once in Gibeon, interrupt the race
Of the undeviating and punctual sun,
How would the world admire; but speaks it less
An agency divine, to make him know
His moment when to sink and when to rise,
Age after age, than to arrest his course?
All we behold is miracle; but, seen
So duly, all is miracle in vain.

Cowper retreated from the over-confidence of the deistic philosophers; man had presumed to know more than he could know:

> So man, the moth, is not afraid, it seems,
> To span omnipotence, and measure might,
> That knows no measure, by the scanty rule
> And standard of his own, that is today,
> And is not ere tomorrow's sun go down.
> But how should matter occupy a charge,
> Dull as it is, and satisfy a law
> So vast in its demands, unless impell'd
> To ceaseless service by a ceaseless force,
> And under pressure of some conscious cause?
> The Lord of all, himself through all diffused,
> Sustains, and is the life of all that lives.
> Nature is but a name for an effect,
> Whose cause is God. He feeds the secret fire,
> By which the mighty process is maintain'd.

In all this, of course, Cowper was speaking with complete sincerity of conviction, yet it was rather as if he had been asked to repeat a lesson learnt by heart. Again he is liable to be misunderstood if we read only his poetry. When he writes:

> Nature, enchanting nature, in whose form
> And lineaments divine I trace a hand
> That errs not, and find raptures still renewed,
> Is free to all men—universal prize,

he appears to be almost Wordsworthian in his approach to nature. But this would be a misinterpretation. To Wordsworth nature was almost a religion; it was the only manifestation of the deity, in a sense it *was* the deity. But this was not so with Cowper. The deity was the Christian God, and nature was indeed his handiwork, but the two were entirely separate and distinct. For his real opinion we must turn to his letters. 'My eyes drink the rivers as they flow.... I delight in baubles, and know them to be so; for rested in, and viewed without a reference to their Author, what is the earth, what are the planets, what is the sun itself but a bauble? Better for a man never to have seen them, or to see them with the eyes of a brute, stupid and unconscious of what he beholds, than not to be able to say, "The Maker of all these wonders is my friend!" Their eyes have never been opened, to see that they are trifles; mine have been, and will be till they are closed for ever.' (3 May 1780.) It was just because Nature was 'baubles' that Cowper could enjoy it so much. It was a relief from the intense strains which his troubled spirit had endured. When he described a threshing scene,

> Wide flies the chaff;
> The rustling straw sends up a frequent mist
> Of atoms, sparkling in the noonday beam

he was describing something which has given him soothing pleasure. We know that, much as he delighted in sunshine, he preferred to walk beneath the shade of trees:

> So sportive is the light
> Shot through the boughs, it dances as they dance,
> Shadow and sunshine intermingling quick,
> And darkening and enlightening as the leaves
> Play wanton.

It was the sights and sounds of nature which gave him most pleasure just because they were a relief from the tensions of deep thought. But he was not a close observer of nature; he did not seek for a meaning in nature, because he knew the answer already. His attitude was much closer to that of Milton than it was to Wordsworth's.

In the same way, deeply influenced as he was by the Evangelical revival, there were times when he appeared to be closer to the thought of Addison and Pope than to the Romantics. Indeed it is possible that it was the tension between the thought of the age of reason and the claims of religion which had done much to worsen his mental break-down. Thus when he drew his picture of the rational life he laid aside the rigorous puritanism of Evangelicalism in order to praise the ideal of the age of classicism:

H

> Blest he, though undistinguished from the crowd
> By wealth or dignity, who dwells secure,
> Where man, by nature fierce, has laid aside
> His fierceness, having learnt, though slow to learn,
> The manners and the arts of civil life.
> His wants, indeed, are many; but supply
> Is obvious, placed within each reach
> Of temperate wishes and industrous hands.
> Here virtue thrives as in her proper soil;
> Not rude and surly, and beset with thorns,
> . . . but gentle, kind,
> By culture tamed, by liberty refresh'd,
> And all her fruits by radiant truth matured.

With the possible exception of the use of the word 'radiant', there is nothing in this passage which would have come amiss to the pen of Addison.

At other times however Cowper was powerfully influenced by Evangelical and Calvinistic thought. He was deeply convinced of the wickedness of London, the city of which he knew so little at first hand:

> Such London is, by taste and wealth proclaim'd
> The fairest capital of all the world;
> By riot and incontinence the worst.

Indeed he was convinced that city-life must needs breed 'rank abundance, sloth and lust'. It was true that cities were also nurseries of the arts, but for this very reason the arts were the more suspect. Nature was always more perfect than art; why then should people prefer pictures to nature? In cities there was an excess of wealth, and this bred selfishness and materialism. The rich by living in the towns failed to set a moral example to the poor in the country:

> The rich, and they that have an arm to check
> The license of the lowest in degree,
> Desert their office; and themselves, intent

On pleasure, haunt the capital, and thus
To all the violence of lawless hands
Resign the scenes their presence might protect.

Yet by how much was the country life superior to the town!
'God made the country, and man made the town.' Cowper called
upon those who knew how to travel only by chariot or sedan and
were fatigued by idleness to take once again the possession of the
countryside.

Cowper made some observant comments on the changes which
were taking place in the countryside in the eighteenth century.
There was first the transformations of Capability Brown:

> Lo, he comes!
> The omnipotent magician, Brown appears!
> Down falls the venerable pile, the abode
> Of our forefathers—a grave, whisker'd race,
> But tasteless. Springs a palace in its stead,
> But in a distant spot; where, more exposed,
> It may enjoy the advantage of the north,
> And aguish east, till time shall have transform'd
> Those naked acres to a sheltering grove.
> He speaks. The lake in front becomes a lawn;
> Woods vanish, hills subside, and valleys rise;
> And streams, as if created for his use,
> Pursue the track of his directing wand,
> Sinuous or straight, now rapid and now slow,
> Now murmuring soft, now roaring in cascades—
> E'en as he bids!

Cowper did not entirely approve, and even less did he approve of
the new capitalist agriculture. There had once, he sighed, been a
time when manors were occupied by the same families from
generation to generation, but now there was a constant change of
tenants, and new men came, bent only on extorting as much quick
profit from the land as possible.

> Mansions once
> Knew their own masters; and laborious hinds

Who had survived the father, served the son.
Now the legitimate and rightful lord
Is but a transient guest, newly arrived
And soon to be supplanted. He that saw
His patrimonial timber cast its leaf,
Sells the last scantling, and transfers the price
To some shrewd sharper ere it buds again.
Estates are landscapes, gazed upon awhile,
Then advertised, and auctioneer'd away.

Cowper had a lively sympathy for the poor. Like Wordsworth, he was much moved by a poor mad woman who roamed the countryside, crazed since her lover was drowned at sea:

She heard the doleful tidings of his death—
And never smiled again! and now she roams
The dreary waste; there spends the livelong day,
And there, unless when charity forbids,
The livelong night. . . .
She begs an idle pin of all she meets
And hoards them in her sleeve; but needful food,
Though press'd with hunger oft, or comelier clothes,
Though pinch'd with cold, asks never.—Kate is crazed!

He condemned the harshness of the law in pressing more heavily on the poor than on the rich:

It is not seemly, nor of good report,
That she (i.e. London) is slack in discipline; more prompt
To avenge than to prevent the breach of law:
That she is rigid in denouncing death
On petty robbers, and indulges life
And liberty, and ofttimes honour, too,
To peculators of the public gold:
That thieves at home must hang; but he, that puts
Into his overgorged and bloated purse
The wealth of Indian provinces, escapes.

He was well acquainted with the problems of poverty among the lace-makers of Olney. In July 1780 he wrote: 'I am an eye-witness of their poverty, and do know that hundreds in this little town are upon the point of starving, and that the most unremitting industry is but barely sufficient to keep them from it', and he strongly condemned the indifference of the government to such suffering. Mrs. Unwin and Cowper did all they could to help by way of private charity, but he lamented that they could do little among so many. Still, blankets and clothes here, a few shillings there, were gratefully received by the 'ragged and hungry poor', and it was a red-letter day when a Mr. Smith in January 1783 sent them forty pounds for distribution. Cowper wrote: 'Olney has not had such a friend this many a day; nor has there been an instance at any time of a few poor families so effectually relieved, or so completely encouraged to the pursuit of that honest industry by which, their debts being paid, and the parents and child-renc omfortably clothed, they are now enabled to maintain themselves.'

Yet Cowper could not get away from the Evangelical belief that suffering was in some ways a blessing. He wrote: 'When I see an afflicted and an unhappy man, I say to myself, there is perhaps a man whom the world would envy, if they knew the value of his sorrows, which are possibly intended only to soften his heart, and to turn his affections towards their proper centre. But when I see or hear of a crowd of voluptuaries, who have no ears but for music, no eyes but for splendour, and no tongue but for impertinence and folly, I say. . . . This is madness! This persisted in must have a tragical conclusion' (5 Nov. 1781). When he heard of a woman dying worth sixty thousand pounds, and leaving it to her poor relations, he added whimsically that 'some of them she has probably ruined by her kindness'. Admirable as his constant acts of charity were, yet he always discriminated carefully between the deserving and the undeserving poor, for

> poverty with most, who whimper forth
> Their long complaints, is self-inflicted woe;
> The effect of laziness or sottish waste.

He described the activities of the poacher; there might be some excuse if he used his ill-gotten gains to feed his hungry family, but more likely they remained hungry while he exchanged his pheasants for drink:

> 'Tis quenchless thirst
> Of ruinous ebriety that prompts
> His every action, and imbrutes the man.

In town or country every twenty paces brought one to a new public house:

> There sit, involved and lost in curling clouds
> Of Indian fume, and guzzling deep, the boor,
> The lackey, and the groom: the craftsman there
> Takes a Lethean leave of all his toil;
> Smith, cobbler, joiner, he that plies the shears,
> And he that kneads the dough; all loud alike,
> All learned and all drunk.

'All learned', for the public houses were the schools of the poor, where they were students of idleness and discontent.

Cowper satirised the false tinsel of eighteenth-century society, with its back-biting, extravagance and gambling. To these he ascribed the loss of an empire:

> . . . be grooms, and win the plate
> Where once your noble fathers won a crown!

The only happy life was the simple life:

> Whom call we gay? That honour has been long
> The boast of mere pretenders to the name.
> The innocent are gay—the lark is gay,
> That dries his feathers, saturate with dew,
> Beneath the rosy cloud, while yet the beams
> Of dayspring overshoot his humble nest.
> The peasant too, a witness of his song,
> Himself a songster, is as gay as he.

But save me from the gaiety of those
Whose headaches nail them to a noonday bed.

Like most Evangelicals, he was extremely critical of the average
run of clergymen, who graced society and did so little for the poor.

But loose in morals, and in manners vain,
In conversation frivolous, in dress
Extreme, at once rapacious and profuse;
Frequent in park, with lady at his side,
Ambling and prattling scandal as he goes;
But rare at home, and never at his books,
Or with his pen, save when he scrawls a card;
Constant at routs, familiar with a round
Of ladyships—a stranger to the poor;
Ambitious of preferment for its gold,
And well-prepared, by ignorance and sloth,
By infidelity and love of world,
To make God's work a sinecure; a slave
To his own pleasures and his patron's pride:—
From such apostles, O, ye mitred heads,
Preserve the Church! and lay not careless hands
On skulls that cannot teach and will not learn.

The danger was that the Evangelical, in expressing his disgust
at the sins of the world, would turn against all which did not savour
of a narrow piety. Wit and humour became suspect, for

'Tis pitiful
To court a grin, when you should woo the soul;
To break a jest, when pity would inspire
Pathetic exhortation. . . .
So did not Paul. Direct me to a quip
Or merry turn in all he ever wrote.

Happily, Cowper did not practise what he preached, for his letters
often reveal a delicate and gentle humour. But in his moral
judgments he was equally austere in his disapproval of popular
heroes:

> Man praises man. Desert in arts or arms
> Wins public honour; and ten thousand sit
> Patiently present at a sacred song
> Commemoration mad; content to hear
> (O wonderful effect of music's power!)
> Messiah's eulogy for Handel's sake.

For in his age Handel was receiving the praise which belonged to the Messiah; and Garrick too was made 'the idol of our worship' and 'the god of our idolatry'. To Cowper the world of business, the world of fashion and the world of the arts, all amounted to vanity.

> I sum up half mankind,
> And add two-thirds of the remaining half,
> And find the total of their hopes and fears
> Dreams, empty dreams.

All this was strictly in accordance with his moral code, and was by no means as detached from the outside world as he often pretended to be. He was the poet who mourned in verse the loss of the *Royal George*; it was he who in Book IV of *The Task* described the impatience with which he awaited the arrival of the post bringing the papers, and the eagerness with which they were scanned. Cowper had his fair share of robust eighteenth-century patriotism:

> England, with all thy faults, I love thee still—
> My country!

In moments like this he forgot his disapproval of the praise of great men:

> Praise enough
> To fill the ambition of a private man,
> That Chatham's language was his mother tongue,
> And Wolfe's great name compatriot with his own.

His letters show the eagerness with which he followed the news of the American War, and the great sadness which came with

England's defeat, a sadness tempered however by the pious sentiment that defeat must have been pre-ordained by God, perhaps in
order to bring the wicked to their knees again in prayer. On the
news of the defeat at Yorktown he wrote: 'We are sorry to hear it,
and should be more cast down than we are, if we did not know that
this catastrophe was ordained beforehand, and that therefore
neither conduct, nor courage, nor any means that can possibly be
mentioned, could have prevented it.' This was a Calvinistic fatalism
which relieved the tension of defeat, and was an antidote to action.
In February 1783 he was humiliated by the terms of the Peace,
but consoled himself with a thought on the nations of the earth
that 'whether they do good or evil, I see them acting under the
permission or direction of that Providence who governs the earth,
whose operations are as irresistible as they are silent and un-
suspected'. Yet he could not resist the remark that it was a 'stain
upon our national honour, and a diminution of our national
property; then, having committed himself so far, he drew back:
'You will suppose me a politician; but in truth I am nothing less.
These are the thoughts that occur to me while I read the newspaper; and when I have laid it down, I feel myself more interested
in the success of my early cucumbers, than in any part of this great
and important subject.'

Cowper all his life was a whig, one who, as he wrote, had
learned as a boy to love his country, and to glow with enthusiasm
at Prior's poetry and the patriotic broadsheets of the time. His
political thought was that of conventional whiggism:

> We love
> The king who loves the law, respects his bounds,
> And reigns content within them: him we serve
> Freely and with delight, who leaves us free:
> But, recollecting still that he is a man,
> We trust him not too far.

He shared with most Evangelicals and many whigs a guilty
conscience at the evils of slavery:

> I would not have a slave to till my ground,

> To carry me, to fan me while I sleep,
> And tremble when I wake, for all the wealth
> That sinews bought and sold have ever earn'd . . .
> We have no slaves at home: Then why abroad?

Like most Englishmen, he regarded French government as the epitome of despotism, of which the Bastille was a gruesome symbol, and five years before the event he looked forward to its fall:

> There's not an English heart that would not leap
> To hear that ye were fallen at last.

In contrast, England was the land of liberty:

> Thee I account still happy, and the chief
> Among the nations, seeing thou art free:
> My native nook of earth!

Liberty was the essential condition of the good life:

> 'Tis liberty alone that gives the flower
> Of fleeting life its lustre and perfume;
> And we are weeds without it. All constraint,
> Except what wisdom lays on evil men,
> Is evil.

It was not the liberty to do as one liked, nor the philosopher's liberty to live as prudence dictated, but the liberty to live according to God's will:

> He is the freeman whom the truth makes free,
> And all are slaves besides.

With Cowper religious faith was accompanied by an anti-intellectualism which was a natural reaction against eighteenth-century philosophy.

> Knowledge and wisdom, far from being one,
> Have ofttimes no connection. Knowledge dwells
> In heads replete with thoughts of other men;
> Wisdom in minds attentive to their own. . . .

Knowledge is proud that he has learn'd so much;
Wisdom is humble that he knows no more.

He was not indeed opposed to learning as such, but only to the philosophy which was so cock-sure in its materialism that it appeared to deny the importance of God. With the thought of Newton, Milton and Hale it was different:

Learning has borne such fruit in other days
On all her branches: piety has found
Friends in the friends of science, and true prayer
Has flow'd from lips wet with Castalian dews.
Such was thy wisdom, Newton, childlike sage!
Sagacious reader of the works of God,
And in his word sagacious. Such too thine,
Milton, whose genius had angelic wings,
And fed on manna! And such thine, in whom
Our British Themis gloried with just cause,
Immortal Hale!

These philosophers strengthened rather than undermined faith in God. For scientific achievements in themselves Cowper cared little. 'One project indeed', he wrote, 'supplants another. The *vortices* of Descartes gave way to the gravitation of Newton, and this again is threatened by the electrical fluid of a modern. One generation blows bubbles, and the next breaks them.' (29 Sept. 1783.) As for the philosophers:

Great contest follows, and much learned dust
Involves the combatants; each claiming truth,
And truth disclaiming both. And thus they spend
The little wick of life's poor shallow lamp
In playing tricks with nature, giving laws
To distant worlds, and trifling in their own.

The trouble with philosophy was that it 'merely lightens the mind with respect to non-essentials'.

Defend me, therefore, common sense, I say,
From reveries so airy, from the toil

> Of dropping buckets into empty wells,
> And growing old in drawing nothing up!

So Cowper turned away from both pietistic practices and philosophy, to seek peace among the 'baubles' of nature and the cares of a practical gardener.

> Ye little know the cares,
> The vigilance, the labour, and the skill,
> That day and night are exercised, and hang
> Upon the ticklish balance of suspense,
> That ye may garnish your profuse regales
> With summer fruits, brought forth by wintry suns.

'My morning', he wrote, 'is engrossed by the garden; and in the afternoon, till I have drunk tea, I am fit for nothing. At five o'clock we walk; and when the walk is over, lassitude recommends rest, and again I become fit for nothing.' In growing his cucumbers, in feeding his hares, and in country walks, he learnt compassion and the brotherhood of man.

> The timorous hare,
> Grown so familiar with her frequent guest,
> Scarce shuns me; and the stockdove unalarm'd
> Sits cooing in the pine-tree, nor suspends
> His long love-ditty for my near approach.

As the sophisticated things of life divided and embittered men, so the simple things increased their sense of interdependence and affection:

> I think, articulate, I laugh and weep,
> And exercise all functions of a man.
> How then should I and any man that lives
> Be strangers to each other?

Not even in his garden, or on his walks, would Cowper find complete contentment:

> O blest seclusion from the jarring world,
> Which he, thus occupied, enjoys! Retreat
> Cannot, indeed, to guilty men restore
> Lost innocence, or cancel follies past;
> But it has peace, and much secures the mind
> From all assaults of evil.

Not complete contentment, then, but the nearest he would ever approach to it.

Cowper was not a Romantic; the passionate turmoils of the Romantic poets still lay ahead when he wrote *The Task*; but in his deeply personal writing, his preference for feeling over knowledge, his love of the country life, his hatred of cruelty, and his concern for the sufferings of the poor and needy, he was a forerunner of much which was typically Romantic. Most of all perhaps he foreshadowed the Evangelical movement which was so potent a force in the period with which this book deals, and this is the subject of the next chapter.

NOTE

[1] He himself recognised this when he wrote in a letter (27 July 1783): 'In former years I have known sorrow, and before I had ever tasted of spiritual trouble.'

7 : The Evangelicals and their Critics

THE general trend of thought in the eighteenth century had been towards a greater humanity and tolerance, but with the triumph of the philosophy of enlightenment and empiricism, had come also latitudinarianism, deism and atheism. 'Good' was interpreted in utilitarian terms, and was practically synonymous with individual and materialistic happiness, and a 'good man' was one who combined prudence with altruism. By the seventeen-eighties there was among a small but influential group of people a growing disquiet which was not unrelated to the political and social changes of the time. Population was increasing faster than at any time in previous history; the growth of towns extended the incidence of thieving, prostitution and debauchery, as well as the risks of riots. The Gordon Riots of 1780 were without precedent in their severity, and left an indelible mark upon the minds of the governing classes. The loss of the American colonies was a great shock to the complacency of the age, and the ideas of liberty and revolution advocated by Tom Paine were disturbing. The rapid growth of wealth consequent upon industrial and commercial development threw into lurid contrast the poverty, ignorance and misery of so many common people, at a time when many thoughtful people were accepting a deeper and more corporate view of society than had been usual in the eighteenth century. The result was that by the seventeen-eighties there were signs of the beginnings of a religious and moral reformation in England.

One answer to the problems of the age was a call to return to religion. Wesley had made just such a call, and his life of toil had left a permanent mark upon the poor and middle classes. But what he had not been able to do was to make any appreciable inroad upon the great, the governing classes. There was a time when the activities of the Countess of Huntingdon suggested that it might be otherwise, and for some years Methodism was a fashionable pursuit among the Society of Bath and London, but it failed to take permanent root. For some the Calvinistic doctrine of Whitefield was too strong for their digestion; but, probably more important for most, was the fact that the movement smacked of impertinence and indiscipline. For Wesley insisted on treating all souls as of equal value, and one sinner as sinful, yet as worth saving, as another. It was impossible to expect that the governing classes would accept the democratic aspects of Wesley's movement, and Wesley recognised towards the end of his life that he had entirely failed to reach them. He once said to a sister of Hannah More: 'Tell her to live in the world; there is the sphere of her usefulness; they will not let *us* come nigh them.' The 'world', of course, to Wesley, was high society, and Hannah More had an entry there which was always denied to him.

The Evangelicals were more successful. They were Anglicans, often people of wealth, always of the utmost respectability, and agreeable companions to the governing classes in a way unthinkable for Methodists. Many of the governing classes were either strongly Evangelical themselves, or at least well disposed towards those who were. Men like the Earl of Dartmouth, Lord Hardwicke, Lord Muncaster, the Earl of Winchelsea, Lord Teignmouth, Sir Charles Middleton and Sir Robert Peel the Elder were among those who gave their support to Evangelical projects. The episcopal bench included some who were equally well disposed. Bishops Porteus of London and Shute Barrington of Durham were their friends, and the undistinguished John Moore, Archbishop of Canterbury often made Evangelical preferments. Above all, George III gave them a hesitant patronage. In 1788 he agreed to issue a Proclamation against Vice and Immorality, and this was followed by the formation of a Proclamation Society under the presidency of Bishop Porteus, to wage war against vice among the lower orders. Its achievements were limited, and most of its attentions were concentrated upon the prosecution of seditious and licentious books. Its most noted exploit was the prosecution of the bookseller of Tom Paine's *Age of Reason*. The unfortunate man went to prison for two years, but it did little to prevent the circulation of the book.[1] As for George III, he became suspicious of a movement which could attack the slave trade.

The leader of the Evangelical movement for forty years was William Wilberforce. A wealthy man, he became M.P. for Hull in 1780 at the age of twenty-one, became a close friend of William Pitt, and for a time led the life of a gay man-about-town. He came under the influence of the ex-slave-dealer-turned-Evangelical, John Newton, and in 1785 he underwent a religious conversion. In 1787 he made his famous entry in his Journal: 'God Almighty has placed before me two great objects, the suppression of the slave trade and the reformation of manners.' He plunged with tireless energy into a life of good works, and was the moving spirit behind dozens of societies devoted to religious works, reform and amelioration; the Bible Society, the Church Missionary Society, the Sunday School Society, the Proclamation Society against Vice and Immorality, the School Society, the Climbing Boys Society, the Anti-Slave Trade Movement, and projects for building hospitals, orphanages, asylums, schools, and charities for aiding widows, indigent clergy and carrying on religious propaganda. He was a generous man, and gave away a large portion of his fortune. One society was the Society for Bettering the Condition and Increasing the Comforts of the Poor (1796); another, the Philanthropic Society (1798), aimed at apprenticing boys to a trade and putting girls into domestic service. Today this might seem like an organisation for providing the governing classes with cheap labour, but there was then a real danger that boys would be driven by hunger to turn thieves and vagabonds, and girls to prostitution, and the motives of the Evangelicals were, according to the standards of the time, entirely charitable. In 1787 Wilberforce introduced in the Commons his first motion for the abolition of the slave trade, and repeated it annually until it was carried in 1807. The success of his campaign in the middle of a great foreign war was an immense personal triumph, and Sir James Mackintosh called it the greatest benefit any individual had ever accomplished. Historians have always seen it as the central achievement of his life; yet to Wilberforce himself, important though the achievement was, it was always subsidiary to the main object of his career.

To him the most important thing was not that a man should be free from slavery, but that he should have a living faith in Jesus Christ. He was of course sensible to the horrors of the slave trade, but even more serious to him was the moral depravity which the trade encouraged among the slave dealers. In his hatred of slavery, he was as much concerned at the vices which slavery encouraged among the masters as the cruelties inflicted upon the slaves. Moreover, so long as slavery continued, it was impossible for missionaries to have free access to the Negroes to attempt the work of conversion. Most Evangelicals believed that it was impossible for any human being to achieve eternal life unless he accepted the Evangelical faith; they rejected the loose eighteenth-century ideas on the subject which had grown up under the influence of Enlightenment. To Wilberforce the work of sending out missionaries to India or elsewhere was more important even than the abolition of the slave trade. The great object of his life's work was nothing less than a complete reformation of the moral life of his age, and he set out his aims in a number of important works which were acclaimed and widely read in his day.

In his *Practical View of the Religious System of Professed Christians Contrasted with Real Christians* (1797) he attacked the nominal Christianity which, it seemed to him, too often passed for the real thing in eighteenth-century life. It was not sufficient merely to be 'good', to be sincere and to perform good works. Complete faith in Christ was the sole condition for holiness, and he looked to the governing classes to set an example to the lower orders. Their attitude should combine gentility and good breeding with a strict regard for morality. 'There will be no capricious humours, no selfish tempers, no moroseness, no discourtesy, no affected severity of deportment, no peculiarity of language, no indolent neglect, no wanton breach, of the ordinary forms of fashions of society.' Religion to Wilberforce was an immensely serious matter, but it did not involve any display of puritan boorishness. A Christian was also a gentleman. In an important

I

passage he indicated the social consequences he envisaged: 'Thus, softening the glare of wealth, and moderating the insolence of power, she (Christianity) renders the inequalities of the social state less galling to the lower orders, whom also she instructs, in their turn, to be diligent, humble, patient: reminding them that their more lowly path has been allotted to them by the hand of God; that it is their part faithfully to discharge its duties, and contentedly to bear its inconveniences; that the present state of things is very short; that the objects, about which wordly men conflict so eagerly, are not worth the contest; that the peace of mind, which Religion offers to all ranks indiscriminately, affords more true satisfaction than all the expensive pleasures which are beyond the poor man's reach; that in this view, however, the poor have the advantage, and that if their superiors enjoy more abundant comforts, they are also exposed to many temptations from which the inferior classes are happily exempted; that "having food and raiment, they should be therewith content", for that their situation in life, with all its evils, is better than they have deserved at the hands of God; finally that all human distinctions will soon be done away, and the true followers of Christ will all, as children of the same Father, be alike admitted to the possession of the same heavenly inheritance. Such are the blessed effects of Christianity on the temporal well-being of political communities.' (p. 406.)

It is this kind of argument which has led so many later writers to dislike the Evangelicals. The suspicion is that Wilberforce was intending religion as an opium for the masses, that it was an instinct for self-preservation which led him to urge that the rich did not flaunt their wealth, and that they should teach the poor resignation and patience, and even that the poor were better off than the rich because they had fewer temptations, or alternatively, that the inequalities of this life were of short duration, and would be followed by just reward in the next life. There is truth in all these suspicions, but they must be seen in the context of the troubled times in which Wilberforce lived. To the governing classes the masses did indeed present a frightening spectacle both in numbers and the brutalised character of their lives. The dangers of revolution and untold destruction seemed very real. How could they be prevented? Education and religion seemed the natural answer to many. The effects would be to soften and humanise, and to inculcate a ready acceptance of the social order and the misfortunes which this life inevitably brought. The alternative was Tom Paine and his solution of revolution. Wilberforce was a deeply sincere Christian, to whom faith in Jesus Christ was the most important thing in the world. He was therefore no humbug in advocating his remedy for the age. To many it has seemed intolerable that he should have advocated Christianity and at the same time supported Pitt's repressive measures, but this again is not to understand the fears of the age nor the instinct for social discipline which was an essential part of it. Those who could remember the Gordon Riots had no need to be reminded of what the alternative might be.

These criticisms of Wilberforce were heard in his own day: many liberals detested him as a steady supporter of tory governments. Hazlitt attacked him as an equivocator, one who would serve both God and Mammon, being too fond of the approval of those in power. He could attack the property of the slave-owners, 'but not a word has he to say, not a whisper does he breathe against the claim set up by the Despots of the Earth over their Continental subjects, but does everything in his power to confirm and sanction it! He must give no offence. Mr. Wilberforce's humanity will go all lengths that it can with safety and discretion: but it is not to be supposed that it should lose him his seat for Yorkshire, the smile of Majesty, or the countenance of the loyal and pious. . . . He preaches vital Christianity to untutored savages; and tolerates its worst abuses in civilized states. He thus shows his respect for religion without offending the clergy, or circumscribing the sphere of his usefulness. . . . He carefully chooses his ground to fight the battles of loyalty, religion, and humanity, and it is such as is always safe and advantageous to himself!' (*Spirit of the Age*, p. 332.) This was intended as a hostile attack on one whom he described as 'a mixture of fashion and fanaticism', but in fact Hazlitt was doing little more than complimenting Wilberforce upon his political sagacity. It is true that he was careful to retain the good opinion which the political powers of the day had of him, but by what other means could he expect to achieve the goal he had set himself? Wesley himself had recognised how much more he could have accomplished if he could have won the support of the governing classes. Wilberforce would have achieved nothing if he had appeared as a dangerous leveller, even supposing that he had the least inclination to be one. Hazlitt's criticism was wide of the mark, for Wilberforce was the most successful reformer of his day.

If Wilberforce was the leader of the Evangelicals, Hannah More was their most successful propagandist. Born in 1745 in Gloucestershire, the fourth of five daughters of humble parents, she and her sisters established a boarding school for young ladies in Bristol, and made enough money to live comfortably. By 1775 Hannah was a precocious literary figure in London, a friend of Dr. Johnson, Burke and Reynolds, and one of the original Bluestockings. In 1777 she wrote a highly successful play which was performed at Drury Lane. She then came under Evangelical influence, and in 1784 retired to Cowslip Green in the Mendips, her 'escape from the world'. In 1788 she published *Thoughts on the Importance of the Manners of the Great to General Society*. It was addressed to 'those who, filling the higher ranks in life, are naturally regarded as patterns, by which the manners of the rest of the world are to be fashioned', and was a call to them to remember how great was the moral responsibility which rested upon them to set an example. She was not attempting to warn against spectacular wickedness; the opportunities which occurred of committing heinous sins were few. Her warnings were of false philosophy and thoughtless conduct. She refers throughout her essay to a 'Good sort of people', good-natured people who were not really wicked. Such people were usually praised, but it was thoughtless praise; good-nature was not enough without holiness. It was quite wrong to suppose that an 'unrestrained indulgence of pleasure' was the mark of 'a liberal, humane and merciful temper', or that libertinism and good-nature were natural allies. 'I am charmed with humanity, generosity and integrity, in whomsoever they may be found. But one virtue must not intrench upon another. Charity must not supplant faith. If a man be generous, good-natured, and humane, it is impossible not to feel for him the tenderness of a brother:

but if, at the same time, he be irreligious, intemperate, and profane, who shall dare to say he is in a safe state?... Without holiness no man shall see the Lord.' Much of the blame for the irreligion of the age she laid upon 'corrupt poets and corrupt philosophers', for they had made pleasure the ultimate goal of life. She was critical also of the stage. *The School for Scandal* for instance was immensely popular, yet it 'exalted liberality and turned justice into ridicule'. She urged that she did not aim to make religion either gloomy or tyrannical; its theme was charity and benevolence. 'The world is a climate which too naturally chills a glowing generosity, and contracts an expanded heart. The zeal of the most sanguine is but too apt to cool.' Religion was not forbidding but inviting, 'not so tyrannising as Appetite, so exacting as the World, nor so despotic as Fashion'. It does not forbid 'the cheerful enjoyments of life'. It does not urge men to fly from society. 'No: the mischief arises not from our living in the world, but from the world living in us; occupying our hearts and monopolising our affections. Action is the life of virtue, and the world is the theatre of action.' Her advice to the Great was certainly moderate, that they should not encourage the non-observance of Sundays by tradesmen nor themselves travel on Sundays, that they should beware of the temptations of newly-gained wealth, and that they should subscribe to Sunday schools. Unless the Great set a good example, how could the penal laws be effective against the poor. 'If the Rich and Great will not, from a liberal spirit of doing right, and from a Christian spirit of fearing God, abstain from those offences, for which the poor are to suffer fines and imprisonments, effectual good cannot be done. It will signify little to lay penalties on the horses of the drover, or on the waggon of the husbandman, while the chariot wheels of the Great roll with incessant motion; and while the sacred day on which the sons of industry are commanded by royal proclamation to desist from travelling, is for that very reason selected for the journeys of the Great, and preferred because the road is encumbered with fewer interruptions.... Will not the common people think it a little inequitable that they are abridged of the diversions of the public-house and the gaming-yard on Sunday evening, when they shall hear that many houses of the first nobility are on that evening crowded with company and such amusements carried on as are prohibited by human laws even on common days?'

Three years later she followed this pamphlet with another, *An Estimate of the Religion of the Fashionable World*, in which she lamented the religious decline in the eighteenth century. 'Under the beautiful mask of an enlightened philosophy, all religious restraints are set at nought; and some of the deadliest wounds have been aimed at christianity, in works written in avowed vindication of the most amiable of all Christian principles. Even the prevalence of a liberal and warm philanthropy is secretly sapping the foundations of christian morals, because many of its champions allow themselves to live in the open violation of the severer duties of justice and sobriety while they are contending for the gentler ones of charity and beneficence. The strong and generous bias in favour of universal toleration, noble as the principle itself is, has engendered a dangerous notion that all error is innocent. . . . While we glory in having freed ourselves from the trammels of human authority, are we not turning our liberty into licentiousness, and wantonly struggling to throw off the *divine* authority too? Freedom of thought is the glory of the human mind, while it is confined within its just and sober limits', but answer for error must be made to God himself, and the real need was that believers should live truly Christian lives.

Completely sincere as her religious attitude was, it will be noted that, even before the outbreak of the French Revolution she felt the need to educate the poor, and to give them as little provocation to discontent as possible. By 1794 this idea was powerfully re-enforced, for there was now the fear of the spread of Jacobinism, and moreover the bad harvests had imposed almost intolerable sufferings upon the peasants. Bishop Porteus was delighted with her writings, and he sought for some means to offset the influence of Tom Paine among the lower classes, many of whom, thanks to the activities of Sunday schools, could read. He therefore pressed Hannah More to write a series of simple stories which would appeal to the people and would inculcate the Christian virtues of industry, charity, patience and resignation. Thus began the Cheap

Repository Tracts, selling at a half-penny or penny each, which proved a phenomenal success, selling over two million copies in the first two years, far outstripping any novel of the period. Hannah More knew intimately the sufferings of the country-folk around her, and she described their predicament with real sympathy. In *Tom White, the Post-Boy* she described 'the hard winter' through which they had just lived. 'In the famous cold winter of the year 1795, it was edifying to see how patiently Farmer White bore that long and severe frost. Many of his sheep were frozen to death, but he thanked God that he had still many left. He continued to find indoor work that his men might not be out of employ. The season being so bad, which some others pleaded as an excuse for turning off their workmen, he thought a fresh reason for keeping them. Mrs. White was so considerate that just at that time she lessened the number of her hogs, that she might have more whey and skim-milk to assist poor families. Nay, I have known her live on boiled meat for a long while together, in a sickly season, because the pot-liquor made such a supply of broth for the sick poor. As the Spring came on, and things grew worse, she never had a cake, a pye, or a pudding in her house, notwithstanding she used to have plenty of these good things, and will again, I hope, when the present scarcity is over; though she says she will never use white flour again, even if it should come down to five shillings a bushel.'

Her simple stories were full of good advice to the poor on the ways in which by thrift they could make their lives more bearable. In *A Cure for Melancholy: Shewing the Way to Do Much Good with Little Money*, written during the famine of 1794, she told the story of Mrs. Jones who was much moved by the parable of the Good Samaritan, and wept that, being so poor, she could not 'go and do likewise'. The vicar however reassured her. 'In the case of the Samaritan, you may observe that charity was bestowed more by kindness and care and medicine than by money.' Poor though she was, she could still 'go about to do good'. This gave Mrs. Jones new heart, and she determined to teach the poor the principles of true economy. First she proved that the baker was giving short weight in his loaves, and as a consequence of this information 'the justices resolved henceforward to inspect the bakers of the district'. Next she proceeded against shops which opened on Sundays. She persuaded the well-to-do to buy the more expensive cuts of meat in order to leave the cheaper for the poor. She urged the latter to do their own baking, of brown bread instead of white, and to brew their own beer instead of visiting the public houses. She used her influence to reduce the number of public houses in the villages. She organised charity schools for the daughters of the village to learn cooking, spinning, weaving and household management, and to make cheap dishes from sheep's heads. Thus Mrs. Jones 'did much good with little money', and she learnt the lesson 'that Providence, in sending these extraordinary seasons of scarcity and distress, which we have twice lately experienced, has been pleased to over-rule these trying events to the general good . . . for without abating any thing of a just subordination, it has brought the affluent to a nearer knowledge of the persons and characters of their indigent neighbours'.

Herein lay the gist of the Evangelical message. Class divisions were the work of divine Providence, and there must be no 'abatement of a just subordination', but if the poor must learn frugality and patience, the rich must recognise a sense of charity and responsibility, and must set an example to those less fortunate than themselves. In this way class hatred will be eliminated, and all people will be brought together in brotherhood and charity. Hannah More could lecture the rich as effectively as the poor. In *A Cure for Melancholy* the Squire was the 'good' landlord and Sir John the example of the landowner who left much to be desired, although he was, of course, a 'good-natured' man. 'His idea of charity was, that a rich man should occasionally give a little of his superfluous wealth to the first object that occurred; but he had no conception that it was his duty so to husband his wealth and limit his expenses as to supply a regular fund for established charity. And the utmost stretch of his benevolence never led him to suspect that he was called to abridge himself in the most idle article of indulgence, for a purpose foreign to his own personal enjoyment.'

If she could lecture equally both rich and poor, she could also idealise the simple life in the full Romantic tradition. The finest of her stories was *The Shepherd of Salisbury Plain,* in which, in Wordsworthian circumstances, Mr. Johnson comes upon a shepherd living with his wife and eight children in a two-roomed hovel and subsisting on the wages of a shilling a day. The hardships are almost unbearable, but the shepherd never loses his cheerfulness and patience. Life was hard, but the shepherd declares, "'tis not near so toilsome as that which my GREAT MASTER led for my sake; and he had every state and condition of life at his choice, and *chose* a hard one; while I only submit to the lot that is appointed me'. 'You are exposed to great cold and heat', said the gentleman. 'True, Sir, but then I am not exposed to great temptations; and so throwing one thing against another, God is pleased to contrive to make things more equal than we poor, ignorant, short-sighted creatures are apt to think. David was happier when he kept his father's sheep on such a plain as this, and employed in singing some of his own psalms perhaps, than ever he was when he became king of Israel and Judah.' For God had specially honoured poverty: 'Oh! Sir, what great or rich, or mighty men have had such honour put on them, or their condition, as shepherds, tent-makers, fishermen and carpenters have had?' The shepherd had learned to read when a boy, 'though reading was not so common when I was a child, as I am told, through the goodness of Providence and the generosity of the rich, it is likely to become now-a-days'; and thus for thirty years he had read the Bible every day.

Although he earned but a shilling a day, some of his girls could earn $\frac{1}{2}d.$ or 1*d.* a day by knitting, the boys could earn 1*d.* or 2*d.* by scaring birds off the corn, or by gleaning in autumn, and the small children could collect wool torn from the sheep by brambles for carding and spinning on winter evenings. Mr. Johnson was appalled at the sight of their hovel, but the shepherd replied: 'The house is very well, Sir; and if the rain did not sometimes beat down upon us through the thatch when we are a-bed, I should not desire a better; for I have health, peace and liberty, and no man maketh me afraid.' Still, in times of winter and famine the misery was great, and Mr. Johnson asked how it was that he could endure such hardship. The answer lay in the promise of religion. 'Suppose, Sir, the King, seeing me hard at work, were to say to me that, if I would patiently work on till Christmas, a fine palace and a great estate should be the reward of my labours. Do you think, Sir, that a little hunger, or a little cold, or a little wet, would make me flinch, when I was sure that a few months would put me in possession? Should I not say to myself frequently—cheer up Shepherd, 'tis but till Christmas! Now is there not much less difference between this supposed day and Christmas than there is between time and eternity.'

Again Hannah More emphasised the importance of greater communication between the classes. 'You great folks', said the Shepherd, 'can hardly imagine how it raises and cheers a poor man's heart, when such as you condescend to talk familiarly to him on religious subjects. It seems to be a practical comment on that text which says, "the rich and poor meet together, the Lord is the maker of them all".' Mr. Johnson, for his part, concluded that 'on the whole he was more disposed to envy than to pity the Shepherd. I have seldom seen, said he, so happy a man'.

The History of Mr. Fantom was a satire on the Tom Paine philosophy in contrast to the practice of true Christian charity. It was the story of a prosperous business man with little true education, who longed to cut a figure. He alighted upon a copy of Tom Paine's book and became carried away by the new philosophy. From him he learned the new phraseology: when speaking of the Church one spoke of narrowness, ignorance, bigotry, prejudice, priestcraft and tyranny, and when speaking of the new philosophy one spoke of the public good, the love of mankind, liberality, candour, toleration, and above all of benevolence. 'Benevolence', he said, 'made up the whole of religion, and all other parts of it were nothing but cant and jargon and hypocrisy.' He was married, but this was unfortunate, for philosophy soon taught him that 'marriage was a shameful infringement on human liberty, and an abridgment of the rights of man'. 'A legitimate self-love, regulated by prudence, and restrained by principle', Hannah More commented, 'produced peaceable subjects and good citizens; while in Fantom a boundless selfishness and inordinate vanity converted a discontented trader into a turbulent politician. . . . Whatever he began with, he was sure to end with a pert squib at the Bible, a vapid jest on the clergy, the miseries of superstition and the blessings of liberty and equality.'

His friend Mr. Trueman was a true Christian who could only lament that the Christians about him were not half so much in earnest about their faith as Fantom was about his philosophy. 'Why is it almost all zeal is on the wrong side?' The two converse:

> *Fantom:* How can a thinking being spend his Sunday better than by going into the country to admire the works of nature?
>
> *Trueman:* I suppose you mean the works of God: for I never read in the Bible that nature made anything. I should rather think that she herself was made by Him who made all things.

Trueman believed in the practice of Christian charity, Fantom did not:

> *Fantom:* I despise a narrow field. O for the reign of universal benevolence! I want to make all mankind good and happy.
>
> *Trueman:* Dear me! sure that must be a wholesale sort of job: had not you better try your hand at a town with a parish priest?
>
> *Fantom:* Sir, I have a plan in my head for relieving the miseries of the whole world ... (and he proceeds to describe a plan for general abolition).
>
> *Trueman:* Sir, among all your abolitions, you must abolish human corruption before you can make the world quite perfect as you pretend. Your philosophers seem to me to be ignorant of the very first seed and principle of misery—sin.

Fantom thought that 'one religion was as good as another, and that no religion was best of all'. He was a friend to all humanity, yet when Trueman asked him to relieve conditions in the local workhouse and aid a friend who had fallen into debt, or when his daughter asked him for a subscription to the local Sunday-school where 'there are two or three hundred to be done good to at once', he refused. Trueman commented that Fantom was 'a wonderful man to keep up such a stock of benevolence at so small an expense'. When a neighbour's house caught fire, Trueman ran to help the inmates, but Fantom was unconcerned, declaring that he was too busy planning how to put out the fire of the Inquisition. He was also working on a 'Treatise on Universal Benevolence and the Blessed Effects of Philosophy and Smuggling'.

Fantom was particularly hostile to religion. He declared: 'All this nonsense of future punishment is now done away. It is *our* benevolence which makes us reject your creed; we can no more believe in a Deity who permits so much evil in the present world, than one who threatens eternal punishment in the next.' 'What!' replied Trueman, 'shall mortal man be more merciful than God?' Fantom stood for the abolition of all punishment and prisons, but when his servant stole some tea-spoons, he declared: 'I hope he will be sent to Botany Bay, if not hanged!' Trueman commented that Jacobinism and impiety were inseparable: 'the reason is obvious. There are restraints in both. There is subordination in both. In both cases the hatred arises from aversion to a superior.' He himself 'did not want any of your farthing-candle philosophy in the broad sunshine of the Gospel'.

.   .   .   .   .   .

With all their success among the governing classes, the Evangelicals aroused powerful enemies. *The Anti-Jacobin Review*, the reactionary journal which opposed every enlightened reform of the period, was equally hostile to Methodists and Evangelicals. 'It is the dread of the predominance of this faction, who are making rapid strides towards ascendancy in the state, that renders it an imperious duty to open the eyes of the public to their real motives and views, as developed by their actions.' The Review strongly criticised those members of the royal family who had lent their patronage to Evangelicalism, and added ominously its 'fervent wish that the House of Brunswick may never forget the principles which seated their family on the throne of these realms'. Parliament and army were being penetrated so as to threaten the security of the State. 'Let churchmen stand firm at their post— let them rally round the altar—let them "cry aloud and spare not", or we be destined to witness a second usurpation without the chance of a second restoration' (Vol. xlix, 1816).

Sydney Smith, when in a famous article in the *Edinburgh Review* of January 1808 he came to consider the incidence of pietistic religion, did not trouble to distinguish between Methodism and Evangelicalism. They were both, he said, 'one general conspiracy against common sense and rational orthodox Christianity'.

He was deeply concerned at its unhealthy aspects, in particular the growth of a superstitious belief that Providence was always at hand to punish men for every petty offence, so that a clergyman dropped dead when playing cards, and a young man when swearing was stung on the tongue by a bee. Such superstition must ultimately produce its antithesis; 'in breeding up a fanatic you have unwittingly laid the foundation of an atheist'. 'The Methodists hate pleasure and amusements; no theatre, no cards, no dancing, no punchinello, no dancing dogs, no blind fiddlers;—all the amusements of the rich and of the poor must disappear, wherever these gloomy people get a footing. It is not the abuse of pleasure which they attack, but the interspersion of pleasure, however much it is guided by good sense and moderation. It is not only wicked to hear the licentious plays of Congreve, but wicked to hear Henry the Fifth, or the School for Scandal. It is not only dissipated to run about to all the parties in London and Edinburgh, but dancing is not *fit for a being who is preparing himself for Eternity*. ... The Methodists are always desirous of making men more religious than it is possible, from the constitution of human nature, to make them.' Sydney Smith objected to the presumptuous and extravagant language of Methodism, as when they described themselves as 'friends of the dear Redeemer'. He was concerned at the extent of the success of Methodism among the poor and ignorant. He saw it as a renewed outburst of the Puritanism of the seventeenth century, and reminded his readers that 'the last eruption destroyed both Church and Throne with its tremendous force'. 'The Methodists have made an alarming inroad into the Church, and they are attacking the Army and Navy. The principality of Wales, and the East-India Company they have already acquired.' He saw them as a powerful force in parliament (namely Wilberforce and the Saints), organising schools throughout the land, distributing millions of tracts, and going abroad in great numbers as missionaries. How was it possible for the Established Church to combat such extravagance as the Methodist conviction that a man could be cured of the scrofula by listening to a sermon, or that an innkeeper had dropped dead for planning a cock-fight? He did not doubt that the Anglican clergy could be more active than they were, but it was difficult to combat such superstition, and the Methodists had 'the facility of mingling human errors with the fundamental truth of religion'. Sydney Smith greatly feared the outcome. 'We most sincerely deprecate such an event; but it will excite in us no manner of surprise if a period arrives when the churches of the sober and orthodox part of the English clergy are completely deserted by the middling and lower classes of the community. . . . At all events, we are quite sure that happiness will be destroyed, reason degraded, sound religion banished from the world; and that when fanaticism becomes too foolish and too prurient to be endured (as is at last sure to be the case), it will be succeeded by a long period of the grossest immorality, atheism and debauchery.'

In 1809 he attacked the Society for the Suppression of Vice as 'a corporation of informers supported by large contributions'. What chance had a Whitechapel butcher or publican when accused by a Society carrying such names as Lord Dartmouth, Lord Radstock and the Bishop of Durham, and when the case came before a bench who were their friends? Such a society could not fail to become tyrannical: 'it is hardly possible that a society for the suppression of vice can ever be kept within the bounds of good sense and moderation'. So zealous a society would not rest until it had probed and interfered in the lives of the great mass of the lower classes. And therein lay Sydney Smith's main objection. 'Nothing has disgusted us so much in the proceedings of this Society as the control which they exercise over the amusements of the poor.' While it was relentless in prosecuting bull-baiting and bear-baiting as sports of the poor, it said nothing about the angling, fox and stag-hunting which were the sports of the rich. 'A man of ten thousand a year may worry a fox as much as he pleases, may encourage the breed of a mischievous animal on purpose to worry it; and a poor labourer is carried before a magistrate for paying sixpence to see an exhibition of courage between a dog and a bear!' The Society said nothing about the gambling houses of the rich: 'to suppose that any society will ever attack the vices of people of fashion is wholly out of the question'. Indeed Sydney Smith suggested that, now there was a society of the rich for the moral reform of the poor, it was only fair that there should be a society of the poor, of barbers, butchers and bakers for the moral reform of the rich!

Dickens, who detested Dissenters and Evangelicals, as much as Sydney Smith did, satirised them on several occasions. Mr. Stiggins, in *Pickwick Papers*, 'was a prim-faced, red-nosed man, with a long thin countenance, and a semi-rattlesnake sort of eye'. He was very partial to Mrs. Weller's fireside and her pineapple rum. At the very mention of old Weller he groaned with moral disapproval, with which Mrs. Weller fully concurred.

'He is a dreadful reprobate', said Mrs. Weller.

'A man of wrath!' exclaimed Mr. Stiggins. He took a large semicircular bite out of the toast and groaned again.

Sam felt very strongly disposed to give the reverend Mr. Stiggins something to groan for, but he repressed his inclination, and merely asked, 'What's the old 'un up to now?'

'Up to, indeed!' said Mrs. Weller. 'Oh, he has a hard heart. Night after night does this excellent man—don't frown, Mr. Stiggins, I *will* say you *are* an excellent man—come and sit here, for hours together, and it has not the least effect upon him.'

'Well, that is odd', said Sam: 'it 'ud have a wery consider-able effect upon me if I wos in his place, I know that.'

'The fact is, my young friend' said Mr. Stiggins, solemnly, 'he has an obderrate bosom. Oh, my young friend, who else could have resisted the pleading of sixteen of our fairest sisters, and withstood their exhortations to subscribe to our noble society for providing the infant negroes in the West Indies with flannel waistcoats and moral pocket handkerchiefs?'

Old Weller had other ideas about flannel waistcoats: 'What's the good o' flannel veskits to the young niggers abroad? But I'll tell you what is it, Sammy,' said Mr. Weller, lowering his voice, and bending across the fireplace: 'I'd come down wery handsome towards straight veskits for some people at home. ... Wot aggrawates me, Samivel, is to see 'em wastin' all their time and labour in making clothes for copper-coloured people as don't want 'em, and taking no notice of the flesh-coloured Christians as do. If I'd my vay, Samivel, I'd just stick some o' these here lazy shepherds behind a heavy wheel-barrow, and run 'em up and down a fourteen-inch-wide plank all day. That 'ud shake the nonsense out of 'em, if anythin' vould.' (Chap. XXVII.)

In *Bleak House*, Mrs. Jellyby was 'a pretty, very diminutive, plump woman, of from forty to fifty, with handsome eyes, though they had a curious habit of seeming to look a long way off. As if they could see nothing nearer than Africa!'

'You find me, my dears', said Mrs. Jellyby, snuffing the two great office candles in tin candlesticks, which made the room taste strongly of hot tallow (the fire had gone out, and there was nothing in the grate but ashes, a bundle of wood, and a poker), 'you find me, my dears, as usual, very busy; but that you will excuse. The African project at present employs my whole time. It involves me in correspondence with public bodies, and with private individuals anxious for the welfare of their species all over the country. I am happy to say it is advancing. We hope by this time next year to have from a hundred and fifty to two hundred healthy families cultivating coffee and educating the natives of Borrioboola-Gha, on the left bank of the Niger.' (Chap. IV.)

Mrs. Pardiggle bullied and neglected her unfortunate children as much as Mrs. Jellyby did hers:

'These', said Mrs. Pardiggle, 'are my five boys. You may have seen their names in a printed subscription list (perhaps more than one), in the possession of our esteemed friend, Mr. Jarndyce. Egbert, my eldest (twelve) is the boy who sent out his pocket-money, to the amount of five-and-threepence, to the Tockahoopo Indians, Oswald, my second (ten-and-a-half) is the child who contributed two-and-ninepence to the Great National Smithers Testimonial. Francis, my third (nine), one-and-sixpence-halfpenny; Felix, my fourth (seven), eight-pence to the Superannuated Widows; Alfred, my youngest (five), has voluntarily enrolled himself in the Infant Bonds of Joy, and is pledged never, through life, to use tobacco in any form.'

We had never seen such dissatisfied children. It was not merely that they were weazened and shrivelled—though they were certainly that too—but they looked absolutely ferocious with discontent. At the mention of the Tockahoopo Indians, I could really have supposed Egbert to be one of the most baleful members of that tribe, he gave me such a savage frown, the face of each child, as the amount of his contribution was mentioned, darkened in a peculiarly vindictive manner, but his was by far the worst. I must except, however, the little recruit into the Infant Bonds of Joy, who was stolidly and evenly miserable.

'They attend Matins with me, at half past six o'clock in the morning all the year round, including of course the depth of winter', said Mrs. Pardiggle rapidly, 'and they are with me during the revolving duties of the day, I am a School lady, I am a Visiting lady, I am a Reading lady, I am a Distributing lady; I am on the local Linen Box Committee, and many general Committees; and my canvassing alone is very extensive —perhaps no one's more so. But they are my companions everywhere; and by these means they acquire that knowledge of the poor, and that capacity of doing charitable business in general—in short, that taste for the sort of thing—which will render them in after life a service to their neighbours, and a satisfaction to themselves.' (Chap. VIII.)

Charlotte Brontë has left an unforgettable picture of a Clergy

K

Daughters' School and of the Yorkshire Evangelical, the Rev. William Carus Wilson, in the description of Lowood, and Mr. Brocklehurst, in *Jane Eyre*.

'Well, Jane Eyre, and are you a good child?'
Impossible to reply to this in the affirmative: my little world held a contrary opinion; I was silent . . .
'No sight so sad as that of a naughty child', he began, 'especially a naughty little girl. Do you know where the wicked go after death?'
'They go to hell', was my ready and orthodox answer.
'And what is hell? Can you tell me that?'
'A pit full of fire.'
'And should you like to fall into that pit, and to be burning there for ever?'
'No, sir.'
'What must you do to avoid it?'
I deliberated a moment; my answer, when it did come, was objectionable: 'I must keep in good health, and not die.'
'How can you keep in good health? Children younger than you die daily. I buried a little child of five years old only a day or two since,—a good little child, whose soul is now in heaven. It is to be feared the same could not be said of you, were you to be called hence . . .
'Deceit's indeed a sad fault in a child,' said Mr. Brocklehurst; 'it is akin to falsehood, and all liars will have their portion in the lake burning with fire and brimstone: she shall, however, be watched, Mrs. Reed . . .'
'I should wish her to be brought up in a manner suiting her prospects, to be made useful and kept humble.'
'Your decisions are perfectly judicious, madam', returned Mr. Brocklehurst. 'Humility is a Christian grace, and one particularly appropriate to the pupils of Lowood; I, therefore direct that especial care shall be bestowed on its cultivation amongst them. I have studied how best to mortify in them the worldly sentiment of pride; and only the other day, I had a pleasing proof of my success: "Oh, dear papa, how quiet and

plain all the girls at Lowood look; with their hair combed back behind their ears, and their long pinafores, and those little holland pockets outside their frocks,—they are almost like poor people's children! and", said she, "they looked at my dress and mamma's as if they had never seen a silk gown before." ' (Chap. IV.)

It is clear that in the attacks upon Methodists and Evangelicals there was both truth and exaggeration and misrepresentation, and both Dickens and Charlotte Brontë were appealing to the ready sympathy of their readers; there was no doubt that their satire would meet with a general approval. It was not true that all Evangelicals were gloomy Sabbatarians breathing hell-fire. Wilberforce himself was mild and gentle, and did not carry his beliefs to extremes, while men like John Thornton, Henry Venn and Fowell Buxton were certainly no ascetics. Even Hannah More did not disapprove of home-brewed ale for the poor. Yet Evangelical clergymen did often give up listening to music or playing cricket. Sunday did often become a day of gloom, and pious ladies like Ruskin's mother on that day turned the pictures to the wall. Thanks to the efforts of Hannah More, several thousand children in Somerset learned to read, but her object was not really to educate them, but to prepare them for religion, and she did not think it necessary to teach them to write. The schools of Joseph Lancaster and Andrew Bell taught thousands of working-class children to read, and they did great work with their flimsy resources. By 1825 the Religious Tract Society had distributed throughout the world over four million Bibles, in a hundred and forty languages. It is impossible to be certain of the extent of the influence this had in forming the social opinions of the British poor, but it was certainly a powerful one. It is significant that many of the later Chartist leaders and trade unionists came from Dissenting and Evangelical homes, and that they had learned to express their ideas of social justice in the very language of dissenting preachers. Often the religious opinions inculcated resembled those of Mr. Brocklehurst, but even such imperfect attempts at Christianity may have saved thousands of the poor from utter brutalisation. The abolition of the Slave Trade in 1807, an enormous personal triumph for Wilberforce, was an indication of the extent to which Evangelical ideas had penetrated the minds of the governing classes. It was not only a matter of flannel waistcoats! Nothing is more remarkable than the upsurge of humanitarianism during the period. As the young Macaulay wrote in 1823: 'This is the age of societies. There is scarcely one Englishman in ten who has not belonged to some association for distributing books, or for prosecuting them; for sending invalids to the hospital, or beggars to the treadmill; for giving plate to the rich, or blankets to the poor.' A mere list of the philanthropic institutions known to have existed in the period 1780–1830 would fill a dozen pages of this book. The reiteration of the theme in Evangelical pamphlets and sermons that the poor should be content with their lot, and happy in their relative freedom from temptation may sound like humbug, but against this must be put the genuine charity which inspired men like Wilberforce and Henry Thornton to give away the greater part of their fortunes, and the many who worked among the poor, in maternity and fever hospitals, in orphanages and among the slums. If the Society for the Prevention of Vice made itself ridiculous by prohibiting the sale of Shelley's *Queen Mab*, it did much good work in preventing some of the hideous tortures inflicted upon animals in the name of sport or profit. If it appeared to take a jaundiced view of pleasure, it saved many young girls from prostitution. With all its shortcomings, the Evangelical movement left an indelible mark upon nineteenth-century life and thought.

NOTE

[1] In 1822 it successfully prosecuted the bookseller of Shelley's *Queen Mab* as an impious work.

8 : The New Jerusalem of William Blake

WILLIAM BLAKE (1757–1827) was by trade an engraver; he made little money from his art, and less from his poetry, and knew by experience the misery and degradation of poverty. He was greatly influenced by the revolutionary events of his day, by the struggle for liberty in America and France, and by the ensuing wars, and was for a time accounted a Jacobin. He wrote in praise of both the American and French Revolutions. Yet he was less interested in politics as such than in the moral problems and conflicts within his own breast, which seemed at times to mirror contemporary political struggles.

Blake was a mystic, a visionary, who always claimed that his poetry was dictated to him by spirits: 'I am under the direction of Messengers from Heaven, Daily and Nightly.' He wrote of his *Jerusalem*: 'I may praise it, since I dare not pretend to be any other than the Secretary; the Authors are in Eternity. I consider it as the Grandest Poem that this World contains.' (Letter to Thos. Butts, 6 July 1803.) In literature he was a complete Romantic. His central plea was for the freedom of the imagination, and all his philosophy was contained in his aphorism that 'All Deities reside in the Human breast'. He emphasised the essential oneness of the Universe and God; God was not some awful judge waiting to condemn the world, but the spirit within each person.

> Why stand we here trembling around
> Calling on God for help and not ourselves, in whom
>   God dwells,
> Stretching a hand to save the falling Man?

How was it possible that men could go on praying to God without attempting to alleviate the suffering they saw around them? Blake expounded a philosophy of brotherhood, not only between human beings, but between all living things. His final plea was for a world controlled by the imagination, in which the arts would flourish, and the old restraints upon men's desires would pass away.

Blake entirely rejected the empirical philosophy of Locke. 'Man's perceptions', he wrote, 'are not bounded by organs of perception: he perceives more than sense can discover.' (*There is No Natural Religion.*) For instance, our five senses give us sense-data about a rose, its colour, scent, weight, etc., but they do not enable us by themselves to perceive beauty. When we perceive beauty we go beyond sense-data and impinge upon the Infinite. Hence he wrote: 'He who sees the Infinite in all things, sees God. He who sees the Ratio only, sees himself only.' (ibid.) The Christian believed that God manifested himself once in Jesus Christ; Blake believed that he manifests himself every time one feels compassion, or beauty, or happiness. Once one steps beyond sense-data, one is using one's imagination, and this to Blake was a spiritual experience, the process by which we perceive the Infinite in even a grain of sand or a wild flower. God was not remote, 'in heaven', but was manifested every time we are aware of the Infinite.

Blake's *Songs of Innocence and Experience* contain some of the most poignant lyrics in the English language. The starting point is the joy of youth and innocence, and the sequel is a tragedy as the 'shades of the prison-house' of experience close upon the life of the adult.

> When the voices of children are heard on the green,
> And laughing is heard on the hill,
> My heart is at rest within my breast,
> And everything else is still.

But the day turns to evening, and this is symbolic of the darkness which comes with age.

Then come home, my children, the sun is gone down,
And the dews of night arise;
Your spring and your day are wasted in play,
And your winter and night in disguise.

Must it always be so? Must life always bring with it hardness and
selfishness and cruelty?

> Break this heavy chain
> That does freeze my bones around.
> Selfish! vain!
> Eternal bane!
> That free Love with bondage bound.

The secret of life lay in the fact that there was an inter-dependence
between all living things, but the love which should bind all men
and nature had become selfish and possessive. This is the theme of
The Clod and the Pebble.

> 'Love seeketh not itself to please,
> Nor for itself hath any care
> But for another gives its ease,
> And builds a Heaven in Hell's despair.'

> So sung a little Clod of Clay
> Trodden with the cattle's feet,
> But a Pebble of the brook
> Warbled out these metres meet:

> 'Love seeketh only Self to please,
> To bind another to its delight,
> Joys in another's loss of ease,
> And builds a Hell in Heaven's despite.'

To Blake joy was impossible without liberty.

> How can the bird that is born for joy
> Sit in a cage and sing?
> How can a child, when fears annoy,

> But droop his tender wing,
> And forget his youthful spring?

It was a terrible thought that every unhappiness of this life was of man's own making. London to Blake was a place of special sadness.

> I wander thro' each charter'd street,
> Near where the charter'd Thames does flow,
> And mark in every face I meet
> Marks of weakness, marks of woe.
>
> In every cry of every Man,
> In every Infant's cry of fear,
> In every voice, in every ban,
> The mind-forg'd manacles I hear.

Certain unfortunate people had Blake's especial sympathy, and chief among these were the child chimney-sweeps. In a terrible indictment, he described how the white skin and curly head of the child were blackened by the grime of his trade, while his parents had 'gone up to the Church to pray':

> 'And because I am happy and dance and sing,
> They think they have done me no injury,
> And are gone to praise God and His Priest and King,
> Who make up a Heaven of our misery.'

Some of Blake's most bitter attacks were against the Church, which encouraged a religiosity and taught of the pains of Hell, while it disregarded the miseries which men created upon earth. To him God was not some being transcending the universe, but within it, in every flower and animal, and in the hearts of men. Men did not inherit Heaven or Hell; they made it within themselves. *The Garden of Love* was a bitter indictment of organised religion:

> I went to the Garden of Love,
> And saw what I never had seen:
> A Chapel was built in the midst,
> Where I used to play on the green.

And the gates of this Chapel were shut,
And 'Thou shalt not' writ over the door;
So I turn'd to the Garden of Love
That so many sweet flowers bore;

And I saw it was filled with graves,
And tomb-stones where flowers should be;
And priests in black gowns were walking their rounds,
And binding with briars my joys and desires.

In place of happiness and love there were condemnation, darkness and death. In *The Little Vagabond* Blake contrasts the warmth and friendship of the ale-house with the cold and forbidding appearance of the church; if only the latter would learn something from the former!

Then the Parson might preach, and drink, and sing,
And we'd be as happy as birds in the spring;
And modest Dame Lurch, who is always at church,
Would not have bandy children, nor fasting, nor birch.

And God, like a father, rejoicing to see
His children as pleasant and happy as He,
Would have no more quarrel with the Devil or the barrel,
But kiss him, and give him both drink and apparel.

How could men of heart accept so readily the poverty and hunger which surrounded them?

Is this a holy thing to see
In a rich and fruitful land,
Babes reduc'd to misery,
Fed with cold and usurous hand?

Is that trembling cry a song?
Can it be a song of joy?
And so many children poor?
It is a land of poverty?

God was not a theological abstraction, but was in every smile, every act of compassion and love. The virtues were *human* attributes, not handed down from above, but created by men in their daily lives.

> For Mercy has a human heart,
> Pity a human face,
> And Love, the human form divine,
> And Peace, the human dress.
>
> Then every man, of every clime,
> That prays in his distress,
> Prays to the human form divine,
> Love, Mercy, Pity, Peace.

The greatest lesson to be learned was the interdependence of mankind:

> Can I see another's woe,
> And not be in sorrow too?
> Can I see another's grief,
> And not seek for kind relief?

Yet even pity and mercy could be misapplied, for pity could be an assumption of superiority, and neither would be necessary if men had not first created the misery and injustice which they then sought to mitigate.

> Pity would be no more
> If we did not make somebody poor;
> And Mercy no more could be
> If all were as happy as we.

Even pity and mercy, then, were symptoms of man's wickedness.

About 1787–8 Blake underwent some deep mystical experience from which he emerged with the conviction that much of the teaching of organised religion over the centuries was false, that for instance it was false that man was divided into two warring principles of body and soul, that all energy of the body was evil, and that the reason which came from the soul alone was good. He rejected the idea that physical love was in some way evil, and that chastity was necessarily good. On the contrary, he wrote that 'Energy is the only life, and is from the Body; and Reason is the bound or outward circumference of Energy. Energy is Eternal Delight. Those who restrain Desire, do so because theirs is weak enough to be restrained; and the restrainer or Reason usurps its place and governs the unwilling.' In the course of time priests had laid the heavy hand of condemnation on much that was natural and good in man; they had forgotten the words of St. Paul that 'he that loveth another hath fulfilled the law', and again that 'love is the fulfilling of the law'. Blake's proverb was that, 'As the caterpillar chooses the fairest leaves to lay her eggs on, so the priest lays his curse on the fairest joys.' Life to Blake was not a negation, but a fulfilment.

This was the theme of his mystical work, *The Marriage of Heaven and Hell*. In a curious way men had come to confuse the two, to mistake Heaven for Hell. Consider for instance Blake's pregnant criticism of Milton's *Paradise Lost*, which was very similar to Shelley's: 'In the Book of Job, Milton's Messiah is called Satan. . . . In Milton the Father is Destiny, the Son a Ratio of the five senses, and the Holy-ghost Vacuum!' God stood for the law, whereas Satan appeared as the individual struggling to be free, and Blake's sympathy, like that of Shelley, was on the side of Satan. He wrote: 'The reason Milton wrote in fetters when he wrote of Angels and God, and at liberty when of Devils and Hell, is because he was a true Poet, and of the Devil's party without knowing it.' Blake's glorification of human desires and energy can be seen in his proverbs:

'The road of excess leads to the palace of wisdom.'
'Prudence is a rich, ugly old maid, courted by Incapacity.'
'He who desires and acts not breeds pestilence.'
'Eternity is in love with the productions of time.'
'The busy bee has no time for sorrow.'
'If the fool would persist in his folly he would become wise.'
'The pride of the peacock is the glory of God.'

'The lust of the goat is the bounty of God.'
'The wrath of the lion is the wisdom of God.'
'The nakedness of woman is the work of God.'

Blake argued that too many prophets had been concerned to pronounce what laws God had laid down for the guidance of men, all beginning with the words 'Thou shalt not . . .!' They forgot that God was not some external law-giver, but was inside each man and woman: 'Men forgot that all Deities reside in the Human breast.' 'Some will say: "Is not God alone the Prolific?" I answer: "God only Acts and Is, in existing beings or Men." ' The good man was not the one who existed in self-agnegation, but one who acted according to the God who was within. In one of his mystical experiences, Blake asked Isaiah whether God had really dictated his writings. His answer was: 'I saw no God, nor heard any, in a finite organical perception; but my senses discover'd the infinite in everything, and as I was then persuaded, and remain confirm'd, that the voice of honest indignation is the voice of God, I cared not for consequences, but wrote.' The chief thing was to be persuaded that what one said was true, 'and in ages of imagination this firm persuasion removed mountains; but many are not capable of a firm persuasion of anything.' (ibid.)

Blake, then, believed in action, not in resignation. He wrote, 'When thou seest an eagle, thou seest a portion of Genius; lift up thy head!' The genius of the human spirit in Blake's poetry was often symbolised by the lion, the tiger or the eagle, and this was also the theme of his magnificent lyric, *The Tiger*.

Tiger! Tiger! burning bright
In the forests of the night,
What immortal hand or eye
Could frame thy fearful symmetry?

In what distant deeps or skies
Burnt the fire of thine eyes?
On what wings dare he aspire?
What the hand dare seize the fire?

The meaning of this poem has been often misunderstood. The tiger is the symbol of the spirit, emerging from the darkness of the material world. The poet is not simply expressing surprise at the beauty and strength of the tiger, but declaring that it *is* God in action. In the last verse, which is otherwise a repeat of the first verse, 'Could' becomes 'Dare', and thus the meaning is underlined. When he wrote:

> Did he who made the Lamb make thee?

Blake was making something more than a comment on the diversity of nature; he was saying that Jesus Christ, the Lamb, shared in the human spirit, and that all men shared the spirit of Christ and of God.

It was at this point in Blake's spiritual development that the French Revolution burst upon him, and the coincidence explains why it made such an impact, for he saw it as an expression in the political context of the very principle which he felt to be working in the hearts of all men. In his *French Revolution*, an epic poem set in type in 1791, but not published for fear of the consequences, Blake expounded his theory of liberty.[1] For five thousand years men had been in chains, and the poet conducts his readers through seven prisons in which through the ages men had been chained, although always they had retained in their hearts the hopes of liberty. But then came the meeting of the States-General in France, and 'the dens shook and trembled: the prisoners look up and assay to shout'. Before the King a great debate takes place, and the Duke of Burgundy, in powerful rhetoric, puts the point of view of tradition:

> Shall this marble-built heaven become a clay cottage, this earth
>   an oak stool, and these mowers
> From the Atlantic mountains mow down all this great starry
>   harvest of six thousand years?[2]
> And shall Necker, the hind of Geneva, stretch out his crook'd
>   sickle o'er fertile France
> Till our purple and crimson is faded to russet, and the king-
>   doms of earth bound in sheaves,

And the ancient forests of chivalry hewn, and the joys of the
combat burnt for fuel;
Till the power and the dominion is rent from the pole, sword
and sceptre from the sun and moon,
The law and gospel from fire and air, and eternal reason and
science
From the deep and the solid, and man lay his faded head down
on the rock
Of eternity, where the eternal lion and eagle remain to devour?

Blake writes without bitterness; he gives Burgundy his due. The
new principles of liberty from America bid fair to destroy six
thousand years of tradition; chivalry would be overthrown,
customary power destroyed, and the moral law and the philosophy
of Reason torn down. From Burgundy's point of view it was a
natural cry. It was natural also that the Archbishop of Paris,
representing organised religion, should add his warning:

for a curse is heard hoarse thro' the land, from a godless race,
Descending to beasts; they look downward, and labour, and
forget my holy law;
The sound of prayer fails from lips of flesh, and the holy hymn
from thicken'd tongues;
For the bars of Chaos are burst.

Here the Archbishop spoke in the name of the moral law which
Blake regarded as a straight-jacket to mankind; his view was
reminiscent of that of St. Paul when he wrote, 'my brethren ye are
become dead to the law by the body of Christ'. In the defence of
his law, the Archbishop became more bloodthirsty than any of the
opponents of revolution:

Let thy soldiers possess this city of rebels, that threaten to
bathe their feet
In the blood of Nobility, trampling the heart and the head:
let the Bastille devour
These rebellious seditious.

Orleans replied as the mouthpiece of revolution; the revolution
stands for health and vigour and liberty, and cannot be suppressed:

Can the fires of Nobility ever be quenched, or the stars by a
stormy night?
Is the body diseased when the members are healthful? can the
man be bound in sorrow
Whose ev'ry function is filled with its fiery desire? can the soul,
whose brain and heart
Cast their rivers in equal tides thro' the great Paradise,
languish because the feet,
Hands, head, bosom, and parts of love follow their high
breathing joy?
And can Nobles be bound when the people are free, or God
weep when his children are happy?

'Fire', Blake writes, in a vivid phrase, 'delights in its form',
and if the Archbishop walks into the flames with his law, he will
be consumed, and if he cannot put out the fire,

'If thou canst not do this, doubt thy theories, learn to consider
all men as thy equals,
Thy brethren, and not as thy foot or thy hand, unless thou
first fearest to hurt them.'

Blake saw the spirit of revolution (which he termed Orc) as
originating in America. In subsequent poems he portrayed the
world as being in the grip of a false spirit who had sent kings and
priests to enslave mankind with these instructions:

Go! tell the Human race that Woman's love is Sin;
That an Eternal life awaits the worms of sixty winters,
In an allegorical abode, where existence hath never come.
Forbid all Joy; and, from her childhood, shall the little Female
Spread nets in every secret path.

Here Blake was writing with a new bitterness and irony. From
this tyranny men were freed by Orc, who in *America* is described
as a red and hairy youth. The coming of revolution is portrayed in

sexual symbolism. Orc sees the beautiful virgin, the daughter of the earth, and 'Round the terrific loins he seiz'd the panting, struggling womb; It joy'd.' A union had been effected which could never be ended, and joy ensued: Orc becomes for the moment the serpent who had tempted Eve to the tree of knowledge:

> The Terror answer'd: 'I am Orc, wreathed round the accursed
>   tree:
> The times are ended; shadows pass, the morning 'gins to
>   break;
> The fiery joy, the Urizen perverted to ten commands,
> What night he led the starry hosts thro' the wide wilderness,
> That stony Law I stamp to dust; and scatter Religion abroad
> To the four winds as a torn book, and none shall gather the
>   leaves;
> But they shall rot on desert sands, and consume in bottomless
>   deeps,
> To make the deserts blossom, and the deeps shrink to their
>   fountains,
> And to renew the fiery joy, and burst the stony roof;
> That pale religious lechery, seeking Virginity,
> May find it in a harlot, and in coarse-clad honesty
> The undefiled, tho' ravish'd in her cradle night and morn;
> For everything that lives is holy, life delights in life;
> Because the soul of sweet delight can never be defil'd.
> Fires enwrap the earthly globe, yet Man is not consum'd.
>
> (*America*, 1.59.)

Blake was no longer thinking of political revolution and its consequences, but of the release of man from the chains of false religion and a false morality. At what point had things begun to go wrong for man? Blake tells us in *Europe*:

> Thought chang'd the Infinite to a Serpent, that which pitieth
> To a devouring flame; and Man fled from its face and hid
> In the forests of night: then all the eternal forests were divided
> Into earths, rolling in circles of Space, that like an ocean
>   rush'd

And overwhelmed all except this finite wall of flesh.
Then was the Serpent temple form'd, image of Infinite,
Shut up in finite revolutions, and Man became an Angel,
Heaven a mighty circle turning, God a tyrant crown'd.

(1.86.)

In short, the moment men invented the Devil, and imagined God
to be a tyrant, men became slaves, and sought to hide themselves
in the forests of night (i.e. the darkness of superstition). At that
point man lost sight of the Infinite, became obsessed with sin,
regarded sexual love as in some sense shameful, and lost the
dignity of his being.

To Blake therefore the two enemies were, first, a narrow
morality springing from religiosity, and second, the philosophy of
reason which confined men to the information gained from their
five senses. The former hate undoubtedly had a strong sexual
content, for Mrs. Blake was a religious prude and at this time of
his life Blake longed for sexual fulfilment. He refers to both in
The Visions of the Daughters of Albion. Oothoon is the daughter of
Albion, and she has become free by throwing off the chains of
slavery:

> I am pure,
> Because the night is gone that clos'd me in its deadly black.
> They told me that the night and day were all that I could see;
> They told me that I had five senses to enclose me up;
> And they enclosed my infinite brain in a narrow circle,
> And sunk my heart into the Abyss, a red, round globe, hot
>   burning,
> Till all from life I was obliterated and erased.
> But all this had gone, for Oothoon is free. Nature has written:
>   Take thy bliss, O Man!
> And sweet shall be thy taste, and sweet thy infant joys renew!

And what are the joys of infancy? Blake tells us, and asks why,
if they were so delightful, men ever allowed themselves to be
deprived of them:

L

Infancy! fearless, lustful, happy, nestling for delight
In laps of pleasure: Innocence! honest, open, seeking
The vigorous joys of morning light, open to virgin bliss,
Who taught thee modesty, subtil modesty, child of night and
   sleep?

Oothoon proclaims her freedom:

The moment of desire! the moment of desire! The virgin
That pines for man shall awaken her womb to enormous joys
In the secret shadows of her chamber: the youth shut up from
The lustful joy shall forget to generate, and create an amorous
   image
In the shadows of his curtains and in the folds of his silent
   pillow.
Are not these the places of religion, the rewards of continence,
The self-enjoyings of self-denial? Why dost thou seek religion?
Is it because acts are not lovely that thou seekest solitude,
Where the horrible darkness is impressed with reflections of
   desire?

Why had religion taught that the most beautiful and natural
expression of human joy, namely physical love, should be treated
as a thing of sin, darkness and shame? Oothoon's cry, on the
contrary, is

Love! Love! Love! happy happy Love! free as the mountain
   wind!

Blake always protested against the principle that there should be
'one law for both the lion and the ox', for men could not be so
cribbed, cabined and confined, and this is a theme which constantly
recurs in his poetry. Men ought not to be weighed down by the
law, but ought to feel their oneness with the Infinite, to remember
that 'All Deities reside in the Human breast.'

   Blake's philosophy of history is contained in his *Song of Los*
(1795), by which time his belief in the French Revolution was
fading.

Adam stood in the garden of Eden,
And Noah on the mountains of Ararat;
They saw Urizen give his Laws to the Nations
By the hands of the children of Los.
Adam shudder'd! Noah faded!

By the stories of the Garden of Eden and the Flood men had received the doctrine of sin; henceforth they were confined by the law. Jesus Christ was identified with Orc, and stood for the release of the human spirit,

Then Oothoon hover'd over Judah and Jerusalem,
And Jesus heard her voice—a Man of Sorrows!—He receiv'd
A Gospel from wretched Theotormon.

From that time 'the human race began to wither', for it became oppressed by the symbols of organised religion:

These were the Churches, Hospitals, Castles, Palaces,
Like nets and gins and traps, to catch the joys of Eternity,
And all the rest a desert.

The next stage was the triumph of the philosophy of the Enlightenment:

Thus the terrible race of Los and Enitharmon gave
Laws and Religions to the sons of Har, binding them more
And more to Earth, closing and restraining;
Till a Philosophy of Five Senses was complete:
Urizen wept, and gave it into the hands of Newton and Locke.

Finally Orc, the spirit of Revolution, triumphed,

The Grave shrieks with delight, and shakes
Her hollow womb, and clasps the solid stem:
Her bosom swells with wild desire;
And milk and blood and glandous wine
In rivers rush, and shout and dance,
On Mountain, dale and pine.

After his writings of 1795 a change came over Blake. He was approaching fifty, his sexual urges burned less impulsively, and he was reconciled to his wife. His main composition of the years 1797–1804 was *The Four Zoas*, a long and extremely intricate work, but happily it is not necessary to attempt to elucidate its recondite themes here. It is sufficient to mention that one was his attempt to reconcile Ratio and Orc, Reason and Energy, just as previously he had sought to separate them. There was now a mood of resignation and sadness, where formerly there had been fire and impulse. There is a famous passage, reminiscent of the Song of Solomon:

> What is the price of Experience? Do men buy it for a song,
> Or Wisdom for a dance in the street? No! it is bought with the
> price
> Of all that a man hath—his house, his wife, his children.
> Wisdom is sold in the desolate market where none come to
> buy,
> And in the wither'd field where the farmer ploughs for bread
> in vain.

Yet the echo of the old theme remains:

> Wherever a grass grows
> Or a leaf buds, The Eternal Man is seen, is heard, is felt
> And all his sorrows, till he reassumes his ancient bliss.
> (VIII, 1.569.)

This period of transition comes to a triumphant conclusion with his greatest epic, *Milton* (1804–9). The old conflicts have subsided, and the issue has now become clear. Man is first and foremost an imaginative being; this is the basis of his claim to share in the Infinite, and all living things have an equal claim. He must first of all overthrow his 'Selfhood', that selfishness which seeks to bend all things to his will.

> I, in my Selfhood, am that Satan! I am that Evil One!
> He is my Spectre! In my obedience to loose him from my
> Hells,

To claim the Hells, my Furnaces, I go to Eternal Death.

(f. 1.21.)

In losing one's selfhood one learns that there is an inevitability about the evolution of the world, that time has never been wasted, that there is purpose in all things:

> for not one moment
> Of Time is lost, nor one event of Space unpermanent;
> But all remain; every fabric of six thousand years
> Remains permanent: tho' on the Earth, where Satan
> Fell and was cut off, all things vanish and are seen no more,
> They vanish not from me and mine; we guard them first and
> last.
> The Generations of Men run on in the tide of Time,
> But leave their destin'd lineaments permanent for ever and
> ever. (f.20 1.19.)

(This was Los speaking, the spirit of time.)

And what, according to this new view, *is* the Universe to man? Is it the mathematical abstractions of the scientists? Blake has a different answer, namely that

> every Space that a Man views around his dwelling-place,
> Standing on his own roof, or in his garden on a mount
> Of twenty-five cubits in height, such Space is his Universe:
> And on its verge the Sun rises and sets, the Clouds bow
> To meet the flat Earth and the Sea in such an order'd Space:
> The Starry Heavens reach no further, but here bend and set
> On all sides, and the two Poles turn on their valves of gold;
> And if he moves his dwelling-place, his Heavens also move
> Where'er he goes, and all his neighbourhood bewail his loss.
> Such are the Spaces called Earth, and such its dimension.
> As to that false appearance which appears to the reasoner,
> As of a Globe rolling thro' Voidness, it is a delusion.

(f.28, 1.5.)

The beginning of wisdom for man is his recognition that he is a part of the Infinite. In a sublime lyric, too long to quote, begin-

ning 'Thou hearest the Nightingale', he describes how the whole
of Nature stands still to hear with wonder the song of the
Nightingale; and the same is true of the flowers:

> Thou perceivest the Flowers put forth their precious Odours;
> And none can tell how from so small a centre comes such
> sweet,
> Forgetting that within that centre Eternity expands . . .
> . . . Every Flower,
> The Pink, the Jessamine, the Wallflower, the Carnation,
> The Jonquil, the mild Lily opes her heavens; every Tree
> And Flower and Herb soon fill the air with an innumerable
> dance,
> Yet all in order sweet and lovely. Men are sick with love!

Against so much loveliness and contentment Blake places the
coldness of the philosophy of the Enlightenment, and the negative
results of Science:

> The Negation is the Spectre, the Reasoning Power in Man:
> This is a false Body, an Incrustation over my Immortal
> Spirit, a Selfhood which must be put off and annihilated alway.
> To cleanse the Face of my Spirit by self-examination,
> To bathe in the waters of Life, to wash off the Not Human,
> I come in Self-annihilation and the grandeur of Inspiration;
> To cast off Rational Demonstration by Faith in the Saviour,
> To cast off the rotten rags of Memory by Inspiration,
> To cast off Bacon, Locke, and Newton from Albion's covering,
> To take off his filthy garments and clothe him with Imagin-
> ation;
> To cast aside from Poetry all that is not Inspiration,
>
> .   .   .   .   .   .
>
> To cast off the idiot Questioner, who is always questioning,
> But never capable of answering; who sits with a sly grin
> Silent plotting when to question, like a thief in a cave;
> Who published Doubt and calls it Knowledge; whose Science
> is Despair,

Whose pretence to knowledge is Envy, whose whole Science is
To destroy the wisdom of ages, to gratify ravenous Envy
That rages round him like a Wolf, day and night, without rest
He smiles with condescension; he talks of Benevolence and
Virtue,
And those who act with Benevolence and Virtue they murder
time on time.
These are the destroyers of Jerusalem! these are the murderers
Of Jesus! who deny the Faith and mock at Eternal Life,
Who pretend to Poetry that they may destroy Imagination
By imitation of Nature's Images drawn from Remembrance.

(f.42, 1.34.)

This passage represents the culmination of Blake's message to
his age, hence his Preface to the poem, in which he called upon the
poets, painters, sculptors and architects of his age to throw off the
domination of the styles of Classicism, and express an inspiration
of their own. 'We do not want either Greek or Roman models if
we are just and true to our own Imaginations, those Worlds of
Eternity in which we shall live for ever, in Jesus our Lord.' There
followed his famous song calling for a building of a new Jerusalem
even 'Among these dark Satanic Mills'. Needless to say, he was not
referring to the new cotton factories. The 'Mills of Satan' meant
for him the intellectual and moral darkness against which he had
always written, and his Jerusalem was the new world of spiritual
freedom, the triumph of the imagination, and to this cause he
dedicated his life:

> 'I will not cease from mental fight,
> Nor shall my sword sleep in my hand,
> Till we have built Jerusalem
> In England's green and pleasant land.'

In his epic *Jerusalem, The Emanation of the Giant Albion*
(1804–20) he portrayed the building of the new land in which the
arts and the imagination would triumph.

> Is that Calvary and Golgotha
> Becoming a building of Pity and Compassion? Lo!

> The stones are Pity, and the bricks well-wrought Affections
> Enamell'd with Love and Kindness; and the tiles engraven
> gold,
> Labour of merciful hands; the beams and rafters are Forgive-
> ness,
> The mortar and cement of the work tears of Honesty . . .
>
> (f.12, 1.28.)

It was a world based securely upon religion, for 'Man must and will have some religion; if he has not the religion of Jesus, he will have the religion of Satan, and will erect the synagogue of Satan, calling the Prince of this World "God", and destroying all who do not worship Satan under the name of God'. Blake's was a religion which eschewed vindictiveness and suffering. 'Every religion', he wrote, 'that preaches Vengeance for Sin is the religion of the Enemy and Avenger, and not of the Forgiver of Sin, and their God is Satan, named by the Divine Name.' The God of the Deists, on the other hand, was simply the God of this world, and a Natural Morality was concerned really with the worship of the self. No longer did Blake attack organised religion: it was true that there had been persecution and wickedness in the history of the Church, for priests and monks were but men, and therefore fallible. But the truth remained, and Blake proclaimed it. 'I know of no other Christianity and of no other Gospel than the liberty both of body and mind to exercise the Divine Arts of Imagination—Imagination, the real and Eternal World of which this Vegetable Universe is but a faint shadow, and in which we shall live in our Eternal or Imaginative Bodies, when these Vegetable Mortal Bodies are no more. . . . O ye Religious, discountenance every one among you who shall pretend to despise Art and Science! I call upon you in the name of Jesus! What is the life of Man but Art and Science?

Blake in his day was almost unknown beyond a very small circle of friends. From his engraving he made a pittance, and from his poetry next to nothing. There is no doubt that he bitterly resented the neglect he experienced:

> The Angel that presided o'er my birth
> Said 'Little creature, form'd of Joy and Mirth,

Go love without the help of anything on Earth.'
(*Misc. Poems & Fragments*, 124.)

and again:

> Since all the Riches of this World
> May be gifts from the Devil and Earthly Kings,
> I should suspect that I worship'd the Devil
> If I thank'd my God for Wordly things.
>
> (ibid., 126.)

Yet there remained a faith in his own genius and in an ultimate recognition:

> My designs unchang'd remain,
> Time may rage but rage in vain.
> For above Time's troubled Fountains
> On the Great Atlantic Mountains,
> In my Golden house on high,
> There they shine eternally.
>
> (ibid., 127.)

Apart from a few lyrics, Blake's poetry has never been popular, for much of it is symbolic, intricate, and difficult to understand, and the nineteenth century hardly knew what to make of his wildly imaginative painting and prints. He was however one of the most original creative geniuses in English literature. His central theme was the need to release the human spirit from bondage. He held the imagination one of the supreme attributes of man, and thus regarded the arts as a supreme expression of man's divine nature. In this he was a complete Romantic, yet all his life he remained a solitary and lonely figure, the most enigmatic figure in a great age of original geniuses and eccentric individualists.

NOTES

[1] It was first published in 1913.
[2] Blake was referring to the ancient tradition that after six thousand years the world would be consumed by fire.

9 : William Wordsworth: The Evolution of a Poet

WORDSWORTH went on a walking holiday in France and Switzerland in the summer of 1790. He landed in France just before the celebrations of July 14, 'that great federal day', and saw something of the festivities. When writing Book VI of the *Prelude* a decade later he commented:

> Europe at that time was thrilled with joy,
> France standing on the top of golden hours,
> And human nature seeming born again.
> (VI, 339.)

But in fact he was not at first deeply moved by the spectacle of revolutionary France, and he tells us why:

> But Nature then was sovereign in my mind
> (VI, 333.)

that is to say, loving nature from his youth, he had not as yet any place for man in his thought. When he reached the Convent of Chartreuse and found it occupied by revolutionary troops, he was deeply shocked that such peace and solitude could be so desecrated:

> Stay, stay your sacriligious hands!—The voice
> Was Nature's, uttered from her Alpine throne;
> I heard it then, and seem to hear it now—
> 'Your impious work forbear: perish what may,
> Let this one temple last . . .'   (VI, 430.)

Sentiment and religion combined to register abhorrence:

But oh! if Past and Future be the wings
On whose support harmoniously conjoined
Moves the great spirit of human knowledge, spare
These courts of mystery, where a step advanced
Between the portals of the shadowy rocks
Leaves far behind life's treacherous vanities,
For penitential tears and trembling hopes
Exchanged—to equalise in God's pure sight
Monarch and peasant.   (VI, 448.)

That he was being essentially truthful to his feelings of 1790 is shown by his letter to his sister at the time: 'Among the awful scenes of the Alps I had not a thought of man, or of a single created being: my whole soul was turned to him who produced the terrible majesty before me.' God, to Wordsworth then, was the author of nature, rather than imminent in it (as in his later poetry); nor was he yet touched by the irreligion which came with the influence of the Revolution. In his *Descriptive Sketches*, written mainly on the banks of the Loire during his thirteen-months' stay from November 1791 until 1792, he wrote of this earlier visit, of the sight of a shrine and its worshippers, and of the emotions the scene aroused in him:

My heart, alive to transports long unknown,
Half wishes your delusion were her own.
(VI, 678.)

Professor Garrod (*Wordsworth*, p. 50) has shown that this senti-ment, as much else in *Descriptive Sketches*, was untruthful, being a transference back to 1790 of the feelings of 1792 (the lines were suppressed in later editions of the poem), but that he was moved by the sight of the worshippers was true enough.

In Book VIII of the *Prelude* Wordsworth is explicit about the periods of his mental development: in childhood he was engrossed in 'animal activities', in youth he was dominated by nature, and it was not until 1791 (he is quite clear about the date) that he became interested in man.

> Yet deem not, Friend! that human kind with me
> Thus early took a place pre-eminent;
> Nature herself was, at this unripe time,
> But secondary to my own pursuits
> And animal activities, and all
> Their trivial pleasures; and when these had drooped
> And gradually expired, and Nature, prized
> For her own sake, became my joy, even then—
> And upwards through late youth, until not less
> Than two-and-twenty summers had been told—
> Was Man in my affections and regards
> Subordinate to her, her visible forms
> And viewless agencies: a passion, she,
> A rapture often, and immediate love
> Ever at hand; he only a delight
> Occasional, an accidental grace,
> His hour being not yet come. Far less had then
> The inferior creatures, beast or bird, attuned
> My spirit to that gentleness of love
> (Though they had long been carefully observed),
> Won from me those minute obeisances
> Of tenderness, which I may number now
> With my first blessings.   (VIII, 340.)

It was in this mood that Wordsworth in November 1791 went a second time to France, and it explains why he was not at first much moved by the Revolution. He did indeed sit in the sunshine among the ruins of the Bastille, and carefully preserved a stone of it as a souvenir, but

> I looked for something that I could not find,
> Affecting more emotion than I felt.   (IX, 72.)

He read the pamphlets and newspapers of the revolutionaries without discovering

> Whence the main organs of the public power
> Had sprung, their transmigrations, when and how

Accomplished, giving thus unto events
A form and body; all things were to me
Loose and disjointed, and the affections left
Without a vital interest.   (IX, 103.)

Moreover, at this time the Revolution had apparently lost much of its impetus; violence had subsided, and the Constituent Assembly were completing the Constitution of 1791. For a time Wordsworth was certainly more concerned with Annette than with politics. Of that affair he tells us nothing in the *Prelude*, but he describes his friendship with a group of military officers, most of whom were royalists thinking of joining the emigrés across the frontier.

'Twas in truth an hour
Of universal ferment; mildest men
Were agitated; and commotions, strife
Of passions and opinions, filled the walls
Of peaceful houses with unquiet sounds.
The soil of common life, was, at that time,
Too hot to tread upon.   (IX, 161.)

Still he failed to understand what the conflict was about, and one reason for this was his failure to understand the difference between English and French society in the eighteenth century. For he describes (IX, 215 seq.) how, having been born into a humble home, he had never in his life met a man who claimed special respect by virtue solely of birth or wealth. Even at Cambridge there was a Republic of Letters

where all stood thus far
Upon equal ground; that we were brothers all
In honour, as in one community,
Scholars and gentlemen; where, furthermore,
Distinction open lay to all that came,
And wealth and titles were in less esteem
Than talents, worth, and prosperous industry.
     (IX, 226.)

And thus the events in France seemed to him to be utterly natural and expected,

> Seemed nothing out of nature's certain course,
> A gift that was come rather late than soon.
>
> (IX, 246.)

One of his officer friends, however, Beaupuy, was different from the others. He was an enthusiastic revolutionary, and it was he who, in long and earnest conversations, instilled in Wordsworth a short-lived revolutionary enthusiasm.

> Oft in solitude
> With him did I discourse about the end
> Of civil government, and its wisest forms;
> Of ancient loyalty, and chartered rights,
> Custom and habit, novelty and change;
> Of self-respect, and virtue in the few
> For patrimonial honour set apart,
> And ignorance in the labouring multitude.
> For he, to all intolerance indisposed,
> Balanced these contemplations in his mind;
> And I, who at that time was scarcely dipped
> Into the turmoil, bore a sounder judgment
> Than later days allowed; carried about me,
> With less alloy to its integrity,
> The experience of past ages, as, through help
> Of books and common life, it makes sure way
> To youthful minds, by objects over near
> Not pressed upon, nor dazzled or misled
> By struggling with the crowd for present ends.
>
> (IX, 321.)

There is no reason to regard this as other than an entirely truthful statement, and if so we can picture Wordsworth discussing 'the end of civil government' in Lockeian terms, and appealing to 'the experience of past ages' to defend 'ancient loyalty', customs and habits, and the combined whig and Greek views of aristocracy, the 'virtue in the few/For patrimonial honour set apart'. In all this, he admits he 'bore a sounder judgment/Than later days allowed', that is to say, when in 1793 he embraced the ideas of Godwin, and became himself a revolutionary. With much of Wordsworth's moderate argument Beaupuy appears to have agreed, for he was no Jacobin, and moreover Wordsworth could go a long way with him in common agreement, for

> though not dead, nor obstinate to find
> Error without excuse upon the side
> Of them who strove against us, more delight
> We took, and let this freely be confessed,
> In painting to ourselves the miseries
> Of royal courts, and that voluptuous life
> Unfeeling, where the man who is of soul
> The meanest thrives the most; where dignity,
> True personal dignity, abideth not;
> A light, a cruel, and vain world cut off
> From the natural inlets of just sentiment,
> From lowly sympathy and chastening truth:
> Where good and evil interchange their names,
> And thirst for bloody spoils abroad is paired
> With vice at home.   (IX, 340.)

Wordsworth, who had no direct experience of Courts or political circles, shared the common view that all politics were corruption and self-interest, in contrast with the purity of Rousseau's simple life.

> We added dearest themes—
> Man and his noble nature, as it is
> The gift which God has placed within his power,
> His blind desires and steady faculties
> Capable of clear truth, the one to break
> Bondage, the other to build liberty
> On firm foundations, making social life,
> Through knowledge spreading and imperishable,
> As just in regulation, and as pure
> As individual in the wise and good.   (IX, 354.)

In these sentiments of the purest Romanticism, Wordsworth and

Beaupuy could find common ground. It was sweet to discuss such ideas in academic circumstances:

> Such conversation, under Attic shades,
> Did Dion hold with Plato;   (IX, 408.)

and still sweeter to feel that the Millenium was maturing before their very eyes. Beaupuy for the first time awakened Wordsworth to the sense of social injustice in a rural instance which would particularly appeal to him:

> And when we chanced
> One day to meet a hunger-bitten girl,
> Who crept along fitting her languid gait
> Unto a heifer's motion, by a cord
> Tied to her arm, and picking thus from the lane
> Its sustenance, while the girl with pallid hands
> Was busy knitting in a heartless mood
> Of solitude, and at the sight my friend
> In agitation said, ''Tis against *that*
> That we are fighting', I with him believed
> That a benignant spirit was abroad
> Which might not be withstood, that poverty
> Abject as this would in a little time
> Be found no more.   (IX, 509.)

In December 1792 Wordsworth returned to London. His money was at an end; Annette's daughter was about to be born, and he had no thoughts of marriage. Had he not returned to England,

> Doubtless, I should have then made common cause
> With some who perished; haply perished too,
> A poor mistaken and bewildered offering.
>   (X, 229.)

But his enthusiasm was undimmed,

> for I brought with me the faith
> That, if France prospered, good men would not long
> Pay fruitless worship to humanity.   (X, 257.)

But in the spring of 1793 the British government dismissed the French ambassador, and the Convention declared war on Britain. To Wordsworth it was the greatest moral shock he had ever experienced.

> No shock
> Given to my moral nature had I known
> Down to that very moment; neither lapse
> Nor turn of sentiment that might be named
> A revolution, save at this one time;
> All else was progress on the self-same path
> On which, with a diversity of pace,
> I had been travelling. (X, 268.)

At first he exulted at early British defeats, but as war gave rise to the revolutionary government of the Jacobins, he was plunged into an agony of doubt and depression:

> It was a lamentable time for man,
> Whether a hope had e'er been his or not;
> A woeful time for them whose hopes survived
> The shock . . .
> Most melancholy at that time, O Friend!
> Were my day-thoughts—my nights were miserable;
> Through months, through years, long after the last beat
> Of those atrocities, the hour of sleep
> To me came rarely charged with natural gifts,
> Such ghastly visions had I of despair
> And tyranny, and implements of death;
> And innocent victims sinking under fear . . .
> (X, 384, 397.)

He describes how, when he heard, as he walked over the sands near Rampside, in Lancashire, of the death of Robespierre and his followers in the Thermidorian reaction of July 1794, he gave thanks to everlasting Justice:

> behold!
> They who with clumsy desperation brought

M

> A river of Blood . . . have been swept away.
>
> (X, 583.)

Yet, writing in 1804, Wordsworth could still recapture the exhilaration of the first revolutionary enthusiasm.

> Bliss was it in that dawn to be alive,
> But to be young was very Heaven! O times,
> In which the meagre, stale, forbidding ways
> Of custom, law, and statute, took at once
> The attraction of a country in romance!
> When Reason seemed the most to assert her rights
> When most intent on making of herself
> A prime enchantress—to assist the work,
> Which then was going forward in her name!
> Not favoured spots alone, but the whole Earth,
> The beauty wore of promise.   (X, 108.)

Wordsworth believed that all poetry should be 'emotion recollected in tranquillity'; the passage of time was necessary to clarify and order the initial emotions and to give them eloquence. In his own poetry the method was triumphantly justified, for the subject of his own mental development, traced with an engaging truthfulness, gained immensely from the pathos which always attends the memory of youthful hopes.

His disgust at the excesses of Jacobin rule did not destroy his faith in the new liberty:

> in the People was my trust. . . .
> I knew that wound external could not take
> Life from the young Republic.   (XI, 11.)

He was forced however to formulate his political theories more carefully. In 1792 they were sheer Rousseau. Liberty was equated with nature; the achievement of liberty meant the release of man's true nature, and this could only be good:

> To Nature, then,
> Power had reverted: habit, custom, law,

> Had left an interregnum's open space
> For her to move about in, uncontrolled. (XI, 31.)

He admitted that he had plunged into the heady world of revolution without due preparation, that Cambridge had not prepared him for the battle:

> I was led to take an eager part
> In arguments of civil polity,
> Abruptly, and indeed before my time.   (XI, 76.)

As a result he had been swept along by youthful emotions rather than by intellectual conviction:

> my likings and my loves
> Ran in new channels, leaving old ones dry:
> And hence a blow that, in maturer age,
> Would but have touched the judgment, struck more deep
> Into sensations near the heart.   (XI, 184.)

He was also, he admitted, open to the influence of what he called 'wild theories', to which he

> lent a careless ear, assured
> That time was ready to set all things right,
> And that the multitude, so long oppressed,
> Would be oppressed no more.   (XI, 191.)

Among these 'wild theories' he certainly included those of Godwin, who exercised a brief but powerful influence in 1793. A decade later he could write of them with contempt:

> This was the time, when, all things tending fast
> To depravation, speculative schemes—
> That promised to abstract the hopes of Man
> Out of his feelings, to be fixed thenceforth
> For ever in a purer element—
> Found ready welcome. Tempting region, *that*
> For Zeal to enter and refresh herself,

> Where passions had the privilege to work,
> And never hear the sound of their own names.
>
> (XI, 223.)

Bitter words these. Wordsworth had come to see Godwin's theories as no more than a cloak under the name of Reason for all the passions of men. But to a young man it looked otherwise:

> What delight!
> How glorious! in self-knowledge and self-rule
> To look through all the frailities of the world
> And, with a resolute mastery shaking off
> Infirmities of nature, time and place,
> Build social upon personal Liberty,
> Which, to the blind restraints of general laws
> Superior, magisterially adopts
> One guide, the light of circumstances.   (XI, 235.)

In short, Godwin's system saw no conflict between the liberty of individuals and the claims of society, or conversely it held that when such a conflict appeared, the latter should always give way to the former. Wordsworth admitted that for a time he was a Godwinian, 'betrayed by present objects, and by reasonings false/From their beginnings' (XI, 287). The result was a period of intellectual and moral confusion,

> till, demanding formal *proof*,
> And seeking it in everything, I lost
> All feeling of conviction, and, in fine,
> Sick, wearied out with contrarieties,
> Yielded up moral questions in despair. (XI, 301.)

From this depression he was rescued, partly by reading Spinoza and Hartley, but above all, he declared, by the influence of his sister Dorothy, who led him gently back to poetry and to a love of nature.

> led me back through opening day
> To those sweet counsels between head and heart

Whence grew that genuine knowledge, fraught with peace,
Which, through the later sinkings of this cause,
Hath still upheld me, and upholds me now.

(XI, 352.)

The character of this 'genuine knowledge' Wordsworth is at pains
to make clear. First, in a passage in Book XI of the *Prelude*,
subsequently suppressed, he drew a distinction between two types
of reason. The true reason was 'the grand and simple Reason',
which he now came gradually to discern, but the other was

> that humbler power
> Which carries on its no inglorious work
> By logic and minute analysis. (XI, 123.)

This was the reason which appealed most naturally to the young
mind, and the one which philosophy most often employed; but it
was dangerous in that it was destructive in its operation.

> Suffice it here
> To hint that danger cannot but attend
> Upon a Function rather proud to be
> The enemy of falsehood, than the friend
> Of truth, to sit in judgment than to feel.
>
> (XI, 133.)

Rejecting rationalism, Wordsworth at once plunged into a review
of the early influences of nature upon him, and the point which he
reiterated time and time again in his poetry was that in his youth
the appeal of nature was entirely to the senses, entirely to the
eye and *ear*.

> I speak in recollection of a time
> When the bodily eye, in every stage of life
> The most despotic of our senses, gained
> Such strength in *me* as often held my mind
> In absolute dominion. (XII, 127.)

And again,

> Powers on whom
> I daily waited, now all *eye* and now
> All *ear*; but never long without the heart
> Employed. (XII, 98.)

The heart however came into operation chiefly in reflection in tranquillity upon the past sensatory experiences. In the time of youth of which he wrote he was content to enjoy nature without a philosophy. Man played no part in his thought. Then came the experience of the French Revolution, and this led him to consider for the first time the place of man in nature.

> Long time in search of knowledge did I range
> The field of human life, in heart and mind
> Benighted. (XIII, 16.)

The study of neither politics nor history helped him,

> seeing little worthy or sublime
> In what the Historian's pen so much delights
> To blazon—power and energy detached
> From moral purpose. (XIII, 41.)

If the pursuit of power was amoral, so was the pursuit of wealth.

> having thus discerned how dire a thing
> Is worshipped in that idol proudly named
> 'The Wealth of Nations' (XIII, 76.)

Godwin merely bemused and misled him, for Godwinianism held that all genuine knowledge, and therefore virtue came from Reason, and by this test the great mass of ordinary people was excluded. This view was aristocratic, in tune with much eighteenth-century thought, and with the whole Neo-Platonic tradition, but it was one which Wordsworth rejected, for

> Why is this glorious creature to be found
> One only in ten thousand? What one is,
> Why may not millions be? What bars are thrown
> By Nature in the way of such a hope? (XIII, 87.)

It was necessary therefore to abandon the whole philosophy of rationalism, and find a new basis of thought. It meant abandoning the whole Platonic tradition in education and philosophy, for he was

> now convinced at heart
> How little those formalities, to which
> With overwhelming trust alone we give
> The name of Education, have to do
> With real feeling and just sense. (XIII, 168.)

And was it really true that virtue was so hard to attain that it was the prized possession of a small élite? Was it really true that all noble qualities could be fostered only in aristocratic surroundings?

> There are who think that strong affection, love
> Known by whatever name, is falsely deemed
> A gift, to use a term which they would use,
> Of vulgar nature; that its growth requires
> Retirement, leisure, language purified
> By manners studied and elaborate;
> That whoso feels such passion in its strength
> Must live within the very light and air
> Of courteous usages refined by art. (XIII, 186.)

It was true that love did not flourish under conditions of barbarity and oppression; nor did he find it

> Among the close and overcrowded haunts
> Of cities, where the human heart is sick.
>   (XIII, 203.)

Yet he rejected the aristocratic view of morality which 'debased the Many for the pleasure of the Few', whereby 'society had parted man from man'. The mistake lay in supposing that virtue was a form of knowledge arrived at by the process of reason, whereas it was the result of feeling, and more readily found in the hearts of simple peasants than in the minds of men of the world.

It was the discovery of this, Wordsworth tells us, that decided him to be a poet.

> I remember well
> That in life's every-day appearances
> I seemed about this time to gain clear sight
> Of a new world—a world too that was fit
> To be transmitted, and to other eyes
> Made visible.   (XIII, 369.)

It is quite wrong therefore to suppose, as is sometimes suggested, that it was the French Revolution which made Wordsworth a poet. The *Descriptive Sketches*, which he wrote in France, and *Guilt and Sorrow*, which he wrote under the influence of Godwin, are not classed among his great poetry. Real inspiration came when, under the influence of his sister Dorothy and Coleridge, he was able to recollect his experiences in tranquillity and order them into a philosophy of his own. The truth was that he had never been as deeply engaged in the events in France as he had supposed, for his nature was too insular to become French in spirit. But the Revolution had forced him to consider the problem of man in society, and it was this which gave him the impetus to become a poet.

His state of mind at this point he explored in his most lyrical poem, *Tintern Abbey*. He had first visited Tintern Abbey in 1793, at the time when he was passing through the mental crisis brought on by the outbreak of war. Five years later he returned, with the crisis resolved. The scene was the same, but now he could recognise that it had actually helped him to find the solution he had lacked in 1793. For the 'beauteous forms' often remembered 'in lonely rooms and 'mid the din of towns and cities' had brought pleasurable sensations, which in turn had persuaded him to cease searching for a rationalist solution to human problems, and had inculcated

> that blessed mood,
> In which the burthen of the mystery,
> In which the heavy and the weary weight
> Of all this unintelligible world,
> Is lightened: that serene and blessed mood,
> In which the affections gently lead us on,—

> Until, the breath of this corporeal frame
> And even the motion of our human blood
> Almost suspended, we are laid asleep
> In body, and become a living soul:
> While with an eye made quiet by the power
> Of harmony, and the deep power of joy,
> We see into the life of things.   (1.37.)

Man had ceased to be insignificant to him, as in his days of youth, and he was no longer the rational and autonomous being of the French Revolutionaries and the philosophy of Godwin, but a part of nature, in which there was an appointed order, and in which love was the motive force. For Wordsworth the sheer delight experienced by his animal spirits when a boy was over.

> That time is past,
> And all its aching joys are now no more,
> And all its dizzy raptures.   (1.83.)

But it had been replaced by something of greater permanence.

> For I have learned
> To look on nature, not as in the hour
> Of thoughtless youth; but hearing oftentimes
> The still, sad music of humanity,
> Nor harsh nor grating, though of ample power
> To chasten and subdue. And I have felt
> A presence that disturbs me with the joy
> Of elevated thoughts; a sense sublime
> Of something far more deeply interfused,
> Whose dwelling is the light of setting suns,
> And the round ocean and the living air,
> And the blue sky, and in the mind of man:
> A motion and a spirit, that impels
> All thinking things, all objects of all thought,
> And rolls through all things.   (1.88.)

These were perhaps the most deeply religious lines Wordsworth ever wrote. His God was not necessarily the Christian God, but there was a spirit throughout nature, the universe and the mind of man and in this Wordsworth found a new contentment.

The subject of the transition which he had experienced from the pleasures of sensation of youth to the philosophical perception of manhood, interested the poet greatly. It was the theme of 'My heart leaps up', and the concluding lines of this poem,

> The child is father of the Man;
> And I could wish my days to be
> Bound each to each in natural piety,

were placed at the head of his *Ode on Intimations of Immortality*, in which he sought, not entirely successfully, to formulate his philosophy on the subject. The *Ode* as it was written in 1802 consisted of the first four stanzas, and thus ended with the cry—

> Whither is fled the visionary gleam?
> Where is it now, the glory and the dream?

To these in 1806 he added further verses, the first four of which set out the Platonic theory of Memory, in which Plato accounted for the intuitive part of the human mind by supposing that it had lived in a previous existence, and thus came 'trailing clouds of glory/...From God, who is our home'. It was a strange theory to find in Wordsworth, who was in general so little influenced by classical philosophy. He had learnt of it from Coleridge, who himself had written a sonnet on the same subject in 1796,[1] and it seemed to accord with a deeply romantic theme which was so important in his thought. This was the idea of tradition and continuity in human affairs. Men were not, as in the Lockeian tradition, primarily independent and autonomous beings, but belonged to a people, a family, a tradition, a brotherhood, and all within the context of nature. This was why life in cities was so hateful to Wordsworth, because it seemed devoid of roots. The countryman on the other hand was a part of nature, a link in a chain of history and tradition, the product of his environment. Moreover man was the product of his early experiences which, to Wordsworth at least, were so deep and vivid. On several occasions in the *Prelude* he recounts experiences of his childhood, to a casual observer trivial and inconsequential, yet to the child deeply impressive, as the terror he had felt when rowing alone on the lake (I, 357–400), or the remorse which he felt at the death of his father (XII, 287–355). It was such deep emotional and irrational experiences as these which moulded the poet's mind, and hence

> The thought of our past years in me doth breed
> Perpetual benediction.   (*Ode*, 1.137.)

As he grew older the ecstacy of his experiences had passed away, but in compensation he had acquired a philosophy. He had indeed 'relinquished one delight', but in its place had learnt 'to live beneath Nature's more habitual sway'. Before long, as we know, Wordsworth's poetical powers would begin to fail, although he was to live for another forty years. But, looking back, in the thirteenth book of the *Prelude*, he recognised that at about the time of the *Tintern Abbey* poem, he had 'gained clear sight of a new world' (XIII, 369). It was a recognition of the fact that the love which he had felt for nature was part of a higher love.

> This spiritual Love acts not nor can exist
> Without Imagination, which, in truth,
> Is but another name for absolute power
> And clearest insight, amplitude of mind,
> And Reason in her most exalted mood.
>   (XIV, 188.)

and from it, he said, he and his sister had

>   drawn
> Faith in life endless, the sustaining thought
> Of human being, Eternity, and God.
>   (XIV, 203.)

It was a conclusion which each person must reach for himself,

> Here must thou be, O Man!

Power to thyself; no Helper hast thou here.

(XIV, 209.)

It was the conclusion of the *Prelude*, and in a way the consummation of Wordsworth's work as a poet.

·   ·   ·   ·   ·   ·

As Wordsworth makes clear, he was led on from his delight in nature to a sympathy for men. He wrote:

> When I began to enquire,
> To watch and question those I met, and speak
> Without reserve to them, the lonely roads
> Were open schools in which I daily read
> With most delight the passions of mankind,
> Whether by words, looks, sighs, or tears, revealed;
> There saw into the depth of human souls,
> Souls that appear to have no depth at all
> To careless eyes. (*Prelude*, XIII, 160.)

This was a new experience for any poet. The peasantry had not hitherto been thought a fitting subject for poetry unless they inhabited the classical landscape of nymphs and shepherdesses, and the grim hardships of their lives had passed largely unrecognised. When Wordsworth settled with his sister Dorothy at Grasmere, they were surrounded by simple peasant life, and Dorothy, as much as Wordsworth, was deeply interested in the lives of their neighbours. They saw their poverty, the women who struggled against ill-health and overwork, the beggars and the hungry children, and it left a deep impression. As early as 1793–4, under the influence of Godwin, Wordsworth had written in indignation in *Guilt and Sorrow* against the evils of war and the press-gangs, and how a 'mild and good man' had been press-ganged into being a sailor, how he had experienced years of suffering, until he committed murder. Meanwhile his wife suffered

> The empty loom, cold hearth, and silent wheel,
> And tears which flowed for ills which patience
>   might not heal. (1.269.)

Eventually, exhausted and ill, she was taken to hospital where

> I heard my neighbours in their beds complain
> Of many things which never troubled me.
>
> (1.390.)

Meanwhile, what justice or hope existed for her misguided and hunted husband? Wordsworth condemned the empty platitudes with which society sought to placate the poor:

> Of social Order's care for wretchedness,
> Of Time's sure help to calm and reconcile,
> Joy's second spring and Hope's long-treasured smile,
> 'Twas not for *him* to speak.

Finally, at the sight of his dead wife, he was overcome by remorse, surrendered himself to the authorities, and was hanged. To Wordsworth war was the source of the sailor's miseries. He well remembered the impact of the American War, and in the Preface to the poem he declared that the French War, 'which many thought would be brought to a speedy close by the irresistible arms of Great Britain being added to those of the Allies, I was assured in my own mind would be of long continuance, and productive of distress and misery beyond all possible calculation', and in this he proved to be right.

Wordsworth came to love shepherds, he wrote,

> not verily
> For their own sakes, but for the fields and hills
> Where was their occupation and abode.
>
> (*Michael*, 1.24.)

The lives of all shepherds and countrymen were hard, with ceaseless grinding toil, and with the threat of misfortune and ruin always hanging over them. Michael, when he had inherited his land, had found it so burdened with debts that

> Till I was forty years of age, not more
> Than half of my inheritance was mine. (1.374.)

He 'toiled and toiled', yet again at the end of his life he was threatened with ruin. In *The Last of the Flock* the theme was the shepherd whose flock had dwindled from fifty sheep to a single one in a hopeless struggle to feed his six children. In *The Sailor's Mother* it is the woman whose son has been lost at sea, and who is left with only his singing bird to steady her reason. Such themes seem morbid, but it must be remembered that they often recorded the everyday experiences of the countryside.

It has sometimes been supposed from this that Wordsworth was recording the agricultural changes of his time, and the worsening conditions of the peasantry which accompanied the agricultural revolution. But this is not to see matter in correct perspective. It is true that much of the suffering of which he wrote was the result of war, and to this extent he was recording a worsening of conditions. But historians do not suppose that enclosure, and other changes of the agricultural revolution, much influenced Cumberland for the worse. Wordsworth was not writing of conditions which had suddenly become worse, but of conditions which had always been part of the lives of the peasantry, yet had not previously been thought worthy of a poet's pen. Gray, in his famous *Elegy*, had been moved by a sense of history as he thought of the generations of simple peasants who had lived and died in the village, and he was aware that

> Chill Penury regress'd their noble rage,
> And froze the genial current of the soul (1.51.)

But he did not pursue the subject in detail, and indeed had almost to apologise for raising it:

> ... Nor Grandeur hear with a disdainful smile
> The short and simple annals of the Poor. (1.31.)

Wordsworth made no such apology, and in poem after poem gave particular instances which had come to his notice of the sufferings of poverty, loneliness and old age.

He himself well knew what poverty was like. For years he lived on a very modest income, during which time his poems did not sell.[2] Even though he received a number of legacies, including that of Raisley Calvert in 1795, and later he had a regular income as stamp-distributor, yet he had always to remain careful about money matters. All the evidence goes to prove his deep concern for the poverty he saw around him at Grasmere. In a poem written in October 1800, which deserves to be better known, the first line of which is 'A narrow girdle of rough stones and crags', he describes how Dorothy, Coleridge and he were walking idly on the edge of the lake, 'observing such objects as the waves had tossed ashore', and listening to the voices of busy reapers in the near-by fields, when they suddenly saw a peasant in the distance fishing.

> 'Improvident and reckless', we exclaimed,
> 'The Man must be, who thus can lose a day
> Of the mid harvest, when the labourer's hire
> Is ample.'

But as they approached him they saw that he was thin and wasted by hunger and sickness, and that, too weak to labour in the harvest field, he was doing all he could 'to gain a pittance from the dead unfeeling lake'. Wordsworth and his companions were deeply moved and guilt-stricken at their over-hasty judgment, and resolved henceforth to 'temper all our thoughts with charity'. That he was concerned also about his own money troubles is revealed in *The Leech-Gatherer* in which he describes how, on a walk he was overcome with 'dim sadness and blind thoughts'. Even though he could enjoy the song of the skylark

> But there may come another day to me—
> Solitude, pain of heart, distress, and poverty.

> We Poets in our youth begin in gladness;
> But thereof come in the end despondency and madness.

Compounded of depression at the social poverty around him, and doubts about his own position, it could be a paralysing and exhausting experience:

>the fear that kills;
>And hope that is willing to be fed;
>Cold, pain and labour, and all fleshly ills;
>And mighty Poets in their misery dead.

In January 1801 Wordsworth sent a copy of the *Lyrical Ballads* to Charles James Fox, particularly recommending to him *The Brothers* and *Michael*, and inviting Fox's sympathies for the social purpose intended. He wrote: 'It appears to me that the most calamitous effect which has followed the measures which have lately been pursued in this country, is a rapid decay of the domestic affections among the lower orders of society. This effect the present rulers of this country are not conscious of, or they disregard it. For many years past, the tendency of society amongst all the nations of Europe, has been to produce it; but recently, by the spreading of manufactures through every part of the country, by the heavy taxes upon postage, by workhouses, houses of industry, and the invention of soup-shops, etc., superadded to the increasing disproportion between the price of labour and that of the necessaries of life, the bonds of domestic feeling among the poor, as far as the influence of these things has extended, have been weakened, and in innumerable instances entirely destroyed. The evil would be the less to be regretted, if these institutions were regarded only as palliatives to a disease; but the vanity and pride of their promoters are so subtly interwoven with them, that they are deemed great discoveries and blessings to humanity. In the meantime, parents are separated from their children, and children from their parents; the wife no longer prepares with her own hands a meal for her husband, the produce of his labour; there is little doing in his house in which his affections can be interested, and but little left in it that he can love. . . . The domestic affections will always be strong amongst men who live in a country not crowded with population, if these men are placed above poverty. But if they are proprietors of small estates which have descended to them from their ancestors, the power which these affections will acquire amongst such men is inconceivable by those who have only had an opportunity of observing hired labourers, farmers, and the manufacturing poor. Their little tract of land serves as a kind of permanent rallying point for their domestic feelings, as a tablet upon which they are written, which makes them objects of memory in a thousand instances when they would otherwise be forgotten. ... The poems are faithful copies from Nature.' Fox however was not to be drawn into so tendentious a discussion. He replied that he was 'no great friend to blank verse for subjects which are to be treated of with simplicity', and of the social implications of the poems he made no mention at all. (Wordsworth: *Prose Works*, II, p. 202.)

Wordsworth was particularly moved by the decline of the domestic system of industry, and its effects upon the poor. He wrote in 1819: 'I could write a treatise of lamentation upon the changes brought about among the cottages of Westmoreland by the silence of the spinning-wheel. During the long winter's nights and wet days, the wheel upon which wool was spun gave employment to a great part of a family. The old man, however infirm, was able to card the wool, as he sate in the corner by the fire-side; and often, when a boy, have I admired the cylinders of carded wool which were softly laid upon each other by his side. Two wheels were often at work on the same floor, and others of the family, chiefly the little children, were occupied in teazing and clearing the wool to fit it for the hand of the carder, so that all, except the infants, were contributing to mutual support. Such was the employment that prevailed in the pastoral vales.' (ibid., III, 55.) What seemed so important to Wordsworth was that in such circumstances there was real social cohesion, each member of the family, and each member of the community, being dependent upon the others, and in this community even the beggar had his allotted part. The Old Cumberland Beggar went his rounds, and

> Among the farms and solitary huts,
> Hamlets and thinly-scattered villages,
> Where'er the aged Beggar takes his rounds,
> The mild necessity of use compels
> To acts of love; and habit does the work
> Of reason.

Charity, not yet cold, was an essential part of the good life, and it was a humanising influence on the poor that they too could play their part, for

> man is dear to man; the poorest poor
> Long for some moments in a weary life
> When they can know and feel that they have been,
> Themselves, the fathers and the dealers-out
> Of some small blessings; have been kind to such
> As needed kindness, for this single cause,
> That we have all of us one human heart.

Instead of charity however there came the Poor Law of 1834, and Wordsworth was bitterly opposed to it. 'This heartless process has been carried as far as it can go by the AMENDED Poor Law Bill, tho' the inhumanity that prevails in this measure is somewhat disguised by the profession that one of its objects is to throw the poor upon the voluntary donations of their neighbours, that is, if rightly interpreted, to force them into a condition between relief in the Union Poor House and alms robbed of their Christian grace and spirit, as being forced rather from the avaricious and selfish; and all, in fact, but the humane and charitable are at liberty to keep all they possess from their distressed brethren.' (ibid., III, 185.)

How grim life could be for the poor when economic hardships broke up the units of the family and the community, Wordsworth described in *The Wanderer*. He was writing of the years of famine in the seventeen-nineties:

> A Wanderer then among the cottages,
> I, with my freight of winter raiment, saw
> The hardships of that season: many rich
> Sank down, as in a dream, among the poor;
> And of the poor did many cease to be,
> And their place knew them not.

While Margaret and her husband sank with them,

shoals of artisans
From ill-requited labour turned adrift
Sought daily bread from public charity,
They, and their wives and children—happier far
Could they have lived as do the little birds
That peck along the hedge-rows, or the kite
That makes her dwelling on the mountain rocks!
(Bk. I, 11541–65.)

It was a picture which Wordsworth never forgot, and it coloured his whole approach to the social question.

In politics Wordsworth was for a time confused and uncertain. At the time of the Jacobin dictatorship in France he wrote: 'I disapprove of monarchical and aristocratical governments, however modified. Hereditary distinctions, and privileged orders of every species, I think, must necessarily counteract the progress of human improvement. Hence it follows that I am not among the admirers of the British constitution. I conceive that a more excellent system of civil policy might be established among us.' Thus far he was merely reciting William Godwin, but then he drew back: 'yet in my ardour to attain the goal, I do not forget the nature of the ground where the race is to be run. The destruction of those institutions which I condemn appears to me to be hastening on too rapidly. I recoil from the very idea of a revolution. I am a determined enemy to every species of violence. I see no connection but what the obstinacy of pride and ignorance renders necessary, between justice and the sword,—between reason and bonds. I deplore the miserable condition of the French, and think that *we* can only be guarded from the same scourge by the undaunted efforts of good men. ... I severely condemn all inflammatory addresses to the passions of men. I know that the multitude walk in darkness. I would put into each man's hands a lantern, to guide him; and not have him to set out upon his journey depending for illumination on abortive flashes of lightning, or the coruscations of transitory meteors.' (*Prose Works*, III, 232.)

Already in this passage it is clear that Wordsworth was recoiling from the dangers of violence which would accompany too hasty a pursuit of liberty. The war with France aided his political transition. Its outbreak was a terrible shock to him, and for years he was opposed to it. Looking back in the year 1821 he declared: 'I disapproved of the war against France at its commencement, thinking, which was perhaps an error, that it might have been avoided; but after Buonaparte had violated the independence of Switzerland, my heart turned against him, and against the nation that could submit to be the instrument of such an outrage. Here it was that I parted, in feeling, from the Whigs, and to a certain degree united with their adversaries, who were free from the delusion (such as I must ever regard it) of Mr. Fox and his party, that a safe and honourable peace was practicable with the French nation, and that an ambitious conqueror like Buonaparte could be softened down into a commercial rival.' (ibid., III, 269.)

Here Wordsworth was clearly indicating 1802-3 as the period of transition, and it coincides with his adoption of a new verse form in which to express his mood. He once described how, one afternoon in 1801, his sister read to him the sonnets of Milton. 'I took fire, and produced three sonnets the same afternoon—the first I ever wrote, except an irregular one at school.' (ibid., III, 52.) In his sonnets *Dedicated to National Independence and Liberty* he recorded the transition in his thought. He mourned the extinction of the Venetian Republic (1802) in 'Once did she hold the gorgeous east in fee', and the fall of Toussaint as a champion of liberty:

> Thou hast left behind
> Powers that will work for thee; air, earth and skies,
> There's not a breathing of the common wind
> That will forget thee: thou hast great allies;
> Thy friends are exultations, agonies,
> And love, and man's unconquerable mind.

He was depressed by the materialism of his age:

> No grandeur now in nature or in book
> Delights us. Rapine avarice, expense,
> This is idolatry.

and

Milton! thou shouldst be living at this hour:
England hath need of thee: she is a fen
Of stagnant waters. . . .
. . . We are selfish men;
Oh! raise us up, return to us again,
And give us manners, virtue, freedom, power.

and

I find nothing great:
Nothing is left which I can venerate;
So that a doubt almost within me springs
Of Providence, such emptiness at length
Seems at the heart of all things.

But the greatest fear of all was that England would fall beneath
the military power of France, and in this danger Wordsworth found
a new version of patriotism and a new need for national security.
Liberty would still remain the objective, but now it signified
national liberty from Napoleonic domination. The English Channel
and sea-power were still the guarantees of national safety. As he
looked across to France from Dover,

I shrunk; for verily the barrier flood
Was like a lake, or river bright and fair,
A span of waters; yet what power is there!
What mightiness for evil and for good!
Even so doth God protect us if we be
Virtuous and wise.

This was why Switzerland seemed to Wordsworth to be of special
significance, for

Two Voices are there; one is of the sea,
One of the mountains; each a mighty Voice:
In both from age to age thou didst rejoice,
They were thy chosen music, Liberty!

In the face of such a foreign danger, class divisions and internal discord seemed unthinkable. In his *Lines on the Expected Invasion* (1803) he called upon monarchists and republicans alike to put aside their differences and to rally to the defence of the nation:

> Come ye—whate'er your creed—O waken all,
> Whate'er your temper, at your Country's call;
> Resolving (this a free-born Nation can)
> To have one Soul, and perish to a man,
> Or save this honoured Land from every Lord
> But British reason and the British sword.

In this way the national emergency led the Romantic poets to discover nationalism as an ideal, and as the indispensable condition for liberty.

This was why Wordsworth and his friends were so deeply interested in the Spanish revolt against French domination in 1808. In December he wrote that he was 'very deep in the subject, and about to publish upon it' (ibid., III, 257). The result was the most notable of his prose works, an extended pamphlet upon *The Convention of Cintra*.

In order to understand Wordsworth's views at this time it is important to remember that the anxiety and gloom which the Napoleonic Wars produced in him were widely shared by the Englishmen of his time. It was believed that, although Britain was invincible on sea, Bonaparte was equally invincible on land. The hopes that had been placed in European coalitions were three times thwarted, and for a time there seemed no alternative principle upon which to rely. The Portuguese and Spanish revolts of 1808 provided another answer; they enabled Britain to use French revolutionary tactics against the French themselves. Just as the French in 1792 had offered fraternity to any of the peoples of Europe who would rise against their rulers, so Canning, the British Foreign Secretary, in June 1808 declared that any nation which would oppose France would automatically become allies of Britain. In August Wellesley defeated the French in Portugal at Vimiero, and was in a position to capture Lisbon and the entire French army under Junot. Instead he was superseded in the command first by Sir Harry Burrard, and then by Sir Hew Dalrymple, who preferred to sign the Convention of Cintra, which allowed the French to retire from Portugal. At the news of this in England there was an outburst of indignation. Burrard and Dalrymple were at once summoned home, and were never employed again. Sir Arthur Wellesley succeeded to the command, but the Commons refused to condemn the Convention of Cintra.

Wordsworth's pamphlet, which appeared in 1809 revealed a grasp of statesmanship which he had never displayed before. He wrote that it had taken Britain (he should have said himself!) some years to be convinced that the French War was necessary, but that the turning-point had come with the subjugation of Switzerland. The French attack on Spain however had been even more important, because it provided Britain with a moral cause which had previously been in doubt. The rising of a people for national liberty was more inspiring than the manoeuvrings of the Austrian and Prussian armies against the French. The struggle was now a moral one, 'of direct and universal concern to mankind', because it involved the freedom of a people. It was therefore a cause which 'calls aloud for the aid of intellect, knowledge, and love, and rejects every other'. Moreover, for the first time it presented Britain with the prospect of an ally capable of defeating the power of France.

'Now, when a new-born power had been arrayed against the Tyrant, the only one which ever offered a glimpse of hope to a sane mind, the power of popular resistance rising out of universal reason and from the heart of human nature—and by a peculiar providence disembarrassed from the imbecility, the cowardice, and the intrigues of a worn-out government—that at this time we, the most favoured nation upon earth, should have acted as if it had been our aim to level to the ground by one blow this long-wished-for spirit, whose birth we had so joyfully hailed, and by which even our own glory, our safety, our existence, were to be maintained'; this was the fact which so angered Wordsworth.

He looked forward, not to the conquest of France by Britain, but to the restoration of a balance of power in Europe, and he was one of the first men in Europe to foresee a new balance of power based upon national states. He looked forward to the time when, not only Spain and Portugal, but Italy and Germany also would be united on the basis of language and culture, free from foreign domination. This would require the disappearance of the petty princedoms of Italy and Germany, but it would be in the interest of European stability. The whole idea of nationalism was so utterly new at that time that it is a remarkable tribute to Wordsworth's prescience that he should have understood it so clearly. He based his belief in nationalism upon what he thought the deepest emotions in men. 'Not by bread alone is the life of Man sustained; not by raiment alone is he warmed—but by the genial and vernal inmates of the breast, which at once pushes forth and cherishes; by self-support and self-sufficing endeavours; by anticipations, apprehensions, and active remembrances; by elasticity under insult, and firm resistance to injury; by joy, and by love; by pride which his imagination gathers in from afar; by patience, because life wants not promises; by admiration; by gratitude which habitually expands itself, for his elevation, in complacency towards his Creator.' And to all this national independence is indispensible. National independence gives a people the sense of being self-governed, and 'where this feeling has no place, a people are not a society, but a herd; man being indeed distinguished among them from the brute; but only to his disgrace'.

The poorest peasant, he wrote, in an independent land, felt this pride because he felt himself in some sense to be self-governed. Man must have love and admiration reaching beyond himself ('otherwise the moral man is killed'), extending not only to fellow-men, but also to ancestry and posterity.[3] National pride grows with a sense of history, and has a warming and civilising influence. 'It is to the worldlings of our own country, and to those who think without carrying their thoughts far enough, that I address myself. Let them know, there is no true wisdom without imagination; no genuine sense;—that the man, who in this age feels no regret for the ruined honour of other Nations, must be poor in sympathy for the honour of his own Country.' Wordsworth did not shrink from applying the consequences of his argument to Ireland. 'Look at the past history of our sister Island for the quality of foreign

oppression: turn where you will, it is miserable at best.' The
Spanish similarly had nothing to gain from French domination.
'The Spaniards are a people with imagination: and the paradoxical
reveries of Rousseau, and the flippancies of Voltaire, are plants
which will not naturalise in the country of Calderon and Cervantes.'
Two years later, in a letter to Captain Pasley (28 March 1811,
Memoirs of Wordsworth (1851), i, 406), Wordsworth stated his
vision even more clearly:

> I think there is nothing more unfortunate for Europe than
> the condition of Germany and Italy. Could the barriers be
> dissolved which have divided the one nation into Neapolitans,
> Tuscans, Venetians, etc., and the other into Prussians,
> Hanoverians, etc., and could they once be taught to feel their
> strength, the French would be driven back into their own land
> immediately. I wish to see Spain, Italy, France, Germany,
> formed into independent nations; nor have I any desire to
> reduce the power of France further than may be necessary for
> that end. Woe be to that country whose military power is
> irresistible! I deprecate such an event for Great Britain
> scarcely less than for any other land. . . . If the time should
> ever come when this island shall have no more formidable
> enemies by land than it has at this moment by sea, the
> extinction of all that it previously contained of good and great
> would soon follow. Indefinite progress, undoubtedly, there
> ought to be somewhere; but let that be in knowledge, in
> science, in civilization, in the increase of the numbers of the
> people, and in the augmentation of their virtue and happiness.
> But progress in conquest cannot be indefinite.

Wordsworth's idea of nationalism stemmed from Burke, and he
owed much also to Coleridge, who introduced him to German
philosophy, and who helped him to write at least a part of the
pamphlet. But the clarity of the political plan which underlay his
thinking was clearly his own, and was not accepted by any of the
politicians of the day. Pitt thought in terms of the need for a new
balance of power in his famous State Paper of 1805, but he did not

go so far as to embrace nationalism as a principle, and neither did Fox, Canning nor Castlereagh, the principal Foreign Ministers until the making of the Treaty of Vienna. Wordsworth's venture into the field of international affairs was therefore a remarkable piece of prescience.

Coleridge appreciated the forces making for German nationalism, but he was more interested in the cultural than in the political consequences. He referred to the subject in his Philosophical Lectures in 1818. He argued that whereas previously in European history intellectual divisions were horizontal and transcended the frontiers of states, in his own day they were determined mainly by national frontiers. Germany, for instance, for the first time had begun to reveal national characteristics. 'Germany never had the advantages that this country has, never had that fulness of occupation by commerce, never that deep interest in the affairs of the whole which constitutes the pride, and is perpetually improving the faculties, of Englishmen, who still carry their country home to their fireside. But on the other hand it had many and great advantages of its own. It was the number of its universities, and the circumstances that the learned or studied men formed a sort of middle class of society correspondent to our middle class, and the very absence of nationality that gave to the Germans, as they became cosmopolites, as they are the only cosmographical people, the only writers truly impartial in their accounts of other nations. If they err, it has been from want of information or wrong premises, but never from any national feeling whatsoever. And the same cause, rendering the outward world of less importance to them, rendered each man of more advantage to them, made them a thinking, metaphysical people. In other words, their defect, for in every nation and every individual put your hand upon the defect of a nation and you will find there its excellence, and upon its excellence you will find there its defect, so it is the defect of Germany to be for ever reasoning and thinking, and in other countries, perhaps happier, to have a great aversion to thinking at all.' (Philosophical Lectures, XIII, Coburn, p. 382.)

In publishing *The Convention of Cintra* Wordsworth recognised a certain incongruity: 'I am aware it will create me a world of enemies, and call forth the old yell of Jacobinism.' As he wrote later: 'I should think that I had lived to little purpose if my notions on the subject of government had undergone no modification: my youth must, in that case, have been without enthusiasm, and my manhood endued with small capability of profiting by reflection. If I were addressing those who have dealt so liberally with the words renegade, apostate, etc., I should retort the charge upon them, and say, *you* have been deluded by *places* and *persons*, while I have stuck to *principles*. *I* abandoned France and her rulers when *they* abandoned the struggle for liberty, gave themselves up to tyranny, and endeavoured to enslave the world.' (ibid., III, 269.)

In 1794 he had declared that 'he was not among the admirers of the British Constitution'; by 1808 he was its staunch supporter. There were three great domestic problems which worried him. The first was Catholic Emancipation, to which he was unalterably opposed. 'If the Roman Catholics, upon the plea of their being a majority merely (i.e. in Ireland) (which implies an admission on our part that their profession of faith is in itself as good as ours, as consistent with civil liberty), if they are to have their requests accorded, how can they be refused the further prayer of being constituted, upon the same plea, the Established Church? I confess I am not prepared for this.' (ibid., III, 258, April 1809.) The second problem was that of the freedom of the press. 'A free discussion of public measures through the press I deem the *only* safeguard of liberty: without it I have neither confidence in kings, parliaments, judges, or divines: they have all in their turn betrayed their country. But the press, so potent for good, is scarcely less so for evil.' In a country where all citizens were educated, subversive propaganda could do no harm, but in England this was not the case. 'I am *therefore* for vigorous restrictions.'

The third problem was that of parliamentary reform. 'When I was young (giving myself credit for qualities which I did not possess, and measuring mankind by that standard) I thought it derogatory to human nature to set up property in preference to person as a title for legislative power. That notion has vanished. I now perceive many advantages in our present complex system of representation which formerly eluded my observation; this has tempered my ardour for reform: but if any plan could be contrived for throwing the representation fairly into the hands of the property of the country, and not leaving it so much in the hands of the large proprietors as it now is, it should have my best support.' (ibid., III, 269–70.)

For Wordsworth the Anglican church rapidly became the great symbol of national solidarity and social stability, and accordingly he was embittered at Wellington's surrender in granting Roman Catholic emancipation. He wrote in February 1829: 'I dare scarcely trust my pen to the notice of the question which the Duke of Wellington tells us is about to be *settled*. One thing no rational person will deny, that the experiment is hazardous. Equally obvious is it that the timidity, supineness, and other unworthy qualities of the government for many years past have produced the danger, the extent of which they now affirm imposes a necessity of granting all that the Romanists demand.' (ibid., III, p. 286.) Equally he regretted the fatuous policy of Charles X and his ministers in France, which led to the 1830 revolution: 'Their stupidity, not to say their crimes, has given an impulse to the revolutionary and democratic spirit throughout Europe which is premature, and from which much immediate evil may be apprehended.' (ibid., III, 308.) Four months later, in November, he was dining at Trinity College, Cambridge, and was horrified to hear 'a Head of a House, a clergyman also, gravely declare, that the rotten boroughs should instantly be abolished without compensation to their owners; that slavery should be destroyed with like disregard of the *claims* (for rights he would allow none) of the proprietors, and a multitude of extravagances of the same sort. Therefore say I, Vive la Bagatelle; motley is your only wear.' (ibid., III, 309.)

He watched the passing of the great Reform Bill with the greatest foreboding, because he could not see how in future any government could withstand the tidal demands of an oncoming democracy. 'Whoever governs, it will be by out-bidding for popular favour those who went before them. Sir Robert Peel was obliged to give way in his government to the spirit of Reform, as it is falsely called; these men are going beyond him; and if ever he shall come back,

it will only, I fear, be to carry on the movement, in a shape somewhat less objectionable than it will take from the Whigs. In the
meanwhile the Radicals or Republicans are cunningly content to
have this work done ostensibly by the Whigs, while in fact they
themselves are the Whigs' masters, as the Whigs well know. . . .
What I am most afraid of is, alterations in the constituency, and in
the duration of Parliament, which will bring it more and more
under the dominion of the lower and lowest classes. On this account
I fear the proposed Corporation Reform, as a step towards household suffrage, vote by ballot, etc. As to a union of the Tories and
Whigs in Parliament, I see no prospect of it whatever. To the great
Whig lords may be truly applied the expression in *Macbeth.*

> They have eaten of the insane root
> That takes the reason prisoner. (ibid., III, p. 321.)

Two years later his opinion had not changed: 'since the night
when the Reform Bill was first introduced, I have been convinced
that the institutions of the country cannot be preserved. . . . It is
a mere question of time'. (ibid., III, 327.)

In his later years Wordsworth did not entirely abandon interest
in public affairs, but he placed his hopes mainly upon the spread
of education under the aegis of the Anglican church. He wrote
in 1843:

> I grieve that so little progress has been made in diminishing
> the evils deplored, or promoting the benefits of education which
> the *Wanderer* anticipates. The results of Lord Ashley's labours
> to defer the time when children might legally be allowed to
> work in factories, and his endeavours to still further limit the
> hours of permitted labour, have fallen far short of his own
> humane wishes, and of those of every benevolent and right-
> minded man who was carefully attended to this subject, and in
> the present session of Parliament Sir James Graham's attempt
> to establish a course of religious education among the
> children employed in factories has been abandoned, in con-

sequence of what might easily have been foreseen, the vehement and turbulent opposition of the Dissenters. . . . Such is my own confidence, a confidence I share with many others of my most valued friends, in the superior advantages, both religious and social, which attend a course of instruction presided over and guided by the clergy of the Church of England, that I have no doubt that if but once its members, lay and clerical, were duly sensible of those benefits, their Church would daily gain ground, and rapidly, upon every shape and fashion of Dissent; and in that case, a great majority in Parliament being sensible of these benefits, the ministers of the country might be emboldened, were it necessary, to apply funds of the State to the support of education on church principles.

(Prose Works, III, 209.)

Of all the social institutions the one for which Wordsworth cared most deeply was the family, and this is well illustrated by a story which late in life he told the bishop of Lincoln: 'As I was riding Dora's pony from Rydal to Cambridge, I got off, as I occasionally did, to walk. I fell in with a sweet-looking peasant girl of nine or ten years old. She had been to carry her father's dinner, who was working in the fields. . . . I wish I had asked her whether she could read, and whether she went to school. But I could not help being struck with the happy arrangement which Nature has made for the education of the heart, an arrangement which it seems the object of the present age to counteract instead of to cherish and confirm. I imagined the happy delight of the father in seeing his child at a distance, and watching her as she approached to perform her errand of love, I imagined the joy of the mother in seeing her return. I am strongly of the opinion that this is the discipline which is more calculated by a thousand degrees to make a virtuous and happy nation than the all-engrossing, estranging, eleemosynary institutions for education, which perhaps communicate more *knowledge*. In these institutions what the pupils gain in *knowledge* they often lose in *wisdom*. This is a distinction which must never be lost sight of.' (ibid., III, p. 466.) It is anecdotes such as this which have led critics so often to deride 'daddy' Wordsworth, but to countless other readers they have brought balm and comfort.

NOTES

[1] On the occasion of the birth of his son, beginning 'Oft o'er my brain', and containing the lines—

And some have said
We lived, ere yet this robe of flesh we wore

Wordsworth himself was not entirely happy with the idea, and wrote later: 'It is far too shadowy a notion to be recommended to faith as more than an element in our instincts of immortality.' (*Prose Works*, III, p. 195.)

[2] When he was nearing sixty Wordsworth wrote that his total earnings from literature did not amount to 'seven score pounds'. (*Prose Works*, III, 291.)

[3] 'There are', he wrote, 'tender and subtle ties by which these principles, that love to soar in the pure region, are connected with the ground-nest in which they were fostered and from which they take their flight.' It is interesting to note that Wordsworth used the same idea and metaphor nearly twenty years later in *To A Skylark*:

Leave to the nightingale her shady wood;
A privacy of glorious light is thine;
Whence thou dost pour upon the world a flood
Of harmony, with instinct more divine;
Type of the wise whose soar, but never roam;
True to the kindred points of Heaven and Home

10 : Coleridge and the Philosophy of Conservatism

At the outbreak of the French Revolution Coleridge was only seventeen. He celebrated the fall of the Bastille with youthful lines:

> I see, I see! glad Liberty succeed
> With every patriot virtue in her train!
> And mark yon peasant's raptured eyes;
> Secure he views the harvests rise;
> No fetter vile the mind shall know,
> And Eloquence shall fearless glow.
> Yes! Liberty the soul of life shall reign,
> Shall throb in every pulse, shall flow thro' every vein.
> *(The Destruction of the Bastille*, 1789.)

For a time, he wrote later, he was 'a sharer in the general vortex, though my little world described the path of its revolution in an orbit of its own'. Like Wordsworth, he was not so much caught up in the events in France, as forced by the new ideas to seek for himself a philosophy which would reconcile the conflicting ideas of his turbulent world. His short-lived enthusiasm for Pantisocracy had little to do with France, and much to do with finding a new moral basis for society in which, as he said, men would become virtuous because there would be no motives for evil. (*Letters*, 21 Oct. 1794. White, *Political Thought of Coleridge*, p. 36.) He was never a democrat but he *was* deeply moved by social injustice. His conscience was touched—as in July 1794, when he wrote to Southey of 'a little girl with a half-famished sickly baby in her arms (putting) her head in at the window of an inn—"Pray give me a bit of bread and meat!" from a party dining on lamb, green peas and salad'. He did not believe that such things could be removed by political nostrums, nor by abusing the government, nor by following what he called 'French *philosophy*', but by finding a new moral basis for society. 'Talk not politics, Preach the Gospel!' (*Letters*, 6 July 1794. White, p. 38.)

What particularly concerned him was the gulf which had emerged between the upper and lower classes, and the brutalised life to which the latter were condemned. 'Can we wonder that men should want humanity, who want all the circumstances of life that humanize? Can we wonder that with the ignorance of brutes they should unite their ferocity' (*Essays*, I, 14–15, White, p. 40). Society, he wrote, did not resemble a chain that ascended in a continuity of links. 'Alas! between the parlour and the kitchen, the tap and the coffee-room, there is a gulph that may not be passed.' How could revolution be prevented in England, how could the poor be humanised, if it was not by education and religion? 'For the incitements of this world are weak in proportion as we are wretched. . . . They, too, who live from hand-to-mouth, will most frequently become improvident. Possessing no *stock* of happiness they eagerly seize the gratification of the moment. . . . Nor is the desolate state of their families a restraining motive, unsoftened as they are by education, and benumbed into selfishness by the torpedo touch of extreme want. Domestic affections depend on association. We love an object if, as often as we see or recollect it, an agreeable sensation arises in our minds. But alas! how should *he* glow with the charities of father and husband who, gaining scarcely more than his own necessities demand, must have been accustomed to regard his wife and children not as the soothers of finished labour but as rivals for the insufficient meal! (ibid., pp. 23–4, 15–16, White, pp. 42–3.)

For a moment Coleridge was influenced by Godwin:

> Nor will I not thy holy guidance bless,
> And hymn thee, Godwin! with an ardent lay;
> For that thy voice, in Passion's stormy day,
> When wild I roam'd the bleak Heath of Distress,

o

> Bade the bright form of Justice meet my way—
> And told me that her name was Happiness.
>
> (*To William Godwin*, January 1795.)

But Coleridge was too deeply influenced by religion to be carried away for long by Godwin's rationalism. On the last day of the year 1796, as he tells us, 'I retired to a cottage in Somersetshire, at the foot of the Quantocks, and devoted my thoughts and studies to the foundations of religion and morals.' (*Biographia Literaria*, p. 103.) He was deeply influenced by the Quaker attitude to religion. Moreover, the ensuing friendship with Wordsworth, which was of such profound consequence to the latter, was also a stabilising influence upon Coleridge. Together they found a deeper understanding of nature:

> Henceforth I shall know
> That Nature ne'er deserts the wise and pure:
> No plot so narrow, be but Nature there,
> No waste so vacant, but may well employ
> Each faculty of sense, and keep the heart
> Awake to Love and Beauty!
>
> (*This Lime-tree Bower my Prison*, June 1797.)

To Coleridge, as to Wordsworth, nature was a complex idea, representing both 'the wisdom and spirit of the Universe', and the beauty of the landscape of the England then under threat from subversion and foreign invasion. Hence in *Fears in Solitude* (April 1798), Coleridge

> found
> Religious meanings in the forms of Nature!
> And so, his senses gradually wrapt
> In a half sleep, he dreams of better worlds,
> And dreaming hears thee still, O singing lark.

All this contrasted painfully with the sense of guilt arising from the political situation:

> We have offended, Oh! my countrymen!

We have offended very grievously,
And been most tyrannous . . .
. . . Like a cloud that travels on,
Steamed up from Cairo's swamps of pestilence,
Even so, my countrymen! have we gone forth
And borne to distant tribes slavery and gangs.

.   .   .   .   .   .

Meanwhile at home,
All individual dignity and power
Engulf'd in Courts, Committees, Institutions,
Associations and Societies,
A vain, speech-mouthing, speech-reporting Guild,
One Benefit-Club for mutual flattery,
We have drunk up, demure as at a grace,
Pollutions from the brimming cup of wealth;
Contemptuous of all honourable rule.
Yet bartering freedom and the poor man's life
For gold, as at a market.

Religion had become an empty ritual:

the very name of God
Sounds like a juggler's charm;

and the nation was plunged into a merciless war which Coleridge
could not as yet condone.

We send our mandates for the certain death
Of thousands and ten thousands! Boys and girls,
And women, that would groan to see a child
Pull off an insect's leg, all read of war
The best amusement for our morning meal!

He wrote, not in anger, but in sadness,

We have been too long
Dupes of a deep delusion!

and in this anguish Coleridge found a deeper love of his country:

O native Britain! O my Mother Isle!
How shouldst thou prove aught else but dear and holy
To me, who from thy lakes and mountain-hills,
Thy clouds, thy quiet dales, thy rocks and seas,
Have drunk in all my intellectual life,
All sweet sensations, all ennobling thoughts,
All adoration of the God in nature,
All lovely and all honourable things,
Whatever makes this mortal spirit feel
The joy and greatness of its future being?
There lives nor form nor feeling in my soul
Unborrowed from my country! O divine
And beauteous island! thou hast been my sole
And most magnificent temple, in the which
I walk with awe, and sing my stately songs,
Loving the God that made me!

Generous financial aid from Josiah Wedgwood enabled Coleridge to spend some months in Germany (1798–9) and thus to come under the influence of German transcendental philosophy. This in turn led him to a close study of mediaeval scholasticism and Neo-Platonism. At one point, he wrote that he was reading Duns Scotus in the Chapter Library at Durham. 'I am burning Locke, Hume and Hobbes under his nose. They stink worse than feather or assafoetida. . . . I am confident that I can prove that the reputation of these three men has been wholly unmerited.' (*Letters*, 22 July 1801. White, p. 50.)

Coleridge reacted directly and passionately against eighteenth-century empirical thought. To him it was the story of 'the long and ominous eclipse of philosophy; the usurpation of that venerable name by physical and psychological empiricism'. (*2nd Lay Sermon*, p. 190. White, p. 98.) The development of empirical science, he admitted, had been accompanied by enormous achievements. 'The sublime discoveries of Newton, and, together with these, his not less fruitful than wonderful application, of the higher mathesis to the movements of the celestial bodies, and to the laws of light, gave almost a religious sanction to the corpuscular system and mechanical theory. .... In short, from the time of Kepler to that of Newton, and from Newton to Hartley, not only all things in external nature, but the subtlest mysteries of life and organisation, and even of the intellect and moral being, were conjured within the magic circle of mathematical formulae. ... Henceforward the new path, thus brilliantly opened, became the common road to all departments of knowledge: and, to this moment, it has been pursued with an eagerness and almost epidemic enthusiasm which, scarcely less than its political revolutions, characterise the spirit of the age.' (*Theory of Life*, ed. Watson, 1848, p. 31, Coburn: *Inquiring Spirit*, Routledge, 1951, pp. 256–7.) The result, he argued, had been that science had tended to dominate all forms of thought, life had been reduced to material or mathematical formulae, and man's mind to the empirical level of Locke's psychology. The result was a false view of man as of an individual unrelated to the past or the future, living in isolation and without a spiritual existence.

To correct this error, Coleridge urged a return to that great Neo-Platonic tradition which was the main artery of European thought until the seventeenth century. (On that tradition see *Reason and Nature in Eighteenth Century Thought*, Ch. II.) 'I refer every man of reflection to the contrast between the present times and those shortly after the restoration of ancient literature.' (He meant the Renaissance.) 'In the latter we find the greatest men of the age, statesmen, warriors, monarchs, architects, in the closest intercourse with philosophy. I need only mention the names of Lorenzo the Magnificent, Picus Mirandola, Ficinus and Politian ... Dante, Petrarch, Spenser, Philip and Algernon Sidney, Milton and Barrow were Platonists. But all men of genius with whom it has been my fortune to converse, either profess to know nothing of the present systems or to despise them.'

In his course of public lectures on philosophy, given at the Crown and Anchor Tavern in the Strand (1818–19) Coleridge returned to the thought of Plato. 'Plato! I really feel, unaffectedly, an awe when I mention his name—when I consider what associations are connected with it.' The essence of Plato's philosophy, he declared, was that 'he taught the idea, namely the possibility, and the duty of all who would arrive at the greatest perfection of the human mind, of striving to contemplate things not in the phenomenon, not in their accidents or in their superficies, but in their essential powers, first as they exist in relation to other powers co-existing with them, but lastly and chiefly as they exist in the Supreme Mind, independent of all material division, distinct and yet indivisible.' (*Philosophical Lectures*, Lecture IV, ed. Coburn, p. 166.) In this lay the origin of Plato's *Idea*, and to Coleridge it was the beginning of philosophic thought. Beneath the transitory and accidental appearances of all things there lay an inner reality which was an essential part of the single whole which we call the universe. It followed that 'there is a moral government in the world—that things neither happen by chance nor yet by any blind agency of necessity'. (Lecture V, Coburn, p. 170.) It followed also that there was a Supreme Being, 'so that what by the efforts of reason we were to acquire painfully, arriving at truth by possession and by the power and force of reasoning, this was to appear in a blessed vision at once—that is the great object. Beautiful passages there are in Plotinus—exquisite morality-fine observations, so that you would believe him to be a Christian'. (Lecture VII, Coburn, p. 241.) Knowledge might be arrived at by two separate ways, one through the senses, and the other by a kind of revelation 'which neither our senses, nor our understanding, nor our reason, could give us the least conception of', and it was with the latter that Coleridge and the Romantics were chiefly concerned.

This led Coleridge to the two conclusions which were the justification for his course of lectures. The first was that 'the human mind never can in a civilized state be without some philosophy or other, and it is an utter mistake to suppose its influence is confined to particular classes'; and the second, 'that without a congenial philosophy there can be no general religion, that a philosophy among the higher classes is an essential condition to the true state of religion among all classes, and that religion is the great centre of gravity in all countries and in all ages, and according as it is good or bad, whether religion or irreligion, so all the other powers of the state necessarily accommodate themselves to it.' (Lecture VII, Coburn, pp. 245–6.)

Coleridge traced the progress of the great Neo-Platonist tradition until the scientific revolution of the seventeenth century, and he paid tribute to the great achievements of empirical science. One consequence however had been a triumph of the philosophy of materialism. Yet this philosophy had entirely failed to fit mind and the process of cognition into its system, and in this lay its fundamental weakness. It was content to take the surface of things as the only reality, whereas the truth was that reality always lay beneath the surface. It tried to explain life in terms of material substance, whereas the material substance was only the outward and visible expression of an inner life or spirit. Plato had seen this, and philosophy therefore needed to return to Plato.

The logical result of scientific materialism, he feared, would be the exclusion of religion. 'For a man who affirms boldly that what the senses have not given to his mind, that he will regard as nothing but words ... such a man cannot pretend to believe in God.' What was needed was that the human heart should rescue the human head. For materialism 'destroys the possibility of free agency, it destroys the great distinction between the mere human and the mere animals of nature, namely the powers of originating an act. All things are brought, even the powers of life are brought, into a common link of causes and effects that we observe in a machine, and all the powers of thought into those of life, being all reasoned away into modes of sensation, and the will itself into nothing but a current, a fancy determined by the accidental copulations of certain internal stimuli. With such a being, to talk of a difference between good and evil would be to blame a stone for being round or angular. The thought itself is repulsive. No, the man forfeits that high principle of nature, his free agency, which though it reveals itself principally in his moral conduct, yet is still at work in all departments of his being. It is by his bold denial of this, by an inward assertion, "I am not the creature of nature merely, nor a subject of nature, but I detach myself from her. I oppose myself as man to nature, and my destination is to conquer and subdue her, to be lord of light and fire and the elements; and what my mind can comprehend that I will make my eye to see. ... And why? Because I am a free being. I can esteem, I can revere myself, and as such a being I dare look forward to permanence . . . for I am capable of the highest distinction, that of being the object of the approbation of the God of the Universe, which no mechanism can be. Nay, further, I am the cause of the creation of the world.' (Lecture XII, Coburn, pp. 362–3.)

This passage contains the central idea of Coleridge's philosophy, by which he sought to reinstate religion as the focal point of man's existence, and to replace scientific materialism by Neo-Platonism. It relates also to Coleridge's philosophy of history, which he set out so clearly in *The Statesman's Manual* (1816).[1] To him the statesman's manual was the Bible, and his argument may be summarised as follows. It was easy to suppose, since contemporary events are always accompanied by so many circumstances which appear to be unique, that there is no point in studying the past as a likely pointer to the interpretation of the present. 'And no wonder', declared Coleridge, 'if we read history for the facts instead of reading it for the sake of the general principles, which are to the facts as the root and sap of a tree to its leaves: and no wonder, if history so read should find a dangerous rival in novels, nay, if the latter should be preferred to the former on the score even of probability'. But this was to misunderstand the meaning of history. Just as the physical universe was governed by physical laws, so human affairs were governed by moral laws, and history was the stage upon which these moral laws were worked out. In a moral sense therefore history was recurrent, and it was meaningful to regard Julius Caesar or Oliver Cromwell as Jacobins, or to see common factors in the fall of the Roman Republic in the first century B.C. and the progress of the French Revolution. It seemed also to Coleridge that all the great developments of history reflected the philosophy current at the time. 'I have known men, who with significants nods and the pitying contempt of smiles, have denied all influence to the corruptions of moral and political philosophy, and with much solemnity have proceeded to solve the riddle of the French Revolution by anecdotes! Yet it would not be difficult, by an unbroken chain of historic facts, to demonstrate that the most important changes in the commercial relations of the world had their origin in the closets or lonely walks of uninterested theorists—

that the mighty epochs of commerce that have changed the face of empires, nay, the most important of those discoveries and improvements in the mechanic arts, which have numerically increased our population . . . have had their origin not in the cabinets of statesmen, or in the practical insight of men of business, but in the closets of uninterested theorists, in the visions of recluse genius. To the immense majority of men, even in civilised countries, speculative philosophy has ever been, and must ever remain, a *terra incognita*. Yet it is not the less true, that all the epoch-forming revolutions of the Christian world, the revolutions of religion and with them the civil, social, and domestic habits of the nations concerned, have coincided with the rise and fall of metaphysical systems.' It will be noted that Coleridge claims here a *coincidence*, and not a direct causation between historical developments and philosophical systems, but as a Neo-Platonist he did not doubt that human affairs were governed by moral principles, and therefore that, if historical developments were the leaves of the tree, moral principles were the root and the sap. He was convinced, he wrote, 'that the fearful blunders of the late dread revolution, and all the calamitous mistakes of its opponents . . . every failure with all its gloomy results, may be unanswerably deduced from the neglect of some maxim or other that had been established by clear reasoning and plain facts in the writings of Thucydides, Tacitus, Machiavel, Bacon, or Harrington'. Above all, they could have been deduced from the Bible. The Jacobinism which Coleridge condemned in the French Revolution, he regarded as springing directly from a false philosophy of natural rights unrelated to any correlative of duty.

Coleridge was deeply read in the seventeenth-century theologians, and his view of man was very similar to that of Milton in *Paradise Lost*. Man was a spiritual being, separate from nature. He was its lord, capable of utilising its forces, but for ever distinct from it because he was a moral being, with powers of free choice. When Coleridge used the word nature it was in one of two senses; he might be referring to 'the aggregate of phenomena' in the universe, or to the active spirit which blew through the universe, rather as a wind which made music on the Aeolian harp:

> And what if all of animated nature
> Be but the organic Harps diversely framed
> That tremble into thought, as o'er them sweeps
> Plastic and vast, one intellectual Breeze
> At once the Soul of each and God of all.
>
> (*The Aeloian Harp*, 1.44.)

Why had this idea, which was so much a part of the Neo-Platonic and Scholastic tradition, been so completely discarded in the late seventeenth century? Coleridge argued that it was partly the consequence of the desire to shake off the despotism of the Stuarts, and with it the whole legacy of the middle ages. Locke's name was associated with the growth of commerce and political freedom. Equally important, however, he thought, was the influence of Descartes. 'Descartes was the first man who made nature utterly lifeless and godless, considered it as the subject of merely mechanical laws.' (Lecture XIII, Coburn, p. 376.) It was true that Descartes' physics were overthrown by Newton, and his metaphysics by Locke, and Locke's philosophy was for the most part given a materialist interpretation in the eighteenth century. When he was answered, the answer came from Germany. 'Mr. Locke's followers had repeated "there is nothing in the mind which was not before the senses". Leibnitz added, "except the mind itself".' (Lecture XIII, Coburn, p. 383.) Above all, the answer came from Kant. He determined the nature of religious truth and its connexion with the understanding and made it felt to the full that the reason itself, considered as merely intellectual, was but a subordinate part of our nature; that there was a higher part, the will and the conscience; and that if the intellect of man was the cherub that flew with wings, it flew after the flaming seraph and but followed in its track. . . . In short, he determined the true meaning of philosophy.' (Coburn, p. 390.)

It was under the influence of the momentous events of the French Wars, quite as much as of German philosophy, that Coleridge turned away from his early views on liberty. Even before his journey to Germany, he wrote: 'I have snapped my squeaking baby-trumpet of sedition, and the fragments lie scattered in the lumber-room of penitence. I wish to be a good man and a Christian, but I am no Whig, no Reformist, no Republican.' (*Letters*, April 1798, White, p. 51.)

> O Liberty! with profitless endeavour
> Have I pursued thee, many a weary hour;
> But thou nor swell'st the victor's strain, nor ever
> Didst breathe thy soul in forms of human power.
> *(France: An Ode*, 1.89.)

What particularly struck him was the futility of changing forms of government. He defined a Jacobin as one who believed that no form of government could be rightful or good which did not spring from universal suffrage. But the form of government told one nothing about the use to which political power would be put, and Coleridge concluded that 'for the present race of men Governments must be founded on property; that government is good in which property is secure and circulates; that government the best, which, in the exactest ratio, makes each man's power proportionate to his property'. (*Morning Post*, 1799, White, 9.56.) On the other hand, 'Jacobinism betrays its mixed parentage and nature by applying to the brute passions and physical force of the multitude (that is, to man as a mere animal) in order to build up government and the frame of society on natural rights instead of social privileges, on the universals of abstract reason instead of positive institutions, the lights of specific experience and the modifications of existing circumstances. Right, in its proper sense, is the creature of law and statute, and only in the technical language of the courts has it any substantial and independent sense. In morals, right is a word without meaning except as a correlative of duty.' (*1st Lay Sermon*, White, p. 90.)

Here then Coleridge adopts the full Burkeian philosophy of conservatism, the rejection of natural rights in favour of privileges acquired within the institutions of a state, and emphasis upon social institutions which carried with them duties as well as rights. Rights acquired meaning only within the framework of institutions, and thus were a product of history, and differed from state to state.

'The reading of *histories* . . . may dispose a man to satire; but the science of HISTORY,—history studied in the light of philosophy, as the great drama of an ever-unfolding Providence,—has a very different effect. It infuses hope and reverential thoughts of man and his destination.' (*Church and State*, p. 34.) For history showed that 'by a happy organisation of a well-governed society, the contradictory interests of ten millions of individuals may neutralise each other, and be reconciled in the unity of the national interest.' (*1st Lay Sermon*, White, p. 95.) The political creed of Tom Paine and the Jacobins was hateful to Coleridge because it seemed a revolt from both religion and the lessons of history.

Hence the bitterness which so often came into the writings of his last years, when he surveyed the consequence of 'French' philosophy: 'State of nature, or the Ourang Outang theology of the origin of the human race, substituted for the Book of Genesis, Ch. I–X. Rights of nature for the duties and privileges of citizens. Idea-less facts, misnamed proofs from history, grounds of experience, etc., substituted for principles and the insight derived from them. State-policy a Cyclops with one eye, and that in the back of the head! Our measures of policy either a series of anachronisms or a truckling to events, substituted for the science that should command them; for all true insight is foresight. . . . Meantime, the true historical feeling, the immortal life of an historical Nation, generation linked to generation by faith, freedom, heraldry, and ancestral fame, languishing and giving place to the superstitions of wealth and newspaper reputation. . . . Gin consumed by paupers to the value of about eighteen millions yearly. Government by journeymen clubs; by reviews, magazines, and above all by newspapers. Lastly crimes quadrupled for the whole country, and in some counties decupled.' (*Church and State*, p. 80.)

Coleridge's solution for the problems of his age was to turn away from the materialist philosophy of the eighteenth century and back to the traditional stream of Neo-Platonism and the Christian religion. 'My system, if I may venture to give it so fine a name, is the only attempt I know ever made to reduce all knowledges into harmony. . . . I wish, in short, to connect by a moral *copula* natural history with political history; or, in other words, to make history scientific and science historical—to take from history its accidentality and from science its fatalism.' (*1st Lay Sermon*, White, p. 104.) The first step was to dethrone the eighteenth-century view of reason, for 'the laws of reason are unable to satisfy the first conditions of human society'. Under its influence society had fragmented into individualism, and society had become meaningless, while the populace had become 'a blind but hundred-armed giant of fearful power, to undermine the foundations of the social edifice, and finally perchance to pull down the all-sheltering roof on its own head, the victim of its own madness!' (*The Courier*, 1814, White, p. 119.) There was, he wrote, 'a natural affinity between despotism and modern philosophy, notwithstanding the proud pretensions of the latter as the emancipator of the human race'. (idem., White, p. 127.)

He rejected Benthamite utilitarianism, because it was plati-tudinous to say that men required the greatest possible happiness for the greatest possible number. 'But *what* happiness? That is the question. . . . *Your* mode of happiness would make *me* miserable.' (*Table Talk*, 20 Aug. 1831.) The root of Coleridge's objection lay in the Benthamite equation that what was pleasurable was good. Coleridge on the other hand held to the Kantian view of the good as an emanation of the categorical imperative.

He rejected also Rousseau's theory of the Social Contract, as being 'a pure fiction, an idle fancy, incapable of historic proof as a fact, and senseless as a theory'. But, he argued, if instead of an original social contract, one thought of a social contract daily renewed, thus expressing the reciprocal duties between subjects and rulers, the idea was a valuable one. (*Church and State*, p. 17.) What Coleridge most feared was that the achievement of universal suffrage would be a preliminary to a general assault upon property. To obviate this danger, he sought a return to a Platonic state in which the different classes lived together in harmony. In a Platonic state, he wrote, 'the integral parts, classes or orders, were so balanced or interdependent as to constitute, more or less, an organic whole'. (*Table Talk*, 14 Aug. 1833.) Coleridge accepted the analogy of the state with an organism. 'Unlike a million of tigers, a million of men is very different from one man. Each man in a numerous society is not only co-existent with, but virtually organised into, the multitude of which he is an integral part.' (idem., White, p. 141.)

This was why he regarded Church and State as essentially complementary. The State thought in terms of classes, or interests, the Church thought in terms of individual souls. 'A Church is, therefore, in idea, the only pure democracy. The Church, so considered, and the State exclusively of the Church, constitute together the idea of a State in its largest sense.' (*Table Talk*, 19 Sept. 1830.) He did not have a high opinion of rulers. 'History has taught me', he wrote, 'that rulers are much the same in all ages, and under all forms of government; that they are as bad as they dare to be.' (*Letters*, April 1798, White, p. 52.) Power therefore was to be feared, unless it was restrained by religion, custom or philosophy. But he was no defender of a *laissez-faire* society; he sought in fact to divert attention from the subject of political reform to what he thought was more important, to social relationships.

He well understood what he called 'the spirit of commerce' which governed his times, but what troubled him was the social misery which appeared to accompany industrial change. He noted the periodic slumps which occurred about every twelve years, and the poverty and suffering which accompanied them. The economists argued that they were inevitable, and must be endured; that 'things would find their own level'. Coleridge replied: 'Go, ask the overseer, and question the parish doctor, whether the workman's health and temperance with the staid and respectful manners best taught by the inward dignity of conscious self-support, have found their level again? Alas! I have more than once seen a group of children in Dorsetshire, during the heat of the dog-days, each with its little shoulders up to its ears, and its chest pinched inward, the very habit and fistures, as it were, that had been impressed on their frames by the former ill-fed, ill-clothed and unfuelled winters.' (*2nd Lay Sermon*, White, p. 189.) He noted the rural depopulation of Scotland, and the words of the village schoolmaster: "O Sir, it kills a man's love for his country, the hardships of life coming by change and with injustice!' Again the economist replied that the growth of Manchester more than compensated for the depopulation of Scotland. Coleridge replied: 'I have passed through many a manufacturing town since then, and have watched many a group of old and young, male and female, going to, or returning from, many a factory, but I could never yet persuade myself to be of his opinion. *Men, I still think, ought to be weighed, not counted.*' (ibid.) Coleridge was not an enemy to commerce, 'to which I attribute the largest proportion of our actual freedom, and at least as large a share of our virtues as of our vices'; but he did think that there had been 'an overbalance of the commercial spirit'. 'Under this head I include the general neglect of all the maturer studies; the long and ominous eclipse of philosophy; the usurpation of that venerable name by physical and psychological empiricism, and the non-existence of a learned and philosophic public.' Equally important was the decline of religion into latitudinarianism. 'Religion and politics, they tell us, require but the application of common sense, which every man possesses, to a subject in which every man is concerned.' If the tendency continued, the result must 'inevitably lead us under the specious names of utility, practical knowledge and so forth, to look at all things through the *medium* of the market and to estimate the worth of all pursuits and attainments by their marketable value. In this does the spirit of trade consist.' (idem., White, p. 197.) The remedy lay in a new attitude to social relationships. 'Our manufacturers must consent to regulations; our gentry must concern themselves in the education as well as in the instruction of their natural clients and dependents, must regard their estates as secured indeed from all human interference by every principle of law and policy; but yet as offices of trust, with duties to be performed in the sight of God and their country.' (idem., White, p. 209.)

In 1817, during the period of distress following the end of the Napoleonic Wars, Coleridge addressed a famous letter to Lord Liverpool, which the Prime Minister had some difficulty in comprehending. Beginning with the customary attack upon empirical philosophy, Coleridge urged that this was one of the main causes of the contemporary decline in religion. 'What indeed but the wages of death can be expected from a doctrine which degrades the Deity into a blank hypothesis, and that the hypothesis of a clockwork-maker . . .: a godless nature, and a natureless, abstract God . . . the Sunday name of gravitation. He welcomed the achievements of science, 'but let it not be forgotten that this is a scion, the one healthy and prosperous gift from the Platonic tree'. Meanwhile 'a few brilliant inventions have been dearly purchased at the loss of all communion with life and the spirit of nature'. For the world had come to be regarded as a mass of independent atoms which met together and formed a society and a government based on individual rights. What had been lost was the sense of growth, and the inter-dependence of duties. 'It is high time, My Lord, that the subjects of Christian Governments should be taught that neither historically or morally, in fact or by right, have men made the State; but that the State, and that alone, makes them men; . . . that states and kingdoms grow, and are not made: and that in all political revolutions, whether for the weal or chastisement of a nation, the people are but the sprigs and boughs in a forest, tossed against each other, or moved all in the same direction, by an agency in which their own will has the least share. As long as the principles of our gentry and clergy are grounded in a false philosophy . . . all the Sunday and national schools in the world will not preclude schism and Jacobinism in the middle and lower classes.' (idem., White, pp. 209–16.)

Of all the social evils of his time, none moved Coleridge more deeply than the consequences of the factory system. 'Those institutions of society which should condemn me to the necessity of twelve hours' daily toil, would make my soul a slave, and sink the rational being in the mere animal. It is a mockery of our fellow creatures' wrongs to call them equal in rights, when by the bitter compulsion of their wants we make them inferior to us in all that can soften the heart, or dignify the understanding. Let us not say that this is the work of time—that it is impracticable at present, unless we each in our individual capacities do strenuously and perseveringly endeavour to diffuse among our domestics those comforts and that illumination which far beyond all political ordinances are the true equalizers of men.' (*Essays on His Own Times*, I, 16–17, Coburn, p. 320.) *Comforts* and *illumination* (that is, education) were to Coleridge far more important than the vote, and their achievement would be the best antidote to Jacobin agitation.

It has been said that government though not the best preceptor of virtue procures us security from the attack of the lower orders.—Alas! why should the lower orders attack us, but because they are brutalized by ignorance and rendered desperate by want? And does government remove this ignorance by education? And does not government increase their want by taxes?—Taxes rendered necessary by those national assassinations called wars, and by that worst corruption and perjury, which a reverend moralist has justified under the soft title of 'secret influence'! The poor infant born in an English or Irish hovel breathes indeed the air and partakes of the light of Heaven; but of its other bounties he is disinherited. The powers of intellect are given him in vain: to make him work like a brute beast he is kept as ignorant as a brute beast. It is not possible that this despised and oppressed man should behold the rich and idle without malignant envy. (ibid., pp. 49–50, Coburn, p. 349.)

Accordingly, in 1818, Coleridge threw himself into the campaign for Sir Robert Peel's Factory Bill. Peel had been moved by the petition of the Lancashire cotton spinners to shorten the hours of work for children, which were then from 5.30 a.m. to 8.30 p.m., and in support of his Bill Coleridge wrote one of the most powerful pamphlets in English social history. The enemies of the Bill proclaimed the need to maintain 'free labour'. Coleridge replied: '*Free* Labour!—in what sense, not utterly sophistical, can the labour of children, extorted from the want of their parents, "their poverty, but not their will, consenting", be called *free*? A numerous body of these very parents are among the petitioners for the measure though at the foreseen diminution of their profits. In what sense then can this be called *free* Labour? . . . It is our duty to declare aloud, that if the labour were indeed free, the employer would purchase, and the labourer sell, what the former has no right to buy, and the latter no right to dispose of: namely the labourer's

P

health, life and well-being. These belong not to himself alone, but to his friends, to his parents, to his King, to his Country, and to God.' And what of the argument that such things could safely be left to the good sense and humanity of the masters themselves? 'This is, doubtless, highly flattering to the present age. ... It is, however sufficient for us to have proved that it remains a mere assertion, and that up to this present hour the asserted increase of human feeling and enlightened self-interest has produced no such effects as are here so confidently promised have exerted no adequate counteraction to the keen stimulants of immediate profit, and the benumbing influences of custom and example.' (*Remarks on Sir Robert Peel's Bill*, 1818. Coburn, pp. 351–359.) Finally Coleridge relied upon the evidence of those best qualified to judge the consequences of factory conditions. 'With especial confidence we refer to the Petition from more than seventeen-hundred of the principal inhabitants of the towns and neighbourhood of Manchester and Salford, among whom are found seven magistrates, nine physicians, twenty-one surgeons, and twenty clergymen, seventeen of whom are of the Established Church. ... They attest the "*fatally injurious consequences* of the present system".' (*The Grounds of Sir Robert Peel's Bill Vindicated*, Coburn, p. 361.) In spite of his arguments, however, the Bill ran into heavy weather, and was emasculated before it reached the statute book. Coleridge was disgusted with what he called 'the Tories, the so called *Conservative* Party', and their readiness to accept *laissez-faire* principles.

What he resented was the fact that both parties appeared to have accepted the *laissez-faire* principles of Malthus. Society had thus been fragmented into atoms with merely a cash relationship between the atoms. 'It is not uncommon', he wrote, 'for a hundred thousand *operatives* (mark this word, for words *in this sense* are things) to be out of employment at once in the cotton districts, and, thrown upon parochial relief, are dependent upon hard-hearted taskmasters for food. The Malthusian doctrine would indeed afford a certain means of relief if this were not a two-fold question. If, when you say to a man, "You have no claim upon me; you have your allotted part to perform in the world, so have I. In a state of nature, indeed, had I food, I should offer you a share from sympathy, from humanity: but in this advanced and artificial state of society, I cannot afford you relief; *you must starve.* You came into the world when it could not sustain you". What would be this man's answer? He would say, "You disclaim all connection with me; I have no claims upon you? *I can then have no duties towards you,* and this pistol shall put me in possession of your wealth. You may leave a law behind you which shall hang me, but what man who saw assured starvation before him, ever feared hanging?".' (*Table Talk*, White, p. 222.) He repeatedly urged that rights could not exist without corresponding duties, and that this applied as much to the rich as to the poor. Indeed, he resented the common practice of referring to *the Poor,* as if they were a permanent class, 'just as in Jamaica I might address myself to *the Negroes.* Now if this have a sound foundation in the fact, it assuredly marks a most deplorable State of Society. The Ideal of a Government is that which under the existing circumstances most effectually affords Security to the Possessors, Facility to the Acquirers, and *Hope* to all.' (Ms. Coburn, p. 366.) The surest way, he was certain, of inducing revolution was to cement the classes into Haves and Have-nots.

Coleridge did not suppose that the unreformed parliamentary system was free from serious criticism. Political power was in too few hands, there was widespread corruption, and taxes fell unjustly upon the poor. 'The actual possessors of power are few, and independent of the people: which is despotism. And the manners of the great are depraved, the sources of corruption incalculable, and consequently the temptations to private and public wickedness numerous and mighty: all which unite in precluding the probability of its proving a *virtuous* Despotism.' (*Essays on His Own Times,* I, 91, Coburn, p. 322.) This was written in 1795, and Coleridge became a good deal more cautious in subsequent years, yet as late as 1830 he could still write: 'Is the House of Commons to be reconstructed on the principle of a representation of interests, or of a delegation of men? If on the former, we may, perhaps, see our way; if on the latter, you can never, in reason, stop short of universal suffrage; and in that case, I am sure that women have as good a right to vote as men.' (*Table Talk*, 21 Nov. 1830.) This in 1830 was to reduce the argument to an absurdity. So long as he feared a really radical Bill, he was opposed to the idea of reform, the effect of which would be, he wrote, 'to destroy our nationality, which consists, in a principal degree, in our representative government, and to convert it into a degrading delegation of the populace. There is no unity for a people but in a representation of national interests.' (*Table Talk*, 25 June 1831.) But when the Whig Reform Bill was about to become law he somewhat shifted the grounds of his opposition. 'The mere extension of the franchise is not the evil; I should be glad to see it greatly extended;—there is no harm in that *per se*; the mischief is that the franchise is nominally extended, but to such classes, and in such a manner, that a practical disfranchisement of all above, and discontenting of all below, a favoured class are the unavoidable results.' (*Table Talk*, 3 March 1832.) In short, the Reform Act would greatly increase the danger of class conflicts, and some interests would now be worse represented than before.

The fullest statement of Coleridge's political theory was set out in his *On the Constitution of the Church and State*, published in 1830 under the impact of Catholic Emancipation (1829) and the prospect of parliamentary reform. In every civilised state, he affirmed, there were always 'two antagonist powers or opposite interests', one standing for permanence and stability, the other for progress and change. In social terms they were represented by the landed and the commercial interests. In constitutional terms they were represented by the Lords and Commons, with the King, as the head of the executive, acting as the arms of the balance. But these alone would not make a civilised people without 'the *third* great venerable estate of the realm', namely the National Church. From one point of view the Anglican Church was merely part of the great Christian Church throughout the world, but it was not with this aspect that Coleridge was concerned, but with its function as a civilising estate of the realm.

In the middle ages the Church was a powerful estate of the realm, concerned with the preservation and extension of learning. 'The object of the national church was to secure and improve that civilisation without which the nation could be neither permanent nor progressive.' (p. 64.) From this point of view the Reformation in England was a great disaster, for many of the resources of the Church (which Coleridge termed the *Nationalty*) were diverted to the benefit of the landed gentry instead of to the encouragement of learning. 'Our eighth Henry would have acted in correspondence with the great principles of our constitution if, having restored the original balance on both sides, he had determined the Nationalty to the following objects: (1) To the maintenance of the Universities and the great liberal schools: (2) To the maintenance of a pastor and schoolmaster in every parish: (3) To the raising and keeping in repair of the churches, schools, and other buildings of that kind; and, lastly, to the maintenance of the proper, that is, the infirm poor, whether from age or sickness'. All this should have been in addition to the strictly spiritual functions of the Church. 'Religion may be an indispensable ally, but is not the essential constitutive end of that national institute which is unfortunately, at least improperly, styled a church.' Originally *clerk* was a word applicable to any man of learning, and it was in this sense that Coleridge wrote of the *clerisy* of the nation as signifying 'the sages and professors of the law; of medicine and physiology; of music; of military and civil architecture; of the physical sciences; with the mathematical as the common organ of the preceding; in short, all the so-called liberal arts and sciences, the possession and application of which constitute the civilisation of the country, as well as the Theological'. Theologians took the lead in the middle ages, simply because thought was then primarily theological in character, and their civilising influence was most marked. 'The church alone relaxed the iron fate by which feudal dependency, primogeniture and entail would otherwise have pre-destined every native of the realm to be lord or vassal. To the church alone could the nation look for the benefits of existing knowledge and for the means of future civilisation. Lastly, let it never be forgotten that under the fostering wing of the church the class of free citizens and burghers were reared. To the feudal system we owe the *forms*, to the church the *substance*, of our liberty.'

Coleridge was a deeply religious man, but he was less concerned in this work with advocating specifically religious teaching than with the whole problem of national education. 'The proper *object* and end of the National Church is civilisation with freedom.' (p. 63.) The National Church should 'secure to the subjects of the realm generally the hope, the chance, of bettering their own or their children's condition.' For education offered to even the humblest families the chance to rise in the world to fame and fortune. 'Our Maker has distinguished man from the brute that perishes by making hope first an instinct of his nature; and secondly an indispensable condition of his moral and intellectual progression. . . . A Natural instinct constitutes a right, as far as its gratification is compatible with the equal rights of others.' Education, extended to all who could profit by it, would be a great solvent of class jealousies and conflicts, and a safeguard against the spread of error.

To Coleridge political wisdom lay in the maintenance of balance between the twin forces of stability and change. The Greek city-states, he argued, fell because they had too much of the latter; Venice fell because it had too much of the former. In England he did not doubt that there was an over-balance in favour of the landed interest, witness 'the obdurate adherence to the jail-crowding Game Laws (which, during the reading of our Church Litany, I have sometimes been tempted to include in the petitions—"from envy, hatred and malice, and all uncharitableness; from battle, murder and sudden death, Good Lord deliver us!")', as well as the Corn Laws and the Statutes against Usury. The balance might be redressed, but must not be overthrown. But with all the constitutional imperfections, there was more liberty in England than had existed in the days of the Commonwealth. 'For little less than a century and a half, Englishmen have collectively and individually lived and acted with fewer restraints than the citizens of any known Republic past or present.' The reason was clear: 'Extremes meet. A democratic Republic and an Absolute Monarchy agree in this: that in both alike the Nation or People delegates its whole power. . . . A Constitution such states can scarcely be said to possess.' (p. 122.) He rejected a class basis for political power. Government existed for the protection of property, but not for the exclusive interests of any section of society, and until this lesson was learnt there would continue to be social unrest.

The trouble had begun at the Restoration. 'With the Restoration came in all at once the mechanico-corpuscular philosophy, which the increase of manufactures, trade and arts, made everything in philosophy, religion and poetry objective; till, at length, attachment to mere external worldliness and forms got to its maximum, when out burst the French Revolution; and with it everything became immediately subjective, without any object at all. The Rights of Man, the Sovereignty of the People, were subject and object both. We are now, I think (1832), on the turning-point again. This Reform Bill seems the *ne plus ultra* of that tendency of the public mind which substitutes its own undefined notions and passions for real objects and historical actualities.' (*Table Talk*, 5 April 1832.) In great measure the danger had arisen from the rationalist attempts to separate matters of the head from matters of the heart. But 'we have hearts as well as heads. We can will and act, as well as think, see, and feel. Is there no communion between the intellectual and the moral? Are the distinctions of the Schools separates in Nature? Is there no Heart in the Head? No Head in the Heart? Is it not possible to find a *practical* Reason, a *Light* of Life, a focal power from the union or harmonious composition of all the Faculties? ... May there not be a yet higher or deeper Presence, the source of Ideas, to which even the Reason must convert itself? Or rather is not this more truly the Reason, and the universal Principles but the Gleam of Light from the distant and undistinguished community of Ideas—or the Light in the Cloud that hides the Luminary? O! let these questions be once fully answered, and the affirmative made sure and evident—then we shall have a Philosophy, that will unite in itself the warmth of the mystics, the definiteness of the Dialectician, and the sunny clearness of the Naturalist, the productivity of the Experimenter and the Evidence of the Mathematician.' (Ms. Egerton, Coburn, p. 126.)

In the same mystic vein he wrote of the deeper reason to be found in nature. 'Throughout all Nature we find evidences of a Will and a Reason, and the Will is *deeper* than Reason. It can no more be called *above* Reason than you would describe the Taproot of an Oak as *above* the Trunk; and it can as little oppose or contradict Reason, as the Foot-sole can go contrary to the Limb— or than the Stuff or matter can contradict the Form.' (ibid., Coburn, p. 308.) Here indeed Coleridge was immersed in mystical Platonism, and there were few in his age who would be willing to follow him into such deep waters. Yet it was Burke and Coleridge who provided the philosophical basis of nineteenth-century conservatism. Gladstone was deeply influenced by Coleridge in the writing of his own *The State in its Relations with the Church* (1838), while Disraeli's views both on history and social reform were remarkably similar to Coleridge's. Although in many ways Coleridge's view of the Church was individual to himself, yet he influenced the coming Oxford Movement. Dean Church commented: 'Coleridge had lifted the subject to a very high level. He had taken the simple but all-important step of viewing the Church in its spiritual character as first and foremost and above all things essentially a religious society of divine institution, not dependent on the creation or will of man.' (*The Oxford Movement*, p. 144.) Coleridge helped to foster a new attitude to history with his respect for institutions and the idea of growth and nationhood, and he powerfully influenced the Tory reformers, such as Lord Ashley, in their attitude to social reform. Altogether he must be regarded as one of the great formative influences upon nineteenth-century thought.

NOTE

[1] *Political Tracts of Wordsworth, Coleridge and Shelley*, ed. R. J. White, C.U.P., 1953.

11 : Romanticism and History:
Sir Walter Scott

LORD ACTON considered the most significant aspect of Romanticism to be its discovery of a sense of history. The seventeenth-century political struggles had encouraged much research into historical precedents, and the age produced numerous antiquarians of stature, but its thought remained predominantly legalistic and theological. The eighteenth century produced great historians in Burnet, Gibbon, Hume and Robertson, three of them Scotsmen, and Hume's *History of England* was a good deal more popular than his philosophical works with the reading public, yet the age did not really become historically minded until the philosophical revolution associated with the thought of Burke and Coleridge had found a new meaning in society and the idea of social growth through time, and until Sir Walter Scott had stirred the imaginations of his age, and indeed of all Europe, with an amazing number of historical novels.

Walter Scott, the son of an Edinburgh attorney and Writer to the Signet, might almost be said to have inherited a sense of history. He once wrote:

My great-grandfather was *out*, as the phrase goes, in Dundee's wars, and in 1715 had nearly the honour to be hanged for his pains ... My father, although a Borderer, transacted business for many Highland lairds, and particularly for one old man, called Stuart of Invernshyle, who had been out both in 1715 and 1745, and whose tales were the absolute delight of my childhood. I believe there never was a man who united the ardour of a soldier and tale-teller, or man of talk, as they call it in Gaelic, in such an excellent degree; and as he was as fond of telling as I was of hearing, I became a valiant Jacobite at the age of ten years old: and, even since reason and reading came to my assistance, I have never quite got rid of the impression which the gallantry of Prince Charles made on my imagination.

(Letter to Robt. Surtees, 17 Dec. 1806. *Letters*, op. cit., I, p. 342.)

In Scott's youth there were still old men and women who could remember vividly the events of the '45 Rebellion, or the exploits of Rob Roy, and he listened eagerly to their stories. All his life he read and memorised the Border ballads, and he spent his spare moments researching into the records of the periods of history about which he was to write.

Scott once described the excitement he had felt as 'a very young boy', at being given a copy of Macpherson's *Ossian* by an old blind poet named Dr. Blacklock; 'and if I have been at all successful in the paths of literary pursuit I am sure I owe much to the success to the books with which he supplied me and his own instructions.' Ossian and Spenser were his two favourites. 'Their tales were for a long time so much my delight that I could repeat without remorse whole cantos of the one & Duans of the other.' Later he was led on to study the question of authorship, and was in no doubt that Ossian was entirely Macpherson's work, and that 'his whole introductions notes &c. is an absolute tissue of forgeries'. But he always felt a sympathy for Macpherson, as one who 'had his imagination fired with the charms of Celtic poetry from his very infancy', and therefore had much in common with Scott himself. (Letter to Anna Seward, Sept. 1806, *Letters*, I, p. 322.) Another book which fired his imagination at the age of twelve was Bishop Percy's *Reliques of Ancient Poetry*, and in 1801 he wrote to the bishop that he could well remember 'the very grass sod to which (when a boy of twelve years old) I retreated from my playfellows, to devour the works of the ancient minstrels.' (Letter to Bishop Percy, 11 Jan. 1801, *Letters*, I, p. 109.)

Scott's letters are full of antiquarian erudition. The Rev.

R. Polwhele writes to him asking for information about 'Sir Tristrem'. Scott replies that 'Tristrem (of whose real existence I cannot persuade myself to doubt) was nephew to Mark King of Cornwall', and he recounts the story, and how 'the loves of Tristrem and Ysonde' were to be found in 'the songs of the King of Navarre, who flourished about 1226, and also in Chretien de Troyes, who died about 1200', and thus passed to Thomas the Rhymer and Robert de Brunne, how by the sixteenth century it was customary to translate the songs of the old minstrels into prose, and how 'Tristrem shared this fate, and his short story was swelled into a large folio now before me, beautifully printed at Paris in 1514.' There were, he added, two important manuscripts, one in the Duke of Roxburghe's Library, and the other in the National Library at Paris, and these were of much greater authority than Mallory's *Morte d'Arthur*, which had been culled from French sixteenth-century sources. In this way the letter continued through pages of erudition, and it is easy to see how it was that Scott was soon regarded as the leading authority on such matters. (Letter to Rev. R. Polwhele, 27 Jan. 1804, *Letters*, p. 207.)[1] Another letter records his excitement when Southey brought him a fifteenth-century manuscript containing several romances in verse, a work which he at once bought for the Advocates' Library in Edinburgh.

His imagination was fired by the old Border ballads, and by mediaeval romances, but he sought also to study the social forces which had gone to shape Scottish history. In 1806 he wrote to Lord Dalkeith an interesting piece of social analysis. There were, he said, few sheep in the Border country in the seventeenth century; cattle were then in high esteem, and there were plenty of hands to tend them. But by the sixteen-eighties 'the bond between chieftain & kinsman seems to have been much broken', and this was accompanied by 'the downfall of the small proprietors'. The old clan system, with all its barbarities, did at least protect its humble members from economic extinction. In 1688 for instance there were a hundred proprietors named Scott living in the Border country:

I think in the same track of country we cannot now find ten. Each of these persons maintained his little stile & had a few cottages round his old tower whose inhabitants made a desperate effort to raise some corn by scratching up the banks of the stream which winded through their glen. These are all gone & their followers have disappeared along with them. I suppose it became more and more difficult for them after the union of the Crowns to keep the 'name & port of gentlemen'; they fell into distress, sold their lands, & the farmers who succeeded them & had rent to pay to those who bought the estates got rid of the superfluous cottagers with all despatch. I have often heard my Grandmother & other old people talk of the waefu' year when seven Lairds of the Forest (all Scotts) became bankrupt at once but how or why I know not. The farmers when they had got rid of the inactive retainers of the small proprietors seem to have gone on for a long time reducing the number of the people on their farms. The ruins of cottages about every farm-house in the country show that this last cause of depopulation continued to operate till a very late period & indeed within the memory of Man. I could name many farms where the old people remember twenty *smoking chimneys* & where there are now not two. . . . In the time of the late Duke of Douglas (d. 1761) the Jedwood forest estate (now entirely a sheep-walk) was divided among sixty or seventy tenants who were bound to furnish three armed men on horseback each for their landlords military service. This was within the memory of man & Lord Douglas's tacks will show it.

(Letter to Lord Dalkeith, 23 Nov. 1806,
Letters, I, p. 329.)

It was the human aspects of such social changes which Scott explored in his Waverley novels. They were not intended to be improbable romances, but an accurate historical picture of social conditions which had once been real enough, and were in Scott's day in the process of passing away.

Scott felt a special sympathy and affection for simple and unlettered country folk. In 1802 he became acquainted with Hogg, the Ettrick Shepherd, and at once wrote to the *Scots Magazine* about this phenomenon 'born in Etterick Forest, and literally bred there in the humble situation of a shepherd. Various causes have concurred in Scotland, to excite and encourage acuteness of observation, and strength of character, even among those who have reaped few or no advantages from fortune and from education. From the remarks of such men, especially upon subjects which they have been accustomed to consider with accuracy, more information may be derived than perhaps the pride of lettered rank will readily allow. . . . Those whose education has commenced with the first opening of their ideas, who have never known what it was to be at large from the trammels of an instructor, who have been as it were, "rocked and craddled, and dandled" into men of literature, may be considered as the denizens of the realms of taste and science. But the uneducated and hardy intruder, whose natural strength of mind impels him to study . . . may . . . view recesses untrod before, and discover beauties neglected by those who have been bred up among them.' (Letter of 26 Sept. 1802, *Letters*, I, p. 158.) In this Scott spoke as a Romantic, and a contemporary of Wordsworth.

All this is reflected in his novels; indeed, he gave the novel new dimensions. Traditionally the eighteenth-century novel was concerned with contemporary society, and although men like Bishop Burnet, Voltaire and Gibbon had written great history, yet there had been no adequate counterpart in fiction. With Scott it might also be said that fiction was often a secondary consideration to the great task of historical reconstruction. His heroes and heroines are often dull and uninteresting, mere excuses enabling the author to surround them with a historical environment at a dramatic moment of time. He was not concerned with profound or intricate problems of character, his characters are often not autonomous individuals, but are borne along by some great historical current; they can hardly help themselves, but are the victims of birth or environment to pre-destined ends. Reason plays small part in their thoughts, the most powerful forces are those of tradition, loyalty, enmity, emulation or love.

The sub-title of *Waverley* was '*Tis Sixty Years Since*, and throughout the book the reader is frequently reminded that the circumstances described have passed away. But they were real enough once, and he is invited to exercise his historical imagination in an attempt to understand why men should have acted in the way they did, even in making a hopeless rebellion. The novel deals with two worlds, the 'reasonable' world of the Hanoverians, and the 'romantic' world of the Scottish clans. Waverley, the somewhat stiff and starchy hero, merely provides the connecting link between them. At the outset readers are warned that 'they will meet in the following pages neither a romance of chivalry nor a tale of modern manners', that the object is 'more a description of men than of manners'. Human nature in all ages remains much the same: 'those passions common to men in all stages of society, which have alike agitated the human heart whether it throbbed under the steel corselet of the fifteenth century, the brockaded coat of the eighteenth, or the blue frock and white dimity waistcoat of the present day. . . . The deep-ruling impulse is the same; and the proud peer who can now only ruin his neighbour according to law, by protracted suits, is the genuine descendant of the baron who wrapped the castle of his competitor in flames. . . . It is from the great book of Nature, the same through a thousand editions.' (*Waverley*: Introductory.) With this tribute to eighteenth-century philosophy, he turns to a picture of England in the first half of the eighteenth century.

At once the contrast appears between the two brothers, Sir Everard and Richard Waverley. The former had inherited the tory and high church views of his ancestors, and therefore he clung with sentimental attachment to the Jacobite cause. His younger brother, Richard, however, having his own way to make in life, 'saw no practicable road to independence save that of relying upon his own exertions, and adopting a political creed more consonant both to reason and his own interest than the hereditary faith of Sir Everard in High-Church and in the house of Stewart', and therefore he attached himself to the Hanoverian interest. (I, Ch. ii.) Sir Everard's support for the Stuarts is an act of loyalty, a product of history, whereas the 'reason' of his brother Richard is merely equated with self-interest. Richard was soon rewarded with 'a seat at one of those boards where the pleasure of serving the country is combined with other important gratifications, which, to render them the more acceptable, occur regularly once a quarter'; and for the rest of the story he is portrayed as a time-server and place-hunter, without parental feelings for his son, or ability to earn a worthy place in English politics. In contrast, Sir Everard lived out his life in loyalty to the traditions of his family, and these were the light of his life. On one occasion when, for a moment, he weakened in his resolution, 'the sun, emerging from behind a cloud, poured at once its checkered light through the stained window of the gloomy cabinet. . . . The baron's eye, as he raised it to the splendour, fell right upon the central scutcheon, impressed with the same device which his ancestor was said to have borne in the field of Hastings.' It was enough; Sir Everard's resolution was restored. (ibid.) He decided to adopt Richard's son, Edward, who thus became the hero of the story.

From childhood Edward was brought up on the stories of history and heraldry, 'till his heart glowed and his eye glistened'. He would hear tales of the family sufferings during the Civil War, and would steal away to the library where 'he would exercise for hours that internal sorcery by which past or imaginary events are presented in action, as it were, to the eye of the muser'. Before his imagination the great scenes of past history would be enacted, and 'through these scenes it was that Edward loved to "chew the cud of sweet and bitter fancy", and, like a child among his toys, culled and arranged, from the splendid yet useless imagery and emblems with which his imagination was stored, visions as brilliant and as fading as those of an evening sky'. This romanticism was sufficient to explain all his subsequent exploits. Meanwhile, as the years passed, 'Sir Everard's Jacobitism had been gradually decaying, like a fire which burns out for want of fuel. His Tory and High Church principles were kept up by some occasional exercise at elections and quarter-sessions, but those respecting hereditary right were fallen into a sort of abeyance' (I, Ch. v). He lived with his memories, embittered with the knowledge that he could expect nothing from a Hanoverian government.

The historical scene being thus set in England, it was Scott's purpose to contrast it with that of Scotland. Edward is sent on a visit to Sir Everard's old Jacobite friend, the Baron of Bradwardine, who had fought in the '15, had been captured at Preston, and then on a memorable occasion, had escaped, but returned to his captors in order to recover his treasured copy of Titus Livy. He was to Scott a figure of gentle fun, with his narrow pedantic learning, his ill-tended estates, his family pride, dating from a charter from King David the First, and his Latin and French tags, which made his conversation almost incomprehensible. Scott described his manor and village of Tully-Veolan with minute accuracy, with its flinty streets, its open fields, its old manor house, and its picturesque poverty, and he added in a note that the details were drawn from actual scenes he had witnessed. This concern for truth continued throughout the book. The anecdote of Bradwardine and Titus Livy actually occurred during the '15 Rebellion. When Edward fails to ask mine host at a slovenly inn to join him at meals, Scott adds a note on the pretensions of Scottish inn-keepers, and another on the practice of drinking a stirrup-cup. The reader is in no doubt that Scott has been meticulous in collecting the social details necessary to give his story authenticity. When Edward comes down to breakfast at Tully-Veolan, Scott cannot resist giving the details of a Scottish breakfast:

> He found Miss Bradwardine presiding over the tea and coffee, the table loaded with warm bread, both of flour, oatmeal, and barley-meal, in the shape of loaves, cakes, biscuits, and other varieties, together with eggs, reindeer ham, mutton and beef ditto, smoked salmon, marmalade, and all the other delicacies which induced even Johnson himself to extol the luxury of a Scottish breakfast above that of all other countries. (I, Ch. xii.)

Edward found it all fascinating, as Scott did, because he was 'warm in his feelings, wild and romantic in his ideas and in his taste of reading, with a strong disposition towards poetry'. He was not a Jacobite, but he and the baron 'met upon history as on a neutral ground, in which they each claimed an interest' (I, xiii). This was Scott's own position. Jacobitism, dead as a political cause, lived again in his imagination as a fascinating human spectacle, and Scott was attempting above all a historical recon- struction of the circumstances which attended the '45 Rebellion.

One day the peace of Tully-Veolan was disturbed by a raid of highland thieves, who carried off the baron's cattle. Bradwardine had ceased to pay protection-money to the neighbouring Highland chieftain, and the raid was a reminder of his obligation. The raid was not the work of the chieftain, the great Vich Ian Vohr, who would not stoop so low, but of Donald Bean Lean; but the chieftain would not restrain the latter unless the protection-money was paid. Such was the barbarous way in which Highlanders were driven to live by the poverty of their circumstances; and the same economic circumstances which drove them to steal would drive them also to Jacobitism and rebellion, should the chance occur. Edward was excited by the romance of the situation, and at once set off to meet Donald, and the chieftain himself. In the moonlight, as he looked at the wild and stirring scenery of a Highland lake, he 'gave himself up to the full romance of his situation'.

Here he sat on the banks of an unknown lake, under the guidance of a wild native, whose language was unknown to him, on a visit to the den of some renowned outlaw, a second Robin Hood. . . . What a variety of incidents for the exercise of a romantic imagination, and all enhanced by the solemn feeling of uncertainty, at least, if not of danger. (I, xvi.)

As his journey progressed, he learnt more of the Highland ways of life and thought. The Highland clans were a complete and ordered hierarchy in which every man had his appointed place, and in which the word of Vich Ian Vohr was law. When Edward referred to Donald as a common thief, he was reproved by Evan Dhu, the flint-like and utterly loyal henchman of the chieftain:

He that steals a cow from a poor widow, or a stirk from a cottar, is a thief; he that lifts a drove from a Sassenach laird is a gentleman-drover. And, besides, to take a tree from the forest, a salmon from the river, a deer from the hill, or a cow

Q

from a Lowland strath, is what no Highlander need ever think shame upon. (I, xviii.)

Such moral attitudes were the product of centuries of history, and individuals were no more responsible for them than they were for the barrenness of the Highlands. Edward gained a further insight into the attitude of the clans when he heard that some of them had been recruited into Highland companies in the service of King George, and that Evan Dhu had served in one. Edward asked Evan whether this did not make him one of King George's soldiers. Evan replied:

Troth, and you must ask Vich Ian Vohr about that; for we are for his king, and care not much which o' them it is.

Clan loyalty required all members to follow wherever the chieftain led them, and for whatever cause, and thus rebellions were likely to continue as long as the clan system continued intact.

Fergus Mac-Ivor, or Vich Ian Vohr, was as much the product of time and place as anyone else. Scott commented that 'had he lived Sixty Years sooner than he did, he would, in all probability, have wanted the polished manner and knowledge of the world which he now possessed; and had he lived Sixty Years later, his ambition and love of rule would have lacked the fuel which his situation now afforded' (I, xix). Having spent some years in France, he had acquired a veneer of culture and polite behaviour, but beneath there were the valour, prickly sense of honour and hot temper of a Highland chieftain. His deepest loyalty was to his clan. No member would ever be turned away, or left in want, and this meant that his estates were overcrowded with a tenantry far beyond the number the land could decently maintain. From his tenants he raised his own army; he kept law and order within his own dominions, had the undisputed power of life and death over his followers, and would allow no other officer of justice to operate anywhere within his jurisdiction. Donald Bean Lean was permitted to carry on his depredations on the fringes of his authority, always so long as he did not overstep a well defined mark, and confined his activities to those not under Mac-Ivor's protection. Mac-Ivor was a devoted

Jacobite, partly as an inherited loyalty, partly because he occasionally received gold from France, and partly because he was flattered by the promise of an earldom from King James the Third and Eighth. In his more reflective moments, however, he was conscious of the wretchedness of his inheritance:

> These stout idle kinsmen of mine account my estate as held in trust for their support; and I must find them beef and ale, while the rogues will do nothing for themselves but practise the broad-sword, or wander about the hills shooting, fishing, hunting, drinking, and making love to the lasses of the strath. But what can I do, Captain Waverley? Everything will keep after its kind, whether it be a hawk or a Highlander. (I, xx.)

Yet his men would follow him even to death, and when the '45 began, it was natural that Mac-Ivor should throw himself into it. Scott makes clear that he could not have acted otherwise, for the logic of history was more powerful than the logic of men.

In order that Edward should understand the passions which moved and united the Highlanders, Mac-Ivor insisted that his sister Flora should lead him along a stream to a wild and rocky place, to sing to him the romantic Gaelic songs. Mac-Ivor declared: 'To speak in the poetical language of my country, the seat of the Celtic Muse is in the midst of the secret and solitary hill, and her voice in the murmur of the mountain stream. He who woes her must love the barren rock more than the fertile valley, and the solitude of the desert better than the festivity of the hall.' (I, xxii.) Mac-Ivor, indeed, admitted that he himself would prefer the fountains of Versailles, but to his sister this spot was Parnassus. His knowledge of France and of the outside world showed him that his native society must pass away, that men like the Baron were driven into Jacobitism and rebellion by the neglect of the Hanoverian government. This was the voice of reason, yet Edward was enthralled with Flora's song, which went deeper than reason, to the heart, and left him in that 'state of mind in which fancy takes the helm, and the soul rapidly drifts passively along with the rapid and confused tide of reflections.' (I, xxiii.)

In spite of his Jacobite and Tory ancestry, Edward had always been unmoved by the claims of any political cause, but when he was received with charm and courtesy by the Young Pretender, he became emotionally involved. Scott portrays the Prince as a charming, handsome and tactful young man, and manages to capture something of the pathos of his flimsy resources and desperate situation; but it is not a vivid character study, and in general the Prince remains as shadowy as his cause. Mac-Ivor, once the rebellion had begun, was 'all air and fire, and confident against the world in arms. . . . He neither asked, expected, nor desired any aid, except that of the clans, to place the Stewarts once more on the throne' (II, xxviii). This enthusiasm however did not prevent him, when the little Jacobite army was marching through Lancashire, from having the most bitter quarrel with Edward over a supposed insult. The scene is the most dramatic in the whole novel. Shortly afterwards the rebellion collapsed. Scott was in some difficulty in extricating Edward from his predicament, and as the reader has little interest in his fate, the remainder of the novel must be pronounced tedious and a failure, except for the tragic trial, imprisonment and execution of the noble Mac-Ivor. At the trial Evan Dhu offered that he and any five others of the clan would gladly die to save Vich Ian Vohr, and when this was refused, he himself refused a pardon and insisted on dying with his chief. That Scott himself was bored with the later chapters he almost admits, for he wrote:

> The earlier events are studiously dwelt upon, that you, kind reader, may be introduced to the character rather by narrative than by the duller medium of direct description; but when the story draws near its close, we hurry over the circumstances . . . (II, xli).

In a Postscript to the novel, Scott commented on the effects of the '45 Rebellion, 'the destruction of the patriarchal power of the Highland chiefs, the abolition of the heritable jurisdictions of the Lowland nobility and barons, the total eradication of the Jacobite party'. All this had gone on rapidly, until in his own day the process was all but complete. Yet, in his early days he had talked with many who could remember those events, and he wished, before all was forgotten, to 'embody in imaginary scenes and fictitious characters a part of the incidents which I then received from those who were actors in them. Indeed, the most romantic parts of this narrative are precisely those which have a foundation in fact'. This was true. Scott is usually accounted one of the great Romantic writers, and the truth of this must depend upon the exact meaning attached to the word. If to be a Romantic signifies the possession of a deep sense of history, a love of nature, and a recognition of the fact that men are more often moved by tradition and sentiment than by reason, then Scott is a Romantic. But in a novel such as *Waverley* he was primarily a historian and sociologist. As he said, the most romantic and vivid incidents in the novel were taken from actuality. All his most vivid characters were social types which went to make up the Scotland of the mid-eighteenth century. The Lowland gentry and subordinate characters, he wrote, 'are not given as individual portraits, but are drawn from the general habits of the period, of which I have witnessed some remnants in my younger days, and partly gathered from tradition'. This to Scott was the real interest of the novel, and it is by its historical accuracy that the novel must stand or fall.

The same is true of Scott's *Heart of Midlothian*, which certainly contains some of his greatest writing. The story grows naturally out of the Scottish scene, for it is the very site of the old Tolbooth prison in Edinburgh (demolished in Scott's day), and the Grassmarket wherein the gallows used to be erected, which gave rise to his reconstruction of the Porteous Riots of 1736. It was a stroke of genius so to entwine the facts of the riots with the deeply interesting story of Jeanie and Effie Deans, that the reader has some difficulty in the first half of the book in regarding the latter as fiction. It is true that Scott took liberties with the details of the events which led to the lynching of Captain Porteous, and it is not always easy to see why, for some of the authentic details, such as those of Robertson's escape from church, are as interesting as those which Scott invented. But Scott knew Edinburgh and its people, and he captured the true spirit of 1736. The portrayal of Jeanie Deans, a plain yet truly noble heroine, reveals deep insight into the Scottish character. Her father, David Deans, a granite-like product of Presbyterianism, the dull and honest Dumbiedikes, Saddletree, with his pedantic absorption in the law, are truly authentic portraits from the Scottish scene. Moreover, the story of the riots, and of the trial of Effie Deans is the most exciting which Scott ever told. The reader waits almost breathlessly for Jeanie to give her evidence, and it is a triumph for Scott's writing that he is convinced that she could not have said otherwise than she did. It is true that the later part of the novel gets out of hand. Scott himself admitted that 'he never could lay down a plan, or, having laid it down, he never could adhere to it', and it is a fact that after Jeanie's interview with Queen Caroline and her return to Scotland, the reader's interest flags, while his credibility is severely strained. But he is ready to forgive much for the great emotional and imaginative experience he has received from the first half of the book.

Scott was at his best when revealing the interplay of character and ideas within a given historical framework. He was particularly fascinated with the interlacing of classes. He wrote:

Perhaps one ought to be actually a Scotchman to conceive how ardently, under all distinctions of rank and situation, they feel their mutual connexion with each other as natives of the same country. There are, I believe, more associations common to the inhabitants of a rude and wild, than of a well cultivated and fertile country; their ancestors have more seldom changed their place of residence; their mutual recollection of remarkable objects is more accurate; the high and the low are more interested in each other's welfare; the feelings of kindred and relationships are more widely extended, and, in a word, the bonds of patriotic affection, always honourable even when a little too exclusively strained, have more influence on men's feelings and actions. (*Heart of Midlothian*, Ch. xiv.)

To David Deans and Jeanie, loyalty to God came first, and thereafter their loyalties were formed by the family, the history of the Cameronians, their friendship with the laird Dumbiedikes, and ultimately to the Duke of Argyle himself. To Scott such social relationships were of the very stuff of history.

Scott's novels are stories of exciting adventure and historical pageant, they are not primarily novels of psychology. He had a massive understanding of socio-historical types, such as of the eighteenth-century Highlander or the seventeenth-century Royalist, and he could create humorous idiosyncratics such as Flibbertigibbet or Richie Moniplies. But in his treatment of the great men and women of history he exercised a judicious restraint. He wrote as a historian rather than a novelist anxious to extort the last ounce of fictional interest from his plot. A modern novelist might have been tempted, in the interest of realism, to have dealt with the relations of Mary, Queen of Scots with Darnley and Bothwell, or to have implicated both Leicester and the Queen in the murder of Amy Robsart, but there was no question of this with Scott. Monarchy and aristocracy were to be given their due. The Queen must never be less than regal, nor Leicester forget his nobility. They would have their human weaknesses, but they must never be such as to overstep a well-defined line; seemliness and the stability of the state would require it.

Scott repeated the pattern of *Waverley* in *The Abbot* (1820). The scene was now the Scotland of the sixteenth century, and the two opposing sides, that of Mary, Queen of Scots and Catholicism, versus the Regent Murray and the Reformed Church. Again the hero, Roland Graeme, finds himself the centre of hostile forces which he does not fully understand, and to neither of which he gives his whole-hearted adherence. 'He had', Scott wrote, 'through various circumstances not under his own control, formed contradictory connexions with both the contending factions, by whose strife the kingdom was distracted, without being properly an adherent of either.' (II, xx.) In this way Scott was able to retain the judicial impartiality of the historian, and reveal something of the strength and weakness of each side. It enabled him also to provide the necessary element of mystery and the supernatural, which always figured in Scott's novels. Roland was puzzled by it all, and on one occasion declared: 'A land of enchantment have I been led into, and spells have been cast around me—every one

has met me in disguise—every one has spoken to me in parables—
I have been like one who walks in a weary and bewildering dream.'
(II, viii.) His grandmother, the mysterious Magdalen Graeme, a
fanatical Roman Catholic, saw to it that the boy received early
training in her faith. But at Avenel, as a page in the household of
Sir Halbert Glendinning, Roland received earnest instruction from
the Protestant Henry Warden. Between these rival fanaticisms he
made no final choice, because there was yet another ethical code,
which he preferred to either of the others, namely that of chivalry,
or loyalty to those who placed their trust in him. Thus he would
never betray the kindness and trust which Sir Halbert and his lady
had shown him, yet when he entered the service of the Queen,
chivalry required that he should be equally loyal to her. When
unwittingly he gave a parcel from the Lady of Lochleven into
Catholic hands, his grandmother applauded the deed, but Roland
declared: 'By Saint Andrew, there were foul mistake; it is the very
spirit of my duty, in this first stage of chivalry, to be faithful to my
trust.' (II, viii.) How else, Scott seems to say, can society continue
in peace, if men are not faithful to their trust? The reply of the
fanatical grandmother, however, was: 'Now, by the love I once
bore thee, I could slay thee with mine own hand, when I hear thee
talk of a dearer faith being due to rebels and heretics, than thou
owest to thy church and thy prince!'

Scott portrayed the Reformed religion as narrow, fanatical and
humourless. Henry Warden, the preacher, declared: 'I seldom jest;
life was not lent to us to be expended in that idle mirth which
resembles the crackling of thorns under the pot' (I, i). He was a
formidable and persistent preacher, for, as Scott wrote, 'the pulpit
was at that time the same powerful engine for affecting popular
feeling which the press has since become' (I, iv). At the same time
Scott's instincts, and his politics[2] were not friendly to Roman
Catholicism. The Abbess of Saint Catherine was 'timid, narrow-
minded and discontented, clung to ancient usages and pretensions
which were ended by the Reformation, and was in adversity, as she
had been in prosperity, scrupulous, weak-spirited and bigoted;
while the fiery and more lofty spirit of her companion suggested a
wider field of effort, and would not be limited by ordinary rules in

the extraordinary schemes which were suggested by her bold and irregular imagination' (I, xii). On the other hand, the Abbot Ambrosius was the personification of wisdom, moderation and true religion. Scott did not defend the ignorance, superstition and fanaticism of the church in mediaeval Scotland, but he regretted the violence and destruction which attended the Reformation. He wrote: 'Although, in many instances, the destruction of the Roman Catholic buildings might be, in the matron's way of judging, an act of justice, and in others an act of policy, there is no doubt that the humour of demolishing monuments of ancient piety and munificence, and that in a poor country like Scotland, where there was no chance of their being replaced, was both useless, mischievous, and barbarous.' (I, viii.) Magdalen Graeme took Roland to witness the destruction: 'Here stood the Cross, the limits of the Halidome of Saint Mary's—here—on this eminence—from which the eye of the holy pilgrim might first catch a view of that ancient Monastery, the light of the land, the abode of saints, and the grave of monarchs—Where is now that emblem of our faith? It lies on the earth—a shapeless block, from which the broken fragments have been carried off, for the meanest uses, till now no semblance of its original form remains' (I, xiii); and Scott added: 'The antiquary may be permitted to regret the necessity of the action, but to Magdalen Graeme it seemed a deed of impiety, deserving the instant vengeance of heaven.' The historian's view he put into the mouth of Sir Halibert: 'the evils of the time are unhappily so numerous, that both churches may divide them, and have enow to spare' (I, xv).

The result of so much bitterness and conflict was to bring both religions into contempt, until men turned away from them both. Peter the Bridgeward declared: 'I will not lower the bridge, come Papist, come Protestant, ye are all the same. The Papists threatened us with purgatory, and fleeched us with pardons;—The Protestant mints at us with the sword, and cuittles us with the liberty of conscience; but never a one of either says, "Peter, there is your penny". I am well tired of all this . . . and I would have you know I care as little for Geneva as for Rome—as little for homilies as for pardons; and the silver pennies are the only passports I will hear of' (I, xvi). Adam Woodcock, the falconer, cared nothing for the relics of the old faith; all he remembered was that the priests 'whillied the old women out of their corn and their candle-end, and their butter, bacon, wool, and cheese, and when not so much as a grey groat escaped tithing'. (ibid.) Yet the Earl of Morton declared that the Reformed church was as bad: 'I think priests of all persuasions are much like each other. Here is John Knox, who made such a nobler puller-down, is ambitious of becoming a setter-up, and a founder of schools and colleges out of the Abbey lands, and bishops' rents, and other spoils of Rome, which the nobility of Scotland have won with their sword and bow, and with which he would now endow new hives to sing the old drone.' (I, xx.)

Roland mistrusts the arguments of *raison d'état* which each side affirms as justification for its policies. To the Abbot he declared that he 'liked not that good service which begins in breach of trust'. The Abbot explained that 'the time which has wrenched asunder the allegiance of Christians to the church, and of subjects to their king, has dissolved all the lesser bonds of society, and, in such days, mere human ties must no more restrain our progress, than the brambles and briers, which catch hold of his garments, should delay the path of a pilgrim who travels to pay his vows'. Roland was not satisfied: 'It is even this which our adversaries charge against us, when they say, that shaping the means according to the end, we are willing to commit great moral evil in order that we may work out eventual good.' The Abbot's defence was that of necessity: 'As well might the hound say to the hare, use not these wily turns to escape me, but contend with me in pitched battle, as the armed and powerful heretic demand of the down-trodden and oppressed Catholic to lay aside the wisdom of the serpent, by which alone they may again hope to raise up the Jerusalem over which they weep, and which it is their duty to rebuild.' (II, viii.) As in all the great conflicts of history, Scott saw a historical necessity which transcended the wickedness or foolishness of individuals. They were all to a large extent the victims of the environment in which they found themselves.

In many ways Scott's treatment of the story of Mary, Queen of

Scots, is unsatisfactory and disappointing. Her beauty, and her tragic story, certainly attracted him. He wrote of 'that brow, so truly open and regal—those eyebrows, so regularly graceful . . . the beautiful effect of the hazel eyes which they over-arched, and which seem to utter a thousand histories—the nose with all its Grecian precision of outline—the mouth so well proportioned, so sweetly formed—the dimpled chin . . .' (II, i). But chivalry prevents him from probing too deeply into her story, or exploring the intricacies of her character. He carefully avoids the most lurid period of her life, that of the life and death of Darnley and of the intrigue with Bothwell. The action of the novel is set in the comparatively tame, but also 'safe', period when Mary is a prisoner in Lochleven castle. Nor will Scott have any truck with the scandalous rumours that she gave birth to a child there, and that she had an affair with George Douglas. All he will admit is that Douglas was secretly in love with her, but of this she is unaware until he has fled. She denies having aided the death of Darnley, but admits to a reckless act: 'I afforded too open occasion for the suspicion— I espoused Bothwell.' (II, ii.) For the most part, however, Scott prefers merely to suggest one of two explanations for her unhappy reign. The first was the romantic one of the hostile fates. The Lady of Lochleven referred to it, and to the Queen's fatal beauty, when, following the flight of George Douglas, she exclaimed: 'O Princess, born in a luckless hour, when will you cease to be the instrument of seduction and of ruin to all who approach you?' (II, x.) Mary herself referred to it as she gazed at the corpse of Douglas, as he lay killed on the battlefield fighting for her: 'Thus has it been with all that loved Mary Stewart!—The royalty of Francis, the wit of Chastelar, the power and gallantry of the gay Gordon, the melody of Rizzio, the portly form and youthful grace of Darnley, the bold address and courtly manners of Bothwell—and now the deep-devoted passion of the noble Douglas—nought could save them— they looked on the wretched Mary, and to have loved her was crime enough to deserve early death!' (II, xvii.)

Scott the historian gave an equally fatalistic explanation, that the fault lay in the darkness of Scottish history. On one occasion, when Mary was being forced to abdicate, Lord Seyton hinted at the dangers if she refused. Mary was horrified: 'Surely Scottish nobles would not lend themselves to assassinate a helpless woman?' Seyton replied: 'Bethink you, madam, what horrid spectacles have been seen in our day; and what act is so dark, that some Scottish hand has not been found to dare it?' (II, ii.) When Lord Ruthven recounted the violence and slaughter of her reign, Mary replied: 'My lord, it seems to me that you fling on my unhappy and devoted head those evils which, with far more justice, I may impute to your own turbulent, wild, and untameable dispositions—the frantic violence with which you, the Magnates of Scotland, enter into feuds against each other, sticking at no cruelty to gratify your wrath, taking deep revenge for the slightest offences, and setting at defiance those wise laws which your ancestors made for stanching of such cruelty, rebelling against the unlawful authority, and bearing yourselves as if there were no king in the land; or rather as if each were king in his own premises. And now you throw the blame on me. . . .' (ibid.) But this was not Scott's final view. Roland on one occasion asked Catherine Seyton if she believed in the Queen's innocence. She had no doubt of it. Roland sighed and looked down. 'Would my conviction were as deep as thine!' That was Scott's view also, but this did not prevent him from a romantic sympathy with her long imprisonment, and sad fate.

Of the broader aspects of the political situation we learn little, except that Scott thought highly of the abilities of the Regent Murray: 'This distinguished statesman, for as such his worst enemies acknowledged him, possessed all the external dignity, as well as almost all the noble qualities, which could grace the power that he enjoyed; and had he succeeded to the throne as his legitimate inheritance, it is probable he would have been recorded as one of Scotland's wisest and greatest kings. But that he held his authority by the deposition and imprisonment of his sister and benefactress, was a crime which those only can excuse who think ambition an apology for ingratitude.' (I, xviii.)

Throughout, Scott maintains his aristocratic view of society. Roland may have within him, as Woodcock said, 'a spice of the devil in his disposition'. Although he was unaware of the circumstances of his birth, Roland was always certain that he came of noble lineage, and acted accordingly, although he was only a page. The Scottish nobility were engaged in their political rivalries, but they normally acted according to the code of chivalry. Mean or wicked deeds, such as the antics of the Lord Abbot of Unreason, or Dryfesdale's attempt to poison the Queen, were always the acts of menials, and were despised by Sir Halbert Glendinning (although he was not a Catholic) or the Lady of Lochleven (although she hated the Queen). The nobility, although often the prisoners of their environment or inherited historical rivalries, generally maintained a moral superiority, according to their own lights, which Scott never allows his readers to forget.

The supernatural was an important part of the equipment of a romantic novelist, but it was a difficult theme, needing most careful handling. The dangers can be seen in Scott's novel, *The Monastery*, in which the White Lady of Avenel, the guardian spirit of a family, appears at regular intervals throughout the book. In setting his story in Scotland at the time of the Reformation, Scott had chosen a magnificent theme, and an environment which he knew intimately. Yet the story was a failure, partly because when he wrote in 1820 he was tired and jaded, and partly because he tried to buttress his story with this recurrent intervention of the supernatural in which he had no pretence of belief. The White Lady makes no appeal to the imagination, and her practice of speaking in verse makes her appearances both tedious and ridiculous. In *Redgauntlet*, on the other hand, in Wandering Willie's Tale, written four years later, Scott writes an absorbing tale based on the supernatural, and the reason for the difference is not far to seek. It was a tale firmly based on seventeenth-century Scottish legend; Scott had heard many such tales, and they had fired his imagination. Second, as written, the story was not told by Scott, but by Wandering Willie, who is re-telling a story he has heard so often that he can recall every detail of his ancestor's story. Also, the fact that it is told in the Scottish dialect adds powerfully to the effect, for here is a story which clearly grows out of the history and folklore of Scotland. Finally, it is a gripping story; the predicament of Steenie Steenson when the rent is missing is an engaging one, and the existence of the jackanapes and Steenie's drinking of whiskey before his vision provides the reader with an alternative explanation for much, though not all, that happened.

Kenilworth (1821) was written in answer to the request of Scott's publisher, Constable, for a picture of Queen Elizabeth which should be a fitting companion-piece to that of Mary, Queen of Scots in *The Abbot*. Unlike Mary, Elizabeth was not a favourite character with Scott, but he chose a story which had an obvious parallel with that of his former novel. The death of Darnley, and Mary's subsequent marriage with Bothwell, might be paralleled by Elizabeth's dalliance with Robert, Lord Dudley, and the murder of Dudley's wife, Amy Robsart. In telling his story, Scott played fast and loose with the historical facts and dates. The Dudley of history, for instance, had married the heiress Amy Robsart in 1550, when he was seventeen, and the Princess Elizabeth, who had been his close friend since the age of eight, attended the wedding. In September 1560, Amy, Countess of Leicester, was found at the bottom of the stairs at Cumnor, with her neck broken. Scott sets his story in the year 1575, when Elizabeth was aged forty-two, at the height of her powers, and the whole plot turns on the fact that the Queen did not know of Leicester's secret marriage with Amy. Scott therefore avoids any temptation he might have felt to implicate Elizabeth in a sordid intrigue with Leicester, still less in the charge that she connived in Amy's death. Leicester was portrayed as a man who had risen to favour entirely by the appeal of his personal beauty: he was a weak character, but not naturally a dishonourable one. For him the stumbling-block was the adamantine will of the Queen. The anticipation of her unreasonable hostility to his marriage with Amy, and his consequent loss of favour, was too much for him; so he lied to Elizabeth, and sought to pass off Amy as the wife of the Iago-like Varney. The fault therefore lay primarily in Elizabeth's tendency to allow her desire to keep Leicester for herself to influence her in what should have been impartial matters of state. Leicester was enflamed by Varney's false stories that Amy had been unfaithful to him with Tressilian, and in a hot moment declared that she was doomed. Varney took this as sufficient mandate to plan and carry out her hideous murder. His motive was the desire to see Leicester, not only continue as the favourite of the Queen, but to become her consort and King of England. Villainy therefore was confined to the lesser characters, those of lower rank; and the central characters, Leicester and the Queen, combined human interest with historical glamour, without being blackened by conscious evil. Amy is portrayed with great skill. She is no pale heroine, but a vigorous and determined girl, tortured by the impossible position in which her secret marriage has placed her. Her interview with the Queen is an exciting episode, for she longs for Elizabeth's help, yet cannot tell all for fear of betraying her husband, and her emotional outbursts lead the Queen to assume that she is insane, and in need of restraint. Thus unwittingly Elizabeth plays into Varney's hands, and the distraught Amy is led away to the remote Cumnor and her death. Leicester's weakness in concealing the truth from the Queen is made plausible by the imperious nature of that daughter of Henry VIII. Scott achieved a considerable measure of accuracy in his estimate of the character of the Virgin Queen. He wrote:

> Queen Elizabeth had a character strangely compounded of the strongest masculine sense, with those foibles which are chiefly supposed proper to the female sex. Her subjects had the full benefit of her virtues, which far predominated over her weaknesses; but her courtiers, and those about her person, had often to sustain sudden and embarrassing turns of caprice, and the sallies of a temper which was both jealous and despotic. She was the nursing-mother of her people, but she was also the true daughter of Henry VIII. (II, Ch. iv.)

Those who were closest to the Queen's affections were often those most likely to suffer. A Burleigh or a Walsingham held their places by virtue of the Queen's 'solid judgment, not her partiality'. Leicester stood on far more volcanic ground: 'the success of Leicester's course depended on all those light and changeable gales of caprice and humour, which thwart or favour the progress of a lover in the favour of his mistress, and she, too, a mistress who was ever and anon becoming fearful lest she should forget the dignity, or compromise the authority, of the Queen, while she indulged the affections of the woman'. (ibid.) With all her caprice, her political sagacity was of the highest order, and her power as firm as a rock. Varney warned Leicester: 'Think upon Norfolk, my lord—upon the powerful Northumberland,—the splendid Westmoreland;—think on all who have made head against this sage Princess. They are dead, captive, or fugitive. This is not like other thrones, which can be overturned by a combination of powerful nobles; the broad foundations which support it are in the extended love and affections of the people. You might share it with Elizabeth if you would; but neither yours, nor any other power, foreign or domestic, will avail to overthrow, or even to shake it.' (II, Ch. xix.) The most vivid and sustained picture of Elizabeth was in the scene at Court in the later chapters of volume I. Scott took great pains to assimilate contemporary evidence at his disposal. In 1810 the *Harleian Miscellany* was published, including the *Fragmenta Regalia* of Sir Robert Naunton, which included the following anecdote:

Bowyer, the gentleman of the black rod, being charged by (the Queen's) express command, to look precisely to all admissions in the privy chamber, one day staid a very gay captain (and a follower of my lord Leicester) from entrance, for that he was neither well known, nor a sworn servant of the Queen; at which repulse, the gentleman (bearing high on my lord's favour) told him that he might, perchance, procure him a discharge. Leicester coming to the contestation said publickly, which was none of his wonted speeches, that he was a knave, and should not long continue in his office, and so turning to go about to the Queen, Bowyer, who was a bold gentleman and well beloved, stepped before him, and fell at her Majesty's feet, relates the story, and humbly craves her grace's pleasure, and in such a manner as if he had demanded, whether my Lord of Leicester was King, or her Majesty Queen; whereunto she replied (with her wonted oath, God's-death) my Lord, I have wished you well, but my favour is not so locked up for you, that others shall not participate thereof; for I have many servants unto whom I have and will, at my

pleasure, bequeath my favour, and likewise resume the same;
and if you think to rule here, I will take a course to see your
forthcoming; I will have here but one *mistress* and no *master*,
and look that no ill happen to him, lest it be severely required
at your hands; which so quailed my Lord of Leicester, that his
faint humility was, long after, one of his best virtues.

(*Harleian Misc.*, V, p. 124.)

Scott followed the incident closely. When Bowyer, the Usher of
the Black Rod complained to the Queen:

> The spirit of Henry VIII was instantly aroused in the bosom
> of his daughter, and she turned on Leicester with a severity
> which appalled him, as well as all his followers.
>
> 'God's death! my lord', such was her emphatic phrase,
> 'what means this? We thought well of you, and brought you
> near to our person; but it was not that you might hide the sun
> from our other faithful subjects. Who gave you license to
> contradict our orders, or control our officers? I will have in
> this court, ay, and in this realm, but one mistress, and no
> master. Look to it that Master Bowyer sustains no harm for
> his duty to me faithfully discharged; for, as I am Christian
> woman and crowned Queen, I will hold you dearly answer-
> able. . . . We will brook no mayor of the palace here.

(*Kenilworth*, I, xvi.)

On numerous occasions Scott includes the results of careful
antiquarian research, and indeed is quite prepared to hold up the
pace of the story in order to include picturesque details. The
castle of Kenilworth and its history are described in great detail.
Scott loved to imagine the scenes of colourful activity which went
on around its walls in Elizabethan days, and to tinge the picture
with a sad nostalgia suitable to the age of Romanticism:

> We cannot but add, that of this lordly palace, where princes
> feasted and heroes fought, now in the bloody earnest of storm
> and siege, and now in the games of chivalry, where beauty
> dealt with prize which valour won, all is now desolate. The

R

bed of the lake is but a rushy swamp; and the massive ruins of the Castle only serve to show what their splendour once was, and to impress on the musing visitor the transitory value of human possessions, and the happiness of those who enjoy a humble lot in virtuous contentment. (II, viii.)

How different was that great day in 1575 when the great Elizabeth came on a state visit to Leicester:

The word was passed along the line, 'The Queen! The Queen! Silence, and stand fast!' Onward came the cavalcade, illuminated by two hundred thick waxen torches, in the hands of as many horsemen, which cast a light like that of broad day all around the procession, but especially on the principal group, of which the Queen herself, arrayed in the most splendid manner, and blazing with jewels, formed the central figure. She was mounted on a milk-white horse, which she reined with peculiar grace and dignity; and in the whole of her stately and noble carriage, you saw the daughter of an hundred kings. (II, xiii.)

Scott had discovered an inventory of the furniture of the castle at the time, and he printed it in full in his notes at the end of the novel. The pageant at Kenilworth is described in minute detail just at the time when the reader is longing to know the fate of the unfortunate Amy. Of course the story was important to so natural a story-teller as Scott, but even more important was the recreation of the atmosphere of a romantic period of history.

. . . . . .

The same is true of *The Fortunes of Nigel*, in which Scott created the most human and humorous portrait of all his monarchs. The plot, which is the adventures of Nigel in the recovery of his inheritance, appealed to Scott as a lawyer, but his real interest lay in the tortuous atmosphere of the Court and Capital of James I and VI in England, and in the pathetic figure of the king himself. The peace-loving and timorous king is vividly, and on the whole justly, drawn, as he struggled against penury and intrigues amidst an English nobility who were essentially alien to him. He is shown pressing on with the building of Inigo Jones's Banqueting Hall in Whitehall, before which his son would one day be executed, and harrassed by petitioners and creditors who made his life a misery. His apartments were as chaotic as his mind, as he sat amidst dusty piles of learned books on kingship, and the manuscripts of his own compositions on poetry and philosophy.

> He was deeply learned, without possessing useful knowledge; sagacious in many individual cases, without having real wisdom; fond of his power, and desirous to maintain and augment it, yet willing to resign the direction of that, and of himself, to the most unworthy favourites; a lover of negotiations, in which he was always outwitted; and one who feared war, where conquest might have been easy. He was fond of his dignity, while he was perpetually degrading it by undue familiarity; capable of much public labour, yet often neglecting it for the meanest amusement; a wit, though a pedant; and a scholar, though fond of the conversation of the ignorant and uneducated . . . laborious in trifles, and a trifler where serious labour was required; devout in his sentiments, and yet too often profane in his language; just and beneficent by nature, he yet gave way to the iniquities and oppression of others. He was penurious respecting money which he had to give from his own hand, yet inconsiderately and unboundedly profuse of that which he did not see. (I, Ch. V.)

There he sat, in his green, quilted, dagger-proof dress, buttoned awry, a clumsy and ungainly figure with spindling legs, the least able, but perhaps the most fortunate, of the Stuarts.

Scott, in one of his most amusing scenes, portrayed James as he teaches Gingling Geordie the money-lender the correct way in which a subject should approach his Sovereign:

> Ye shall approach the presence of majesty thus,—shadowing your eyes with your hand, to testify that you are in the presence of the Viceregent of Heaven.—Vera weel, George, that is done in a comely manner.—Then, sir, ye sall kneel, and make as if

ye would kiss the hem of our garment, the latch of our shoe, or such like.—Very weel enacted—whilk we, as being willing to be debonair and pleasing towards our lieges, prevent thus,—and motion to you to rise; whilk, having a boon to ask, as yet you obey not, but, gliding your hand into your pouch, bring forth your supplication, and place it reverentially in our open palm. (ibid.)

George seizes the opportunity to present a real petition, at which the king explodes when he realises how easily he has been trapped. James acknowledges his debts, but has to admit that 'our Exchequer is as dry as Dean Giles's discourses in the penitential psalms'.

James's essential humanity was his most engaging quality, and it gave rise to an attractive sense of humour. To Lord Huntinglen he declared: 'My English lieges here may weel make much of me, for I would have them to know, they have gotten the only peaceable man that ever came of my family' (I, IX). This was true, for James was so timid that he could not bear even to look upon a naked sword, so deeply had his early experiences impressed him; and he cuts a ridiculous figure when out hunting he comes upon Nigel alone in the wood, and is convinced that it is an attempted assassination (II, X). Feeling the awful insecurity of being without attendants, and being on foot, he rushes to his horse ('I'll hear ye best on horseback. I canna hear a word on foot, man, not a word'), and screams for help. Yet, with all his indignity and ineffectualness, James is an attractive character in Scott's portrait, and the latter brings out the pathos, loneliness and anxieties of royal power when it falls to one not capable of bearing them. As James declares, 'My lieges keep a' their happiness to themselves; but let bowls row wrang wi' them, and I am sure to hear of it.'

· · · · · ·

Scott was a prolific writer; his collected novels ran to forty-eight volumes, and in addition there were twelve volumes of verse, and numerous short stories. His influence upon the nineteenth-century novel was very great; he was admired and imitated by such diverse writers as Pushkin, Manzoni, Victor Hugo, Mickiewicz, Maria Edgeworth and Fenimore Cooper. He was the first novelist in Britain to become wealthy by his writings, and he gave the novel an impeccable morality, from which Dickens dared not stray far, and which made it difficult for even the strictest parent to deny his daughter the opportunity of reading. Above all, he inculcated a new attitude to history which was to leave so profound a mark upon the nineteenth century.

The new attitude was not easy to acquire. Hazlitt, in one of his most brilliant pieces of criticism, showed how difficult he himself found it. (*The Spirit of the Age: Sir Walter Scott.*) Scott, he wrote, represented half the human intellect: 'if you take the universe, and divide it into two parts, he knows all that it *has been*; all that it *is to be* is nothing to him'. His criticism was that in admiring the past, Scott had no regard for the present. 'The land of pure reason is to his apprehension like Van Dieman's Land;—barren, miserable, distant, a place of exile, the dreary abode of savages, convicts and adventurers'. Hazlitt admitted that Scott's novels were a stimulus to the imagination: 'they are a relief to the mind, rarefied as it has been with modern philosophy, and heated with ultra-radicalism'. He admitted also that his influence was to soften old animosities: 'Sir Walter is a professed *clarifier* of the age from the vulgar and still lurking old-English antipathy to Popery and Slavery.' What Hazlitt the old Jacobin feared was that Scott's influence would reinforce conservative and reactionary political views, that in examining anew the claims of the House of Stuart, he would legitimise the House of Hanover, and reinforce the legitimacy of the House of Bourbon. By romanticising the Middle Ages, 'he administers charms and philtres to our love of Legitimacy, makes us conceive a horror of all reform, civil, political, or religious, and would fain put down the *Spirit of the Age.*' What Hazlitt preferred was what has come to be called the Whig Interpretation of History, with Wyclif, Luther, Hampden, Sidney, Somers and the whigs as the heroes, enlightening and civilising their times, and passing on the torch of progress to their successors. Scott had no such intention. It is true that he had little sympathy with the reformers of his day, but in his novels he was advocating no political creed, Protestant, Catholic or Jacobite. Instead he was fascinated with the problem of human nature placed in a historical environment from which it could not escape, and his conclusion was that men and women in the same historical predicament would always act in the same way, that Protestants and Catholics, Cavaliers and Roundheads, Jacobites and Hanoverians were made by the historical circumstances in which they found themselves, because men's loyalties were stronger than their reason, and that on the whole it was good that it should be so. Ruskin was deeply influenced by the sense of history he found in Scott; Carlyle was fiercely critical of Scott, but learnt more from him than he cared to admit; Bagehot admired his contribution to the study of history; and so the broad stream of British historiography flowed on in the nineteenth century, enriching in turn both conservative and liberal philosophies, and saving the latter from the bleak extremities of Utilitarianism.

NOTES

[1] Scott published an edition of *Sir Tristrem* in that year.

[2] Cf. Sir Walter Scott's attitude to Catholic Emancipation:

> As for Catholic Emancipation—I am not, God knows, a bigot in religious matters, nor a friend to persecution; but if a particular sect of religionists are *ipso facto* connected with foreign politics—and placed under the spiritual direction of a class of priests, whose unrivalled dexterity and activity are increased by the rules which detach them from the rest of the world— I humbly think that we may be excused from intrusting to them those places in the State where the influence of such a clergy, who act under the direction of a passive tool of our worst foe, is likely to be attended with the most fatal consequences. If a gentleman chooses to walk about with a couple of pounds of gunpowder in his pocket, if I give him the shelter of my roof, I may at least be permitted to exclude him from the seat next to the fire.
> Letter to Robert Southey, 15 Dec. 1807.
> *Letters of Sir Walter Scott.* Ed. Grierson, I, p. 400.

12 : Robert Southey: Toryism and the Social Question

Of all the tory writers, none was more deeply concerned with the social problems of the time than Robert Southey. At the age of eighteen, as an undergraduate of Balliol, he had celebrated the French Revolution with an epic on Joan of Arc. He despised what he called 'the pedantry, prejudice, and aristocracy' of the university, gave up powdering his hair, and was accounted a Jacobin. Under the influence of Coleridge, and with his friend Robert Lovell, he threw himself into Pantisocracy, a plan for a perfect social life on the banks of the Susquehanna. He incorporated his republican sentiments in a drama called *Wat Tyler*, which however he was prudent enough not to publish, and which appeared only in a pirated edition in 1817. When his enemies attacked him for the expression of views so unlike those he held in 1817, he replied in the *Quarterly Review* that *Wat Tyler* expressed the errors of youth and ignorance, but that at least 'they bore no indication of an ungenerous spirit, or of a malevolent heart' (*Essays*, II, 9).

In Southey's youth, Jacobinism in England had seemed an exotic creed confined to a small number of the educated classes, but the situation had changed when it threatened to become a mass movement for the subversion of society. Moreover the French had shown that Jacobinism could lead to military dictatorship. Southey had dreamed of being a poet, but by 1810 he wrote: 'I have an ominous feeling that there are poets enough in the world without me, and that my best chance of being remembered will be as a historian' (Southey to Landor, 26 March 1810). Without any fortune of his own, he had to maintain his family by his pen, and he wrote ceaselessly a stream of reviews, essays and histories in order to earn a living. His early views changed under the successive influences of a visit to Portugal in 1795, which left a deep mark upon him, and his reading of history. For years he was engaged in amassing a great quantity of material for a History of Portugal, which was never written, but which gave him a new insight into the historical evolution of a people. He was deeply moved by the British struggle against the French. 'Never before', he wrote, 'had the country been engaged in so long or so arduous a struggle: never had any country, in ancient or in modern times, made such great and persevering exertions' (*Essays*, II, 327). He was particularly excited by the struggle of the Spanish people against the French, and predicted that Napoleon's Spanish War would lead to his ruin. As with Wordsworth and Coleridge, the Spanish resistance gave him a new understanding of nationalism, and with it came a new sense of history. He wrote a *History of the Peninsular War*, but without much military information the work was a failure. On the other hand his *Life of Nelson* was a popular and patriotic work. As the years passed, fear of French military power was equalled in his mind by fear of Jacobinism, and the possibility in Britain of what he always called a *bellum servile*. He turned more and more therefore to the study of the social question, and the reading of the history of other turbulent times, in order to seek for precedents which would suggest ways out of the dangers which he felt to be so real.

In 1801 the first census in Great Britain was taken. The population was found to be 10,942,646, and great comfort was taken from the fact that of these 2,700,000 were men capable of defending their country, so that it was apparent, as Southey wrote, that 'we might defy the world in arms'. But at the same time it came as a shock to discover that nearly one person in nine was dependent upon parochial aid, and therefore that 'there was something rotten in our internal policy'. (Southey: *On the State of the Poor* (1812) *Essays*, 1, 75.) In these circumstances Southey gravely feared a social upheaval. The central feature of the problem was the rapid growth of population. He entirely rejected Malthus's argument as 'too foolish, as well as too wicked, ever to become permanently prevalent'. The real danger was not economic privation but that, just as the Reformation had thrown up wild characters, such as fifth-monarchy-men, so the French Revolution had thrown up materialist and atheistic revolutionaries.

Southey argued that if Malthus's theory was sound, 'it would be hopeless to seek for any alleviation of existing misery.' It was a gloomy thought that mankind was, and always had been, pushing beyond the margin of subsistence, and could be kept down only by moral restraint, vice and misery. It was not true that men had outrun the means of subsistence. There were areas of the world, capable of cultivation, which had not one man per square mile. 'In England the inhabitants might be multiplied to ten-fold their present number, and the island still produce enough for the subsistence of all. . . . If a country be over-peopled, and crowded and distressed in regard to its system of society, before it be half peopled in proportion to its extent and its power of production, the fault lies in that system of society, not in the system of nature.' (ibid., I, 86–7.) In short the fault lay, not with God, but with man. Southey was shocked at Malthus's remedy for the existing evil, which was 'simply to abolish the poor rates, and starve the poor into celibacy. A plan for the abolition of the poor rates as practicable as it is humane! The rich are to be called upon for no sacrifices; nothing more is required of them than that they should harden their hearts. They have found a place at the table of nature, and why should they be disturbed at their feast?' (ibid., I, 92.) Malthus had written that nature had laid no place at the feast for those without subsistence, and that they had no right to expect one. Southey replied that those so excluded would very soon fight for one, and thus that Malthus's way led to a social struggle.

Southey argued that a great social breach had been made at the Reformation, and a great opportunity lost to provide a national system of education, and so for two centuries nothing had been done to improve the lot of the poor. Since 1770, with the onset of industrialism, although the wealth of the nation had greatly increased, the conditions of the lower classes had worsened. For the new industrialism 'Adam Smith's book is the code, or confession of faith; a tedious and hard-hearted book, greatly over-valued even on the score of ability, for fifty pages would have comprised its sum and substance. ... That book considers man as a manufacturing animal; it estimates his importance, not by the sum of goodness and of knowledge which he possesses, not by the virtues and charities which should flow towards him and emanate from him, not by the happiness of which he may be the source and centre, not by the duties to which he is called, not by the immortal destinies for which he is created; but by the gain which can be extracted from him.' (I, 112.) The result had been the worst evils of the factory system. 'The London workhouses supplied children by waggon-loads to those manufactories which would take them off the hands of the parish; a new sort of slave-trade was invented; a set of child-jobbers travelled the country, procuring children from parents whose poverty was such as would consent to the sacrifice, and undertaking to feed, clothe, and lodge them for the profits of their labour. In this manner were many of our great manufactories supplied!' (I, 115.) The result was the creation of a race of manufacturing poor without health, education, religion or hope, for whom the pot-house offered the only relief, with the consequences of profligacy and pauperism.

Behind these grim facts there always lurked the spectre of revolution. The riots of 1780 and 1790, and the Luddite activities of 1811, seemed to provide ample justification for the fear. 'That there is any organised plan for effecting a revolution in this country we are far from asserting or believing; but it by no means follows that the preparatory work of revolution is not going on. There is no commissariat for supplying London, and yet London is supplied with a regularity and abundance which no commissariat, however perfect, could possibly accomplish.' (I, 119.) What Southey feared was the constant wearing away of authority until the whole system of government should fall into contempt. The manufacturing system was preparing thousands of wretched people who would be ready followers of revolutionaries and demagogues. 'The weekly epistles of the apostles of sedition are read aloud in tap-rooms and pot-houses to believing auditors, listening greedily when they are told that their rulers fatten upon the gains extracted from their blood and sinews; that they are cheated, oppressed and plundered; that their wives are wanting bread, because a corrupt majority in parliament persists in carrying on a war which there was no cause for beginning, and to which there can be no end in view; that there is neither common sense nor common honesty in the government; that the liberty of the press has been destroyed, and they are, in fact, living under military law.' (I, 121.) The seven hundred thousand people in receipt of poor relief would provide a ready reservoir of discontent. 'When the Luddites began to organize themselves, the funds of the societies to which they belonged afforded them a ready supply. ... In this country, journeymen have long been accustomed to combine for the purpose of obtaining higher pay from their employers; each trade has its fund for such occasions, raised by weekly or monthly payments; the different trades assist each other in their combinations, and the business is managed by secret committees. ... Such are the means which the disaffected part of the populace have in their hands. ... These are fearful circumstances.' The danger, as Southey saw it, was that whereas the principles of the French Revolution had at first appealed to young intellectuals, 'young men of ardent mind and generous inexperience', yet by 1812 'jacobinism, having almost totally disappeared from the educated classes, has sunk down into the mob'. (I, 126.) He feared direct incitement to revolution much less than the constant attacks upon the government, war policy, the Monarchy, corruption, and social distress. The nation was being slowly poisoned by hostile propaganda. Above all he feared the viciousness of the press. Were not bonfires lit, and flags flown by the mob to celebrate the murder of Percival, one who was 'the model of every virtue'? 'Healths were drunk, accompanied with ferocious exultation for what had been done. ... The imagination of a dramatist could conceive no fitter prelude to the most dreadful tragedy of popular madness.' (I, 137.) The blame, Southey argued, lay mainly with the press. 'The first duty of government is to stop the contagion; the next, as far as possible, to remove the causes which have predisposed so large a part of the populace for receiving it.' It was not sufficient to quell the Luddites if the causes of their discontent were not removed.

As remedies Southey made several important proposals. A century before J. M. Keynes, he proposed a great programme of public works in order to stimulate employment:

> Never indeed was there a more senseless cry than that which is at this time raised for retrenchment in the public expenditure as a means of alleviating the present distress. That distress arises from a great and sudden diminution of employment, occasioned by many coinciding causes, the chief of which is that the war-expenditure of from forty to fifty millions yearly has ceased. Men are out of employ: the evil is that too little is spent, and as a remedy we are exhorted to spend less! Everywhere there are mouths crying out for food because the hands want work; and at this time, and for this reason, the state-quack requires further reduction! Because so many hands are unemployed, he calls upon government to throw more upon the public by reducing its establishments and suspending its works!
>
> (Letter to Wm. Smith, M.P., 1817. *Essays*, II, 26.)

It did not much matter what the programme of public works consisted of. It might be improving roads or draining fens, or recovering land from the sea. In any case, 'better would it be for the state to build pyramids in honour of our Nelsons and Wellingtons, or Towers of Babel for star-gazing, than that men who have hands, and are willing to work, should hunger for want of employment.' (*Essays*, I, 145.) Any occupation was preferable to unemployment and poor relief.

Second, Southey advocated a system of national education, with a school in every parish 'as an outwork and bulwark of the national church'; so that 'as none can die for want of food in England, so none should be suffered to perish for lack of knowledge'. (I, 146.) 'Lay but this foundation, and the superstructure of prosperity and happiness which may be erected will rest upon a rock; the rains may descend, and the floods come, and the winds blow and beat upon it, and it will not fall.'

The third proposal was for imperial expansion; Canada, Cape Colony, Australasia were countries favourable to British settlement. 'It is time that Britain should become the hive of nations, and cast her swarms; and here are lands to receive them. . . . The seas are ours, and to every part of the uninhabited or uncivilized world our laws, our language, our institutions, and our Bible may be communicated. Fear not, if these seeds be sown, but that God will give the increase!' (I, 154–5.)

Four years later (1816) in another essay on the same subject, Southey commented that the days were gone by when philosophers talked easily of achieving a millenium. 'We are now but too feelingly convinced that no violent and rapid melioration in society is possible, and that great and sudden changes are evils in themselves and in their consequences.' (I, 162.) But cautious reform was another matter. The central problem of society was that whereas the nation had grown rapidly richer, the lower classes had not shared in the benefits. Yet 'the well-being of the people is not of less importance than the wealth of the collective body'. (I, 178.) Estates had grown larger and more productive, 'but look at the noblest produce of the earth, look at the children of the soil, look at the seeds which are sown here for immortality! Is there no deterioration there?' (I, 179.) Southey lamented the passing of the yeoman farmer; 'this was the right English tree in which our heart of oak was matured. . . . The sense of family pride and family character was neither less powerful nor less beneficial in this humble rank, than it is in the noblest families when it takes its best direction. But old tenants have been cut down with as little remorse and as little discrimination as old timber, and the moral scene is in consequence as lamentably injured as the landscape!' (I, 180.) In their place has emerged a depressed, feckless and discontented class dependent upon the poor law. 'A large proportion of the misled multitude who have been burning barns and corn-stacks, would have been siding the civil power to repress these frantic outrages, if they had had their own little property to defend. Let us not deceive ourselves! governments are safe in proportion as the great body of the people are contented, and men cannot be contented when they work with the prospect of want and pauperism before their eyes, as what must be their destiny at last. If you would secure the state from within as well as from without, you must better the condition of the poor.' (I, 183.)

What Southey looked for was a great process of amelioration and humanisation, with the poor re-settled on the land, and a greater concern shown by society for relieving their misfortunes. In this respect he particularly commended the work of the Society for Bettering the Condition and Increasing the Comforts of the Poor, founded by the bishop of Durham, William Wilberforce and Sir Thomas Bernard about 1796, and Southey quoted numerous examples of their work, and of the evidence they collected of the social problems of the time. They were stories of great human interest, such as of a widow with fourteen children, who refused to put her younger children in the work-house, but strove to cultivate a small-holding in order to maintain them. Most of them were stories of self-help, and in general they reflected the humanity of the authorities in aiding those who sought to aid themselves. Sir Thomas Bernard urged that the poor should be treated as free and national beings. 'Let us endeavour to operate by individual kindness and encouragement, by the prospect of acquiring property, and by every other incitement to industry and prudence; and we shall find that when the component parts of the body politic become sound and perfect, the state itself will be healthy and strong.' (I, 211.) This, Southey declared, was 'true radical reform. Too long has that foul philosophy prevailed which considers men either as mere machines, or as mere animals, whose animal wants are all that are to be taken into account of statistic economy.' (I, 214.)

Southey was fertile with proposals of his own. He would establish savings banks for the poor, prohibit bull-baiting and cock-fighting. He was bitterly opposed to the Game Laws, which were responsible for three-fourths of the crimes among the poor. He wanted Factory Acts to limit the hours of work of children in cotton factories, and he wanted the employment of boys as chimney-sweeps to be prohibited. Such practices, he wrote, were more akin to savagery than to civilised conduct. Above all, he wished for a national system of education. In 1816 the National Society had about seven hundred schools, with over a hundred thousand children, but Southey regarded this as no more than a beginning, when in London alone there were a hundred and thirty thousand children without the means to education, and many of them weie beggars. He regarded 'Dr. Bell's intellectual steam-engine' as rendering the cost of a national system trifling, and his main concern was that it should be under the control of the Anglican church. Indeed, he was much more concerned to see that children received religious instruction than any other kind of learning, and he was anxious to see that education did not fall into the hands of either Dissenters or atheists. He estimated that one schoolmaster, on the Madras system, could run a school of a thousand children at a cost of two hundred pounds a year, so that all the poor children of London could be educated for twenty-six thousand pounds. 'If it were necessary to raise that sum by a specific tax, is there man or woman throughout England upon whom it might be levied that would not cheerfully pay?' (II, 161.) With education for all, with new laws to curb the radical press, with factory acts to protect children, and with a great programme of land settlement in place of the system of poor relief, Southey believed that the dangers from social discontent would pass.

Southey's *Colloquies on the Progress and Prospects of Society* (1829) were written in the form of a dialogue between himself and Sir Thomas More. This gave him the opportunity to make historical comparisons, and to assess his age in the perspective of history. The result was a sombre picture of a guilt-ridden age, perplexed by problems deeper than any which had faced the nation since the sixteenth century. That was why Southey found More a congenial companion, for the tempests which accompanied the Reformation seemed to him to be similar to those of his own age.

Southey asked whether the early nineteenth century had any cause for self-congratulation on grounds of progress. The eighteenth century had been over-optimistic about the age of reason, and had regarded religion as the superstition of simpletons. But the nineteenth century could not be so sure, for men could appear reasonable one moment, and become raging madmen the next. 'Think how the dog, fond and faithful creature as he is, from being the docile and obedient of all animals, is made the most dangerous, if he becomes mad; so men acquire a frightful and not less monstrous power when they are in a state of moral insanity, and break loose from their social and religious obligations.' (I, 31.) Certainly progress was possible; 'the sum both of moral and physical evil may be greatly diminished by good laws, good institutions, and good governments'. But progress was far from inevitable.

Nor would the millenium be brought about by 'the triumph of what you call liberal opinions; nor by enabling the whole of the lower classes to read the incentives to vice, impiety and rebellion, which are prepared for them by an unlicensed press; nor by Sunday Schools, and Religious Tract Societies; nor by the portentous bibliolatry of the age!' (I, 35.)

Even if progress could be discerned in certain limited respects, it could not be regarded as of general application, for even if there was progress in England, there was perhaps regress in other parts of the world, and even in England it did not extend to all classes. 'Consider your fellow-countrymen, both in their physical and intellectual relations: and tell me whether a large portion of the community are in a happier or more hopeful condition at this time, than their forefathers were when Caesar set foot upon the island?' (I, 45.) Not, he wrote, that he had ever been deluded 'even in the ignorance and presumptuousness of youth, when I first perused Rousseau', into supposing that the savage state was preferable to the social. Yet it was true that there had been no general melioration. 'Look, for example, at the great mass of your populace in town and country, a tremendous proportion of the whole community! Are their bodily wants better, or more easily supplied? Are they subject to fewer calamities? Are they happier in childhood, youth and manhood, and more comfortably or carefully provided for in old age, than when the land was uninclosed, and half-covered with woods?' (I, 46.)

It was true that England had for long been spared the horrors of civil war, but was it certain that this happy state would continue? 'If the seeds of civil war should at this time be quickening among you, if your soil is everywhere sown with the dragon's teeth, and the fatal crop be at this hour ready to spring up, the impending evil will be an hundred fold more terrible than those which have been averted.' (I, 49.) The tranquillity of England, indeed, appeared to depend upon the weather, for a plague or bad harvest could plunge

THE REFORMATION · 273

the country into disaffection. The dangers appeared to Southey to be immense. London, for instance, had grown to enormous size. What was to prevent the outbreak there of a pestilence or plague greater than any in history? 'Physically considered, the likelihood of their recurrence becomes every year more probable than the last' (I, 51), and men stood helpless in view of their ignorance as to the causes of disease. 'In this, as in all things, it behoves the Christian to live in a humble and grateful sense of his continual dependence upon the Almighty.' One could look forward to the control of disease by scientific knowledge, but that stage in human progress had not yet been reached. Meanwhile, for the great mass of the working classes, 'they are worse fed than when they were hunters, fishers, and herdsmen; their clothing and habitations are little better, and, in comparison with those of the higher classes, immeasurably worse. Except in the immediate vicinity of the collieries, they suffer more from cold than when the woods and turbaries were open. They are less religious than in the days of the Romish faith; and if we consider them in relation to their immediate superiors, we shall find reason to confess that the independence which has been gained since the total decay of the feudal system, has been dearly purchased by the loss of kindly feelings and ennobling attachments. They are less contented, and in no respect more happy.' (I, 60.)

Such thoughts naturally led Sir Thomas More back to pre-Reformation days, when, he believed, the church was a good landlord, and took care of the poor. The dissolution of the monasteries had meant hardship for the peasants. 'As far as they were concerned, the transfer of property was always to worse hands. The tenantry were deprived of their best landlords, artificers of their best employers, the poor and miserable of their best and surest friends. There would have been no insurrections in behalf of the old religion, if the zeal of the peasantry had not been inflamed by a sore feeling of the injury which they suffered in the change.' (I, 88.) But the beggars created by the agricultural revolution of the eighteenth century were no better off than those created by that of the sixteenth century, and in this as in so many other ways there was no certainty of progress. Indeed in his own day Southey estimated that one-eighth of the population were paupers (I, 92).

Altogether Southey judged the century between the Glorious Revolution of 1688 and the outbreak of the French Revolution to be the happiest years England had ever known. 'The morals of the country recovered from the contagion which Charles II imported from France, and for which Puritanism had prepared the people. Visitations of pestilence were suspended. Sectarians enjoyed full toleration, and were contented. The Church proved itself worthy of the victory which it had obtained. The Constitution, after one great but short struggle, was well-balanced and defined; and if the progress of art, science, and literature was not brilliant, it was steady.' Yet there was a reverse side to the coin, with the triumph of a false philosophy of a selfish materialism. Sir Thomas More reminded Southey the historian that 'God is above, but the devil is below. Evil principles are, in their nature, more active than good. The harvest is precarious, and must be prepared with labour, and cost, and care; weeds spring up of themselves, and flourish and seed whatever the season. Disease, vice, folly and madness are contagious; while health and understanding are incommunicable, and wisdom and virtue hardly to be communicated!' (I, 37.) Thus London, 'the heart of your commercial system, is also the hot-bed of corruption. It is at once the centre of wealth and the sink of misery; the seat of intellect and empire, and yet a wilderness. . . . Many thousands in your metropolis rise every morning without knowing how they are to subsist during the day; or, many of them, where they are to lay their heads at night. . . . Moral evils are of your own making; and undoubtedly the greater part of them may be prevented.' (I, 108–100.) The Poor Law cost ten times the whole expenses of government under Charles I, yet 'not a winter passes in which some poor wretch does not actually die of cold and hunger in the streets of London! With all your public and private eleemosynary establishments, with your eight million of poor-rates, with your numerous benevolent associations, and with a spirit of charity in individuals which keeps pace with the wealth of the richest nation in the world, these things happen, to the disgrace of the age and country, and to the opprobrium of humanity.' (I, 112.)[1]

Southey felt instinctively that the problem needed legislation, but he was vague as to the measures needed. Yet the danger of a *bellum servile* was real enough, and if it came, it would be more terrible than the peasant revolts of history. 'Imagine the infatuated and infuriated wretches, whom not Spitalfields, St. Giles's and Pimlico alone, but all the lanes and alleys and cellars of the metropolis would pour out. . . . Its possibility at least ought always to be borne in mind. The French Revolution appeared much less possible when the Assembly of Notables was convoked; and the people of France were much less prepared for the career of horror into which they were presently hurried.' (I, 115.)

The three men whom Southey thought to have given the greatest moral impetus to their age were Thomas Clarkson, of the anti-slavery movement, Dr. Bell, the educationalist, and Robert Owen of Lanark. Owen, he was convinced, would have achieved much more than he had done, 'if he had not alarmed the better part of the nation by proclaiming upon the most momentous of all subjects, opinions which are alike fatal to individual happiness and to the general good'. (I, 133.) He had made the mistake of opposing religious instruction for children. What could he not have achieved if he had had the support of the religious sects? 'With all Owen's efforts and all his eloquence, (and there are few men who speak better, or who write so well,[2]) he has not been able in ten years to raise funds for trying his experiment; while during that time the Bible Society has every year levied large contributions upon the public, and more than once a larger sum within the year than he has asked for. Had he connected his scheme with any system of belief, though it had been as visionary as Swedenborgianism, as fabulous as Popery, as monstrous as Calvinism, as absurd as the dreams of Joanna Southcote, or perhaps even as cold as Unitarianism, the money would have been forthcoming.' (I, 144.) More teased Southey that perhaps he would not think so favourably of Robert Owen's scheme for villages of co-operation if it had not so resembled Southey's youthful ideal of Pantisocracy. Southey replied that 'that consideration is more likely to put me on my guard against illusion', but he considered that 'what they aimed at was plainly practicable if it could have been fairly started, and the direct results must have been of unquestionable advantage to themselves, and utility to the commonwealth'. (I, 140.) Southey never entirely lost his early enthusiasm for some such solution to the land problems of his age.

Time and time again Southey returned to the dilemma which lay at the centre of his thought. The new industrialism was undoubtedly 'a necessary stage in the progress of society' (I, 158), and it was productive of great benefits. Without it, for instance, he did not see how it would have been possible to beat Napoleon. The problem then was how to eliminate the social evils, while retaining the social benefits? History provided no lessons for guidance in such a novel situation (I, 161). Industrialism had happened without plan or system, and it had deformed everything which it had touched. 'From the largest of Mammon's temples down to the poorest hovel in which his helotry are stalled, the edifices have all one character. Time cannot mellow them; Nature will neither clothe nor conceal them; and they remain always as offensive to the eye as to the mind'! (I, 174. The influence of such passages as this upon Carlyle is obvious.) The life of the peasant had improved little since the sixteenth century, when Southey envisaged happy cottages humming with the noise of spinning-wheels. Since then peasants had learnt to eat the potato and to drink tea, but apart from these things, there had been little improvement. The only outlets from so grim an existence were provided by emigration to the United States, or 'perhaps one in a thousand, by good conduct and good fortune, obtains an employment in the cotton mill which places him in a respectable station; and one in a myriad becomes a master manufacturer himself, and founds a family who take their place among the monied aristocracy of the land.' (I, 176.) But for the great mass of workers there was no hope of social improvement. Yet the age was dominated by the spirit of commerce, and Southey had to admit that 'the natural consequences of commerce are every way beneficial; they are humanizing, civilizing, liberalizing' (I, 197). The problem therefore remained to modify the evils by some form of paternalism, without attempting to put back the clock of progress.

In many ways Britain's problems were unique, but to Southey

the European situation seemed equally full of dangers. French aggression remained a threat; the German states were threatened with 'a struggle of opinions between governments which grant too little, and enthusiasts who demand too much', while the weakness of the small German states remained a temptation to the aggressor. 'Italy is in a worse condition; a condition disgraceful to itself and reproachful to all its rulers. It suffers under the double curse of foreign dominion and of its own fatal superstition; the pestilent influence of that Upas (the Catholic Church) extends far and wide, but Italy lies under the droppings of that poison tree.' (I, 231.) The eighteenth century had fostered the idea that man's reason would be a sufficient guide for all the problems of this life, but once the French Revolution had broken through the crust of custom, this was shown to be false. What then remained? 'To what can you look for the preservation of peace, or for a mitigation of war?' Not to the new science, nor to the Holy Alliance, which was a mere brotherhood of individual monarchs (I, 232–3), nor to public opinion. 'Proceed as you are proceeding in this country, and the affairs of government will ere long be regulated by that opinion, as the weather-cock is by the wind.' (I, 234.) Indeed 'the supremacy of public opinion is the worst evil with which, in the present state of the world, civilized society is threatened'.

'The science of politics', Southey declared, 'has been erected by shallow sophists upon abstract rights and imaginary compacts, without the slightest reference to habits and history; but in ignorance of the one, and contempt of the other' (I, 254), and this led him to resist Roman Catholic Emancipation as an invasion of the rights of the Established Church. His prejudices against the Roman religion were unalterably fixed: it was a religion of super-stition, it was largely responsible for the ignorance and fanaticism of the Irish, and on the continent it was the ally of the despot. The four brightest days in English history were those of the signing of Magna Carta, the accession of Queen Elizabeth, the Restoration of Charles II and the landing of William of Orange; and the two blackest days in the history of Ireland were those on which Catholics received the vote and 'a Protestant Government gave its sanction and support to a seminary for the Romish Priesthood'.

Although he wrote much of the evil consequences of the Reformation, Southey never doubted the benefits of a process which, he wrote, had placed a Bible instead of a rosary in the homes of Britain. On the subject of the Catholic Church and Ireland Southey was most prejudiced, and had little of value to offer.

His staunch support for an Established Church arose from his conviction that 'nothing but religion can preserve our social system from putrescence and dissolution' (II, 88). It was not that he believed that the Anglican church was fulfilling its functions adequately. For instance, with the great increase in population, whose communities had been left without charge. Yet without religion there was little hope for society. 'Alas! for human nature, when hopes and fears are no longer under the regulation of a reasonable faith!' (II, 108.) For this purpose it must be made available to all, and this was why Southey was so interested in the extension of education. He objected to the fact that schools, originally founded for the education of poor scholars, had become the preserves of the rich. The lot of the poor commoner at the universities was worse than it had been in the sixteenth century. 'Is not inferiority of condition in your Universities made more humiliating than it was in times when the distinction of ranks was more broadly marked, and is not that humiliation of a kind which is likely to produce anything rather than humility?' (II, 131–3.) In consequence many men had been driven into Nonconformity. But for the great mass of the poor, it was very difficult to achieve any education at all, and those who did learn to read were at the mercy of radical literature. Southey wanted a great extension of education under the aegis of the Church, and he advocated the foundation of another English university, perhaps at Durham or Jarrow, in tribute to the memory of the Venerable Bede. (II, 144. Bede was buried at Durham.) Religion was to be the great bulwark against the disintegration of society.

Southey held William Pitt responsible for making needless concessions to the tendencies of his age. Not only had he granted the vote to the Irish Catholic, and given government support to Maynooth, but by his frequent creation of peers he had weakened the House of Commons. 'When Mr. Pitt removed from thence so many of the great land-holders into the House of Lords, their place in the Commons was to be supplied, at best, with men who had less of that influence which properly belongs to property in a commonwealth constituted as is ours; and room was made for men of a lower class and of a dangerous description, who, before the structure of Parliament was thus, almost it may be said, revolutionized, would never in the march of their ambition have approached its doors.' Thus while those whom he called Lord Cucumber and Earl Mushroom carried little weight, in the Commons a new kind of voice was heard. 'I cannot but think that there is no place in which a demagogue, well-armed with impudence, would feel more conscious of the strength which audacity supplies: nor where he could be so mischievous and so dangerous.' (II, 231–2.) The result was that, whereas church property was raided at the Reformation, 'already voices are heard in Parliament recommending a second spoliation!' (II, 125.)

Southey felt that he lived in an age of explosive change. 'Never was there so stirring an age as the present! From yonder little town, which with its dependent hamlets contains not more than four thousand inhabitants, adventurers go not only to the all-devouring metropolis, and to the great commercial and manufacturing towns of Lancashire and Yorkshire, but to Canada and the United States, to the East and West Indies, to South America, and to Australia. I could name to you one of its natives who is settled at Moscow, and to another whose home is among the mountains of Caucasus. In these days there is not perhaps one man in a thousand (except among the higher families) who, if he lives to manhood, is buried with his fathers.' (II, 259.) In all this there was much good. Indeed 'there is no profession which more truly may deserve to be called liberal when carried on by a just and honourable man' than that of commerce. But the whole of Europe was in ferment in a struggle between the forces of feudalism and 'the levelling principle of democracy' (II, 414), and Britain had not escaped its influence. In addition 'you have a great and increasing population, exposed at all times by the fluctations of trade to suffer the severest privations in the midst of a rich and luxurious society, under little or no restraint from religious principle, and if not absolutely disaffected to the institutions of the country, certainly not attached to them: a class of men aware of their numbers and of their strength; experienced in all the details of combination; improvident when they are in receipt of good wages, yet feeling themselves injured when those wages, during some failure of demand, are so lowered as no longer to afford the means of comfortable subsistence; and directing against the Government and the laws of the country their resentment and indignation for the evils which have been brought upon them by competition and the spirit of rivalry in trade. They have among them intelligent heads and daring minds; and you have already seen how perilously they may be wrought upon by seditious journalists and seditious orators in times of distress.' (II, 415.)

'On what do you rely for security against these dangers? On public opinion? You might as well calculate upon the constancy of wind and weather in this uncertain climate. On the progress of knowledge? It is such knowledge as serves only to facilitate the course of delusion. On the laws? the laws is weak as a bulrush if it be feebly administered in time of danger. On the people? they are divided. On the Parliament? every faction will be fully represented there. On the Government? it suffers itself to be insulted and defied. ... The principle of duty is weakened; that of moral obligation is loosened; that of religious obedience is destroyed.' (ibid.)

Yet Southey discerned another side to the picture. Literature was having a humanizing effect; the worst evils of the criminal law were being reformed, the slave trade had been abolished, and missionary activity abroad had greatly increased. 'There is a general desire throughout the higher ranks for bettering the condition of the poor, a subject to which the Government has also directed its patient attention'; education was being extended, so that 'in a few generations this whole class will be placed within the reach of moral and intellectual gratifications'; corruption in government had been eliminated, so that the scandalous jobbery of the eighteenth century had almost disappeared; in the fine arts 'a levelling principle is going on, fatal perhaps to excellence, but favourable to mediocrity', and 'accomplishments which were almost exclusively professional in the last age, are now to be found in every family within a certain rank of life'.[3] 'In all this I see the cause as well as the effect of a progressive refinement, which must be beneficial in many ways.' But all this supposed that the danger of political convulsion could be withstood long enough for the amelioration of society to take effect. And this brought Southey to his central recommendation: 'There can be no health, no soundness in the state, till Government shall regard the moral improvement of the people as its first great duty. The same remedy is required for the rich and for the poor. Religion ought to be blended with the whole course of instruction. . . . We are, in a great degree, what our institutions make us.' (II, 420–25.)

Southey chose to write his book in the form of a dialogue with Sir Thomas More because it seemed to him that the upheavals associated with the Reformation afforded the nearest parallels with those of his own age, and Southey regarded himself as in some respects in the same position as More had been. In this way More commented: 'I grieved over a spoliation which cannot even now be called to mind without regret; I resisted opinions which in their sure consequences led to anarchy in all things, tending not only to overthrow the foundations of authority both in church and state, and thus to the destruction of all government and all order, but to subvert the moral law, and dethrone conscience from its seat in the heart of man. The evil which I apprehended came to pass. That I did not with the same perspicuity foresee the eventual good, was because it was less certain, and more remote.' (II, 40.) In the last resort it was a sense of history which gave Southey perspective in judging of the problems of his age. The same sense which led him to reject the philosophy of the millennium gave rise to belief in the possibility of an evolutionary progress. To this extent in his philosophy he was a Kantian.

Southey learnt from Coleridge to admire Kant. What particularly appealed to him was his view of history as the great unfolding of a rational plan, 'that there may be discovered in the course of human history a steady and continuous, though slow development of certain great predispositions in human nature: and that although men neither act under the law of instinct like brute animals, nor under the law of a preconcerted plan like rational cosmopolites, the great current of human actions flows in a regular stream of tendency towards this development: individuals and nations, while pursuing their own peculiar and often contradictory purposes, following the guidance of a great natural purpose, and thus promoting a process, which even if they perceived it, they would little regard.' The ultimate object was 'the unravelling of a hidden plan of nature for accomplishing a perfect state of civil constitution for society in its internal relations as the sole state of society in which the tendencies of human nature can be all and fully developed.' What he disliked about Kant was that he supposed that man could be guided by reason alone, without the aid of religion.

Southey's book brought a devastatingly hostile article in the *Edinburgh Review* by the young Thomas Babington Macaulay. If Southey may be said to have summarised the tory philosophy of 1829, Macaulay certainly summarised the whig philosophy of 1830, and it will be as well to consider the arguments of the latter here at the point when we reach the year which concludes this study.

Macaulay was profoundly dissatisfied with Southey's book because he dissented from all the fundamental assumptions from which the latter wrote. To Southey government was a fine art, to Macaulay it was a science. 'Government is to Mr. Southey one of the fine arts. He judges of a theory, of a public measure, of a religion or a political party, of a peace or a war, as men judge of a picture or a statue, by the effect produced on his imagination.' Southey seemed destined to jump to extremes, at first as a republican, and at last as an ultra-tory. 'His political system is just what we might expect from a man who regards politics, not as matter of science, but as matter of taste and feeling.' It was beyond Macaulay's comprehension that Southey should find Robert Owen of greater importance than Hallam or Lingard. 'He has passed from one extreme of political opinion to another, as Satan in Milton went round the globe, contriving constantly to "ride with darkness". Wherever the thickest shadow of the night may at any moment chance to fall, there is Mr. Southey.'

Southey could see only the social miseries of the Industrial

Revolution; Macaulay emphasised its achievements. Southey was concerned at the burden of the poor rates: Macaulay pointed out that they were much less in the industrial towns than in the counties, that in 1825 they were twenty shillings a head in Sussex, and only four shillings in Lancashire. Southey was concerned at the heavy mortality rates. Macaulay replied that in 1750 the rate was about one in twenty-eight in Manchester, and that in 1830 it was about one in forty-five. 'We might with some plausibility maintain that the people live longer because they are better fed, better lodged, better clothed, and better attended in sickness, and that these improvements are owing to that increase of national wealth which the manufacturing system has produced.' Macaulay poked fun at Southey's romantic picture of peasants living in rose-covered cottages, 'rose-bushes and poor-rates, rather than steam-engines and independence'. It was no doubt true that a cottage was more picturesque than a factory, but 'does Mr. Southey think that the body of the English peasantry live, or ever lived, in substantial or ornamental cottages, with box-hedges, flower-gardens, bee-hives and orchards?' Southey moreover looked to the government to relieve the distress of the poor and unemployed; to this Macaulay replied with the arguments of *laissez-faire*. The powers of governments were limited, and did not extend to relieving every misfortune and misery which befell in life. Southey advocated a paternalism which Macaulay rejected: 'Mr. Southey entertains as exaggerated a notion of the wisdom of governments as of their power.'

Southey had wished to see religion as the basis of civil government; this was an assertion which came near to the heart of the difference of outlook between him and Macaulay. To Macaulay the purpose of government was utilitarian; it existed for the good of mankind, and would have to exist whether there was a religious basis of government or not. 'However pure or impure the faith of the people might be, whether they adored a beneficent or a malignant power, whether they thought the soul mortal or immortal, they have, as soon as they ceased to be absolute savages, found out their need of civil government, and instituted it accordingly. It is as universal as the practice of cookery.' From a false premiss Southey proceeded to what Macaulay thought a dangerous principle, namely that as religion is the basis of government, it is the first duty of the state 'to train the people in the way in which they should go'. Macaulay rejected this because 'A religion may be false. A government may be oppressive. And whatever support government gives to false religions, or religion to oppressive governments, we consider as a clear evil.' Governments are no wiser than other men in deciding what is true or false in religion. Similarly laws do not necessarily reflect some higher wisdom; the only safe principle is that they should reflect public opinion. 'What are laws but expressions of the opinion of some class which has power over the rest of the community?[4] By what was the world ever governed but by the opinion of some person or persons? By what else can it ever be governed? What are all systems, religious, political, or scientific, but opinions resting on evidence more or less satisfactory? The question is not between human opinion and some higher and more certain mode of arriving at truth, but between opinion and opinion, between the opinions of one man and another, or of one class and another, or of one generation and another. Public opinion is not infallible; but can Mr. Southey construct any institutions which shall secure to us the guidance of an infallible opinion? . . . The duties of government would be, as Mr. Southey says that they are, paternal, if a government were necessarily as much superior in wisdom to a people as the most foolish father, for a time, is to the most intelligent child, and if a government loved a people as fathers generally love their children. But there is no reason to believe that a government will have either the paternal warmth of affection or the paternal superiority of intellect.'

There was also the greatest danger in rulers prescribing morals and beliefs to their people. Such matters could be decided only by free discussion, not by authoritarian pronouncement. Macaulay pointed to the consequences of the Arminian attempt to enforce uniformity in the reign of Charles I, and a similar Puritan attempt during the period of the Commonwealth. Southey feared the decline of religion. 'Mr. Southey thinks that the yoke of the church is dropping off because it is loose. We feel convinced that it is borne only because it is easy, and that, in the instant in which an attempt is made to tighten it, it will be flung away.' Macaulay declared that he found it impossible to reconcile Southey's argument with a full acceptance of a principle of toleration; apparently his opinion was 'that everybody is to tolerate him, and that he is to tolerate nobody'. The true power of the Christian Church lay in its charity and benevolence, not in any power of persecution. 'The whole history of Christianity shows that she is in far greater danger of being corrupted by the alliance of power, than of being crushed by its opposition.'

On the whole Southey took a gloomy view of the prospects of society, Macaulay took an optimistic view. Men were better fed, better clothed and better housed in England than in the sixteenth century, and certainly much better than in those European countries which had not experienced the benefits of steam power. It was also true that men were more humane and more critical. 'For this very reason, suffering is more acutely felt and more loudly bewailed here than elsewhere.' Yet, apart from America, 'we must confess ourselves unable to find any satisfactory record of any great nation, past or present, in which the working classes have been in a more comfortable situation than in England during the last thirty years.' Indeed the whole range of history showed the steady advance of progress, and the astounding advance in wealth and the size of the population, and there was no reason to suppose that the progress would not continue. It would not indeed be impossible that England in 1930 might have 'a population of fifty millions, better fed, clad, and lodged than the English of our time'. 'We rely on the natural tendency of the human intellect to truth, and on the natural tendency of society to improvement. ... We know of no country which, at the end of fifty years of peace and tolerably good government, has been less prosperous than at the beginning of that period.'

For Macaulay the law of progress was writ large in history. 'History is full of the signs of this natural progress of society. We see in almost every part of the annals of mankind how the industry of individuals, struggling up against wars, taxes, famines, conflagrations, mischievous prohibitions, and more mischievous protections, creates faster than governments can squander, and repairs whatever invaders can destroy. We see the wealth of nations increasing, and all the arts of life approaching nearer and nearer to perfection, in spite of the grossest corruption and the wildest profusion on the part of rulers.'

Such was the philosophy of optimism of the whigs as stated by Macaulay on the eve of the whig victory in 1830 and the Great Reform Bill of 1832. It was a philosophy which gave the party the impetus for a long run of political power during the next thirty-six years.

NOTES

[1] Sir Walter Scott also regarded the Poor rates as the most serious social problem of the time. He wrote to Southey in March 1818:

> The times look gloomy enough. I do not fear the usual strain of popular discontent, but the Poor rates, like the snakes of your eastern tyrant, are gnawing into the bowels of England. It is deep and spreading gangrene and the question is whether the patient may not bleed to death in the attempt to extirpate it. Fortunately we have in this respect no common cause of discontent with you. Our very poverty has saved us from the misfortunes attending too general and indiscriminate a system of providing for the poor and I think we feel the advantage so much that we will not easily forfeit it. Last year, which was a very severe one among the poor people, we had the prudence in this and other parishes to anticipate the evil by agreeing upon the propriety of carrying through certain improvements on the high roads and such other public works as served to employ the population, who might otherwise have robbed and starved. This was done so cautiously and with so little ostentation that the people never found out that it was done for the *nonce*. It is the last of degradation so far as I have been able to observe when the honest and independent labourer has become an object of eleemosynary relief. His proud spirit is broken like that of a seduced female and he ceases to possess one great impulse to every honourable exertion-self-estimation. I speak with some confidence on this subject, for being naturally fond of the country people and spending among them all that I can possibly spare I have many opportunities to remark their motives and manners.
>
> (*Letters*, 23 March 1818.)

[2] This must indicate the extent to which Southey was impressed by his arguments, for Owen was no stylist.

[3] 'By means of two fortunate discoveries in the art of engraving, the graphic representations are brought within the reach of whole classes who were formerly precluded by the expense of such things from these sources of gratification and instruction. Artists and engravers of great name are now, like authors and booksellers, induced to employ themselves for this lower and wider sphere of purchasers.' (II, 423.) See p. 385.

[4] Karl Marx's theory of law originally stated by Harrington, is thus seen to have been a commonplace among the whigs while he was still a boy.

13 : Shelley and the Spirit of Liberty

THERE are a number of themes which may be said to run through Shelley's poetry, and one of the most important is that of the necessity of liberty to the human spirit. Much of his thought was influenced by Plato, from whom he borrowed the metaphor of the cave, and the shadows which reflected reality. From the Neo-Platonic tradition he borrowed the idea of nature, and the Chain of Being which linked man with the spiritual unity of the universe, and this idea was reinforced by his intense interest in science, which led him to study the proliferation of natural forms, and the wonders of the physical universe. He was thus aware of some pattern in the universe, of which man was a part; yet man had in some way taken a wrong turning. The Greeks had discovered the nature of liberty, and had given civilisation to the west, but the meaning had been lost as men sank beneath the twin tyrannies of kings and priests. In his own day the idea of liberty had returned, but it had to fight against the combined forces of the Holy Alliance, and hence Shelley showed a passionate interest in the Peterloo Massacre in England, and the revolts in Spain and Greece, which he took to be the beginnings of a new age of liberty for Europe. What exactly 'liberty' meant to him in a political sense it is not often easy to say, and it is true that the 'liberalism' of European revolts was often a very inadequate creed. But Shelley was not the child in politics which he has sometimes been made out to be. A close study of his ideas will show that he had a clear grasp of realities, and that politically he was more moderate than he seemed. But he was less interested in political forms than in the *spirit* of liberty, and that to him meant in some way the release of the personality of men and women from economic, intellectual and spiritual bonds. He spoke often in support of 'revolution', but it was not a revolution of violence which he advocated, but a moral transformation whereby individualism and social justice would be released, and tyranny would succumb simply because it was obscurantist, outmoded and inadequate. How society would then be organised, and how individualism would be reconciled with social obligations he did not enquire too deeply. In a new era of universal love such problems would solve themselves.

Queen Mab (1813) was a poem of youthful exuberance, written before Shelley was twenty-one, and expressing most completely his debt to the ideas of Godwin. Of all the poems of the period it was the one which most completely expressed the romanticism of revolt, and being a juvenile poem, although already showing the poet's power of words and promising mastery of verse form, it stated his philosophy in clear and forthright terms. Man, to Shelley, was a pure and noble being who should enjoy the fruits of the earth in happiness and peace, but alas, he had been perverted and borne down by the weight of power. It was the nature of the spirit to be free, but man's spirit had been imprisoned, and his nature corrupted:

> Power, like a desolating pestilence,
> Pollutes whate'er it touches; and obedience,
> Bane of all genius, virtue, freedom, truth,
> Makes slaves of men, and, of the human frame,
> A mechanised automaton.   (III, 176.)

For Shelley political power was symbolised by kings and courts, around which corruption fattened while the poor starved:

> Those gilded flies
> That, basking in the sunshine of a court,
> Fatten on its corruption!—what are they?
> —The drones of the community; they feed
> On the mechanic's labour.   (III, 106.)

Their influence pervaded society, and corrupted all men; was it so strange therefore that men had forgotten the nobility of their nature in the atmosphere of decadence?

> Is it strange
> That this poor wretch should pride him in his woe?
> Take pleasure in his abjectness, and hug
> The scorpion that consumes him? Is it strange
> That, placed on a conspicuous throne of thorns,
> Grasping an iron sceptre, and immured
> Within a splendid prison, whose stern bounds
> Shut him from all that's good or dear on earth,
> His soul asserts not its humanity?
> That man's mild nature rises not in war
> Against a king's employ? No—'tis not strange,
> He, like the vulgar, thinks, feels, acts and lives
> Just as his father did; the unconquered powers
> Of precedent and custom interpose
> Between a *king* and virtue.   (III, 88.)

This was the explanation why men had not risen long ago to overthrow tyranny and to 'dash kings from their thrones'. It follows that when men learn to understand their true nature they will destroy the political powers which have oppressed men and made misery and wars:

> Nature rejects the monarch, not the man;
> The subject, not the citizen: for kings
> And subjects, mutual foes, forever play
> A losing game into each other's hands.
> Whose stakes are vice and misery. The man
> Of virtuous soul commands not, nor obeys.
>   (III, 170.)

The contrast was always between the peace, beauty and harmony of nature, and the misery created by man:

> Look on yonder earth:
> The golden harvests spring; the unfailing sun
> Sheds light and life; the fruits, the flowers, the trees,

T

> Arise in due succession; all things speak
> Peace, harmony, and love. The universe,
> In Nature's silent eloquence, declares
> That all fulfil the works of love and joy—
> All but the outcast, Man. He fabricates
> The sword which stabs his peace; he cherisheth
> The snakes that gnaw his heart; he raiseth up
> The tyrant, whose delight is in his woe. (III, 192.)

The fruits of the earth were meant to be enjoyed by all alike, yet in practice they were the preserves of a few. The Spirit of Nature was in all men, just as it pervaded the whole universe, the life of minute creatures, and inanimate nature alike, and once men recognised the need to follow its lead there would follow a reign of eternal peace. Addressing the Spirit of Nature, the poet declared:

> 'Man, like these passive things,
> Thy will unconsciously fulfilleth:
> Like theirs, his age of endless peace,
> Which time is fast maturing,
> Will swiftly, surely come;
> And the unbounded frame, which thou pervadest,
> Will be without a flaw
> Marring its perfect symmetry.'   (III, 233.)

Shelley did not answer the various questions which arise concerning his attitude to nature. If man was in every respect a part of nature, how was it that he had become corrupted? If man was, as he said 'unconsciously fulfilling the Spirit of Nature', why was it necessary to call upon him to turn away from his present state, since the Spirit of Nature would inexorably guide him anyway? It is clear that Shelley was drawing in part on traditional ideas. The Spirit of Nature, which pervaded alike the motions of the stars and the lives of the smallest microbes, was a new version of the traditional concept of the Great Chain of Being, and the corruption which had entered men's lives was only another way of stating the Fall and the expulsion from the Garden of Eden. The wickedness of Satan was transformed into the wickedness of kings, who had corrupted man from his true nature. Similarly the ideal future which awaited man was a secularised version of the changeless eternity of Paradise.

How important these concepts were to the literature of revolt may be seen if we compare Shelley's ideas with those of the greatest philosopher of revolt of the period, Karl Marx. Marx too believed in the innate goodness of human nature. He too believed that men had been corrupted—his word was 'alienated'—not by kings, although that was part of the story, but by the economic system, and by the modern world of capitalism. He too believed that there were sufficient fruits of the earth for all if only they were fairly distributed, and that in order to achieve this desirable state of affairs it was necessary to overthrow the existing system, to destroy political power (so that the State would 'wither away') and establish an eternity of changeless peace and equality. Moreover the same uncertainty arose with Marx's theory that arose with Shelley's. For if the whole universe was actuated by the Spirit of Nature (in Marx's version it was the historical process, inexorable and scientific in its character), why was it necessary to change it by force, and if man stood outside the order of Nature (having the power to choose alternative courses of action), how could it be certain that he was bound by any of its laws?

Neither Shelley nor Marx would have anything to do with a doctrine of original sin. Men were not corrupt by nature, but only by circumstances. To Marx they were the victims of the economic system under which they lived; to Shelley they were the products of bad education.

> The child,
> Ere he can lisp his mother's sacred name,
> Swells with the unnatural pride of crime, and lifts
> His baby-sword even in a hero's mood.
> This infant-arm becomes the bloodiest scourge
> Of devastated earth.   (IV, 107.)

The child has no chance to develop according to his nature.

> It is bound
> Ere it has life; yea, all the chains are forged

> Long ere its being: all liberty and love
> And peace is torn from its defencelessness;
> Cursed from its birth, even from its cradle doomed
> To abjectness and bondage!   (IV, 133.)

To Shelley the instruments of this bondage were always the same;
kings, surrounded by corrupt and flattering courtiers and 'hoary-
headed' (with Shelley they were always 'hoary-headed') hypocrites,
wilfully misleading the people. And Shelley would have been in full
agreement with Marx that the economic system was unjust and
oppressive:

> The iron rod of Penury still compels
> Her wretched slave to bow the knee to wealth,
> And poison, with unprofitable toil,
> A life too void of solace to confirm
> The very chains that bind him to his doom.
>   (IV, 127.)

The world was tainted by what Carlyle later called Mammonism.

> All things are sold: the very light of Heaven
> Is venal; earth's unsparing gifts of love,
> The smallest and most despicable things
> That lurk in the abysses of the deep,
> All objects of our life, even life itself,
> And the poor pittance which the laws allow
> Of liberty, the fellowship of man,
> Those duties which his heart of human love
> Should urge him to perform instinctively,
> Are bought and sold as in the public mart.
>   (IV, 177.)

Men were the prisoners of the system under which they lived:

> War is the statesman's game, the priest's delight,
> The lawyer's jest, the hired assassin's trade.

They were prisoners, but not permanently corrupted; they had

before them a clear choice of liberty or slavery, of life or death.
There was no middle way.

> Man is of soul and body, formed for deeds
> Of high resolve, on fancy's boldest wing
> To soar unwearied, fearlessly to turn
> The keenest pangs to peacefulness, and taste
> The joys which mingled sense and spirit yield.
> Or he is formed for abjectness and woe,
> To grovel on the dunghill of his fears.
>
> .   .   .   .   .   .
>
> The one is man that shall hereafter be;
> The other, man as vice has made him now.
>
> (IV, 154.)

In his general indictment against history Shelley was particularly
severe in his condemnation of the Church. At the age of nineteen
he had written a pamphlet entitled *The Necessity of Atheism*, for
which he had been sent down from Oxford, and the harsh penalty
only confirmed him in his view that the God of orthodoxy was an
evil and vengeful being. The God of the priests had entrapped Adam
into sin, and had then punished him for it. Slaves had built massive
temples; priests had instituted bloody persecutions and fomented
religious wars. God appeared as a vengeful being, choosing to save
his Elect, but ready to condemn the mass of mankind to perdition.
If this was the God of history, it could not be Shelley's God. In its
place he fell back upon a God of his own, the Spirit of Nature.

> Spirit of Nature! all-sufficing Power
> Necessity! thou mother of the world!
> Unlike the God of human error, thou
> Requir'st no prayers or praises; the caprice
> Of man's weak will belongs no more to thee
> Than do the changeful passions of his breast
> To thy unvarying harmony . . .   (VI, 197.)
> No love, no hate thou cherishest; revenge
> And favouritism, and worst desire of fame

Thou know'st not: all that the wide world contains
Are but thy passive instruments, and thou
Regard'st them all with an impartial eye,
Whose joy or pain thy nature cannot feel,
Because thou hast not human sense,
Because thou art not human mind.   (VI, 212.)

Now this God of Shelley's is clearly the God of Voltaire and the eighteenth-century Enlightenment, the God which science had appeared to confirm. Shelley was fascinated with the development of science since the age of Newton, and to him it seemed to confirm the age-old idea of the Great Chain of Being which stemmed from Plato, in which every detail had its appointed place in the pattern of the universe. Indeed, he specifically referred to it in words which we have placed in italics:

There is no God!
Nature confirms the faith his death-groan sealed:
Let heaven and earth, let man's revolving race,
His ceaseless generations tell their tale;
Let every part depending on the chain
That links it to the whole, point to the hand
That grasps its term! let every seed that falls
In silent eloquence unfold its store
Of argument; infinity within,
Infinity without, belie creation;
The exterminable spirit it contains
Is nature's only God; but human pride
Is skilful to invent most serious names
To hide its ignorance.   (VI, 13.)

In the hands of priests the God of history had been the instrument of oppression:

Earth groans beneath religion's iron age,
And priests dare to babble of a God of peace,
Even whilst their hands are red with guiltless blood.
                                (VII, 43.)

In contrast, the Spirit of Nature to Shelley stood for justice, peace and love.

Herein lay the weakest link in Shelley's argument, for his Spirit of Nature was not in truth the spirit which science had revealed, but the old view of Paradise which would come for all eternity once men had regained liberty. It was also Marx's view of the classless society. Shelley envisaged the frozen hills and deserts turned to green fields, the lion lying down with the lamb, and

> Here now the human being stands adorning
> This loveliest earth with taintless body and mind.
>
> .   .   .   .   .   .
>
> All things are void of terror: Man has lost
> His terrible prerogative, and stands
> An equal amidst equals: happiness
> And science dawn though late upon the earth;
> Peace cheers the mind, health renovates the frame;
> Disease and pleasure cease to mingle here,
> Reason and passion cease to mingle there;
> Whilst each unfettered o'er the earth extend
> Their all-subduing energies. (VIII, 198.)

All this was attainable, for man was capable of perfectibility; for

> every heart contains perfection's germ

if only it was allowed free expression.

In *The Revolt of Islam* (1818) Shelley continued the theme of the conflict between liberty and tyranny. At first it is a struggle between an eagle and a snake, representing respectively tyranny and goodness. Laon, a noble youth, representing Shelley himself, and Cythna, a beautiful maiden, are caught up in the struggle. Sometimes the struggle is given a straightforward political context:

> Such is this conflict—when mankind doth strive
> With its oppressors in a strife of blood,
> Or when free thoughts, like lightnings, are alive,
> And in each bosom of the multitude

> Justice and truth with Custom's hydra brood
> Wage silent war; when Priests and Kings dissemble
> In smiles or frowns their fierce disquietude,
> When round pure hearts a host of hopes assemble,
> The Snake and Eagle meet—the world's foundations
>   tremble.   (I, xxxiii.)

Often however Laon is fighting vague enemies simply described as Tyrants. Battles are curiously dreamlike, and Laon often passes from one scene to another in Shelley's favourite symbol of a boat gliding through troubled waters. The whole poem is insubstantial and inordinately long, and the reader may be forgiven for agreeing with Lamb's complaint that it was full of 'theories and nostrums, ringing in their own emptiness'. The whole picture is fraught with Shelley's contempt for man's life as it has been lived throughout history:

> I heard, as all have heard, the various story
> Of human life, and wept unwilling tears.
> Feeble historians of its shame and glory,
> False disputants on all its hopes and fears,
> Victims who worshipped ruin,—chroniclers
> Of daily scorn, and slaves who loathed their state
> Yet, flattering power, had given its ministers
> A throne of judgement in the grave.   (II, iii.)

The history of man had been the history of misery because it had been the history of tyranny:

> For they all pined in bondage; body and soul,
> Tyrant and slave, victim and torturer, bent
> Before one Power.   (II, viii.)

Man has enslaved himself by his willing submission to tyrants, not least to his lust for gold:

> Man seeks for gold in mines, that he may weave
> A lasting chain for his won slavery;—
> In fear and restless care that he may live

He toils for others, who must ever be
The joyless thralls of like captivity;
He murders, for his chiefs delight in ruin;
He builds the altar, that its idol's fee
May be his very blood; he is pursuing—
O, blind and willing wretch!—his own obscure
    undoing.   (VIII, xiv.)

But man had the power to escape from such bondage; he had once tasted Paradise, and might return to it again. Indeed, the whole poem is powerfully influenced by the ideas of *Paradise Lost*.

Such man has been, and such may yet become!
Ay, wiser, greater, gentler, even than they
Who on the fragments of yon shattered dome
Have stamped the sign of power . . .
. . . Hope is strong,
Justice and Truth their winged child have found—
Awake! arise! until the mighty sound
Of your career shall scatter in its gust
The thrones of the oppressor.   (II, xii, xiii.)

Once tyranny was overthrown, mankind would live in blissful enjoyment of the rich fruits of the earth, but not meat, for blood should never again flow. Conversation would be of liberty, hope and justice, and

Our toil from thought all glorious forms shall cull,
To make this Earth, our home, more beautiful,
And Science, and her sister Poesy,
Shall clothe in light the fields and cities of the free!
                          (V, lvi.)

In the new world woman would at last be free, for

Can man be free if woman be a slave?
Chain one who lives, and breathes this boundless air,
To the corruption of a closèd grave!   (II, xliii.)

When Laon and Cythna escape from the Tyrant, they consummate the achievement of a final liberty by an idyllic sensual love in perfect natural surroundings. Shelley's first thought had been to make them brother and sister, for incest was an idea which fascinated the Romantics, both as an unusual experience, and as likely to satisfy the need for a perfect identity of feelings and interests.

> And such is Nature's law divine that those
> Who grow together cannot choose but love,
> If faith or custom do not interpose,
> Or common slavery mar what else might move
> All gentlest thoughts. (VI, xl.)

But prudence persuaded Shelley at the last moment to change his mind, and Cythna became an orphan. None the less, it was clear that to him that the consummation of liberty lay in sexual bliss between man and woman who were in all spiritual matters equals. We cannot regard the intellectual content of the poem as of great significance, nor does it contain Shelley's best poetry, but he himself regarded it as an important work. 'I felt the precariousness of my life, and I engaged in this task, resolved to leave some record of myself.' This he did, for Laon is clearly Shelley's image of himself.

It was such poems as *The Revolt of Islam* which led Matthew Arnold to his famous estimate of Shelley as a 'beautiful and ineffectual angel, beating in the void his luminous wings in vain'. The judgment is a fair one in that the *liberty* which Laon pursues throughout the poem is a vague and nebulous concept, insubstantial in either an intellectual, moral or social sense. But that Shelley had a clear view of what he meant by liberty in a political and social sense, is shown by two works both written in 1819, *The Mask of Anarchy*, and his prose pamphlet, *A Philosophical View of Reform*, the latter of which Matthew Arnold may not have read, as it was not published until 1920. *The Mask of Anarchy* was written in anger at the news of the Peterloo Massacre. It was cruelly satirical of Castlereagh, Foreign Minister and Leader of the Commons:

> I met Murder on the way—
> He had a mask like Castlereagh—
> Very smooth he looked, yet grim;
> Seven blood-hounds followed him.

Eldon, the Lord Chancellor (against whom Shelley had a personal grudge), who appeared as Fraud, and Sidmouth, the Home Secretary, as Hypocrisy. They are attendants in a masque in honour of Anarchy, but as the ghastly procession moves onwards against the people, a young maiden, Hope, bars their way. She calls upon the men of England to

> Rise like Lions after slumber
> In unvanquishable number,
> Shake your chains to earth like dew
> Which in sleep had fallen on you—
> Ye are many—they are few.

This at first sight appears to be a call to revolution, but this is not its purpose. It was not revolution and violence that Shelley advocated, but a recognition by the people of the meaning of freedom. And what *is* freedom? The people knew well enough what slavery was:

> 'Tis to work and have such pay
> As just keeps life from day to day
> In your limbs, as in a cell
> For the tyrants' use to dwell

> 'Tis to see your children weak
> With their mothers pine and peak,
> When the winter winds are bleak—
> They are dying whilst I speak.

Slavery, then, is poverty, hardship and toil.

> 'Tis to be a slave in soul
> And to hold no strong control
> Over your own wills, but be
> All that others make of ye.

Freedom, accordingly was the contrary. Shelley's view was no longer nebulous, but practical and forthright:

> Thou art clothes, and fire, and food
> For the trampled multitude—
> No—in countries that are free
> Such starvation cannot be
> As in England now we see.
>
> To the rich thou art a check,
> When his foot is on the neck
> Of his victim, thou dost make
> That he treads upon a snake.

Freedom meant just laws for 'high and low', and wisdom, which would show men that the priests' warnings of eternal damnation were false, and finally it was peace and love. What Shelley called for was not revolution, but understanding of the true nature of freedom:

> Let a vast assembly be,
> And with great solemnity
> Declare with measured words that ye
> Are, as God has made ye, free.

When they are attacked by oppression, they do not rebel, but stand with folded arms, calm and resolute until the fury passes:

> With folded arms and steady eyes,
> And little fear, and less surprise,
> Look upon them as they slay
> Till their rage has died away.
>
> Then they will return with shame
> To the place from which they came,
> And the blood thus shed will speak
> In hot blushes on their cheek.
>
> Every woman in the land
> Will point at them as they stand—

> They will hardly dare to greet
> Their acquaintance in the street.

This was a measure of Shelley's political maturity by 1819. With all his deep sympathy with the people, he called, not for revolution, but for restraint in the full realisation of the true nature of man. He sensed that public opinion would ultimately triumph, and he was right. There was no second Peterloo Massacre, there was no revolution, and by the eighteen-twenties the spirit of reform had begun to make itself felt. Men 'with folded arms and steady eyes', and a strong sense of the justice of their cause, were to achieve more in nineteenth-century England than any revolutionary. Not that Shelley's poem may be said to have influenced events, for Leigh Hunt feared to publish it until 1832, when the worst fears of revolution were passing.

His political views were worked out more fully in his main political prose work, *A Philosophical View of Reform*, which included also his philosophy of history. He saw the English revolutions of the seventeenth century doing little to limit the power of either monarchy, aristocracy or episcopacy, because what they lost in power they made up for in security of tenure. The real step towards liberty was not in politics, but in the scientific revolution which began with Bacon and Locke, and led on to the philosophy of the Enlightenment. Although he regarded the philosophy of Locke as 'superficial', yet he regarded it as bearing fruit, both in the formation of the United States, and the coming of the French Revolution. The United States provided a perfect example of a free government. The French Revolution, with all its disappointments, had set in motion a chain of events which would lead ultimately to the overthrow of tyrants throughout Europe, and indeed the world. In England there was a great literary and philosophical renaissance. 'It is impossible to read the productions of our most celebrated writers, whatever may be their system relating to thought or expression, without being startled by the electric life which there is in their words. They measure the circumference or sound the depths of human nature with a comprehensive and all-penetrating spirit at which they are themselves perhaps most sincerely astonished, for it is less their own spirit than the spirit of their age.'

Accompanying this great literary upsurge there was a popular desire for change in the forms of government, which could not long be resisted. The Revolution of 1688 established government by oligarchy, government by the rich: 'the name and office of king is merely the mask of this power. . . . Monarchy is only the string which ties the robbers' bundle'. Shelley reserved his most bitter hostility for the aristocracy, who had inherited power. 'They eat and drink and sleep, and in the intervals of these things performed with most vexatious ceremony and accompaniments they cringe and lie. They poison the literature of the age in which they live by requiring either the antitype of their own mediocrity in books, or such stupid and distorted and inharmonious idealisms as alone have the power to stir their torpid imaginations. Their hopes and fears are of the narrowest description. Their domestic affections are feeble, and they have no others.' Under this oligarchy the condition of the poor became worse, for men were required to work fourteen hours a day for wages which had once been earned in seven, and women and children were forced to work in order to maintain the existence of the family. Shelley felt deeply the injustice of the economic system which created so much misery, for 'happiness is a principle of nature', yet it was denied to the poor. He bitterly opposed the cold doctrines of Malthus whereby they were 'required to abstain from marrying under penalty of starvation'. How heartless to preach sexual restraint to the poor, when it was the most difficult thing in the world for even the most intelligent to practise, and how heartless to require the poor 'to abstain from sexual intercourse, while the rich are to be permitted to add as many mouths to consume the products of the labour of the poor as they please'.

The fact was that 'the majority of the people of England are destitute and miserable, ill-clothed, ill-fed, ill-educated'; the danger was that they would be forced into revolution in order to obtain their rights. Shelley wrote, not to foment revolution, but to forestall it. He feared an immediate achievement of democracy as likely to lead to a general assault upon property. He believed in the justice of private property. 'Labour and skill and the immediate wages of labour and skill is a property of the most sacred and indisputable right, and the foundation of all other property. And the right of a man to property in the exertion of his own bodily and mental faculties, or on the produce and free reward from and for that exertion is the most inalienable of rights.' But there was another kind of private property, founded upon injustice, and the sudden achievement of democracy might well lead to a dispossession. It was necessary therefore to see that there was timely reform, before revolution gained momentum. 'The first principle of political reform is the natural equality of men, not with relation to their property but to their rights.' Shelley was not proposing either universal or manhood suffrage. 'Any sudden attempt at universal suffrage would produce an immature attempt at a Republic', while the suggestion that women might be given the vote seemed to him to be 'somewhat immature'. This sentence must be remembered when we read Shelley's frequent fulminations against kings; he did not really contemplate the overthrow of monarchy in England. What he wanted was gradual reform, beginning with the disfranchisement of rotten boroughs, and the establishment of triennial parliaments and a voting qualification based on the possession of private property. That there was risk even in these reforms he did not deny, but 'it is in politics rather than in religion that faith is meritorious'. He wanted the cause of reform to be undertaken by the poets and philosophers of the time. 'Suppose the memorials to be severally written by Godwin, Hazlitt and Bentham and Hunt, they would be worthy of the age and of the cause; radiant and irresistible like the meridian sun they would strike all but the eagles who dared gaze upon its beams with blindness and confusion.' Moderate reform would be an antidote to revolution; it would forestall what Shelley called 'certain vulgar agitators' who preached Retribution, and would open a new age of liberty, equality and social justice.

Shelley incorporated the same philosophy of life of the earlier poems in his lyrical drama *Prometheus Unbound*, which was based on Aeschylus's version of the legend. Prometheus was the great benefactor of man, having brought fire and the arts down from heaven, thereby incurring the wrath of Jupiter, who had him chained to a rock in the Caucasus. There he remained, undergoing

great torture and suffering, during millennia, so long as the tyranny
of Jupiter remained. That tyranny would be overthrown by the
only force among the human emotions which was not subject to it,
namely Love. For the lovely maiden Asia, symbolising Nature,
loved Prometheus, and she descended to the depths to learn from
Demorgorgon, a shrouded figure symbolising Eternity, when
Prometheus might obtain his release. While there, she questioned
Demorgorgon about the nature of things. First, 'Who made the
living world?' 'God', was the reply. It was easy to accept that God
had made the beautiful things of life, but

> who made terror, madness, crime, remorse,
> Which from the links of the great chain of things,
> To every thought within the mind of man
> Sway and drag heavily, and each one reels
> Under the load towards the pit of death?
>
> (II, iv, 19.)

Demorgorgon's answer was enigmatic: it was *he who reigns*. But
this raised the whole question. Who *did* reign? Was it the tyrant
Jupiter?

> To know nor faith, nor love, nor law; to be
> Omnipotent but friendless is to reign;
> And Jove now reigned; for on the race of man
> First famine, and then toil, and then disease,
> Strife, wounds, and ghastly death unseen before,
> Fell.

But in establishing this tyranny, Jupiter was only employing, and
misusing, the power of knowledge which he had obtained from
Prometheus, for

> Prometheus
> Gave wisdom, which is strength, to Jupiter,
> And with this law alone, 'Let man be free',
> Clothed him with the dominion of wide Heaven.

Jupiter had misused knowledge to enslave men, and to bring

misery and suffering into the world. Yet the Promethean knowledge which Jupiter had employed was available to all men, and indeed there were reserves which Jupiter had not used, for

> Love he (i.e. Prometheus) sent to bind
> The disunited tendrils of that vine
> Which bears the wine of life, the human heart;
> And he tamed fire which, like some beast of prey,
> Most terrible, but lovely, played beneath
> The frown of man; and tortured to his will
> Iron and gold, the slaves and signs of power,
> And gems and poisons, and all subtlest forms
> Hidden beneath the mountains and the waves.
> He gave man speech, and speech created thought,
> Which is the measure of the universe;
> And Science struck the thrones of earth and heaven,
> Which shook, but fell not; and the harmonious mind
> Poured itself forth in all-prophetic song;
> And music lifted up the listening spirit
> Until it walked, exempt from mortal care,
> Godlike, o'er the clear billows of sweet sound,
>
> (II, iv, 63.)

and all the arts glorified the mind of man. Who, then, *did* reign? Was it in truth Jupiter, who used knowledge to enslave, or Prometheus, who had given man some godlike qualities? The answer of Demorgorgon was still enigmatic, for was not Prometheus still chained to his rock? But Love was now abroad, and it was irresistible. Asia learned that Jupiter's hour had come.

In the third act Prometheus was released from his bonds, and echoes reached him.

> The echoes of the human world which tell
> Of the low voice of love, almost unheard,
> And dove-eyed pity's murmured pain, and music,
> Itself the echo of the heart, and all
> That tempers or improves man's life, now free.
>
> (III, iii, 44.)

v

The arts of painting, sculpture and poetry, all told the same story

> Of all that man becomes, the mediators
> Of all that best worship, love, by him and us
> Given and returned.

The Spirit of the Earth hurried in to tell of the transformation which had come over the world, and how

> All things had put their evil nature off.
>
> (III, iv, 77.)

The Spirit of the Hour confirmed the change:

> And behold, thrones were kingless, and men walked
> One with the other even as spirits do.
> None fawned, none trampled; hate, disdain or fear,
> Self-love or self-contempt, on human brows
> No more inscribed, as o'er the gate of hell,
> 'All hope abandon ye who enter here';
> None frowned, none trembled, none with eager fear
> Gazed on another's eye of cold command,
> Until the subject of a tyrant's will
> Became, worse fate, the abject of his own,
> Which spurred him, like an outspent horse, to death.
>
> .   .   .   .   .   .
>
> The loathsome mask has fallen, the man remains
> Sceptreless, free, uncircumscribed, but man
> Equal, unclassed, tribeless, and nationless,
> Exempt from awe, worship, degree, the king
> Over himself; just, gentle, wise: but man
> Passionless?—no, yet free from guilt or pain,
> Which were, for his will made or suffered them,
> Nor yet exempt, though ruling them like slaves,
> From chance, and death, and mutability,
> The clogs of that which else might oversoar
> The loftiest star of unascended heaven,
> Pinnacled dim in the intense inane. (III, iv, 131.)

Such was the ideal world of Shelley, and it was in contrast to the disjointed world of existence which a Fury described in Act I, in which

> The good want power, but to weep barren tears.
> The powerful goodness want: worse need for them.
> The wise want love; and those who love want wisdom;
> And all best things are thus confused to ill.
> Many are strong and rich, and would be just,
> But live among their suffering fellow-men
> As if none felt: they know not what they do.
>
> (I, 625.)

It is essential to realise that to Shelley the ideal was *attainable*. As Mary Shelley wrote in a Note to the play: 'Shelley believed that mankind had only to will that there should be no evil, and there would be none. . . . That man could be so perfectionised as to be able to expel evil from his own nature, and from the greater part of the creation, was the cardinal point of his system.' He was not thinking in terms of some political revolution; Jupiter was not overthrown by force, but by the moral superiority of his opponent. The new world came about peacefully, when men realised the nature of the power which knowledge had placed in their hands, when science had opened up unlimited possibilities for human advancement, and when the arts had disseminated the ideals of truth, beauty, compassion and love. The whole work was conceived and written in the purest spirit of poetry. Indeed, Sir Herbert Read has called it 'the greatest expression ever given to humanity's desire for intellectual light and spiritual liberty'. (*The True Voice of Feeling*, p. 271.)

The theme of liberty recurs in his *Ode to Liberty* (1820) in which, in spite of his natural repugnance to violence, he celebrated the Spanish revolts of that year:

> My soul spurned the chains of its dismay,
> And in the rapid plumes of song
> Clothed itself, sublime and strong.

He glorified Athens as the true home of liberty in that it had first
released the human spirit,

> One Sun illumines Heaven; one Spirit vast
> With life and love makes chaos ever new,
> As Athens doth the world with thy delight renew.

It was impossible that God had intended man to discover his
liberty only to fall under the heel of the twin tyrants, king and
priest:

> Oh, that the free would stamp the impious name
> Of KING into the dust!
> Oh, that the wise from their bright minds would kindle
> Such lamps within the dome of this dim world,
> That the pale name of PRIEST might shrink and dwindle
> Into the hell from which it first was hurled.

> He who taught man to vanquish whatsoever
> Can be between the cradle and the grave
> Crowned him the King of Life. Oh, vain endeavour!
> If on his own high will, a willing slave,
> He has enthroned the oppression and the oppressor.

At the time of the sordid quarrel between George IV and his wife
Caroline in 1820, Shelley attempted a raucous satire, *Swellfoot the
Tyrant*, in which it might be said that he attempted to apply the
techniques of Rowlandson to verse. The unfortunate king appears
bloated with gout and over-indulgence; his

> kingly paunch
> Swells like a sail before a favouring breeze,
> And these most sacred nether promontories
> Lie satisfied with layers of fat.

His subjects appear as a chorus of pigs, lean and hungry, ready to
devour the hogwash which their royal master lets fall. The Tory
ministers are represented as corrupt sycophants; and the royal
agents, Leech, Gadfly and Rat, pursue the reputation of the Queen

Iona across Europe. Wellington is accused of having 'drunk more wine, and shed more blood, than any man in Thebes'. Lord Liverpool is accused of a tyranny under the name of a glorious constitution:

> The Lean-Pig rates
> Grow with the growing populace of Swine,
> The taxes, that true source of Piggishness
> (How can I find a more appropriate term
> To include religion, morals, peace, and plenty,
> And all that fit Boetia as a nation
> To teach the other nations how to live?)
> Increase with Piggishness itself.

Queen Iona appears to throw herself on the mercies of the Pigs, and at the end of the play she rides off triumphant on the back of John Bull. Shelley had a poor opinion of Queen Caroline, and it was no part of his purpose to exalt that foolish lady. The whole work has little but a mild historical interest, for Shelley lacked the pen of a Pope or a Byron to make a success of satire.

In 1821 Shelley was fired by the spectacle of the Greek revolt against the Turks. He assumed that the British Government would support the Turks. 'The English', he wrote, 'permit their own oppressors to act according to their natural sympathy with the Turkish tyrant, and to brand upon their name the indelible blot of an alliance with the enemies of domestic happiness, of Christianity and civilisation. . . . Should the English people ever become free, they will reflect upon the part which those who presume to represent their will have played in the great drama of the revival of liberty, with feelings which it would become them to anticipate. . . . This is the age of the war of the oppressed against the oppressors, and every one of those ringleaders of the privileged gangs of murderers and swindlers, called Sovereigns, look to each other for aid against the common enemy, and suspend their mutual jealousies in the presence of a mightier fear.' But, he continued, a new age of liberty was near; Spain was already free, Greece was in revolt, and 'the world waits only the news of a revolution in Germany to see the tyrants who have pinnacled themselves on its suppineness precipitated into the ruin from which they shall never arise'. In this mood he wrote his lyrical drama *Hellas*, a tribute to the glories of the Greek tradition. 'We are all Greeks', he wrote. 'Our laws, our literature, our religion, our arts have their root in Greece. But for Greece . . . we might still have been savages and idolators.'

> Let there be light! said Liberty,
> And like sunrise from the sea,
> Athens arose! Around her born,
> Shone like mountains in the morn
> Glorious states;—and are they now
> Ashes, wrecks, oblivion? (I, 682.)

The Sultan Mahmud listens to the prophecies of the inevitable destruction of his tyrannical empire, and throughout the poem the choruses foretell the inevitable return of liberty, and finally proclaim that 'Greece, which was dead, is arisen!'

> The world's great age begins anew,
> The golden years return,
> The earth doth like a snake renew
> Her winter weeds outworn:
> Heaven smiles, and faiths and empires gleam,
> Like wrecks of a dissolving dream. (1, 1060.)

> Oh, write no more the tale of Troy,
> If earth Death's scroll must be!
> Nor mix with Laian rage the joy
> Which dawns upon the free.

Hellas was among the last of Shelley's compositions, and it was dedicated to Prince Alexander Mavrocordato, the rebel leader with whom Byron later co-operated in western Greece. As a poem it is not a great success; its chief beauties are to be found in the lyrics of the choruses, in which Shelley poured forth, with great excitement and optimism his simple faith in liberty.

Shelley was aged thirty when he was drowned off Leghorn in July 1822. Whether, if he had lived a normal life-span, he would have retained his early optimism on the subject of liberty, may well be doubted. Four days before his death he was writing verses which began

> The hours are flying
> And joys are dying
> And hope is sighing.

More enigmatic is the major poem *The Triumph of Life*, which he left unfinished, in which, under the guidance of Rousseau, he surveys the careers of the great men of history, from Plato and Alexander to Voltaire and Napoleon, all of whom had in some way failed. As for Napoleon:

> I felt my cheek
> Alter, to see the shadow pass away,
> Whose grasp had left the giant world so weak
> That every pigmy kicked it as it lay;
> And much I grieved to think how power and will
> In opposition rule our mortal day,
> And why God made irreconcilable
> Good and the means of good.

The poem has a deeply serious and almost sombre note about it, as if Shelley was on the verge of a new period in his thinking. It breaks off with the agonising question,

> Then, what is life? I cried.

and Shelley wrote no more.

14 : The Mansion of the Mind: John Keats

THE sensuous nature of much of romantic poetry should not obscure the fact that romantic poets were often concerned with serious attempts to arrive at answers to philosophical, social, and even political problems. In this respect Keats has sometimes been misunderstood; he too was concerned with the philosophical problems posed by Romanticism, but his life was cut short before he could arrive at the formulation of his answers. Had all three poets achieved a normal life-span, he might well have had more to say than Shelley, and certainly more than Byron.

In a letter to J. H. Reynolds (2 May 1818) Keats set out his famous simile of human life:

I compare human life to a large Mansion of Many Apartments, two of which I can only describe, the doors of the rest being as yet shut to me. The first we step into we call the infant or thoughtless Chamber, in which we remain as long as we do not think— We remain there a long while, and notwithstanding the doors of the second Chamber remain wide open, showing a bright appearance, we care not to hasten to it; but are at length imperceptibly impelled by the awakening of this thinking principle within us—we no sooner get into the second Chamber, which I shall call the Chamber of Maiden-Thought, than we become intoxicated with the light and the atmosphere, we see nothing but pleasant wonders, and think of delaying there for ever in delight: However among the effects this breathing is father of is that tremendous one of sharpening one's vision into the heart and nature of Man—of convincing

one's nerves that the world is full of Misery and Heartbreak,
Pain, Sickness and oppression—whereby this Chamber of
Maiden Thought becomes gradually darken'd and at the same
time on all sides of it many doors are set open—but all dark—
all leading to dark passages—We see not the balance of good
and evil. We are in a Mist. *We* are now in that state—We feel
the 'burden of the Mystery'.

This passage is essential to the understanding of Keats' mind.
Most of the Romantics carried through life idyllic memories of
their childhood, of flowers and streams and carefree days, and had
a subconscious longing for their return. John Clare wrote of the
delights of his boyhood and longed in vain for their return:

> Those joys which childhood calls its own,
> Would they were kin to men!
> Those treasures to the world unknown,
> Then known, are withered then!

Blake too could hardly bear to think of the happiness of childhood:

> The days of my youth rise fresh in my mind,
> My face turns green and pale

for he, like Wordsworth, felt that 'there had passed away a glory
from the earth'. Keats was very conscious of the mental stages
through which men passed in life:

> Four seasons fill the measure of the year;
> Four seasons are there in the mind of man,
> He hath his lusty Spring when fancy clear
> Takes in all beauty with an easy span:
> He hath his Summer, when luxuriously
> He chewed the honied cud of fair Spring thoughts,
> Till, in his soul dissolved they come to be
> Part of himself.

In fact he had hardly reached summer, when his short life was
ended by disease, but it is clear from his writings that he was loath

to leave the period of springtime, when happiness could be *felt* unaccompanied by the chill winds of thought. Just a year before his death, he wrote: 'Like poor Falstaff though I do not babble, I think of green fields. I must with the greatest affection on every flower I have known from my infancy—their shapes and colours are as new to me as if I had just created them with a superhuman fancy. It is because they are connected with the most thoughtless and happiest moments of our lives. I have seen foreign flowers in hothouses of the most beautiful nature, but I do not care a straw for them. The simple flowers of our spring are what I want to see again.' (14–16 Feb. 1820.)

By 1817 Keats had begun to wrestle with the problems presented by a philosophy of life, and it then seemed to him that the only truth lay in the imagination. In a letter of 22 November 1817, he wrote: 'I am certain of nothing but of the holiness of the heart's affections and the truth of imagination. What the imagination seizes as beauty must be truth, whether it existed before or not, for I have the same idea of all our passions as of love: they are all in their sublime creative of essential beauty.' What he meant was this, that when we normally speak of knowledge we imply that what is in our minds corresponds, so to speak, to something outside it. But can we be *certain* of the correspondence? With the imagination it is different. If we feel love, or a sense of beauty, then that love and that sense of beauty, are *real* (i.e. true) and are not open to question. Note the phrase 'whether it existed before or not'; there is no need for a correspondence with something outside the mind; the mind has created it, and therefore it is true. And so Keats continued: 'The imagination may be compared to Adam's dream— he awoke and found it truth. I am the more zealous in this affair, because I have never yet been able to perceive how anything can be known for truth by consequitive reasoning—and yet', he added significantly, 'it must be.' In short, Keats did not deny the existence of knowledge; it was simply that he had not yet discovered a basis for it which satisfied him.

For a time indeed Keats dallied with the idea that man should seek to live within his imagination, having as little contact as possible with the outside world, and to explain his meaning he took the metaphor of a spider's web which is suspended in air, and has the fewest possible contacts with material things: 'It appears to me that almost any man may, like the spider, spin from his own inwards his own airy citadel—the points of leaves and twigs on which the spider begins her work are few, and she fills the air with a beautiful circuiting. Man should be content with as few points to tip with the fine web of his soul, and weave a tapestry empyrean full of symbols for his spiritual eye, of softness for his spiritual touch, of space for his wandering, of distinctness for his luxury. . . . It is more noble to sit like Jove than to fly like Mercury—let us not therefore go hurrying about and collecting honey-bee like, buzzing here and there impatiently from a knowledge of what is to be arrived at; but let us open our leaves like a flower and be passive and receptive' (Letter, 19 Feb. 1818). On 3 May he was writing that extensive knowledge was necessary to some people—'it takes away the heat and fever, and helps, by widening speculation, to ease the burden of the mystery'—but for himself as the imagination enabled him to soar upwards, knowledge brought him crashing down, and he declared that it was 'impossible to know how far knowledge will console us for the death of a friend and the ill "that flesh is heir to".'

Keats had a deep respect for Milton's poetry, but the poet who influenced him most in grappling with these problems was Wordsworth. Wordsworth, he declared, had 'in truth epic passion, and martyrs himself to the human heart', and from him Keats learnt that 'axioms in philosophy are not axioms until they are proved upon our pulses'. It was from a consideration of Wordsworth's thought that Keats was led on to set out his metaphor of the mansion with which we began.

We may illustrate the complexities of Keats' thought from his poem *Lamia*. Lamia, a spotted snake, takes on the form of a beautiful woman in order to pursue the love of a youth of Corinth. She helps the god Hermes to see a beautiful nymph:

> It was no dream; or say a dream it was,
> Real are the dreams of Gods, and smoothly pass
> Their pleasures in a long immortal dream.

Here is Keats' view of the imagination; to a god a dream is a reality because it does not end. Lamia achieves her idyllic love with Lycius, the youth of Corinth, but she always knows that it cannot last, for this world is 'empty of immortality and bliss':

> Thou art a scholar, Lycius, and must know
> That finer spirits cannot breathe below
> In human climes and live.

And Lycius, with all his love, could not stifle thought, at which Lamia began to moan and sigh

> Because he mused beyond her, knowing well
> That but a moment's thought is passion's
> passing bell.

Finally, at the appearance of the old philosopher Apollonius, Lamia disappeared, and Lycius was found to be dead. How is this poem to be interpreted? Lycius comes through the ordeal to receive the crown of thyrsus, the Bacchic symbol of forgetfulness, the best that can be expected in this life of sorrow. There is little sympathy for Lamia. She is first met with as a lurid snake, and this prepares the reader to assume that she is intended as a seductress. In the end she receives a crown of willow and adder's tongues, but as this is the gift of the philosopher Apollonius, it is not clear whether Keats intends this to be her just reward, or whether he is saying that philosophy will always put the worst construction upon idyllic love. As for the philosopher himself, he is crowned with 'spear-grass and the spiteful thistle', to indicate the bitterness of philosophers' tongues. Here the moral indeed is clear enough:

> Do not all charms fly
> At the mere touch of cold philosophy?
> There was an awful rainbow once in heaven
> We know her woof, her texture; she is given
> In the dull catalogue of common things.
> Philosophy will clip an Angel's wings,
> Conquer all mysteries by rule and line,

Empty the haunted air, and gnomed mine—
Unweave a rainbow, as it erewhile made
The tender-person'd Lamia melt into a shade.

Yet even without the intervention of Apollonius, this idyllic love
was doomed, for Lycius was mortal, and this was why Lamia had
'moaned and sighed'. Keats made plain that he regarded physical
love as the greatest of earthly pleasures:

Let the mad poets say whate'er they please
Of the sweets of Fairies, Peris, Goddesses,
There is not such a treat among them all,
Haunters of cavern, lake and waterfall,
As a real woman.

To some commentators this has seemed banal or tasteless, but it
undoubtedly reflected Keats' own desires, and it contains the real
meaning of the poem. Lamia was a goddess, and could presumably
have used magical powers over Lycius, but she 'judged, and
judged aright' that there was no power more potent than that
exercised by a beautiful woman. Neither mad poets nor sane
philosophers could alter that fact; but, as with all human things,
there was the accompanying regret that physical ecstasy was
transitory, and knowledge of this acted as a blight even at the
moment of consummation.

How deeply Keats longed for sexual satisfaction is revealed in
numerous poems. In his *Dedication to Leigh Hunt*, he wrote that
the only thing which would be likely to distract him from con-
templating the beauties of nature would be the rustling of a
maiden's gown:

Were I in such a place, I sure should pray
That nought less sweet, might call my thoughts away,
Than the soft rustle of a maiden's gown
Fanning away the dandelion's down;
Than the light music of her nimble toes
Panting against the sorrel as she goes.
How she would start, and blush, thus to be caught
Playing in all her innocence of thought!

In *Woman! when I behold thee flippant* he is again haunted:

> Light feet, dark violet eyes, and parted hair;
> Soft dimpled hands, white neck, and creamy breast;
> Are things on which the dazzled senses rest
> Till the fond, fixed eyes, forget they stare,

and he has little strength to resist the power of such a vision:

> In truth there is no freeing
> One's thoughts from such a beauty.

Herein lay the danger, that he would simply submit to sensuous desires, and in *Sleep and Poetry* he showed that he was aware of it. It was so easy, he wrote, to argue that 'life is but a day, a fragile dewdrop on its perilous way', and that one need do no more than to enjoy it. But Keats had great ambitions:

> O for ten years, that I may overwhelm
> Myself in poesy! so I may do the deed
> That my own soul has to itself decreed.

First there must be a period of sensuous experience:

> First the realm I'll pass
> Of Flora, and Old Pan: sleep in the grass,
> Feed upon apples red, and strawberries,
> And choose each pleasure that my fancy sees.

The sexual symbolism returns as he pursues fair nymphs, and ultimately achieves the joy he seeks:

> Another will entice me on, and on,
> Through almond blossoms and rich cinnamon;
> Till in the bosom of a leafy world
> We rest in silence, like two gems upcurl'd
> In the recesses of a pearly shell.

But this is not an end, but a beginning. There is no doubt that Keats subconsciously believed that sexual satisfaction was a necessary preliminary to his maturity, but once that was achieved, he had a nobler task to perform:

> And can I ever bid these joys farewell?
> Yes, I must pass them for a nobler life,
> Where I may find the agonies, the strife
> Of human hearts.

This task was no less than the restoration of poetry and the imagination to their rightful places, following the chill winter of Augustan rationalism.

> Yes, a schism
> Nurtured by foppery and barbarism,
> Made great Apollo blush for this his land.
> Men were thought wise who could not understand
> His glories.

Philosophers had become insensible to the things of the imagination:

> Beauty was awake!
> Why were ye not awake? But ye were dead
> To things ye knew not of,—were closely wed
> To musty laws lined out with wretched rule
> And compass vile: so that ye taught a school
> Of dolts to smooth, inlay, and clip, and fit,
> Till, like the certain wands of Jacob's wit,
> Their verses tallied. Easy was the task:
> A thousand handcraftsmen wore the mask
> Of Poesy. Ill-fated, impious race!
> That blasphemed the bright Lyrist to his face,
> And did not know it,—no, they went about,
> Holding a poor, decrepit standard out,
> Mark'd with most flimsy mottoes, and in large
> The name of one Boileau!

Keats' task, then, was to proclaim anew the poetry of the imagination:

> A drainless shower
> Of light is poesy; 'tis the supreme of power.

As yet the dream was vague, but of one thing he was sure, that it would take the form of a pursuit of wisdom which would not depend upon knowledge:

> What though I am not wealthy in the dower
> Of spanning wisdom; though I do not know
> The shiftings of the mighty winds that blow
> Hither and thither all the changing thoughts
> Of man: though no great minist'ring reason sorts
> Out the dark mysteries of human souls
> To clear conceiving; yet there ever rolls
> A vast idea before me, and I glean
> Therefrom my liberty.

Of the nature or extent of that vast idea we can only guess, for Keats died when he was twenty-five, but there are some clues as to the direction his mind was taking.

One reason why he was so loath, in the language of his metaphor of the Mansion of the Mind, to leave the second Chamber, was that he was loath to face the deeper problems of human life, those of evil, sickness and death. Yet it was clear to him that such problems must one day be faced, for poetry was not a form of escapism, but the highest expression of wisdom. It was a subject to which he returned again and again. In a letter of 27 October 1818, he wrote: 'I will speak of my views, and of the life I purpose to myself—I am ambitious of doing the world some good. If I should be spared that may be the work of maturer years—in the interval I will essay to reach to as high a summit in poetry as the nerve bestowed upon me will suffer. The faint conceptions I have of poems to come brings the blood frequently into my forehead. *All I hope is that I may not lose all interest in human affairs.*' It is quite wrong to suppose that Keats was not interested in politics; in the struggle between liberty and authority which was going on in his day, he placed himself clearly on the side of liberty. It would be wrong also to take too seriously his attack upon philosophy in *Lamia*. He was attacking a

1 George Romney:
William Cowper

National Portrait Gallery

National Portrait Gallery

2 B. R. Haydon:
William Wordsworth

3 George Richmond: William Wilberforce
(watercolour)

4 Thomas Girtin: Kirkstall Abbey in Yorkshire
(watercolour)

5 Sir Henry Raeburn: Col. Alistair MacDonell of Glengarry

6 Sir David Wilkie: Blind Man's Buff

7 Sir Thomas Lawrence: Pope Pius VII

8 John Crome: Landscape with Cottages

9 J. M. W. Turner: Inside Tintern Abbey

10 J. M. W. Turner: Crossing the Brook

11 John Constable: Boat-building near Flatford Mill

12 John Constable: The Leaping Horse

13 John Nash: The Royal Pavilion, Brighton

14 John Nash: Banqueting Room in the Royal Pavilion, Brighton

15 John Nash: Carlton House Terrace

16 James Wyatt: The
Library, Oriel
College, Oxford

17 James Wyatt: Fonthill Abbey

18 Richard Payne Knight: Downton Castle, Shropshire

19 Gillray: The Knight of the Woeful Countenance (1790). Burke, on a Papal donkey, rides to do battle with the French Revolution in defence of aristocracy and despotism.

20 Gillray: Light expelling Darkness: Pitt drives the chariot of British power, and by the light of the Constitution disperses the darkness of Jacobinism, and the Whigs are swept away in the clouds

21 Gillray: The Frenchman enjoys the rags and meagre diet of liberty, while John Bull, grumbling as usual, carves the roast beef of old England.

The Genius of France Triumphant — or — BRITANNIA petitioning for PEACE. — Vide The Proposals of Opposition. — To the Patriotic Advocates for Peace, this Scenely Sight is dedicated

22 Gillray: Britannia petitioning for Peace (1795): National opposition to an ignominious peace with France. Fox and the Whigs ready to surrender the fleet and Bank of England to the French.

Shrine at S.t Ann's Hill.

23 Gillray: Fox worshipping at the shrine of the Rights of Man (1798)

24 Gillray: The Turks, Russians and Austrians dislodge the French from Italy (1799), while British sea-power renders the French helpless

BRITANNIA between DEATH and the DOCTORS ; —— *" Death may decide when Doctors disagree. "*

25 Gillray: Pitt ousts Addington, and treads on Fox, while Bonaparte appears from behind the bedcurtains and prepares to kill Britannia

particular philosophy, but not philosophy in general. Here Milton came to his aid, for he had combined philosophy with sublime poetry, and Keats quoted with approval his lines:

> How charming is divine Philosophy
> Not harsh and crabbed as dull fools suppose
> But musical as is Apollo's lute.

When Keats came to his *annus mirabilis*, 1819, he was beginning to face this problem. In a most important letter of 19 March he wrote that he was still young, 'writing at random, straining at particles of light in the midst of a great darkness, without knowing the bearing of any one assertion of any one opinion'. He was still, he said, absorbed in a contemplation of nature, in 'the alertness of a stoat or the anxiety of a deer'. But was this enough?

> Though a quarrel in the streets is a thing to be hated, the energies displayed in it are fine; the commonest man shows a grace in his quarrel. By a superior being our reasonings may take the same tone—though erroneous they may be fine. This is the very thing in which consists poetry; and if so it is not so fine a thing as philosophy, for the same reason that an eagle is not so fine a thing as truth.

Now this is a very remarkable statement, for it implies that Keats was already regarding all his poetry so far as merely preparatory explorations, emotional expressions as he groped his way towards *truth*. An eagle was a fine thing, but it was not so fine as truth; poetry was a fine thing, but the finest poetry must be the embodiment of a philosophy of life. And thus he commented in the same letter upon his sonnet *Why did I laugh tonight?* 'it was written with no agony but that of ignorance; with no thirst of anything but knowledge when pushed to the point though the first steps to it were through my human passions'. Knowledge was the only thing for which Keats thirsted, but the first steps towards it had to be by way of the human passions.

If we have read Keats aright so far, we shall put a somewhat different interpretation upon the great Odes from that which is usually given. The nightingale is indeed the symbol of the imagin-

w

ation, less a bird than an immortal presence in all ages in the minds of men:

> The voice I heard this passing night was heard
> In ancient days by emperor and clown:
> Perhaps the self-same song that found a path
> Through the sad heart of Ruth, when, sick for home,
> She stood in tears amid the alien corn.

Keats' first instinct is to follow the nightingale into the ideal world of the imagination,

> That I might drink and leave the world unseen,
> And with thee fade away into the forest dim.

Or alternatively the beauty of its song has made him 'half in love with easeful Death'. Yet the poet knows that neither of these solutions will do. He recognises the existence of two worlds, the ideal world of the imagination, and the world of here-and-now; and a philosophy which embraces the former without taking into account the latter simply will not do. We know that the poem was preceded by Keats' long walk and talk with Coleridge, and under the stimulus of that great mind he was continuing to wrestle with the problem of knowledge. The early Keats had indeed wished to

> Fade far away, dissolve, and quite forget
> What thou among the leaves hast never known,
> The weariness, the fever, and the fret
> Here, where men sit and hear each other groan;
> Where palsy shakes a few, sad, last grey hairs,
> Where youth grows pale, and spectre-thin, and dies
> Where but to think is to be full of sorrow
> And leaden-eyed despairs;
> Where Beauty cannot keep her lustrous eyes
> Or new Love pine at them beyond tomorrow.

The long illness of his brother Thomas had put a great strain upon him[1]; here indeed was a real world, and it was a world of sorrow. But it was not the only real world. Differing equally from the world

of sorrow and from the ideal world of the nightingale there was the
world which was at his feet:

> I cannot see what flowers are at my feet,
> For what soft incense hangs upon the boughs,
> But, in embalmed darkness, quess each sweet
> Wherewith the seasonable month endows
> The grass, the thicket, the fruit trees wild;
> White hawthorn, and the pastoral eglantine;
> Fast-fading violets cover'd up in leaves;
> And mid-May's eldest child,
> The coming musk-rose, full of dewy wine,
> The murmurous haunt of the flies on summer eves.

A philosophy which rested upon the immortal world of the
nightingale but ignored the other two worlds of reality was inadequate, and it was the realisation of this which might have made
1819 a new point of departure for Keats, had he been spared the
ravages of tuberculosis.

The same quest was pursued in the *Ode on a Grecian Urn*. The
idea had long been forming in his mind. In a letter of 19 March
1818, he described how he was going through a period of lethargy,
and added: 'Neither poetry, nor ambition, nor love have any
alertness of countenance as they pass by me: *they seem rather like
three figures on a Greek vase*—a man and two women whom no one
but myself could distinguish in their disguisement. *This is the only
happiness: and is a rare instance of advantage in the body over-
powering the mind.*' In the next sentence he mentions that he has
heard from William Haslam (one of his closest friends) of the
imminent death of Haslam's father. The juxtaposition of these
ideas is significant. Poetry and the pursuit of the ideal was Keats'
relief from the real world of sadness and death. The fascination of
the Grecian Urn was that, like the nightingale's song, it was
immortal and unchangeable, but only because it was divorced from
the real world. Or, to put it another way, it lived only in the
imaginations of those who viewed it. It was a 'still unravish'd bride
of quietness'; it kept its purity only because it had never reached
the point of consummation which living beings could achieve:

> Bold Lover, never, never canst thou kiss,
> Though winning near the goal—yet, do not grieve;
> She cannot fade, though thou hast not thy bliss,
> For ever wilt thou love, and she be fair!

Ideal love, like ideal beauty, must be unending and immortal, and with the aid of the Urn Keats can imagine that it is a reality.

> More happy love! more happy, happy love
> For ever warm and still to be enjoy'd,
> For ever panting and for ever young;
> All breathing human passion far above,
> That leaves a heart high-sorrowful and cloy'd
> A burning forehead, and a parching tongue.

It is a seductive idea, and one which leads Keats near to the ideal world of Plato:

> Thou, silent form! dost tease us out of thought
> As doth eternity.

Yet, and this is the real point, it remains a 'Cold Pastoral!' It is not life, but a work of art. It remains in all ages 'a friend to man' because it points to the existence of an ideal world of the imagination, yet it is not the whole story, but part of a complex philosophical system which Keats has not yet been able to comprehend. How, then, shall we interpret the last two lines of the poem? For often they have been misinterpreted:

> 'Beauty is truth, truth beauty'—that is all
> Ye know on earth, and all ye need to know.

Often they are interpreted as if Keats had written 'We' instead of 'Ye'. But he did not. The 'Ye' is the Urn, the symbol of immortal art, and for the ideal world of art 'Beauty is truth, truth beauty' may be a sufficient principle. In the scenes on the Urn the young men and maidens, the pipes, the trees in eternal springtime, have eternal beauty and are therefore true (i.e. real). But the point to which Keats has come in his thought is that this is *not* all *we* need to know in this brief life of ecstacy and disappointment, hope and sorrow. Something more is needed which the ideal world of the imagination cannot alone supply; and there can be little doubt that had Keats lived he would have sought to discover a more adequate philosophy.[2]

That we are not here merely interpellating ideas beyond Keats' intention is proved by the letter which he wrote to his brother George in March 1818. Keats was considering whether the ideal happiness was ever attainable in this life, and he concluded that it was not, since the knowledge that it must end by death must always make the experience less than ideal:

> But in truth I do not at all believe in this sort of perfectibility—the nature of the world will not admit of it. . . . The point at which man may arrive is as far as the parallel state in inanimate nature and no further. For instance, suppose a rose to have sensation, it blooms on a beautiful morning, it enjoys itself—but there comes a cold wind, a hot sun—it cannot escape it, it cannot destroy its annoyances—they are as native to the world as itself; no more can man be happy in spite, the worldly elements will prey upon his nature. The common cognomen of this world among the misguided and superstitious is 'a vale of tears' from which we are to be redeemed by a certain arbitrary interposition of God and taken to heaven. What a little circumscribed straightened notion! Call the world if you please 'The vale of soul-making'. Then you will find out the use of the world (I am speaking now in the highest terms for human nature admitting it to be immortal which I will here take for granted for the purpose of showing a thought which has struck me concerning it). I say 'Soul-making', soul as distinguished from an intelligence. There may be intelligences or sparks of the divinity in millions—but they are not souls till they acquire identities, till each one is personally itself. Intelligences are atoms of perception—they know and they see and they are pure, in short they are God. How then are souls to be made? How then are these sparks which are God to have identity given them—so as ever to possess a bliss

peculiar to each one's individual existence? How, but by the medium of a world like this? This point I sincerely wish to consider because I think it a grander system of salvation than the Christian religion—or rather it is a system of spirit-creation. This is effected by three grand materials acting the one upon the other for a series of years. These three materials are the *intelligence*, the *human heart* (as distinguished from intelligence or mind) and the *world* or *elemental space* suited for the proper action of *mind and heart* on each other for the purpose of forming the *soul* or *intelligence destined to possess the sense of identity*. I can scarcely express what I but dimly perceive—and yet I think I perceive it. . . . As various as the lives of men are—so various become their souls, and thus does God make individual beings, souls, identical souls of the sparks of his own essence.

No excuse is needed for quoting so long but so important a passage. The three elements which, according to Keats, go to the make-up of a human personality are his intelligence (an earlier age would have said his reason), his heart and the world around him. Keats argued that an intelligence without a heart lacked personal identity, and an intelligence and heart which failed to come to terms with the world would fail to find a reason for being. Any philosophy which failed to take account of all three would be inadequate. This is a sound and business-like conclusion, and very different from the philosophy to be learnt from the Grecian Urn.

To understand the great Odes of Keats we must remember what he conceived to be the function of a poet at the time he was writing them. In a letter of 27 October 1818 he wrote that the important point to recognise about a poetical character was that it had no character: 'it enjoys light and shade; it lives in gusto, be it foul or fair, high or low, rich or poor, mean or elevated. It had much the same delight in conceiving an Iago as an Imogen. What shocks the virtuous philosopher, delights the chameleon poet. It does no harm from its relish of the dark side of things any more than from its taste for the bright one; because they both end in speculation. *A poet is the most unpoetical of anything in existence, because he has no identity*—he is continually in for, and filling, some other body—the sun, the moon, the sea, and men and women who are creatures of impulse are poetical and have about them an unchangeable attribute—the poet has none; no identity— he is certainly the most unpoetical of all God's creatures. . . . It is a wretched thing to confess, but is a very fact, that not one word I ever utter can be taken for granted as an opinion growing out of my identical nature—how can it, when I have no nature?' In short, Keats regarded the poet as a kind of mirror held up to nature, reflecting rather than creating. He may for a moment identify himself with the nightingale or with the Grecian Urn, but there is no reason why we should take this as meaning more than Keats himself intended it to mean. We do not suppose that Shakespeare in creating Iago or Imogen necessarily permanently identified himself with all his characters said. Keats was a young man, fervently anxious for experiences of life, and therefore ready momentarily to identify himself with many diverse situations without regarding them as more than a passing phase.

If we have interpreted Keats aright, it would seem that he was struck down by disease just at the time when he was on the verge of a great leap forward in philosophy. What form it might have taken we cannot even guess, but that his poetry of 1819 was preparatory for such a leap seems certain. It is wrong therefore to regard Keats merely as a sensuous poet; he was aware of a deeper and nobler task, and his early death, perhaps far more than that of Shelley or Byron deprived the world of something of infinite value.

NOTES

[1] Cf. his letter of 21 Sept. 1818: 'Although I intended to have given some time to study alone I am obliged to write, and plunge into abstract images to ease myself of his countenance his voice and feebleness. . . . If I think of fame of poetry, it seems a crime to me, and yet I must do so or suffer.'

[2] How much Keats owed to Elizabethan and subsequent themes, cf. *Reason and Nature*, pp. 29-36.

15 : Childe Harold and Don Juan

Macaulay, when he came to assess the life and work of Lord Byron (in the *Edinburgh Review* of June 1830), came to the conclusion that he was the true populariser of the Romantic approach to nature, because he reached a vastly wider audience than Wordsworth had been able to do. He also for a short time created a vogue in England without parallel in literature. 'Among that large class of young persons whose reading is almost entirely confined to works of imagination, the popularity of Lord Byron was unbounded. They bought pictures of him; they treasured up the smallest relics of him; they learned his poems by heart, and did their best to write like him, and to look like him. Many of them practised at the glass in the hope of catching the curl of the upper lip, and the crowl of the brow, which appear in some of his portraits. A few discarded their neckcloths in imitation of their great leader. For some years the Minerva press sent forth no novel without a mysterious, unhappy Lara-like peer. The number of hopeful undergraduates and medical students who became things of dark imaginings, on whom the freshness of the heart ceased to fall like dew, whose passions had consumed themselves like dust, and to whom the relief of tears was denied, passed all calculation. This was not the worst. There was created in the minds of many of these enthusiasts a pernicious and absurd association between intellectual power and moral depravity. From the poetry of Lord Byron they drew a system of ethics, compounded of misanthropy and voluptuousness, a system in which the two great commandments were, to hate your neighbour, and to love your neighbour's wife.' By 1830, Macaulay was glad to record, the affectation had passed away.

Lord Byron was by nature a rebel, a rebel, not so much in politics, but against the narrow and canting spirit of his age. Hazlitt, with his usual perception, commented that 'his ruling motive is not love of the people, but of distinction; not of truth, but of singularity. ... We do not like Sir Walter's gratuitous servility: we like Lord Byron's preposterous *liberalism* little better. He may affect the principles of equality, but he resumes his privilege of peerage upon occasion.' There was much truth in this, but Hazlitt was too near in time to his subject to see just what it was that Byron was revolting against. Under the influence of the long French Wars England had become the home of *cant*, in which a narrow religiosity passed for true religion, in which hypocrisy and an outward show of respectability passed for true morality. 'In these days', Byron wrote, 'the grand *primum mobile* of England is *cant*; cant political, cant poetical, cant religious, cant moral; but always cant.' This to him was the true enemy.

Byron came of a turbulent family. His grandfather, Admiral John Byron, was known as Foul-weather Jack; his uncle, the fifth Lord Byron, 'the Wicked Lord', killed a man in a duel, and was thought to deal in black magic. His father, John Byron, was a profligate who died when the child was three. His mother, born Catherine Gordon, was proud of her Scottish ancestry, but was a vulgar, drunken and turbulent woman, who drove the boy to desperation by her taunts and tantrums. In 1798 Byron inherited from his uncle the title, together with Newstead Abbey. Educated at Harrow and Cambridge, he published his first book of poetry, *Hours of Idleness* in 1807. It received a scathing notice in the *Edinburgh Review*. In 1809 he replied with a brilliant satire, *English Bards and Scotch Reviewers*, and then left England for a two-years' jaunt through Spain, Albania and Greece. It was this experience which really made Byron a poet, for his imagination was fired by contact with the Mediterranean and the classical world. On his return he published the first two Cantos of *Childe Harold* and, as he said, 'I awoke one morning and found myself famous.' His poetry was intensely romantic, very easy reading, and with a spice of audacity which, coming from the pen of a noble lord, made it irresistible to the age. It was an unparalleled success and went through seven editions in four weeks. He was lionised in society, and besieged by amorous women, not least by Lady Caroline Lamb, the daughter of Lady Bessborough and wife of William Lamb, later Lord Melbourne.

Already there was the Byronic pose. At the age of twenty-one he had written:

> His home, his hope, his youth are gone,
> Yet still he loves, and loves but one.

In *Childe Harold*, at the age of twenty-four it became:

> For he through Sin's long labyrinth had run,
> Nor made atonement when he did amiss,
> Had sigh'd to many though he loved but one,
> And that loved one, alas! could ne'er be his.
> Ah, happy she! to 'scape from him whose kiss
> Had been pollution unto aught so chaste.
>
> (Canto, I, v.)

No wonder the *Edinburgh Review* hinted darkly that neither his morals, nor his politics nor his religious views were safe! By 1812 there was in England a built-in fear of romantic liberalism, and Byron seemed to go out of his way to shock. It is true that it was the age of Dandyism, the age of the Prince Regent, Beau Brummell and Captain Gronow. There was plenty of immorality in society, numerous women like Lady Oxford, an accomplished lover, whose children were known by the wits as the Harleian Miscellany. But there were certain conventions to be observed, and when these were flouted society could be hard in defence of its privileges.

Lady Caroline Lamb pursued Byron until she was the talk of the town. Her first impression, that he was 'Mad, bad and dangerous to know', made her all the more determined. In 1813, in a lurid scene at a ball, she attempted to kill herself in an ecstasy of unrequited love. Meanwhile Byron was enjoying other affairs, not least with the experienced Lady Oxford. He was also deeply attached to his elder half-sister, Augusta Leigh. It is not necessary to suppose incest between them; he loved her because she was a Byron, and he could relax with her as he could with no other woman. In exile, four years later, he wrote:

> My sister! my sweet sister! if a name
> Dearer and purer were, it should be thine.
> Mountains and seas divide us, but I claim
> No tears, but tenderness to answer mine:
> Go where I will, to me thou art the same—
> A loved regret which I would not resign.
> There yet are two things in my destiny—
> A world to roam through, and a home with thee.
> The first were nothing—had I still the last,
> It were the haven of my happiness;
> But other claims and other ties thou hast,
> And mine is not the wish to make them less.

'The first were nothing—had I still the last.' With all his restiveness, there were times when Byron sought the security of a home which he had never known. If he was in love with Augusta, and if they committed incest in 1813, then her daughter Medora might be Byron's daughter. But on the whole it seems unlikely, for Byron never showed any interest in the child, whereas he always had great sentimental attachment to his other two daughters.

Still, perhaps Augusta had something to do with Byron's marriage in January 1815 to Annabella Milbanke, which is otherwise one of the most inexplicable events in his life. Annabella was a dowdy bluestocking, a prude with an innate dislike of sex, and Byron chose her in preference to any of the cohort of glamorous women who pursued him. He himself regarded the courtship as an oddity: 'What an odd situation and friendship is ours!—without one spark of love on either side, and produced by circumstances which in general lead to coldness on one side, and aversion on the other', he wrote in his Journal (Moore, II, p. 285). This was a fair assessment. The marriage was arranged like a piece of business, was icily cold, and a disaster from the start. A daughter, Ada, was born in December, and in January 1816 Lady Byron left him, declaring that he was not of sound mind, and that nothing would induce her to return to him. He never saw her again.

His poetry of these years was concerned with romantic action, and heroes whose youthful idealism was warped and embittered by the harsh world of reality. Both *The Corsair* and *Lara* are imaginary portraits of Byron himself. Thus Conrad:

> His heart was form'd for softness—warp'd to wrong
> Betray'd too early, and beguiled too long;
> Each feeling pure—as falls the dropping dew
> Within the grot; like that had harden'd too;
> Less clear, perchance, its earthly trials pass'd,
> But sunk, and chill'd, and petrified at last.
> Yet tempests wear, and lightning cleaves the rock
> If such his heart, so shatter'd it the shock.
>
> (The Corsair.)

Even more closely did he identify himself with the chieftain Lara, who after years of wandering, had returned to his patrimony:

> 'Twas strange—in youth all action and all life,
> Burning for pleasure, not averse from strife;
> Woman—the field—the ocean—all that gave,
> Promise of gladness, peril of the grave,
> In turn he tried—he ransack'd all below,
> And found his recompense in joy or woe,
> No tame, trite medium; for his feelings sought
> In that intenseness an escape from thought . . .
>
> .   .   .   .   .   .
>
> There was in him a vital scorn of all:
> As if the worst had fall'n which could befall,
> He stood a stranger in this breathing world,
> An erring spirit from another hurl'd . . .
>
> .   .   .   .   .   .
>
> With more capacity for love than earth
> Bestows on most of mortal mould and birth,
> His early dreams of good outstripp'd the truth
> And troubled manhood follow'd baffled youth;
> With thought of years in phantom chase misspent,

And wasted powers for better purpose lent;
And fiery passions that had pour'd their wrath
In hurried desolation o'er his path,
And left the better feelings all at strife
In wild reflection o'er his stormy life;
But haughty still, and loth himself to blame,
He call'd on Nature's self to share the shame,
And charged all faults upon the fleshly form
She gave to clog the soul, and feast the worm
Till he at last confounded good and ill,
And half mistook for fate the acts of will. (*Lara.*)

Thus the picture of the Byronic hero gradually took shape. But it was all strong meat for the time, and the *Anti-Jacobin Review* in March 1814 enquired whether Byron had 'written one single sentence worthy to be impressed on the mind of youth, whether he had composed one single line serviceable to the cause of religion, morality or virtue'. After his wife left him he was gradually excluded from society. At a ball at Lady Jersey's in April 1816 he and Augusta were shunned by the guests. On April 25th he left England, never to return.[1] In the succeeding cantos of *Childe Harold* he described his leisurely journey through Belgium and down the Rhine to Switzerland, where he met Shelley, Mary Godwin and Clare Clairmont, step-daughter of William Godwin. There were pleasant talks with Shelley, and a love affair with Clare, but the old restiveness returned. He settled in Venice, and sought relief in a succession of mistresses and a life of sexual orgy, which soon exhausted him physically.[2]

Yet these were the years of his greatest poetry. The essence of Byronism lay in the theme of the struggle of the human spirit to achieve autonomy against the forces of oppression:

'Tis to create, and in creating live
A being more intense, that we endow
With form our fancy, gaining as we give
The life we image, even as I do now,
What am I? Nothing: but not so art thou,
Soul of my thought! (*Childe Harold*, III, vi.)

Yet always there was the battle against time; at some time in youth
he had taken a wrong turning:

> untaught in youth my heart to tame,
> My springs of life were poison'd. 'Tis too late!
>
> (III, vii.)

Yet this 'too late!' merely heightened the heroism of the struggle,
because in fact there was no giving up. The goal was always to
achieve an autonomy independent of all other beings. The Byronic
hero must stand alone:

> He would not yield dominion of his mind
> To spirits against whom his own rebell'd;
> Proud though in desolation; which could find
> A life within itself, to breathe without mankind.
>
> (III, xii.)

The spirit of man was to be expressed, not in communities, but
against the background of nature:

> Where rose the mountains, there to him were friends;
> Where roll'd the ocean, thereon was his home;
> Where a blue sky, and glowing clime, extends,
> He had the passion and the power to roam;
> The desert, forest, cavern, breaker's foam,
> Were unto him companionship; they spake
> A mutual language, clearer than the tome
> Of his land's tongue, which he would oft forsake
> For Nature's pages glass'd by sunbeams on the lake.
>
> (III, xiii.)

All this was in marked contrast to the discomfort he had experienced in society:

> But in Man's dwellings he became a thing
> Restless and worn, and stern and wearisome,
> Droop'd as a wild-born falcon with clipt wing
> To whom the boundless air alone were home.
>
> (III, xv.)

So again he had gone on his travels,

> Self-exiled Harold wanders forth again,
> With nought of hope, but with less of gloom.
>
> (III, xv.)

In this there was much of the aristocratic disdain for the crowd, and something of the Stoic concern for internal peace as the supreme objective:

> To fly from, need not be to hate, mankind:
> All are not fit with them to stir and toil,
> Nor is it discontent to keep the mind
> Deep in its fountain, lest it overboil
> In the hot throng, where we become the spoil
> Of our infection. (III, lxix.)

Man must indeed live as a part of nature, yet he was more than nature, for his goal was to transcend it, to rise above its limitations. Only thus could he achieve autonomy:

> I live not in myself, but I become
> Portion of that around me; and to me
> High mountains are a feeling, but the hum
> Of human cities torture: I can see
> Nothing to loath in nature, save to be
> A link reluctant in the fleshly chain,
> Class'd among creatures, when the soul can flee,
> And with the sky, the peak, the heaving plain
> Of ocean, or the stars, mingle, and not in vain.
>
> (III, lxxii.)

Life was a struggle, but not pointless if the spirit triumphed in the end:

> And thus I am absorb'd, and this is life;
> I look upon the peopled desert past,
> As on a place of agony and strife,
> Where, for some sin, to sorrow I was cast,

> To act and suffer, but remount at last
> With a fresh pinion.   (III, lxxiii.)

Always there was that promise of final triumph:

> And when, at length, the mind shall be all free
> From what it hates in this degraded form,
> Reft of its carnal life, save what shall be
> Existent happier in the fly and worm,—
> When elements to elements conform,
> And dust is as it should be, shall I not
> Feel all I see, less dazzling, but more warm?
> The bodiless thought? the Spirit of each spot?
> Of which, even now, I share at times the immortal lot?
> (III, lxxiv.)

> Are not the mountains, waves, and skies, a part
> Of me and of my soul, as I of them?
> Is not the love of these deep in my heart
> With a pure passion? should I not contemn
> All objects, if compared with these? and stem
> A tide of suffering, rather than forego
> Such feelings for the hard and worldly phlegm
> Of those whose eyes are only turn'd below
> Gazing upon the ground, with thoughts which dare
>   not glow?   (III, lxxv.)

The life of the poet was lonely and painful, yet ecstatic, and Byron
thought of himself as occupying a proud and lonely eminence:

> I have not loved the world, nor the world me;
> I have not flatter'd its rank breath, nor bow'd
> To its idolatries a patient knee,—
> Nor coin'd my cheek to smiles,—nor cried aloud
> In worship of an echo; in the crowd
> They could not deem me one of such; I stood
> Among them, but not of them; in a shroud
> Of thoughts which were not their thoughts, and still
>   could,

Had I not filed my mind, which thus itself subdued.

(III, cxiii.)

This last line was a genuine and deeply tragic confession. With all his nobility of nature, he *had* defiled his mind, and this he could not forget. The succeeding canto is one of the most moving he ever wrote:

> I have not loved the world, nor the world me,—
> But let us part fair foes; I do believe,
> Though I have found them not, that there may be
> Words which are things,—hopes which will not deceive,
> And virtues which are merciful, nor weave
> Snares for the failing; I would also deem
> O'er others' griefs that some sincerely grieve;
> That two, or one, are almost what they seem,—
> That goodness is no name, and happiness no dream.

(III, cxiv.)

Here was no pose, but a noble mind speaking the truth as he saw it.

In this, the third Canto of *Childe Harold*, Byron was at his most metaphysical. In the fourth Canto he touched momentarily on the European scene. It grieved him that liberty had been overthrown, first by the Jacobins, then by Napoleon, and finally by the Holy Alliance. For,

> France got drunk with blood to vomit crime,
> And fatal have her Saturnalia been
> To Freedom's cause, in every age and crime;
> Because the deadly days which we have seen,
> And vile Ambition, that built up between
> Man and his hopes an adamantine wall,
> And the base pageant last upon the scene,
> Are grown the pretext for the eternal thrall
> Which nips life's tree, and dooms man's worst—
>   his second fall.   (IV, xcvii.)

It seemed that in overthrowing one form of power, men were doomed to set up another:

X

> Can tyrants but by tyrants conquer'd be,
> And Freedom find no champion and no child . . .?
>
> (IV, xcvi.)

It was from Byron that his age learnt to love the beauties of
Italy, its art and history, and to mourn its weak and divided state
beneath the Austrian yoke:

> Italia! oh Italia! thou who hast
> The fatal gift of beauty, which became
> A funeral dower of present woes and past,
> On thy sweet brow is sorrow plough'd with shame,
> And annals graved in characters of flame.
> Oh, God! that thou wert in thy nakedness
> Less lovely or more powerful, and couldst claim
> Thy right, and awe the robbers back, who press
> To shed thy blood, and drink the tears of thy distress.
>
> (IV, xlii.)

Often Byron acts as an admirable guide to the English visitor:

> I stood in Venice, on the Bridge of Sighs;
> A palace and a prison on each hand.   (IV, i.)

Or in Santa Croce, in Florence, he pays homage at the tombs of
Michelangelo, Alfieri, Galileo and Machiavelli:

> These are four minds, which, like the elements,
> Might furnish forth creation.   (IV, lv.)

Over the ruins of past glory there is always a romantic nostalgia,
and a realisation of the futility of human ambition. As he surveys
the Palatine Hill in Rome he comments, ''tis thus the mighty falls'.

> There is the moral of all human tales;
> 'Tis but the same rehearsal of the past,
> First Freedom and then Glory—when that fails
> Wealth, vice, corruption,—barbarism at last.
> And History, with all her volumes vast
> Hath but *one* page.   (IV, cviii.)

From past glories Italy had become an Austrian province:

> The Suabian sued, and now the Austrian reigns—
> An Emperor tramples where an Emperor knelt;
> Kingdoms are shrunk to provinces, and chains
> Clank over sceptred cities; nations melt
> From power's high pinnacle, when they have felt
> The sunshine for a while, and downward go
> Like lauwine loosen'd from the mountain's belt;
> Oh for one hour of blind old Dandolo!
> Th'octogenerian chief, Byzantium's conquering foe.
>
> (IV, xii.)

But if individuals and human affairs were transitory, beauty and truth were not; the things of the spirit were timeless:

> Those days are gone—but Beauty still is here.
> States fall, arts fade—but Nature doth not die ...
>
> (IV, iii.)

In this he suggests that Beauty and Nature are permanent, in contrast to the transitory affairs of men, yet, perplexingly, he goes on to suggest that the ideal world was in the mind of man, and that it did not simply reflect some world outside itself:

> The beings of the mind are not of clay;
> Essentially immortal, they create
> And multiply in us a brighter ray
> And more beloved existence. (IV, v.)

The mind may create an ideal world, or it may become infatuated with false values; it may transcend Nature, or fall far below her:

> Of its own beauty is the mind diseased,
> And fevers into false creation:—where,
> Where are the forms the sculptor's soul hath seized?
> In him alone. Can Nature show so fair?
> Where are the charms and virtues which we dare
> Conceive in boyhood and pursue as men,

> The unreach'd Paradise of our despair,
> Which o'er informs the pencil and the pen,
> And overpowers the page where it would bloom again?
> (IV, cxxii.)

The tragedy of the romantic lay in the fact that the reality of life always fell short of the ideals which the mind conceived, and thus

> We wither from our youth, we gasp away—
> Sick—sick; unfound the boon—unslaked the thirst,
> Though to the last, in verge of our decay,
> Some fantom lures, such as we sought at first—
> But all too late,—so are we doubly curst.
> Love, fame, ambition, avarice—'tis the same,
> Each idle—and all ill—and none the worst—
> For all are meteors with a different name,
> And Death the sable smoke where vanishes the flame.
> (IV, cxxiv.)

In this way there was an element of fraud in human life, that men should have the power to conceive the ideal, yet never attain it:

> Few—none—find what they love or could have loved.
> (IV, cxxv.)

and

> Our life is a false nature—'tis not in
> The harmony of things,—this hard decree,
> This ineradicable taint of sin,
> This boundless upas, this all-blasting tree,
> Whose root is earth, whose leaves and branches be
> The skies which rain their plagues on men like dew.
> (IV, cxxvi.)

The very qualities, Byron argued, which made him a poet, which lifted him above other men, were those which made him suffer:

> Have I not—
> Hear me, my mother Earth! behold it, Heaven!—

Have I not had to wrestle with my lot!
Have I not suffer'd things to be forgiven?
Have I not had my brain sear'd, my heart riven,
Hopes sapp'd, name blighted, Life's life lied away?
And only not to desperation driven,
Because not altogether of such clay
As rots into the souls of those whom I survey.

(IV, cxxxvi.)

The critic might well regard this as a mixture of exaggeration,
self-pity and aristocratic superiority, but it was a preliminary to a
typical Byronic climax, when the spirit triumphs over all difficulties:

But I have lived, and have not lived in vain:
My mind may lose its force, my blood its fire,
And my frame perish even in conquering pain;
But there is that within me which shall tire
Torture and Time, and breathe when I expire;
Something unearthly, which they deem not of,
Like the remembered tone of a mute lyre,
Shall on their soften'd spirits sink, and move
In hearts all rocky now the late remorse of love.

(IV, cxxxvii.)

The only forces which did justice to man's unconquerable spirit
were provided by the mountains and the sea, and so

Roll on, thou deep and dark blue Ocean—roll!
Ten thousand fleets sweep over thee in vain;
Man marks the earth with ruin—his control
Stops with the shore;—upon the watery plain
The wrecks are all thy deed, nor doth remain
A shadow of man's ravage, save his own,
When, for a moment, like a drop of rain,
He sinks into thy depths with bubbling groan,
Without a grave, unknell'd, uncoffin'd and unknown.

(IV, clxxix.)

In politics Byron was always a radical. In England he was naturally in opposition to the tories, and he was a friend to Lord Holland and a number of leading whigs. On his return to England in 1811 he took his seat in the House of Lords and on three occasions spoke on public affairs. In February 1812 he opposed the Nottingham Frame-breaking Bill. He wrote to Lord Holland that by the use of the frame, which did the work of seven men, six were thrown out of work: 'Surely, my Lord, however we may rejoice in any improvement in the arts which may be beneficial to mankind, we must not allow mankind to be sacrificed to improvements in mechanism. The maintenance and well-doing of the industrious poor is an object of greater consequence to the community than the enrichment of a few monopolists. . . . My own motive for opposing the bill is founded on its palpable injustice.' (Moore, II, 123.) In his speech he declared: 'I have traversed the seat of war in the Peninsula: I have been in some of the most oppressed provinces of Turkey; but never, under the most despotic of infidel governments, did I behold such squalid wretchedness as I have seen since my return, in the very heart of a Christian country.' And the only solution the government could devise was to invent new crimes to be punished by death. 'Is there not blood enough upon your penal code, that more must be poured forth to ascend to heaven and testify against you. . . . Are these the remedies for a starving and desperate populace. . . . When a proposal is made to emancipate or relieve, you hesitate, you deliberate for years, you temporise and tamper with the minds of men; but a death-bill must be passed off hand, without a thought of the consequences.' (Moore, II, 127.) His other important speech was in favour of Catholic Emancipation.

He assumed that any revolt, as a blow against authority, was worthy of support. As he put it,

> When a man hath no freedom to fight for at home,
> Let him combat for that of his neighbours;
> Let him think of the glories of Greece and of Rome,
> And get knock'd on the head for his labours.
>
> To do good to mankind is a chivalrous plan,
> And is always as nobly required;

Then battle for freedom wherever you can.
And, if not shot or hang'd, you'll get knighted.

To overthrow tyranny did not seem to him to be a difficult task; all that was needed was the will to win on the part of the people. 'As to political slavery, so general, it is men's own fault: if they *will* be slaves let them! Yet it is but "a word and a blow". See how England formerly, France, Spain, Portugal, America, Switzerland, freed themselves! There is no one instance of a long contest in which *men* did not triumph over systems.' (Moore, V, 53.) In 1821 he was involved with the Carbonari in their plans for revolts in Italy, and was made what he called 'the Chief of the Coalheavers'. His advice was always to strike a blow for freedom. He was ready to fight himself, and his house at Venice became a miniature arsenal. He talked gaily of 'a war between the Powers and the people'. 'It is a grand object—the very *poetry* of politics. Only think—a free Italy!!! Why there has been nothing like it since the days of Augustus.' But he soon found that the Carbonari could not muster a thousand men; the reason, he said, was that only the upper and middle classes were interested, and that the populace were quite unmoved. 'Thus the world goes; and thus the Italians are always lost for lack of union among themselves. . . . I always had an idea that it would be bungled; but was willing to hope, and am so still.' (Moore, V, 107.) In fact the revolts were suppressed by Austrian troops, and, as an Italian said sorrowfully to Byron, 'Alas! the Italians must now return to making operas.' The family of Byron's mistress, Teresa Guiccioli, as well as he himself, were implicated in the Carbonari movement, and were forced to leave Venice. In 1821 Byron moved to Ravenna, where he did what he could to ease the plight of the refugees. 'It has been a miserable sight to see the general desolation in families. I am doing what I can for them, high and low, by such interest and means as I possess or can bring to bear. There have been thousands of these pro-scriptions. . . .' (Moore, V, 215.) All his life Byron was extremely generous with money to those less fortunate than himself.

In 1823 he determined to go to fight for the Greeks. The decision was not made without considerable hesitation, but, as he put it, 'a man ought to do something more for society than write verses'. It was a heroic gesture, but was without any clearly defined objective. He soon learnt to despise the Greeks: 'I am of St. Paul's opinion, that there is no difference between Jews and Greeks,—the character of both is equally vile.' He found the Greeks quarrelsome, deceitful and divided, and he soon doubted whether the cause could ever succeed. But the Greek chieftain Mavrocordato was a good leader, and Byron was able to supply the cause with money, without which, he wrote, he believed the resistance in western Greece might have collapsed. Always however there was in his mind a presentiment of his fate, or else a romantic vision of how a hero should die. In January 1824, on his thirty-sixth birthday he wrote,

> My days are in the yellow leaf;
> The flowers and fruits of love are gone;
> The worm, the canker, and the grief
> Are mine alone!

Three months later he was dead.

Byron's politics and his heroism made him a great spiritual force with European liberals in the nineteenth century, yet in fact there is little evidence that he ever thought deeply about the problems of politics. He inherited the eighteenth-century aristocratic view of liberty, and he kept it untarnished during the long Napoleonic Wars. He had an instinctive dislike of governments, and an instinctive sympathy for any people struggling to be free, but he never thought deeply about the problems of political power. He believed passionately in freedom of thought and expression, but he thought little about the wider implications of democracy. His whole instinct was aristocratic. He was generous and humane in his dealings with his social inferiors, but he never for a moment forgot that they *were* his inferiors. In espousing the cause of first the Carbonari and then the Greeks, he assumed the role of a nationalist, and yet there is little evidence that he appreciated the force of nationalism as Wordsworth did. Rather he was simply supporting a cause which implied resistance to the hated Austrian in Italy, and the Turkish rulers in Greece, and that was enough.

He was not inspired by thoughts of either Italian or Greek national-ism, but he was fighting for the historical glories of Rome, Venice and classical Greece. He was a cultural crusader rather than a modern nationalist, but as such he was an immense inspiration to European liberals of his time.

His attitude to politics was nearer to that of the Manfreds and Dandolos of history, and to Napoleon in his own day, than to constitutionalism or democracy. His ideal was the heroic leader, leading his men on some great and noble exploit. There is a most interesting example of the working of his mind in this respect. On 20 March 1814 he wrote in his Journal: 'Lord Erskine thinks that ministers must be in peril of going out. So much the better for him. To me it is the same who are in or out;—we want something more than a change of ministers, and some day we will have it.' This at first sight might seem to suggest that he was presaging some liberal or democratic revolution. But the Journal immediately continues: 'I remember, in riding from Chrisso to Castri (Delphos), along the sides of Parnassus, I saw six eagles in the air. It is uncommon to see so many together; and it was the number, not the species, which is common enough, that excited my attention.' This apparently inconsequential remark is in fact deeply significant. Byron was very superstitious, and at the time he had been con-vinced that the sight of six eagles together at so revered a place as Parnassus was an omen of some heroic future awaiting him. (Hence his annoyance when his sober companion, Hobhouse, argued that they were not eagles, but vultures!) In his imagination he always tended to identify himself with Napoleon, and thus Lord Erskine's reference to the expected fall of the government touched off a subconscious wish. That he was not fully aware of the connection is shown by the fact that he added: 'I wonder what put these two things into my head just now?' (Moore, III, 17.)

Sir Walter Scott, who knew him well, perhaps best understood Byron's politics. He wrote: 'On politics, he used sometimes to express a high strain of what is now called Liberalism; but it appeared to me that the pleasure it afforded him as a vehicle of displaying his wit and satire against individuals in office was at bottom of this habit of thinking, rather than any real conviction of the political principles on which he talked. He was certainly proud of his rank and ancient family; and, in that respect, as much an aristocrat as was consistent with good sense and good breeding. Some disgusts, how adopted I know not, seemed to me to have given this peculiar and, as it appeared to me, contradictory cast of mind: but, at heart, I would have termed Byron patrician on principle.' (Moore, III, 163.) This was true. Byron was genuinely humanitarian, warm-hearted and generous in relieving distress when he saw it, and it was part of his image to be against the establishment; yet his whole outlook was aristocratic. Immensely proud of his ancestry, title and rank, he expected everyone of lesser rank to be fully conscious of the hierarchy to be observed in society. His interest in European revolutions was of the most superficial kind, and even his final expedition to Greece was a matter of divided loyalties, for if he had a romantic attachment to the heritage of classical Greece, he greatly admired the Turks as an exotic people.

There was much else about Byron which Walter Scott discerned. He noted how the gloomy melancholy which Byron assumed in public disappeared under the stimulus of conversation. Byron was never really at ease in society. The air of melancholy on his first appearance may have been, as has often been assumed, something of a pose, but it originated in an instinctive dislike of meeting people, and his boredom with conventional conversation. Scott wrote: 'When I observed him in this humour, I used either to wait till it went off of its own accord, or till some natural and easy mode occurred of leading him into conversation, when the shadows almost always left his countenance, like the mist rising from a landscape. In conversation he was very animated.' That Byron was instinctively ill at ease in society was revealed by the suspicions he always had that there were innuendoes in other people's remarks. Scott commented: 'I think I remarked in Byron's temper starts of suspicion, when he seemed to pause and consider whether there had not been a secret, and perhaps offensive, meaning in something casually said to him. In this case, I also judged it best to let his mind, like a troubled spring, work itself clear, which it did in a minute or two.' (Moore, III, 165–6.) It is possible that Byron felt himself at a disadvantage in the presence of Scott, for the latter was a much older man, already famous, and Byron certainly had great admiration for him, adjudging him the greatest writer of the age. Byron's letters to Sir Walter Scott have an awkwardness and sense of inferiority about them which are not to be found in any other of his letters. He himself recognised it in one of his letters to Scott. 'I can only account for it on the same principle of tremulous anxiety with which one sometimes makes love to a beautiful woman of our own degree, with whom one is enamoured in good earnest; whereas, we attack a fresh-coloured housemaid without (I speak, of course, of earlier times) any sentimental remorse or mitigation of our virtuous purpose.' It is significant that Byron should try to hide his embarrassment by a gauche display of his wicked past. (Moore, V, 299; 12 Jan. 1822.)

In Byron gloom and nostalgia were mixed in an extraordinary way with felicity and brilliant wit. It was not only Scott who noticed how rapidly his countenance changed from one mood to another during conversation. 'His face appeared tranquil like the ocean on a fine spring morning; but, like it, in an instant became changed into the tempestuous and terrible, if a passion, a thought, a word, occurred to disturb his mind. His eyes then lost all their sweetness, and sparkled so that it became difficult to look at them. . . . The natural state of his mind was the tempestuous.' (Moore, IV, 216.) With all his moods, his letters scintillate with shafts of wit:

The Apollo Belvidere is the image of Lady Adelaide Forbes—
I think I never saw such a likeness.

I have seen the Pope alive, and a cardinal dead,—both of whom looked very well indeed.

> My dear Mr. Murray
> You're in a damned hurry
>   To set up this ultimate Canto;
> But (if they don't rob us)
> You'll see Mr. Hobhouse
>   Will bring it safe in his portmanteau.

Do you think I would not have shot myself last year, had
I not luckily recollected that Mrs. Clermont and Lady Noel,
and all the old women in England would have been delighted?[3]

Such examples are to be found in profusion.

Don Juan was the most scintillating and, to his age, the most
shocking of Byron's poems:

> They accuse me—Me—the present writer of
> The present poem—of—I know not what—
> A tendency to under-rate and scoff
> At human power and virtue, and all that;
> And this they say in language rather rough.
> Good God! I wonder what they would be at!
> I say no more than hath been said in Dante's
> Verse, and by Solomon and by Cervantes.
>
> (VII, iii.)

His publisher, he jested, had told him that the poem was impossible
for family reading:

> 'Tis all the same to me; I'm fond of yielding,
> And therefore leave them to the purer page
> Of Smollett, Prior, Ariosto, Fielding,
> Who say strange things for so correct an age.
>
> (IV, xcviii.)

To his publisher, Murray, Byron wrote, '*Don Juan* will be known,
by and by, for what it is intended—a satire on *abuses* in the present
state of society, and not an eulogy of vice. It may be now and then
voluptuous;—I can't help that. Ariosto is worse. Smollett ten times
worse; and Fielding no better. No girl will ever be seduced by
reading *Don Juan*'. In vain he urged during the poem that it was a
cautionary tale, with a highly moral purpose:

> Besides, in Canto Twelfth, I mean to show
> The very place where wicked people go.
>
> (I, ccvii.)

But all this was written with his tongue in his cheek, and in the age of Thomas Bowdler and Hannah More it was all very shocking.

Critics were indeed acquainted with the farcical tumbling in and out of bed such as they found in *Tom Jones*. There was just such a scene in the first Canto of *Don Juan*, in which Julia conceals Juan under the bedclothes while her irate husband searches the bedroom, and the critic Jeffrey termed it 'indelicate but very clever, merely comic and a little coarse'. But what shocked him was that the poet should mingle deeply serious and immoral thoughts with what would otherwise be a hilarious farce. For Julia is sent to a convent, and yet writes passionate love-letters to Juan. 'The poet chooses to make this shameless and abandoned woman address to her young gallant an epistle breathing the very spirit of warm, devoted, pure and unalterable love—thus profaning the holiest language of the heart, and indirectly associating it with the most hateful and degrading sensualism. Thus our notions of right and wrong at once confounded—our confidence in virtue shaken to the foundation—and our reliance on truth and fidelity at an end for ever. Of this it is that we complain.' In short, the infidelity of the wife might be regarded as an amusing, though coarse, theme, but the unrestrained expression of passionate physical love in her letters, in disregard of her convent vows, struck at the roots of the moral order, and was too much for Jeffrey to tolerate.

It was also disconcerting to the age to find physical love described with such passionate sensuousness, and to know that the poet was writing from intimate experience of his subject. The most passionate stanzas in the poem are the love scenes between Haidee and Juan in the second Canto:

> A long, long kiss, a kiss of youth, and love,
> And beauty, all concentrating like rays
> Into one focus, kindled from above;
> Such kisses as belong to early days,
> Where heart, and soul, and sense, in concert move,
> And the blood's lava, and the pulse a blaze,
> Each kiss a heart-quake,—for a kiss's strength,
> I think, it must be reckon'd by its length.
> (II, clxxxvi.)

This stanza illustrates one of Byron's devastating tricks, the use of bathos to deflate a moment of high seriousness, to remind the reader that the poet has been playing with him, that he is not really serious, because there is so little in life which is worth being really serious about.

It was Byron's declared aim to prick the bubble of numerous social conventions, to show how many of the cherished beliefs of the age were the result of humbug and cant. Heroics, for example:

> In case our lord the king should go to war again,
> He learned the arts of riding, fencing, gunnery,
> And how to scale a fortress—or a nunnery.
>
> (I, xxxviii.)

Donna Inez had Juan most carefully educated, with the classics thoroughly expurgated. Even the family Missal she kept to herself because it had lewd illuminations in the margin.

> Her maids were old, and if she took a new one,
> You might be sure she was a perfect fright,
> She did this during even her husband's life—
> I recommend as much to every wife.   (I, xlviii.)

Yet this was not the education Byron recommended. If he had had a son,

> I'd send him out betimes to college,
> For there it was I pick'd up my own knowledge.
>
> (I, lii.)

Byron's barbs of irony sting the reader when he least expects them:

> A quiet conscience makes one so serene!
> Christians have burnt each other, quite persuaded
> That all the Apostles would have done as they did.
>
> (I, lxxxiii.)

To those satisfied with the scientific achievements of the age:

> I said the small-pox has gone out of late;
> Perhaps it may be follow'd by the great. (I, cxxx.)

And the frailty of women:

> A little still she strove, and much repented,
> And whispering 'I will ne'er consent'—consented.
>
> (I, cxvii.)

For, so Byron liked to think,

> Man's love is of man's life a thing apart,
> 'Tis woman's whole existence.　　(I, cxciv.)

The autobiographical nature of the poem increased both the interest and the embarrassment of contemporaries. Donna Inez was a most skilful satirical portrait of Lady Byron. Julia's affair with Juan brought on a divorce,

> The nine days' wonder which was brought to light,
> And how Alfonso sued for a divorce,
> Were in the English newspapers, of course . . .
>
> There's more than one edition, and the readings
> Are various, but they none of them are dull.
>
> (I, clxxxviii.)

The most poignant theme in the poem is the exquisite beauty of first love:

> But sweeter still than this, than these, than all,
> Is first and passionate love—it stands alone,
> Like Adam's recollection of his fall;
> The tree of knowledge has been pluck'd—all's known—
> And life yields nothing further to recall
> Worthy of this ambrosial sin, so shown,
> No doubt in fable, as the unforgiven
> Fire which Prometheus filch'd for us from heaven.
>
> (I, cxxvii.)

But the very transitory nature of such ecstasy, for Byron, leaves the rest of life a sad and regretful experience, and so,

> Man, being reasonable, must get drunk;
> The best of life is but intoxication:
> Glory, the grape, love, gold, in these are sunk
> The hopes of all men, and of every nation;
> Without their sap, how branchless were the trunk
> Of life's strange tree, so fruitful on occasion.
>
> (II, clxxix.)

With Byron there is always beneath the surface the bitterness at not having achieved a constant love. Usually it is turned away with an acid joke; how useless is philosophy in controlling the human passions!

> Love, constant love, has been my constant guest,
> And yet last night, being at a masquerade,
> I saw the prettiest creature, fresh from Milan,
> Which gave me some sensations like a villain.

> But soon Philosophy came to my aid,
> And whispered, 'Think of every sacred tie!'
> 'I will, my dear Philosophy!' I said
> 'But then her teeth, and then, oh Heaven! her eye!
> I'll just enquire if she be wife or maid,
> Or neither—out of curiosity!' (II, ccix–ccx.)

The essential honesty with which Byron displayed his love-life in Italy was something quite new in English literature, and too much in the spirit of Rousseau and Casanova to be other than shocking. And Byron would have been very disappointed if he had not shocked, for to him it was a form of revenge against the English society which had shunned him. In the final Canto Don Juan visits England, and Byron concealed his secret desire to return there under a rather tired satire:

> I've no great cause to love that spot of earth,
> Which holds what *might have been* the noblest nation;
> But though I owe it little but my birth,
> I feel a mix'd regret and veneration

For its decaying fame and former worth.
Seven years (the usual term of transportation)
Of absence lay one's old resentments level,
When a man's country's going to the devil.
(X, lxvi.)

With all its wit and bravado, *Don Juan* has its sadness and
nostalgia. There is the recurrent theme of the physical ecstasies of
youth which can never be recovered:

And the sad truth which hovers o'er my desk
Turns what was once romantic to burlesque.
And if I laugh at any mortal thing,
'Tis that I may not weep; and if I weep
'Tis that our nature cannot always bring
Itself to apathy. (IV, iii, iv.)

Life starts with its glories of hope, but one by one they fade with
experience:

All, when life is new,
Commence with feelings warm, and prospects high;
But time strips our illusions of their hue,
And one by one in turn, some grand mistake
Casts off its bright skin yearly like a snake.
(V, xxl.)

Always with Byron there is the hint of the 'grand mistake' which
has blighted his life:

Love's the first net which spreads its deadly mesh;
Ambition, Avarice, Vengeance, Glory, glue
The glittering lime-twigs of our later days,
Where still we flutter on for pence or praise.
(V, xxii.)

Herein lay the morality of the poem, for

By setting things in their right point of view,
Knowledge at least is gained.

Y

With all the metaphysical similarities between Byron and the contemporary Romantics, there was little fellow-feeling between them. In his Dedication to Don Juan he was contemptuous of Southey, the revolutionary who became Poet Laureate and a tory.

> Bob Southey! You're a poet—Poet-laureate,
> And representative of all the race,
> Although 'tis true that you turn'd out a Tory at
> Last,—yours has lately been a common case,—
> And now, my Epic Renegade! what are ye at?
> With all the Lakers, in and out of place?
> A nest of tuneful persons, to my eye
> Like 'four and twenty Blackbirds in a pye;
>
> Which pye being opened they began to sing'
> (This old song and new simile holds good),
> A dainty dish to set before the King',

Wordsworth also had his place in the Excise, with a safe salary:

> You're shabby fellows—true—but poets still,
> And duly seated on the immortal hill.

Coming from Byron, with his assured princely income, these attacks were in poor taste, but he thought he discerned apostacy for the sake of money, and he himself was a whig:

> Sir Laureate—I proceed to dedicate,
> In honest simple verse, this song to you.
> And if in flattering strains I do not predicate,
> 'Tis that I still retain my 'buff and blue'.

Moreover he disliked the poetry of the 'Lakers' because he thought that it merely pandered to the cant of the time, lacked sincerity or was merely drivelling:

> Thou shall believe in Milton, Dryden, Pope;
> Thou shalt not set up Wordsworth, Coleridge, Southey;
> Because the first is crazed beyond all hope,

The second drunk, the third so quaint and mouthy.

(I, ccv.)

Of *The Excursion* he writes: 'A drowsy frowsy poem, Writ in a manner which is my aversion.'

> Pedlars, and 'Boats', and 'Waggons!' Oh! ye shades
> Of Pope and Dryden, are we come to this?
> That trash of such sort not alone evades
> Contempt, but from the bathos' vast abyss
> Floats scumlike uppermost, and these Jack Cades
> Of sense and song above your graves may hiss!—
> The 'little boatman', and his 'Peter Bell',
> Can sneer at him who drew 'Achitophel'.

(III, c.)

Such was Byron's reply to Wordsworth's unfortunate remark that Dryden's verses had been forgotten.

In his early days Byron thought Walter Scott incomparably the greatest contemporary poet, with Rogers, Moore and Campbell next, and the 'Lakers', Wordsworth, Coleridge and Southey trailing far behind. Later he thought Shelley, alone of his contemporaries, his superior as a poet. In 1817 he wrote that 'with regard to poetry in general, I am convinced, the more I think of it that Scott, Southey, Wordsworth, Moore, Campbell and I are all in the wrong, one as much as another; that we are upon a wrong revolutionary poetical system, or systems, not worth a damn in itself, and from which none but Rogers and Crabbe are free; and that the present and next generations will finally be of this opinion.' The mistake, he argued, was to have departed from the style of Pope, whom Byron regarded as incomparably the greatest poet. 'I was really astonished (I ought not to have been so) and mortified at the ineffable distance in point of sense, learning, effect, and even *imagination*, passion and *invention*, between the little Queen Anne's man, and us of the Lower Empire. . . . Crabbe's the man, but he has got a coarse and impracticable subject.' (Moore, IV, 64.) It was the denigration of Pope by Wordsworth and Coleridge which turned Byron so unalterably against them. Why should they, he asked, have attacked Pope for what was his chief glory, namely his adherence to the precepts of reason? Whether one's test for a poet was reason, imagination, passion or invention, Pope was the supreme poet. 'There will be found as comfortable metaphysics and ten times more poetry in the *Essay on Man*, than in *The Excursion*. If you search for passion, where is it to be found stronger than in the epistle from Eloisa to Abelard, or in Palamon and Arcite? Do you wish for invention, imagination, sublimity, character? seek them in the Rape of the Lock, the Fables of Dryden, the Ode on Saint Cecilia's Day, and Absalom and Achitophel. . . . We are sneeringly told that Pope is the "Poet of Reason", as if this was a reason for his being no poet. Taking passage for passage, I will undertake to cite more lines teeming with *imagination* from Pope than from any two living poets, be they who they may.' (Moore, V, 18–19.) So long as Keats was alive, Byron never had a good word to say for his poetry, and he admitted that it was Keats' inability to appreciate Pope which lay at the root of his prejudice: 'My indignation at Mr. Keats's depreciation of Pope has hardly permitted me to do justice to his own genius.' This belated recognition of 'genius' was written only after Keats' death. He was equally hostile to the view that the Lake poets were superior to Pope in their attitude to nature. 'Is it not a shame to hear our Lakers in "Kendal green", and our Bucolical Cockneys, crying out (the latter in a wilderness of bricks and mortar) about "Nature", and Pope's "artificial indoor habits"?' Was it not Pope who had inspired Kent to lay out English grounds tastefully? Were not his descriptions of Windsor Forest, or his influence upon the gardens of Stowe, worthy of note? 'His various excellence is really wonderful: architecture, painting, gardening, all are alike subject to his genius.' (Moore, V, 167.) 'In the present day there have sprung up two sorts of Naturals,—the Lakers, who whine about Nature because they live in Cumberland; and their under-sect (which someone has maliciously called the "Cockney School"), who are enthusiastical for the country because they live in London.' Wordsworth, Coleridge and Southey had at least travelled in Europe, and seen Nature in her varied moods, but what had Keats and the others seen, except *bricks*! Byron concluded, 'If they had said nothing of Pope, they might have remained "alone with their glory" for aught I should have said or thought about them or their nonsense. But if they interfere with the little "Nightingale" of Twickenham, they might find others who will bear it—*I* won't. Neither time, nor distance, nor grief, nor age, can ever diminish my veneration for him, who is the great moral poet of all times, the delight of my boyhood, the study of my manhood, perhaps (if allowed to me to attain it) he may be the consolation of my age. His poetry is the Book of Life.' (Moore, V, 169.)

In April 1821 Robert Southey, the Poet Laureate, published a highly patriotic poem entitled *The Vision of Judgement*. Dedicating his poem to George IV, Southey praised the glorious military achievements of the age, the 'perfect integrity of the whole adminis-tration of public affairs' in Britain, the advance of religion, George IV's architectural contributions to London, and in general the 'sciences, arts and letters which are flourishing beyond all former example'. The genuineness of Southey's patriotism was not in doubt, but the poem itself verged on the ridiculous. It described how the poet, as he listened to the death bell of old George III, fell into a trance, and how an angel showed him the King's spirit rising to heaven, where he was welcomed by his illustrious pre-decessors, and by Shakespeare and Milton. Southey's preface showed that he intended his poem to be an object-lesson in how literature should serve a moral, religious and political purpose. He argued that poetry traditionally had been noble and pure, capable of being read by the whole family. Recently however there had emerged a 'Satanic school' of poets whose 'diseased hearts and depraved imaginations' had rebelled against religion, and had sought to corrupt by their lascivious writings, and their 'images of atrocities and horrors'. The reference to Byron and *Don Juan* was obvious. Byron detested Southey as the arch-priest of cant, and as a renegade from the cause of liberalism, and the opportunity of making a crushing retort to Southey was irresistible. He replied with *The Vision of Judgement* (1821), the most perfect of all his satires.

The opening lines established the mood of wit and sophisticated disbelief:

> Saint Peter sat by the celestial gate:
> His keys were rusty, and the lock was dull,
> So little trouble had been given of late;
> Not that the place by any means was full . . .
>
> .   .   .   .   .   .
>
> The angels all were singing out of tune,
> And hoarse with having little else to do . . .

In this way he scoffed at what he took to be Southey's religiosity and the outworn ideas which the new intelligentsia no longer took seriously. Southey, moreover, had glorified the achievements of war. Byron wrote that the recording angel was exhausted at inscribing the names of those slaughtered in war:

> Each day too slew its thousands six or seven,
> Till at the crowning carnage, Waterloo,
> They threw their pens down in divine disgust—
> The page was so besmear'd with blood and dust.

Southey had glorified George III. Byron declared that he was a good farmer, but a bad king, and that his death was of very little significance. Blind and insane, he had ceased to matter, and his elaborate funeral was merely part of the cant of the time. Southey had talked of George being in heaven, and his enemies in hell. Byron never forgot his Calvinist childhood; he hated talk of damnation, and seized the opportunity to condemn the narrowness of Anglicanism:

> I know this is unpopular; I know
> 'Tis blasphemous; I know one may be damn'd
> For hoping no one else may e'er be so;
> I know my catechism; I know we are cramm'd
> With the best doctrines till we quite o'erflow;
> I know that all save England's church have shamm'd,
> And that the other twice two hundred churches
> And synagogues have made a *damn'd* bad purchase.

In Southey's poem the arrival of George III at the gates of heaven was the occasion for a special fanfare. Byron sought to set the event in truer perspective:

> 'George the Third is dead'
> 'And who *is* George the Third?' replied the apostle:
> '*What George? what Third?*'

Byron was making no attack upon religion itself, but only wittily suggesting the blasphemy in Southey's poem in the suggestion that God himself must be impressed by the arrival of the British monarch. The Archangel Michael then appeared to conduct the trial of George III, and Satan arrived to claim his victim. The scene obviously owed much to Milton. They treated each other with great mutual respect, rather as lordly statesmen. Michael makes it clear to Satan:

> I ne'er mistake you for a *personal* foe;
> Our difference is *political*, and I
> Trust that, whatever may occur below,
> You know my great respect for you.

Satan presents the case against the King; it is the whig case the influence of Bute, the loss of America, the war against France, five million Catholics refused political equality.

> He ever warr'd with freedom and the free:
> Nations as men, home subjects, foreign foes,
> So that they utter'd the word 'Liberty!'
> Found George the Third their first opponent.

The case was neatly put, and John Wilkes and Junius were summoned as witnesses. Byron treats them with great skill. It was not really his purpose to condemn George III, nor to write a diatribe against his reign. It was not the King, but Southey, who was the villain of the piece. Wilkes and Junius appear because they had appeared in Southey's poem, but neither of them gives evidence against the King. They had, they said, written all they had to say on earth:

> I don't like ripping up old stories, since
> His conduct was but natural in a prince.

Finally Southey arrives to read his poem in praise of the King, and Byron satirised his political apostacy:

> He had written praises of a regicide;
> He had written praises of all kings whatever;
> He had written for republics far and wide,
> And then against them bitterer than ever:
> For pantisocracy he once had cried
> Aloud, a scheme less moral than 'twas clever;
> Then grew a hearty anti-jacobin—
> Had turn'd his coat—and would have turned his skin.

> . . . . . .

> He had written much blank verse, and blanker prose,
> And more of both than any body knows.

Southey proceeded to attempt to read his poem, but at the sound of the first lines the spirits howled and fled, and thus the trial was never completed.

> All I saw farther, in the last confusion,
> Was, that King George slipp'd into heaven for one;
> And when the tumult dwindled to a calm,
> I left him practising the hundredth psalm.

The ending was most skilfully managed: it was no part of Byron's purpose to be hard on George III, or to rake up old controversies, but to set the record straight in view of Southey's exaggerations, and Southey was left to look ridiculous as the arch-priest of cant.

The Vision of Judgement was the most perfect of Byron's satires. In the *English Bards and Scotch Reviewers* he had written:

> Such is the force of wit! but not belong
> To me the arrows of satiric song;
> The royal vices of our age demand
> A keener weapon, and a mightier hand.

Still there are follies, e'en for me to chase,
And yield at last amusement in the race:
Laugh when I laugh, I seek no other fame;
The cry is up, and scribblers are my game.

For this amusement poor Southey proved fair game, and in the process Byron struck a blow for honesty.

When Byron died at Missolonghi in April 1824 the Greek Provisional Government proclaimed a general mourning for twenty-one days, and all Europe acknowledged the passing of the most famous of living Englishmen. It was a death entirely in accord with the Byronic idea, that of a noble spirit fighting against overwhelming odds. In France he had a devoted following among the liberals, and Taine declared that he was the only contemporary English poet who reached the supreme height. Goethe called him 'without question the greatest talent of the age'. To European liberals of the nineteenth century he was the great symbol of English political idealism in the struggle against the forces of conservatism and reaction. In England he was a more controversial figure, but he was widely read, and Matthew Arnold regarded Byron and Wordsworth as the two greatest poets of the age. Yet English society had driven Byron out; indeed it is significant that Byron, Shelley, Keats and Landor all found the intellectual atmosphere of England uncongenial, and preferred to live abroad. Byron's greatest qualities lay in his vivid personality and his intellectual honesty. He detested or despised most of the public figures of his day, George III, Castlereagh, Wellington, Brougham; indeed he was correct when he wrote: 'I have simplified my politics into an utter detestation of all existing governments.' He stemmed from the aristocratic anarchism which created an imaginary world in so many eighteenth-century minds, and he found the caustic style of Pope the most effective means of expressing it. His greatest impact was as a liberating force, but for most of his age he went too far. Madam de Staël once said to Byron in Switzerland: 'You should not have warred with the world; it is too strong always for any individual: I myself once tried it in early life, but it will not do.' Macaulay summed up the reaction of his age in a famous passage:

'We know no spectacle so ridiculous as the British public in one of its periodical fits of morality. In general, elopements, divorces, and family quarrels, pass with little notice. . . . But once in six or seven years our virtue becomes outrageous. We cannot suffer the laws of religion and decency to be violated. We must make a stand against vice. We must teach libertines that the English people appreciate the importance of domestic ties. Accordingly some unfortunate man, in no respect more depraved than hundreds whose offences have been treated with leniency, is singled out as an expiotary sacrifice. If he has children, they are taken from him. If he has a profession, he is ruined. He is cut by the higher orders and hissed by the lower. He is, in truth, a sort of whipping-boy, by whose vicarious agonies all the other transgressors of the same class are, it is supposed, sufficiently chastised. . . . At length our anger is satiated. Our victim is ruined and heart-broken. And our virtue goes quietly to sleep for seven years more.' Macaulay was writing of Byron.

.   .   .   .   .   .

With Byron's tempestuous career may be compared that of Walter Savage Landor (1775–1864), who all his life described himself as an 'aristocratic radical', who started life as a kind of miniature Byron, spent long years in exile in Italy, and lived long enough to become a Conservative in mid-Victorian England.

Walter Savage Landor (1775–1864) was all his life an individualist. Born at Warwick, of an old landowning family, he was heir to a fortune and did not need to earn a living. At Rugby he showed a linguistic brilliance, but was by nature so turbulent and arrogant that he was asked to leave before his time. At Oxford he was the centre of a group of young bloods who imagined themselves to be Jacobins, and he was one of the first to cease powdering his hair. Southey wrote later: 'I remember he was a contemporary of mine at Oxford, of Trinity, and notorious as a mad Jacobin; his Jacobinism would have made me seek his acquaintance, but for his madness: he was obliged to leave the University for shooting at one of the Fellows through the window.' This was not quite accurate, but he did fire a gun through the window at the shutters of a fellow-undergraduate's rooms, and in consequence was rusticated for two terms in 1794. He never returned as a student to Oxford.

His views at this time were very similar to those of Wordsworth and Coleridge, and they were expressed in his first notable poem, *Moral Epistle* (1795). 'I was then in raptures', he wrote later, 'with what I now despise.' *Gebor* appeared in 1798, within a few weeks of the *Lyrical Ballads*, and was written in the same direct language which Wordsworth and Coleridge claimed as such a novelty in their work. Charles Lamb indeed thought *Gebor* 'quasi Gibberish', De Quincey thought it 'too Tom-Painish', and others thought parts of it blasphemous, but Southey regarded it as one of the greatest poems ever written, and gave it an excessively enthusiastic notice in the *Critical Review*. The poem contained an idealistic picture of Bonaparte as 'a mortal man above all mortal wise'. In his enthusiasm for the French Revolution, Landor was contemptuous of British politicians. He was hostile to Pitt, and although he sometimes affected to follow Fox, he never liked him. The House of Commons he called 'the most costly exhibition in Europe', and when he met Tom Paine he found him 'in fact a monstrous clever man'. A visit to Paris following the Peace of Amiens of 1802 began a revolution in his thinking when he saw how effectively the French had been deprived of political liberty by the First Consul. He wrote to his brother Henry: 'Doubtless the government of Buonaparte is the best that can be contrived for Frenchmen. Monkeys must be chained, though it may cost them some grimaces. If you have read the last senatus consultum, you will find that not an atom of liberty is left. This people, the most inconstant, and therefore the most contemptible in the world, seem'd to have recovered their senses when they had lost their freedom. ... As to the cause of liberty, this cursed nation has ruined it for ever.' (Malcolm Elwin: *Landor*, Macdonald (1958), p. 92.) Years later Landor commented: 'In my boyhood I was a fierce democrat and extolled the French. In a few years it was evident how incapable was that people of Liberty, and how prone to despotism. Let me never be called inconsistent if I praised the good and true, abhorring and detesting the vicious and the false.' (R. H. Super: *Walter Savage Landor*, John Calder (1957), p. 65.)

With the renewal of war, and the intensification of the Anglo-French struggle, Landor, like Wordsworth, discovered a new patriotism. The fall of the Ministry of All the Talents in 1807 completed his conversion from the whig cause, and the Spanish revolt against the French in 1808 gave him a new enthusiasm. Declaring, 'May every Frenchman out of France perish! May the Spaniards not spare one!', he announced his intention of going to Spain to fight as an ordinary soldier for the Spaniards. Southey was thrilled at the heroism of the decision, and at once fell to imagining the consequences if Landor personally captured King Joseph,—'he would infallibly hang him on the nearest tree'. Landor saw some action, but the Convention of Cintra cut short his activities, and he was back in England by November 1808. King Ferdinand made him an honorary colonel in the Spanish army, but when years later Ferdinand became a despot, Landor returned his commission, saying 'that he was willing to aid a people in the assertion of its liberties against the antagonist of Europe, but that he could have nothing to do with a perjuror and traitor'. Landor, like Southey, always retained a special admiration for the Spanish people and their culture. In his play *Count Julian* he wrote of Spain as

> Unconquerable land! unrivalled race!
> Whose bravery, too enduring, rues alike
> The power and weakness of accursed kings.

Landor's attempt to set up as a country gentleman at Llanthony was a complete failure. He failed to become a magistrate, or to unseat the political interest of the Beauforts; he was in financial difficulties, and there was constant trouble with his tenants.[4] Finally, disillusioned with England, and with lack of recognition for his genius, and heavily in debt, he withdrew abroad. He was at Tours during the Hundred Days, and later settled first at Como, and then at Florence. By 1820 he could write to Southey: 'I think of England as if I were in another world, and had lost all personal interest in it.' His outlook now was cosmopolitan; he hated the Holy Alliance, and supported the Neapolitan rebels of 1821 by writing a pamphlet on their behalf. He spent much of his time writing, and in collecting pictures. Monckton Milnes, who visited him at Fiesole in 1833 found his walls covered with 'such masters as Masaccio, Ghirlandaio, Gozzoli, Filippo and Fra Angelico', some of which Landor said he had bought for a few shillings.

When the 1830 Revolution broke out in France, Southey wrote to Landor that 'Italy cannot be long inactive in the day of regeneration', and he feared lest Landor might become involved, as in the Neopolitan revolt of 1821. But Landor, although he always supported the Greek rebels, had lost much of his revolutionary enthusiasm, and he was contemptuous of contemporary Florentines. He replied, 'Be assured there is not a patriot in Florence who would have a single pane of glass broken in his window to bring about any change whatever. At my time of life, and with my utter indifference what befalls so rascally a race, you need not apprehend that, in case of a bustle, I should take any part in it.' (Elwin, p. 248.) Yet he welcomed the coming of the Reform Bill in England. All his life he had been in favour of religious toleration and parliamentary reform, and he was much less worried about the consequences of the latter than many of his contemporaries. He wrote to his sister in May 1831: 'The misfortune is that the change had not taken place fifty-five years earlier. Then we should not have lost America, except as a colony and a dependant, and by no means a Confederate and friend.' He had always tended to have a contempt for the politicians; he was always severely critical of Pitt, was contemptuous of what he called 'the vices, the profligacy and the perfidy' of Fox, he thought ill of Canning and Liverpool and he hated Brougham. When he talked of parliamentary reform he was seeking for a means to diminish government influence at elections and increase the electoral power of property. He never supposed that there was a depository of political wisdom in the mob, towards whom his attitude was always paternalistic. In 1844 he declared that 'my heart sinks and aches every time I go out of doors, such is the misery of the poor', and in 1854 he wrote that he hated to go to London because of the scenes of poverty and misery he so often encountered there. (Elwin, p. 309.) By 1836 he was calling himself a Conservative, and expressing views similar to those of the later

Coleridge and Wordsworth. He explained that he was particularly anxious that the Anglican Church should retain control of education. 'But if Bishops are to sit in the House of Lords as Barons, voting against no corruption, against no cruelty, not even the slave trade, the people ere long will knock them on the head. Conservative I am, but no less am I an *aristocratic radical*. I would eradicate all that vitiates our constitution in church and state, making room for the gradual growth of what altered times require, but preserving the due ranks and orders of society, and even to a much greater degree than most of the violent tories are doing.' (Elwin, p. 325.) In his later years he was chiefly worried alternatively by the prospect of the advance of Roman Catholicism in England, and the decline of religion. In a pamphlet of 1851, *Popery, British and Foreign*, he wrote: 'It would grieve me to foresee a day when our cathedrals and our churches shall be demolished or desecrated; when the tones of the organ, when the symphonies of Handel, no longer swell and reverberate along the groined roof and dim windows. But let the old superstitions crumble into dust; let Faith, Hope and Charity be simple in their attire; let few and solemn words be spoken before Him "to whom all hearts are open, all desires known".' In 1851, the year of the Great Exhibition, Jacobinism was but a distant memory.

NOTES

[1] Byron wrote: 'I retired from the country, perceiving that I was the object of general obloquy; I did not indeed imagine, like Jean Jacques Rousseau, that all mankind was in a conspiracy against me, though I had perhaps as good grounds for such a chimera as ever he had: but I perceived that I had to a great extent become personally obnoxious in England, perhaps through my own fault, but the fact was indisputable.' He added that 'I can hardly conceive that the common and everyday occurrence of a separation between man and wife could in itself produce so great a ferment.' (Thos. Moore: *The Works of Lord Byron* (1832), V, 7.)

[2] He wrote quite openly of his affairs and his attempts to drink deep, e.g. 'It is the height of the Carnival, and I am in the extreme and agonies of a new intrigue with I don't exactly know whom or what, except that she is insatiate of love, and won't take money, and has light hair and blue eyes, which are not common here, and that I met her at the Masque, and that when her mask is off, I am as wise as ever. I shall make what I can of the remainder of my youth.' (Moore, IV, 79.)

[3] Mrs. Clermont had been his wife's governess; Lady Noel was his mother-in-law.

[4] Landor was a difficult man, but anyone who believes that in those days tenants were always ground down by triumphant landlords should study the facts presented in Mr. Elwin's *Landor*, Chap. 6.

16 : Painting and Architecture in the Age of the Picturesque

During the course of the eighteenth century Hogarth, Reynolds and Gainsborough did much to create an English tradition in painting, and the Palladians and their successors achieved the zenith of classical English architecture. Hogarth was entirely a native product, scorning continental models, but Reynolds, in his *Discourses* more than in his painting, pointed to the need for artists to continue to study the Italian tradition of Raphael, Michelangelo and the Carracci, and to adjudge heroic and historical painting as superior to all other forms. In this respect 1780 does not provide a particularly significant dividing line, for Gainsborough had another eight years to live, Reynolds' *Discourses* would continue for another decade, and Robert Adam did not die until 1792. Nevertheless other influences were beginning to make themselves felt. Literature and Horace Walpole were popularising Gothic styles of mediaevalism, darkness and mystery; Indian and Chinese art forms were providing exotic alternatives, and Romanticism was beginning to encourage a new regard for nature and the simple peasant life. For the first time in the century it might be said that literature greatly surpassed painting and architecture in importance, for there was a growth of a middle-class audience more concerned with reading than with the visual arts. The foundation of the Royal Academy in 1768 was a necessary, and on the whole beneficial, step towards producing an English tradition in painting, but it did tend to cast artists in a certain mould, and to encourage them to paint, if not like Sir Joshua, at least according to his precepts. In general therefore there was a tendency to uncertainty about the artistic achievements of the period 1780–1830 which was absent from those of the previous sixty years.

The point is illustrated by a dilemma to which R. B. Haydon drew his readers' attention. Haydon was a choleric man, and an unequal artist, but at his best he has been unduly neglected. When he came up to London from Plymouth in 1804 he was full of Sir Joshua's teaching that 'High Art' was the only art worth pursuing, and that for this purpose it was necessary 'to unite nature and the antique'. But to do this he found an impossible task: 'I had nature of course, but if I copied her, my work was mean, and if I left her, it was mannered. What was I to do? . . . In my model I saw the back vary according to the action of the arms. In the antique these variations were not so apparent. Was nature or the antique wrong? Why did not the difference of shape from difference of action appear so palpably in the antique, as in nature? This puzzled me to death. If I copied what I saw in life, Fuseli said, "This is too much like life!" If I copied the marble, Wilkie said, "That looks as if you had painted from stone!" ' (*Life of B. R. Haydon*, I, 81–2.) It was a dilemma which sprang from the artistic cross-currents of the time. Haydon was not a great artist, but he was an immensely industrious one, and he frequently found himself having to tackle grandiose subjects far beyond his capacity.

In one respect Reynolds' injunction was clearly in accord with the spirit of the time, for the high regard paid to historical themes enabled artists of the day to express the powerful current of patriotism which accompanied the French Wars. Benjamin West, a Quaker from Pennsylvania, had a great reputation in his day as the painter of religious and historical scenes, and he became President of the Royal Academy in 1794. Today he is chiefly remembered for his picture 'The Death of General Wolfe' (1771), in which he created a sensation by ignoring the urgent advice of Sir Joshua Reynolds and painting the figures in eighteenth-century dress, instead of the traditional classical costume. John Singleton Copley, another American, from Boston, won fame with such pictures as 'The Death of the Earl of Chatham', 'The Death of Major Pierson', described by Wellington as the best battle piece he had ever seen, and 'The Siege and Relief of Gibraltar', all fine action pieces.

The force of precept, tradition and Italian example often led artists to continue to paint classical themes in the classical style, but under the influence of Romanticism taste was changing, and there was a new interest in what the eighteenth century had called Gothic themes of history, conflict, terror and fantasy. Moreover, since the greatest influence in English literary history was Shakespeare, and since Garrick and Mrs. Siddons had again made Shakespeare's characters household words, it was natural that artists should turn to Shakespeare for inspiration. In 1786 John Boydell, an engraver, established a Shakespeare Gallery, to which almost all the great artists of the day, including Reynolds, contributed. The gallery was open to the public, and engravings of the pictures were sold throughout the country. After Shakespeare, the greatest literary influence was that of Milton, and Henry Fuseli started a Milton Gallery, for which he painted forty pictures. Neither project was a success, Boydell died in debt, and in 1805 the entire gallery of a hundred and seventy pictures was sold for a little over six thousand pounds. The reason was not far to seek. Great art is more than book illustration or records of stage sets, and most of the pictures were painted without conviction. At best therefore they were melodramatic, and at worst dull. Moreover, the historical painter, if he was to be accurate, required a considerable amount of archaeological knowledge, and this Boydell's contemporaries did not possess. Soon the general knowledge possessed by the public surpassed that of the artists, and then the pictures became ludicrous.

After Shakespeare and Milton, and soon to surpass both, was the new interest in history. The Histories of Hume and Robertson had been widely read, and for the first time the middle ages were beginning to exercise a fascination. Before Hume there had been almost a conspiracy of silence about the events of the reign of Charles I, but now the struggles of Cavalier and Roundhead took on a romantic significance. John Singleton Copley painted 'Charles I demanding the Five Members', John Opie painted 'The Assassination of David Rizzio', and 'James I of Scotland Assassinated by Graham'; and James Northcote painted 'The Murder of the Princes in the Tower', 'The Death of Wat Tyler', and 'The Death of Mortimer'. In many of such pictures, of course, history and Shakespeare came together.

z

It was in such subjects as were presented by Shakespeare and mediaeval legend that Henry Fuseli found his most congenial themes. The son of a Zürich artist, he had spent some early years translating and illustrating literary works, and his painting never lost some of the characteristics of book-illustration. He had studied in Italy, and was chiefly influenced by Michelangelo, from whom he learnt to paint bulging muscles. An awkward man in his move-ments, he included odd distortions in his drawings. He was the most obviously Romantic painter of his time, with a vivid imagin-ation, a love of the macabre, darkness and terror, and of heroic themes mingled with erotic fancies. He spent some years in painting pictures for the Shakespeare and Milton Galleries, which were not a success, but they were widely known through engravings. Recently drawings by him have come to light in New Zealand, and they leave one in no doubt that he was one of the most original and inventive artists of his time.

With the influence of Italian art apparent in most of the artists of the period, it might be supposed that religious subjects would be among the most important of their pictures. But here there was a difficulty. Puritanism had left its mark in the eighteenth-century attitude to art in churches, and pictures were suspect as products of popery. When in 1773 the members of the Royal Academy, led by Sir Joshua Reynolds, offered to decorate St. Paul's Cathedral at their own expense, the offer was happily turned down, not because the artists had neither the knowledge nor ability for so large a work, but for fear of possible papist influences in the subject-matter. However, with the growth of the influence of Evangelical-ism, religious subjects again became less unlikely, especially in the form of prints for the poor. Benjamin West in his last years painted 'Our Saviour healing the Sick' (1811) and 'Christ rejected by Caiaphas' (1814).

Reynolds had shown that, although 'high art' was the noblest form of art, portraiture was the most lucrative. Although he remained pre-eminent in popular esteem until his death in 1798, there had been times at which George Romney had appeared to be a dangerous rival. Romney was a good colourist and draftsman, but lacked psychological depth in his portraits. His most famous subject was Emma Hart, later Lady Hamilton, whom he painted no less than fourteen times; and among his best portraits are those of Mrs. Mark Currie (Tate Gallery) and the poet Cowper (National Portrait Gallery). Always of a nervous and suspicious character, his mind gave way in 1798; he returned to his wife whom he had deserted thirty years before, and died in 1802. His removal from the scene left Thomas Lawrence in indisputed pre-eminence in the world of portraiture. Lawrence had been a boy prodigy, elected R.A. at the age of twenty-four in 1794, by which time he had painted a number of celebrated portraits, including those of George III, his Queen, and the royal children. He was an immensely fluent painter, with a tendency to superficiality and prettiness, without the psychological depth of Reynolds or Gainsborough. In his own day, however, he was thought to be unsurpassed. He was particularly attracted by the romantic roles of the actor Kendall, and painted him as Coriolanus and Hamlet, in which he could emphasise the new romantic mood of dark and Byronic melancholy brooding against a turbulent sky. His children were pretty without the insight and pathos which Reynolds put into his portraits of children. He did have however a genius for the painting of limpid eyes which Delacroix found irresistible.

Lawrence's great moment came in 1814, when the Prince Regent decided to have painted a gallery of portraits of the rulers and their ministers who had aided in the overthrow of Napoleon. Between 1814 and 1820 Lawrence painted the Prince Regent, the Tsar Alexander, the Emperor Francis I of Austria, the King of Prussia, Blücher, Wellington on horseback (his only equestrian picture), and others. Two of his most successful studies were those of Pope Pius VII and Cardinal Consalvi; in the portrait of the Pope Lawrence achieved his deepest psychological study. Many of the pictures were copied and sent all over Europe, and Lawrence achieved a European reputation unequalled by any of his predecessors. Yet he had had to work too quickly to achieve great art, and today no one who views them in the Waterloo Gallery at Windsor can regard them as more than works of craftsmanship. Many of the portraits he painted after 1820 were done in a more leisurely fashion, and were a good deal better. 'Countess of Blessington', 'Master

Lambton' and 'Lady Robert Manners' are fine portraits. He continued his prolific work until his sudden death in 1830.

Lawrence's Scottish contemporary, Sir Henry Raeburn, apart from a period of study in Italy and short visits to England, painted all his life in Edinburgh, and was a fine portraitist. His portrait, 'Dr. Nathaniel Spens', is a vigorous action piece, in which Spens is practising archery. 'Colonel Alastair MacDonell of Glengarry' is a romantic portrait of a highland chieftain that might have been a study for Scott's Fergus McIvor, in which Raeburn makes exciting use of light and shade. His female portraits have a simplicity and truth devoid of flattery, and bordering on the prosaic. Raeburn never attempted subjects other than portraits, and thus his range was limited, but it says much for the growth of Edinburgh as a cultural centre that he was kept busy and prosperous with his portraits for thirty-six years, until his death in 1823. Had he chosen to move to London, he might have been a serious rival to Sir Thomas Lawrence.

Growing interest in natural scenery, in space, cloud effects and mountains brought about the sense of need for a new medium which would indicate light and transitory effects better than could be achieved in oils. Hence the development by the end of the eighteenth century of the use of water-colours, both in England and on the Continent. Previously water-colours had been confined mainly to topographers who wished to record landscapes, buildings or ruins; now they were developed into a full art form. The earliest eighteenth-century water-colours were those of Alexander Cozens (1715–86), once thought to be a natural son of Peter the Great, and his son, John Robert Cozens (1752–97), whom Constable once described as 'the greatest genius that ever touched landscape'. J. R. Cozens was perhaps the first water-colourist to bring real poetry into his landscapes. Even more remarkable were the water-colours of Thomas Girtin (1775–1802), who was one of the first artists to make extensive excursions through the countryside, towns and villages, in order to paint on the spot. He delighted to paint ruins, with highlights and cool shadows, often with gloomy skies. Unfortunately his colours have not well survived, so the full force of his paintings has been lost.

Water-colours, being regarded at first as an inferior art, were confined to one small room of the Academy exhibitions. In 1805 therefore a number of artists broke away to form the Water-colour Society, and to hold their own exhibitions. Among them were John Varley, an attractive artist who reduced the rules of composition almost to a science, George Barret, whose landscapes were painted with deep feeling, Joshua Cristall, and others.

We may consider here a group of artists who studied directly from nature, and who may be considered as showing special characteristics of Romanticism in consequence. George Stubbs was the greatest of the animal painters. He studied animal anatomy with great care, and in 1776 published *The Anatomy of the Horse*, illustrated with his own drawings. He did a great deal to emphasise the nobility of his subject, and his paintings were in great demand by owners and breeders. At the same time he was fascinated with the power and cruelty of wild animals, and he developed the theme in such pictures as 'Lion Killing a Horse', 'Tigers at Bay' and 'The Horse Frightened at a Lion'. Even closer to rustic life was George Morland, a drunken, quarrelsome man, who lived rough, was often heavily in debt, and eventually drank himself to death, in 1804, at the age of forty-one. In spite of his turbulent life, he painted quiet rural scenes of stables, horses, gypsies and land-scapes. His pictures were in great demand, indeed it is said that many were copied and passed off as Morlands. They were always painted with the closest attention to naturalistic accuracy, and no one knew better than he did the cottages and fields of the peasantry among whom he lived. More sober in his private life, but more turbulent in his pictures was Morland's brother-in-law, James Ward (1769–1859). His fascination with the themes of power and conflict in nature is seen in such pictures as 'The Bull', 'Fighting Horses' and 'Napoleon's Charger, Marengo', and they make him a noted interpreter of the Romantic spirit, and a forerunner of Delacroix.

Although naturally London was the centre of the world of painting, yet Norwich, in its prosperous seclusion, was able to produce a school of painting of its own. John Crome (1768–1821) of Norwich had little education or formal training, and started life as a house- and sign-painter. Like Gainsborough at Ipswich, he was inspired by the flat East Anglian scenery, and much influenced by Dutch painting. He could find inspiration in any gnarled tree or winding stream, and he soon built up a considerable reputation as a teacher, and for his studies of the fields, heaths and streams of his native country-side. He was also the central figure in 'The Norwich Society' formed for the study and advancement of the arts. How closely some of his pictures adhered to the Dutch style is shown by the fact that the Redgraves, the historians of the period, could remember seeing Crome's work sold as a Wynants.

One of his friends and associates was John Sell Cotman (1782–1842), son of a Norwich draper. Cotman studied art in London, and for some years painted water-colours of landscapes in which he developed a technique of large flat washes. He was fascinated by archaeology, and by romantic subjects such as the Yorkshire abbeys and Conway Castle. Indeed Conway Castle was a favourite subject with Romantic painters. Cotman was a master of the picturesque; he could find poetry in almost any rural scene. Specially romantic also are the water-colours of David Cox (1783–1859) in their wild and turbulent scenery, stormy skies, twisted and storm-rent trees, fiery horses, and wind-swept heaths.

Girtin died in 1802, the year in which J. M. W. Turner became a Royal Academician. There is an apochryphal remark ascribed to Turner that 'if Girtin had lived I should have starved', an unlikely possibility, for Turner was a towering genius, and the most revolutionary influence in the history of English painting. Born in 1775 of lower middle class parents, he won acclamation at an early age. As early as 1797 a critic of the Royal Academy Exhibition referred to his 'undeniable proof of the possession of genius and judgement, and what is uncommon, in this age, is, that it partakes but very little of the manner of any other master: he seems to view Nature and her operations with a peculiar vision'. Turner was exhibiting a sea piece, in which he was attempting to portray the power and movement of the ocean, and *The Times* commented: 'we never beheld a piece of the kind possessing more imagination or exciting more awe and sympathy in the spectators'. By 1799 he was producing some of his finest water-colours,

'Abergavenny Bridge' and 'Harlech Castle' being among the best, and it was the latter which produced the first comparison between Turner and Claude. A contemporary critic wrote: 'This landscape, though it combines the style of Claude and of our excellent Wilson, yet wears an aspect of originality that shows the Painter looks at Nature with his own eyes.' Throughout the period Claude set the standard for landscape painting.

Turner's life is almost indistinguishable from his art; he never married, had few wants, and spent all his life absorbed in the study of nature and light. He made no attempt to pander to public taste; he did not tell anecdotes in his pictures, such as Victorians came to love, he had no social message. As Stephen Rigaud characteristically commented in 1855: 'He worshipped nature with all her beauties; but forgot God his Creator, and disregarded all the gracious invitations of the Gospel.' In short, he was solely concerned with the artistic aspects of visual experience.

It is still sometimes suggested that Ruskin 'discovered' Turner and made him acceptable to his age, but this is to underestimate Turner's early success, as well as to exaggerate Ruskin's value as an interpreter of Turner. It is true that Turner always had many unsold pictures, but he was a prolific worker, he sold much and became a wealthy man, with substantial investments before he had reached middle age. His water-colours of Yorkshire and Wales sold well. He sold his 'Fifth Plague of Egypt' to William Beckford for hundred and fifty guineas, and Beckford also bought a series of drawings of Fonthill at thirty-five guineas each. He sold his 'Sun rising through Vapour' to Sir John Leicester for three hundred and fifty guineas in 1807, and twenty years later bought it back for four hundred and ninety guineas in order to leave it to the nation. The truth was that Turner's artistic career represented a steady evolution as he sought to proceed from mere representation to artistic interpretation, and as time passed his pictures became more and more difficult for contemporaries to understand. Ruskin was almost entirely concerned with these later pictures, and at the time when he was writing he knew little of his earlier works. Still, although Turner's early works never lacked admirers, especially among experts, yet they presented to contemporaries some of the difficulties which presented themselves to the next generation.

John Hoppner put his finger on the main difficulty when he told Farington in 1803 that he 'reprobated the presumptive manner in which he (Turner) paints, and his carelessness. He said that so much was left to be *imagined* that it was like looking into a coal fire, or upon an Old Wall, where from many varying and undefined forms the fancy was to be employed in conceiving things'. Turner indeed was providing a new visual experience in which he was relying more on the imagination and on the subconscious reactions of his viewers, whereas many of his critics wanted him simply to paint according to one or other of the traditional styles. Northcote complained that Turner's pictures 'were too much compounded of art and had too little of nature'. Now by 'nature' he did not mean precisely what the artist saw, as in a mirror, but the way in which natural themes had been treated in the past by the great masters. For Northcote it was too much for an artist to ask his viewers to look with a new vision. It was true that Turner was not finishing every detail; parts of his pictures were left vague and undefined, whereas the foreground was often clearly defined. In this way a sense of distance was achieved, and the whole was enveloped in a vaporous mystery. Figures were often not conceived in the round, but merely suggested as parts of a coherent whole. Turner had studied Titian, Poussin, Claude and Ruysdael (he was less impressed by Rembrandt, remarking that some things were 'miserably drawn and poor in expression', and he thoroughly disliked Rubens), and he attempted throughout his life to assimilate what he had learnt from them.

This was too much for some critics. One wit called him 'over-Turner'. One of his most persistent critics was Sir George Beaumont, who as early as 1806 told Farington that Turner's pictures 'appeared to him to be like the works of an *old man* who had lost the power of execution'. Constable followed suit, declaring that 'Turner becomes more and more extravagant, and less attentive to nature'. David Wilkie thought Turner's style 'the most abominable I ever saw: some pieces of the picture you cannot make out at all and although his pictures are not large, yet you must be at the other end of the room before they can satisfy the eye'. The remark is instructive, for Wilkie was accustomed to read a picture from detail to detail, as if it were a Hogarth print, instead of attempting to comprehend it as a coherent whole, and a single emotional experience. Benjamin West, the President of the Royal Academy, declared in 1807 that he was 'disgusted' with Turner's views of the Thames, as being merely 'crude blotches, nothing could be more vicious'. Yet this was the period of such masterpieces as 'Conway Castle' (1802) which Turner treated in the full romantic spirit, a gloomy, mysterious and forbidding castle suggested against turbulent and angry skies, in startling contrast to the solidly painted debris on the beach. It is the period also of 'The Shipwreck' (1805), in which Turner showed mastery of a raging and turbulent sea; and the 'Sun rising through Vapour' (1807), a grey picture in which Turner showed his fascination with the representation of atmosphere. John Landseer understood Turner's achievement, and wrote in the *Review of Publications of Art* (1808): 'Perhaps no landscape painter has ever before so successfully caught the living lustre of Nature herself, under her varying aspects and phenomena of seasons, storms, calms, and time of day. The verdant and cheerful hues of spring, the rich mellowness of autumn, and the gleams and gloom of equinoxial storms, are to him alike familiar; and he dips his pencil with equal certainty and with equal success in the grey tints of early dawn, the fervid glow of the sun's meridian ray, and the dun twilight of evening.' Sir Thomas Lawrence described Turner as 'indisputably the first landscape painter in Europe', and Thomas Phillips told Farington that he thought Turner the greatest landscape painter that had ever lived.

In 1815 Turner exhibited his 'Dido building Carthage' and 'Crossing the Brook', both in the tradition of Claude. Indeed the *St. James's Chronicle* called the latter 'a fine work which, in grandeur and ideal beauty Claude never equalled'. Sir George Beaumont however was so bounded by the eighteenth-century tradition that he called it 'weak and like the work of an old man, one who no longer saw or felt colour properly; it was all of *pea-green* insipidity'. However absurd this may seem today, it is an indication of how strange Turner's colours seemed to traditionally-minded viewers. Yet the limits of Beaumont as an art critic may be judged from his remark to Farington that he thought Benjamin West the greatest artist since C. F. Le Brun!

It seemed strange to contemporaries that Turner should often give a banal title to a picture which in all other respects was highly romantic. To those brought up in the eighteenth-century tradition great art had to be ennobling, and this in effect meant that it had to be in accord with the great Neo-Platonic or Christian tradition of Europe. Turner himself followed that same tradition with subjects such as 'The Deluge' (1802), 'Dido and Aeneas' (1814) and 'Dido building Carthage' (1815), and these were entirely acceptable themes to contemporaries, and moreover were reminiscent of similar subjects undertaken by Claude. However in other pictures Turner broke completely with this tradition and used such titles as 'The Harbour of Dieppe', and this was more difficult to accept. Hence Crabb Robinson wrote in his diary: 'No one could find fault with a Garden of Armida, or even of Eden, so painted. But we know Dieppe, and can't easily clothe it in such fairy hues. I can understand why such artists as Constable and Collins are preferred.'

It was impossible that so great and revolutionary an artist as Turner should have been universally accepted in his own day, yet the degree to which he was accepted and appreciated by connoisseurs was much greater than those who know only Ruskin's version of the subject would suppose. Under the influence of Ruskin there was a tendency to concentrate too much upon Turner's later pictures, to the exclusion of his earlier works. Even today 'Rain, Steam and Speed' is probably the best known of his pictures, and it is not always recognised that this was the final product of a great artistic experiment spread over fifty years, some of the pictures of which are not so easily seen as those in the National Gallery. Hazlitt understood what that great experiment was about, although he did not entirely approve of it. In his Round Table essays in *The Examiner* he wrote of Turner as, 'the ablest landscape painter now living, whose pictures are however too much abstractions of aerial perspective, and representations not properly of the objects of nature as of the medium through which they were seen. . . . They are pictures of the elements of air, earth and water.' This was true, and by adopting this intensely scientific attitude to the problems of representation, Turner pointed the way to the most important artistic developments of the nineteenth century.

Sir George Beaumont's hostility to Turner is all the more interesting because in so many ways he was a noted and beneficent patron of the arts. He came of an old landed family which included Henry I and the dramatist Francis Beaumont among its progenitors. A wealthy man, with estates in Leicestershire and Essex, he was all his life devoted to art. He painted and sketched constantly, and was a notable collector. His prize possession, which he always carried about with him, was Claude Lorrain's 'Hagar and the Angel'. He was indeed so devoted to the great works of the past that he feared lest any contemporary artist should break away from the canons of good behaviour in art which he had learnt so meticulously from Sir Joshua Reynolds, and never modified. Yet he was a generous patron of young artists. He took an instant liking to the young and penniless David Wilkie. Wilkie had a genius for genre painting in which simple peasants were portrayed realistically, with humour, and without romantic overtones. When however he painted the story of King Alfred and the cakes, this realism offended Beaumont, who wrote to him that a historical subject must be dealt with with dignity: 'Whatever may have been the fact, a certain classical veil should be thrown over each trivial circumstance; and it is upon this ground I rather object at present to the expression of the girl who is taking up the cakes, as a little too ludicrous. The same natural manner of taking them up, nay, the same expression of countenance, may be preserved, only it should be softened, and the face more refined and delicate.'

Sir George Beaumont tried also to be a good friend to B. R. Haydon, but the latter had so irrascible a temper, and so exalted an opinion of his own genius as an artist, that he was a difficult man to patronise or befriend. More significant was the long and genuine friendship which grew up after 1803 between Sir George and Wordsworth and Coleridge. Lady Beaumont was devoted to Wordsworth's poetry, and Sir George once told Farington that 'he was infinitely indebted to Wordsworth for the good he had received from his poetry, which had benefited him more, had more purified his mind, than any sermons had done'. Wordsworth once told him that 'he wished to be considered as a teacher or nothing', and it was as such that they accepted him. It was a genuine friendship. Sir George gave Wordsworth a small property, helped Coleridge with money, and later helped Wordsworth to pay his son's expenses at the university, all without embarrassing the recipients. As late as 1809 he still found it necessary to warn Haydon against Wordsworth's dangerously democratic opinions, but they seem never to have retarded the friendship between them.

Among the artists, the most important of Sir George Beaumont's protégés was John Constable. Born at East Bergholt, Suffolk, in 1776, Constable was the son of a prosperous miller, a fact of which he was always proud, for was not Rembrandt also the son of a miller? Although he resisted his father's attempts to induce him to follow the same occupation, yet the mill and the surrounding countryside had always a special meaning for him. He did not need to study in Italy; all the inspiration for his painting was to be found within a few miles of his birthplace. His origins go far to explain why from the first he rejected the heroic forms of painting, much as a working-class man might refuse to wear a top hat and frock coat, because they did not suit him. He once declared: 'The sound of water escaping from mill-dams, etc., willows, old rotten planks, slimy posts, and brickwork, I love such things. . . . I shall never cease to paint such places. . . . Painting is with me but another word for feeling, and I associate "my careless boyhood" with all that lies on the banks of the Stour; those scenes made me a painter.' Wordsworth had a similar background, and it was similar experiences of rural life which made him a poet.

It was only slowly that Constable made a mark on the artistic world of his day. He had difficulty in assimilating the academic training which he received. A year younger than Turner, he had only just had a picture accepted by the Royal Academy in 1802, the year in which Turner was elected a full Academician. Time and time again he failed in his attempts to become an Associate, and finally succeeded only in 1819, when he was forty-three. Meanwhile he continued with his experiments, sold few landscapes, and for a time lived by painting portraits of local worthies at a few guineas a time. It is wrong however to suppose that he was simply self-taught, for, as he said himself, anyone who was self-taught had a very poor teacher. In fact he made the most careful study of certain works of Poussin, Claude, Alexander Cozens, Girtin and Gainsborough. Any artist who seeks to ignore the past does so at his peril, and Constable was not so foolish as to attempt it. It is true that his biographer Leslie reported: 'I remember to have heard him say, when I sit down to make a sketch from nature, the first thing I try to do is to forget that I have seen a picture.' This would be a sensible attitude for any artist to adopt, but it would take no account of the operation of the subconscious part of the mind. That Constable did not mean all that he appeared to mean by it is revealed by another of his remarks, upon the Suffolk country-side: 'It is a most delightful landscape for a painter. I fancy I see Gainsborough in every hedge and hollow tree.' The great problem for any painter is how to translate what he sees into the conventions of oils and a canvas, and it was with interpretation that Constable was really concerned. 'The art of seeing nature', he once said, 'is a thing almost as much to be acquired as the art of reading the Egyptian hieroglyphs.' He believed, as Wordsworth did, that the task of the artist was to educate the public, and not simply to give them what they expected. For this purpose there must be constant experimentation. As he said in his Hampstead lectures, 'Painting is a science, and should be pursued as an inquiry into the laws of nature. Why, then, may not landscape painting be considered as a branch of natural philosophy, of which pictures are experiments?' Here again we see that, so far from there being any sense of conflict between art and science, the artist regards himself as a kind of scientist, experimenting in the representation of nature.

Constable by no means rejected tradition in painting, but he did seek to go beyond it. He himself put the matter very clearly: 'In Art as in Literature, there are two modes by which men aim at distinction; in the one the Artist by careful application to what others have accomplished, imitates their works, or selects and combines their various beauties; in the other he seeks excellence at its primitive source—NATURE. The one forms a style upon the study of pictures, and produces either imitative or eclectic art, as it has been termed; the other by a close observation of nature discovers qualities existing in her, which have never been portrayed before, and thus forms a style which is original.' What he sought above all was to break out from the tradition of eighteenth-century painting, to go beyond it, and in doing so he was bound to give offence. In this he might have taken the warning of William Gilpin, who in 1791 had written that the public would not stand for blue or purple trees: 'Neither poetry or painting is a proper vehicle of learning. The painter will do well to avoid every uncommon appearance in nature.' Instead Constable preferred to experiment, to paint the sun *in* the picture, and not merely as shining from behind the artist, to paint luxurious foliage glistening with moisture, rolling clouds and boisterous breezes. No artist has ever studied cloud formations more carefully nor painted them more truthfully. Fuseli had the right idea when he said that Constable's landscapes made him call for his great-coat and umbrella. In an attempt to capture the sparkle of moist leaves in sunshine Constable flecked his paintings with what became known as 'Constable's snow'. Contemporaries found it difficult to accept, and Constable's biographer Leslie reports that picture dealers took out these flecks with a coat of blacking laid on with water and a coat of mastic varnish, as an aid to selling the pictures. Constable was bitter about the subject: 'rubbed out and dirty canvases take the place of God's own works', he wrote: and hearing of a possible purchaser of one of his landscapes he wrote cynically: 'Had I not better grime it down with slime and soot, as he is a connoisseur, and perhaps prefers filth and dirt to freshness and beauty?'

Everyone knows the story of Sir George Beaumont remonstrating with Constable because his foregrounds had not the mellow brown of an old violin, and how Constable placed an old violin on green grass to emphasise the difference. Of course Beaumont was aware of the greenness of grass; what he was concerned with was the tonality of the whole picture, which according to eighteenth-century usage had required a brown foreground. To us Constable's greens do not appear particularly green, and this is not simply the effect of the darkening of age and dirt, nor even the blackening by picture-dealers anxious to sell the pictures. There was a limit to the greenness which even Constable could accept, and it fell short of that of the later French Impressionists. To see Constable in perspective, we should look at eighteenth-century pictures before looking at his, just as we should look at his before we look at the French Impressionists, and we can then see what the artist's aim was. As he put it himself, 'Lights—dews—breezes—blooms and freshness, not one of which has yet been perfected by any painter in the world.'

Breaking away, then, from the academic tradition, Constable attempted a direct study of nature. As he wrote at the time, 'there is room enough for a natural painter. The great vice of the present day is *bravura*, an attempt at something beyond the truth. In endeavouring to do something better than well they do what in reality is good for nothing. Fashion always had and ever will have its day; but truth (in all things) only will last and can have just claims on posterity'. If we compare three pictures, his 'Dedham Vale' (R. G. Proby, Esq.), 'Malvern Hall, Warwickshire' (National Gallery) and 'Wivenhoe Park, Essex' (National Art Gallery, Washington), we can see the gradual evolution of a personal style. In the first he has adopted Claude's composition of a sunlit plain viewed between trees, but there is none of the exotic romanticism such as Turner infused into his 'Crossing the Brook', but instead simply a quiet observation of nature. In 'Malvern Hall' there is the use of flat areas of colour such as Girtin employed in his water-colours, while in 'Wivenhoe Park' Constable has arrived finally at a mature style of his own. The three pictures represent a span of fourteen years, during which he was repeatedly rejected as an Associate at the Royal Academy, and his great friend Archdeacon Fisher explained why. Constable's pictures, he told him, did not 'solicit attention'. His themes did not strike contemporaries as noble works of art, and when he aimed at achieving a total visual impression by eliminating details from his pictures, he offended Academicians who concluded that his pictures were simply un-finished. Yet his technique was to point the direction in which nineteenth-century painting was to develop.

In the period 1817–29 Constable reached his fullest maturity with such pictures as 'Flatford Mill' (1817), 'The White Horse' (1819), 'The Hay Wain' (1821), 'Salisbury Cathedral from the Bishop's Grounds' (1824), 'The Leaping Horse' (1825) and 'The Opening of Waterloo Bridge' (1829). Of 'The White Horse' the *Examiner* commented: 'He does not give a sentiment, a soul, to the exterior of nature as Mr. Turner does; he does not at all exalt the spectator's mind, which Mr. Turner eminently does, but he gives her outward look, her complexion and physical countenance. He has none of the poetry of nature like Mr. Turner, but he has more of her portraiture.' In order to establish an artist's reputation at the Royal Academy large paintings were thought to be necessary, and Constable tried to send in one a year. For these he usually made a preliminary study. Those for 'The Hay Wain' and 'The Leaping Horse', now in the Victoria and Albert Museum, make an interesting study in contrast to the finished works, for they have a sparkling liveliness which has been carefully eliminated by the more sedate finished works. Even so the pictures made no great sensation, and were difficult to sell. Eventually Constable sold 'The Hay Wain' to a French dealer, who exhibited it at the Louvre, where it made a considerable stir, and caused Delacroix hastily to repaint one of his landscapes.

Constable was embittered at the English public's lack of interest in landscapes: 'Londoners', he declared, 'with all their ingenuity as artists, know nothing of the feelings of a country life, the essence of landscape, any more than a hackney coach horse knows of pasture.' He had few friends, for as the Redgraves said, he was 'eminently sarcastic, and very clever at saying the bitterest things in a witty manner', and consequently he found it easy to make enemies. His wife died in 1829, and his last years were clouded by ill-health and disappointment. He died in 1837.

It is customary to link the names of Constable and Wordsworth as allies in a common cause, and certainly the two men had similar ideas about natural scenery. When Constable wanted to express his love for England he often quoted Wordsworth; moreover both became convinced tories. Yet, although the two men met several times, they never became friends. Constable's favourite poet was not Wordsworth, but Cowper.[1] He had reservations about

Wordsworth's poetry. He wrote to his wife in October 1823: 'Last evening Sir George (Beaumont) read a good deal of Wordsworth's *Excursion*. It is beautiful, but has some sad melancholy stories, and as I think only serve to harrow you up without a purpose, it is bad taste—but some of the descriptions of landscape are beautiful.' Perhaps it was the social content of Wordsworth's poem which offended him, for Constable was interested only in naturalistic observation. A book about which he had no such reservations was Gilbert White's *Natural History of Selborne*. Also he was alienated by Wordsworth's pomposity, of which Farington gives an absurd instance: 'Constable remarked upon the high opinion Wordsworth entertains of himself. He told Constable that while he was going to Hawkshead school, his mind was often so possessed with images, so lost in extraordinary conceptions, that he has held by a wall not knowing but he was part of it.—He also desired a lady, Mrs. Lloyd, near Windermere, when Constable was present, to notice the singular formation of his skull.—Coleridge remarked that this was the effect of intense thinking.—I observed to Constable, if so, he must have thought in his mother's womb.' (Diary, 12 Dec. 1807.) Wordsworth, with all his greatness as a poet, unfortunately lacked a sense of humour.

·　　·　　·　　·　　·　　·

The period 1780–1815, the period of Gillray, Rowlandson and Cruikshank, was the golden age of English caricature. Conditions were just right for it; Hogarth had pointed the way, political and social issues were lively and controversial, and publication was unmuzzled. English oppression versus American rebellion, Liberty versus Jacobinism, Protestantism versus Popery, Regency immorality versus Evangelical puritanism, English liberty versus Napoleonic tyranny, these were admirable themes for caricature. Moreover, public opinion was sufficiently advanced to make caricature profitable, and print-shops in Bond Street, Piccadilly and elsewhere did a brisk business. Indeed the vogue for caricature marks a definite step along the road to popular government, for it depended upon the contrast between ostensible and real motives, between the spoken word and the underlying intention, between the

AA

good of the community and the selfish interests of those in power. Gradually the figure of John Bull emerged, not yet the stereotyped figure he became in the Victorian Age, but in general representing the simple citizen or countryman, sometimes the butt, but often the foil of those who thought themselves cleverer than he. The basic idea of caricature is a salutary one because it breeds a healthy realism about the dangers inherent in the exercise of political power.

As Dr. Dorothy George has shown,[2] the tides of public opinion can be followed in the political caricatures of the time. They did not necessarily express the political opinions of the artist; they were commissioned by one or other of the publishers of prints, and sometimes they were commissioned by some important figure connected with the government or opposition. An artist might very well find himself engraving a pro-Pitt and a pro-Fox plate in turn. But caricatures were by no means simply products of the political powers, but often expressed the currents of public opinion, and when this is combined with wit and brilliant execution they become of absorbing interest to the student of the period.

In the great struggles between Fox on the one hand and George III and Pitt on the other, Fox on the whole came off badly. The Fox-North Coalition of 1783 was a grave miscalculation on Fox's part, and the caricaturists branded him variously as Cromwell, Catiline and Carlo Khan, the man who paraded liberty while seeking to gather Indian patronage into his own hands. Rowlandson produced a strip cartoon of the story of the Fox and the Badger, in which the fox, the badger and the devil conspire to seize political power and hold John Bull in bondage, ending with the song

> Come we're all rogues together
> The People must pay for the play
> Then let us make Hay in fine weather
> And keep the cold winter away.
> Come we're all rogues together.
> (George, op. cit., I, plate 68.)

When George III replaced the Coalition by the Pitt government, Rowlandson produced a cartoon entitled *Britania Roused*, in which an enormous Britannia hurls the two diminutive figures of Fox and North through the air. (ibid., plate 69.) When Pitt destroyed Fox's following and swept to victory in the elections of 1784, Rowlandson portrayed 'The Hanoverian Horse and the British Lion', in which Pitt was riding the spirited horse, the Royal Prerogative, which was trampling on the Constitution and kicking its heels at the House of Commons, while Fox was riding the British Lion, and demanding that he take Pitt's place, while the Lion grumbled that if this horse was not tamed it would soon be 'the Absolute King of our Forest'. (ibid., plate 70.) On the whole George III was treated with affection and respect by the cartoonists, although the miserliness of the Queen was sometimes satirised. The Prince of Wales' marriage with Mrs. Fitzherbert (1785) and its subsequent disavowal was often hinted at, and he was on occasion likened to Charles Surface, in *The School for Scandal*, and shown to be racketing about with his whig friends with complete disregard to filial piety. Fox and his friends came off badly from the Regency Crisis in 1788, when they were shown to be hungry for political power in complete disregard to propriety and respect for the sick monarch, and to be busy sharing out political power among themselves, only to have their hopes dashed when the King's recovery was announced. His illness brought forth a wave of sympathy and affection for George III greater than anything he had ever known before. Thus at the point at which the royal power began to decline, the royal popularity was on the increase.

At the beginning of the French Revolution the caricaturists united in taking the side of the Revolution, and in lauding liberty, Necker, Orleans and Lafayette. Doubts however began to be expressed when the revolutionary cause was taken up with such enthusiasm by Joseph Priestley, Dr. Price and the dissenters. Still, as Dr. George has shown (op. cit., 1,209), the caricaturists were by no means immediately convinced by the arguments of Burke's *Reflections*. After Fox and Pitt, Burke among the politicians had been the chief butt of the cartoonists, and had not come well out of the long-drawn-out impeachment of Hastings (which after 1788 soon lost public interest) and the Regency Crisis. Usually he was represented as an Irish Jesuit. His romantic defence of Marie

Antoinette did not strike an immediate note of acceptance, and caricaturists were inclined to show him as Don Quixote defending the age of chivalry which was already dead, and riding on a mule with the pope's head. Burke was not a sufficiently popular figure readily to be accepted as leader of a national reaction. On the other hand, caricaturists during 1791–2 increasingly voiced the suspicions of the time against the dissenters and their threat to both Church and King. But the period was one of great political confusion, in which caricaturists did not simply take sides for or against the Revolution. Gillray, for instance, produced a bitter satire upon the Queen, entitled *Sin, Death and the Devil*, based on Milton and an engraving by Hogarth, in which the Queen appears as a hideous Sin defending Pitt (Death) from his disloyal colleague, Thurlow (the Devil), and wearing about her waist the keys to the Back Stairs (op. cit., I, plate 91). When in November 1792 the French proclaimed fraternity and assistance to the peoples of Europe, Cruikshank was ready to take them at their word, and his print portrayed a young woman wearing the cap of liberty decreeing death to tyrants. But shortly afterwards in a print entitled *The Friends of the People* (the name of the whig reform society) he made a bitter attack on Tom Paine and Joseph Priestley as men anxious to shed British blood for their version of liberty. Gillray also attacked them, but on the whole during 1792 he seems to have been concerned to play down the dangers from France and to warn his countrymen against being stampeded into a war.

It was Gillray who, perhaps more than any other, raised caricature to an art, by seeking to give visual effect to the sort of thing which Dr. Arbuthnot (the inventor of John Bull), Swift, Pope, Gay, Fielding and Charles Churchill had said in words. Born in Chelsea in 1756, Gillray was the son of an ex-soldier who had lost his right arm at Fontenoy. He had a strict Moravian upbringing, and this no doubt added an edge to the morality of his caricatures. He was apprenticed to an engraver, and in 1778 was admitted as a student to the Royal Academy. His first political comments began to appear about 1782, and were part of the national reaction against the misconduct of the American War. As he was paid an average of two guineas a plate, this could be a profitable occupation. Moreover, his contemporary James Sayers, another caricaturist, obtained from Pitt an Exchequer appointment together with two other sinecures, for his attacks upon Fox during 1783–4, and this was a tempting prospect for any rival. There is no reason to suppose that Gillray would not have worked for anyone who was prepared to pay him for his work. His caricature *The Rights of Man* (May 1791) was dedicated ironically to the 'Jacobine Clubs of France and England', and was thus probably the first anti-Jacobin satire published in England. Henceforth most of his caricatures were anti-revolutionary. His *The Zenith of French Glory* (12 Feb. 1793) was a brilliant satire on the execution of Louis XVI. (Nat. Portrait Gallery). From this time onwards he was clearly on the tory side: there would have been no money to be earned on the other side, and he was clearly expressing the weight of public opinion in his caricatures.

With the outbreak of war in 1793 there was an upsurge of patriotism in most of the caricatures of the time, but as the war went badly during the first few years, there was a good deal of unease expressed at mismanagement and incompetence, especially of the Commander-in-Chief, the Duke of York, who was portrayed as dining in great luxury while his troops suffered. One interesting feature is Gillray's special sympathy for the lot of the common soldier. By 1795 the war had become unpopular, there was social unrest at home, and Pitt's stock was at the lowest point it had ever been. But so too was that of Fox and his friends for their open sympathy with France. One cartoon portrayed Pitt as the doctor bleeding his patient to death by taxes, and there were others drawing attention to social problems, and the situation whereby the poor were reduced to starvation while the rich continued to live in prodigal plenty.

An important event occurred in November 1797 when Canning launched his enterprise, *The Anti-Jacobin*, and asked Gillray to join him. The paper was not to have illustrations, but Gillray's help elsewhere would be useful, and Canning, now Under Secretary for the Foreign Department, secured a government pension of two hundred pounds a year for Gillray.[3] The paper lasted only eight months, for both Pitt and Canning found it an embarrassment, but Gillray continued to support Canning. The threat of a French invasion was too serious for any attitude less than patriotic resolution, and Gillray found it easy to attack the irresponsibility of the Foxite opposition. Whig prestige reached a new low point in 1798 with the outbreak of the Irish Rebellion shortly after Fox's drinking a toast to Irish freedom. Pitt and Tierney fought a duel, and there was an audible sigh of relief when it was known that Pitt was unhurt. Nelson's victory at the Battle of the Nile gave the nation new heart at the unaccustomed experience of victory, and Gillray produced a print of Fox hanging himself in chagrin at the failure of the Irish rebellion and the loss of the French fleet. Although the introduction of Income Tax in 1799 was resented, and the financial burdens of the Second Coalition satirised, yet victory appeared to be near in 1799, and hopes were high. The triumph of Bonaparte changed all that, and hopes fell again in 1800. Gillray produced a pointed cartoon showing Bonaparte banishing liberty from France at his *coup d'état*. When Pitt resigned in 1801 there was no stir, and only Gillray produced a dignified print honouring Pitt for resigning over Catholic Emancipation and thus putting principle before office. On the other hand, few had much hope that the Peace of Amiens would be lasting, and cartoonists soon saw the Addington government as pygmies, and Pitt as the only man capable of renewing the war against the French. Gillray's caricature *Lilliputian-Substitutes Equiping for Public Service* (1801) showed Addington in Pitt's jack-boots, which came up to his chin, and an enormous Windsor coat, and all his colleagues in clothes much too big for them. On 28 May 1802 Canning arranged a birthday dinner for Pitt at which his song, 'The Pilot that weathered the Storm' was sung:

And oh! if again the rude whirlwind should rise,
The dawning of peace should fresh darkness deform,
The regrets of the good and the fears of the wise
Shall turn to the Pilot that weathered the Storm.

Gillray continued the same theme. On 14 March 1804 his *The State Waggoner and John Bull* showed Addington's waggon stuck fast in the mire, and John Bull asks why he does not harness better horses, such as those which were frisking on the heath, Pitt, Fox, Grenville and Canning. In a caricature of 20 May 1804, *Britannia between Death and the Doctors*, Gillray showed Pitt kicking Addington out of the sick room, and treading upon Fox's face, as he brings new medicine, labelled 'Constitutional Restoration' to the sick Britannia, while 'Boney' tries to stab her from behind the bed curtains. (George, op. cit., plate 30.) Later Gillray harassed the Ministry of All the Talents on every possible occasion, sometimes showing them as greedy little pigs for whom the sow (England) had too few teats.

The caricatures of Bonaparte during the period were legion; there were a hundred and seventy-six prints on 'Little Boney' in 1803 alone. Sometimes they showed him bestriding the narrow world like a colossus, sometimes as a diminutive Gulliver whom an enormous George III could see only with the aid of a magnifying glass. The theme of national unity was now much more apparent in the face of a tyrant who, but for British sea power and the Russian winter, appeared likely to dominate the world.

After the war there were still some fine caricatures, as for instance against the brutality of the Peterloo Massacre, and, on the other side, of Radicalism shown as bent on destroying English liberties, but after 1820 the art rapidly declined. Political issues became less burning, and public opinion turned against unbridled political comment. Moreover, the technical difficulties of producing prints by means of copper plates no longer made them a profitable business, and artists turned to other art forms. Gillray died in 1815, Rowlandson in 1827, Cruikshank not until 1878, but the great age of caricature was over.

·   ·   ·   ·   ·   ·

In architecture perhaps the most peculiar feature of the period 1780–1830 was its eclectic nature, and the way in which classical and Gothic styles were attempted indifferently by the same architect, and often combined in the same building. Since Horace Walpole had built Strawberry Hill much more had been learnt about the spirit and techniques of Gothic architecture, and James

Wyatt (1747–1813) became its recognised authority. He built Lee Priory, Canterbury (recently demolished) with great understanding of the needs of Gothic; and his Fonthill Abbey for William Beckford must have been fantastic and sensational. But he was equally prepared to build the Library of Oriel College, Oxford, in the traditional classical style. Richard Payne Knight (1750–1824) made a particularly successful experiment in an irregular castellated building in Downton Castle, Shropshire in 1774, and this set a fashion for the next three-quarters of a century. Humphrey Repton (1752–1818) became a successful landscape gardener, breaking away from the style of Capability Brown, and, relying more on what he called the 'character' of a place, using more naturalistic forms. He was strongly in favour of Gothic architecture. He recommended that 'a castle which, by blending a chaste correctness of proportion with bold irregularity of outline, its deep recesses and projections producing broad masses of light and shadow, while its roof is enriched by turrets, battlements, corbles and lofty chimneys, has infinitely more picturesque effect than any other style of building'. 'Picturesque' was the new fashionable word, and it has given a name to the architecture of the period.

A notable change in aesthetic theory came with the publication of Archibald Alison's *Principles of Taste*, first published in 1790, which included a full statement of the Principle of Association. The Platonic tradition had given rise to the idea that beauty was a quality inherent in an object, which could therefore be analysed, and perhaps isolated. Hogarth for instance had been led on to try to formulate the principles of beauty and to isolate the line of beauty and the line of grace.[4] Burke had seen the fallacy of this, and had sought to give a more psychological interpretation of the sublime and the beautiful. Beauty was an expression of sexual feelings, and sublimity of our fears. The Principle of Association went further; beauty was not inherent in any object, but depended upon the feelings of association which were aroused in the minds of those who experienced it. Thus there might be little real difference between the howl of a dog and the howl of a wolf, yet the one was banal, and the other sublime. A peasant might be quite unmoved by the lowing of a cow, which the cultivated mind might find idyllic. The sense of pleasure arose, not from the object itself, but from the memories or associations invoked.

This recognition of the psychological aspects of aesthetic pleasure suggested the need for another aesthetic category. The influence of Platonic thought, and the Greek artistic experience, were still sufficiently strong to lead men to suppose that there was a category of the beautiful, expressing perfection, the ideal of human experience, while Burke's definition of the sublime catered for the sense of awe and mystery associated with some aspects of Romanticism. A third category was added by the whig squire, Sir Uvedale Price, in his *Essays on the Picturesque* (1794). The word *picturesque* derived from the Italian *pittoresco*, meaning 'after the manner of painters'. It was occasionally used in this sense in the eighteenth century, but was not included by Dr. Johnson in his Dictionary. Uvedale Price made it a part of aesthetic theory. By the eighteenth century connoisseurs were deeply appreciative of the landscapes of Claude, Salvator Ross and Gaspar Poussin. When therefore they came upon scenes which reminded them of those landscapes they were naturally gratified, and termed them *picturesque*, that is to say, such as Claude or Poussin might have painted. It would then occur to them that the scene was very different from the 'improved' landscapes of Capability Brown. This was no discovery on the part of Uvedale Price, for James Thomson as early as 1748 had written of

> Whate'er *Lorrain* light-touched with softening Hue,
> Or savage *Rosa* dashed, or learned *Poussin* drew.
> (*The Castle of Indolence.*)

but Price raised the subject to the level of aesthetic theory. In place of the arranged clumps and undulating paths of Capability Brown, Price advocated the thickets, gnarled oaks, banks, and hollows such as one saw in the favourite painters, and as really existed in nature. 'These hollows are frequently overgrown with wild roses, with honeysuckles, periwinkles, and other trailing plants, which, with their flowers and pendant branches, have quite a different effect when hanging loosely over one of these recesses, opposed to its deep shade, and mixed with the fantastic roots of trees and the varied tints of the soil, from that which they produce when they are trimmed into bushes, or crawl along a shrubbery, where the ground has been worked into one uniform slope.' Man must not order nature more than was absolutely necessary. Brown's gravel walks had become tedious: 'A gravel walk cannot have the playful variety of a by-road; there must be a border to the gravel, and that and the sweeps must, in great measure, be regular, and consequently formal.' (Sir Thomas Dick Lauder's Edition, p. 72.) Price's complaint against Capability Brown was that in rationalising the landscape he had removed the element of mystery and surprise. 'there is one improvement which I am afraid almost all who had not been used to look at objects with a painter's eye would adopt, and which alone would entirely destroy its character—that is smoothing and levelling the ground. The moment this mechanical commonplace operation, by which Mr. Brown and his followers have gained so much credit, is begun, adieu to all that the painter admires—to all intricacies—to all the beautiful varieties of form, tint, and light and shade; every deep recess—every bold projection—the fantastic roots of trees—the winding paths of sheeps—all must go; in a few hours, the rash hand of false taste completely demolishes what time only, and a thousand lucky accidents can mature, so as to make it become the admiration and study of a Ruysdael or a Gainsborough; and reduces it to such a thing as an oilman in Thames Street may at any time contract for by the yard at Islington or Mile-End.' (p. 73.)

Uvedale Price argued that a Greek temple in its complete state would be beautiful, but as a ruin it was picturesque; Greek architecture was beautiful, but Gothic architecture was picturesque, a young beech or tender ash tree might be beautiful, but a rugged old oak or knotted wych elm would be picturesque; a race horse would be beautiful, but an ass picturesque, a youth might be beautiful, but a rough and rugged forester would be picturesque. A placid lake was beautiful, but a mountain stream was picturesque. He paid tribute to the beauty of Claude's landscapes, but it was clear that he preferred those of Rubens. 'His landscapes are full of the peculiarities and picturesque accidents in nature—of striking contrasts in form, colour, and light and shadow: sunbeams bursting through a small opening in a dark wood— a rainbow against a stormy sky—effects of thunder and lightning, torrents rolling down, trees torn up by the roots, and the dead bodies of men and animals—are among the sublime and picturesque circumstances exhibited by his daring pencil. These sudden gleams, these cataracts of light, these bold oppositions of clouds and darkness which he has so nobly introduced, would destroy all the beauty and elegance of Claude: on the other hand, the mild and equal sunshine of that charming painter, would as ill accord with the twisted and singular forms, and the bold and animated variety of the landscapes of Rubens.' (p. 117.)

His suggestions for landscaping and buildings included the natural use of woods and water, the value of old and gnarled trees, the aesthetic effect of mixed architecture, and the need to preserve all that remained of castles, manor houses, cottages, mills, outhouses and hovels. 'An exclusive attention', he wrote, 'to what is strictly beautiful, will lead towards monotony'; it was more important to aim at the picturesque than at the attainment of beauty. Herein lay the special virtue of Gothic architecture. 'Gothic buildings are full of breaks and divisions, and the parts highly and profusely enriched; the correspondence between the parts being much less obvious than in Grecian architecture, the whole has often an apparent irregularity, and from these circumstances many Gothic structures, even in their entire and perfect state, display a marked picturesque state', and moreover, 'that character cannot but be increased by decay' (p. 364).

The subject of the picturesque was explored further by the Shropshire squire, Richard Payne Knight in his *Principles of Taste* (1805). In some respects he was critical of Uvedale Price's theories, and he based his own theory squarely on Alison's principle of association. He knew enough of the history of taste to recognise the importance of fashion. In one age 'high-dressed heads, tight-laced stays, and wide hoops' were thought highly becoming; to another age they would appear ridiculous. 'Let no one imagine that he solves the question by saying that there have been errors of taste'; it was all a matter of association. Knight did not dispute the beauty of Greek sculpture and architecture, but this was not to say that men must continue to build in that style in all ages. 'Grecian temples have been employed as decorations by almost all persons who could afford to indulge their taste in objects so costly. ... They are unquestionably beautiful, being exactly copied from those models which have stood the criticism of many successive ages. In the rich lawns and shrubberies of England, however, they lose all that power to please which they so eminently possess on the barren hills of Agrigentum and Segesta, or the naked plains of Paestum and Athens' (p. 169). Since Knight's thesis was that taste was simply a matter of association, it would have been reasonable to admit that those who built these temples in England were moved by the classical associations thus aroused, but to him these associations had failed to continue to excite, and he looked else-where for new stimuli. 'To a mind richly stored, almost every object of nature or art that presents itself to the senses either excites fresh trains and combinations of ideas, or vivifies and strengthens those which existed before: so that recollection enhances enjoyment, and enjoyment brings recollection' (p. 143). Whatever fulfilled these qualifications Knight termed the pic-turesque, and he was critical of Price for unnecessarily confining the meaning of the word. 'The boors of Ostade, the peasants of Gainsborough, and the shepherds of Berghem are picturesque; but so likewise are the warriors of Salvator Rosa, the apostles of Raphael, and the bacchanalians of Poussin: nor is the giant oak of Ruysdael, or full-grown pine or ilex of Claude, less so than the stumpy decayed pollard of Rubens or Rembrandt: nor the shaggy worn-out hack or cart-horse of Morland or Asselyn, than the pampered war-horse with luxuriant mane and flowing tail which we justly admire in the pictures of Wovermans. The dirty and tattered garments, the dishevelled hair, and general wild appear-ance of gipsies and beggar girls are often picturesque: but the flowing ringlets, fine shawls, and robes of delicate muslin thrown into all the easy, negligent and playful folds of antique drapery by polished grace and refined elegance, are still more so' (p. 155). It was all a matter of education, experience and association. To Knight beauty might consist of regularity, neatness or congruity, but what excited the imagination he termed the picturesque.

Knight found this power to excite a particular quality of Gothic architecture. 'The contrivers of this refined and fantastic Gothic seem to have aimed at producing grandeur and solemnity, together with lightness of effect; and incompatible as these qualities may seem, by attending to effect only, and considering the means of producing it as wholly subordinate, and in their own power, they succeeded to a degree which the Grecian architects, who worked by rule, never approached.' (p. 176.) Herein lay the clue to the reason why Knight and his friends were turning away from the classical in architecture. To them it was rational, able to be explained in terms of rules and measurements, while Gothic was intricate, surprising, mysterious and exciting. 'Ruined buildings, with fragments of sculptured walls and broken columns, the mouldering remnants of obsolete taste and fallen magnificence, afford pleasure to every learned beholder, imperceptible to the ignorant, and wholly independent of their real beauty, or the pleasing impressions which that make on the organs of sight; more especially when discovered in countries of ancient celebrity, renowned in history for learning, arts, or empire. The mind is led by the view of them into the most pleasing trains of ideas.' (p. 195.) In other words, the appeal was intellectual, to one's knowledge of history and literature; it arose from the power of association, not from an inherent beauty. Scenery which was 'wild, abrupt and fantastic' Knight called romantic, 'not only because it is similar to that usually described in romances, but because it affords the same kind of pleasure as we feel from the incidents usually related in such of them as are composed with sufficient skill to afford any pleasure at all'.

Knight did not advocate that contemporaries should simulate mediaeval castles. The best style seemed to him to be 'that mixed style which characterises the building of Claude and the Poussins: for as it is taken from models which were built piecemeal during many successive ages, and by several different nations, it is distinguished by no particular manner of execution, or class of ornaments; but admits of all promiscuously, from a plain wall or buttress, of the roughest masonry to the most highly wrought Corinthian capital: and, in a style professedly miscellaneous, such contrasts may be employed to heighten the relish of beauty, without disturbing the enjoyment of it by any appearance of deceit or imposture' (p. 225). It was this mixed style which he himself attempted at Downton Castle.

Knight denied that there were any universally applicable rules of architecture. 'What we call the laws of nature are merely certain rules of analogy which we draw from the general results both of mathematical demonstration and habitual association.' 'Truth is naturally circumstantial, especially in matters that interest the feelings' (p. 283). 'The words genius and taste are, like the words beauty and virtue, mere terms of general approbation, which men apply to whatever they approve, without annexing any specific ideas to them' (p. 432). If there was an infallible criterion it was 'the unsophisticated sentiments of the most natural taste and inclination of mankind' (p. 15). In this way Knight sought to blend the acquisitions of learning and experience with the history and natural surroundings of the countryside. Under the guidance of such writers as Price and Knight architects accepted eclecticism as a principle, and a building might be castellated, with ogee windows, and yet retain classical features; or it might be Italianate, such as might be seen in a Claude picture, with a circular tower, overhanging eaves and a tall colonnade; or it might be cottage-style, with Gothic hips, gables, verandahs and porches.

Subsequent ages have not regarded the result with much favour, nor did it escape criticism from contemporaries. Jane Austen, who was keenly interested in houses and landscapes, satirises the cult of the picturesque in *Sense and Sensibility*:

'It is very true,' said Marianne, 'that admiration of landscape scenery has become mere jargon. Everybody pretends to feel and tries to describe it with the taste and elegance of him who first defined what picturesque beauty was.'

'I like a fine prospect', said Edward, 'but not on picturesque principles. I do not like crooked, twisted, blasted trees, I admire them much more if they are tall, straight and flourishing. I am not fond of nettles or thistles or heath blossoms.'

Marianne looked with amazement at Edward.

She returned to the same subject again in *Northanger Abbey*, when Henry Tilney lectured Catharine in the new jargon:

> He talked of foregrounds, distances and second distances; side screens and perspectives; lights and shades; and Catharine was so hopeful a scholar, that when they gained the top of Beechen Cliff, she voluntarily rejected the whole city of Bath, as unworthy to make part of a landscape.

In such matters Jane Austen preferred to remain a child of the eighteenth century.

Often the changes in matters of taste were linked with changes in social outlook, as may be illustrated from Wordsworth's correspondence for 1805. His friend Sir George Beaumont had consulted Wordsworth about proposals for a new lay-out for his gardens at Coleorton. It would be naturally in accordance with eighteenth-century tradition that he should adopt some such design as might have been approved by William Kent or Capability Brown; but to this Wordsworth was strongly opposed: 'Nothing of that lofty or imposing interest, formerly attached to large property in land, can now exist; none of the poetic pride, pomp, and circumstance; nor anything that can be considered as making amends for violation done to the holiness of Nature.' To Wordsworth, the mansion standing in the centre of undulating grasslands, with interesting woodlands stretching away to the horizon was overbearing and offensive, shutting out, as it did, village life and happy homesteads which were the real life-blood of the countryside. He was not an egalitarian, but he did believe that landowners had a social duty to perform, and that they should live as part of an integrated country-side, not as solitary monarchs isolated from it. Constable had something of the same idea in mind when he said that a gentleman's park was his aversion. Wordsworth continued: 'In the present state of society, I see nothing interesting either to the imagination or the heart, and, of course, nothing which true taste can approve, in any interference with Nature, grounded upon any other principle. . . . Nature had greatly the advantage in those days, when what has been called English gardening was unheard of.

This is now beginning to be perceived, and we are setting out to travel backwards. Painters and poets have had the credit of being reckoned the fathers of English gardening; they will also have hereafter the better praise of being fathers of a better taste . . . in other words, we are submitting to the rule which you at present are guided by, that of having our houses belonging to the country, which will of course lead us back to the simplicity of Nature.' (Prose Works, II, 184.)

Some features of the picturesque were to be found in the architecture of John Nash (1752–1835) before he became the favourite architect of the Prince Regent. His own country house, East Cowes Castle, was a most entertaining example, with battlements, square-headed windows, Gothic library and drawbridge, and a wild garden laid out by his partner, Humphry Repton. Contemporaries called the style 'Moorish', for no particular reason. Nash really knew little about Gothic building, and indeed declared: 'I hate this Gothic style; one window costs more trouble in designing than two houses ought to do.' For the most part it was sufficient for him to introduce a few features, such as battlements or ogees. In 1811 however at Blaise Castle, near Bristol, he built nine Gothic cottages, complete with hips, gables, verandas and porches, which were his most successful attempts at being what Sir John Summerson has called 'a cottage romanticist'. At that time Augustus Pugin was bringing out his *Specimens of Gothic Architecture*, and establishing a great reputation as the authority on the subject.

The most impressive of John Nash's projects was that for the laying out of a royal park at Marylebone, somewhat reminiscent of Bath, with a circus, crescent, terraces and villas. This garden city was to be connected with the south by a 'royal mile' which would lead from the Park to Carlton House, the home of the Prince Regent. The plan was laid before the Prince in 1811, and he was delighted with it. Henceforth Nash was his close confidant in architectural matters. The whole plan was intended, not only to glorify Carlton House, but to have great significance for the development of London. 'My purpose', Nash wrote, 'was that the new street should cross the eastern entrance to all the Streets occupied by the higher classes, and to leave out to the east all the bad streets.' In other words, the future Regent Street would cut off the squares and mansions of the rich of the West End from the maze of poor streets which ran to the east into the City. He envisaged this great street with an arcade, and he hoped that members of parliament and others would be able to walk two-thirds of the way to Westminster under cover, while genteel folk could promenade and gossip as in so many Italian cities. Regent Street was laid out as he planned, but much else in his plan was abandoned, and Regent's Park became no more than a shadow of his original intentions, while the buildings in Regent Street were allowed to develop piecemeal, and without the arcade. In this way it was finished by 1823, although not before there had been much grumbling about the cost, and much hostility to his use of stucco as a cheap method of building. As the *Quarterly Review* put it in 1826:

Augustus at Rome was for building renown'd,
And of marble he left what of brick he had found;
But is not our Nash, too, a very great master?—
He finds us all brick and he leaves us all plaster.

Still, Nash proved himself to be a great town-planner. It was he who planned such works as York Terrace, Sussex Place, Cumberland Terrace, Clarence Terrace and Kent Terrace. He also planned Trafalgar Square, although he erected none of its buildings, and he produced a fine plan for the environs of the British Museum which, if it had been carried out, would have given it a noble setting.

Meanwhile, the Prince Regent had other work for him. Since 1783 he had been much attached to Brightelmstone, and Henry Holland had built him a charming country house, or Pavilion, to which the Prince constantly added until, with Nash's help, he had made it a fantastic fairy palace, with Chinese and Indian additions. Finally it was finished in 1823 at the huge cost of a hundred and sixty thousand pounds, and at this point the King began to lose interest. He did not spend long there in the following years, and the Royal Pavilion became, what it has always subsequently remained, the most striking product of the Age of the Picturesque. Nash had become very unpopular both as being a confidant of the monarch, and also because of the expenditure which his work entailed, and this was increased when George IV, who had come to detest Carlton House, required the building of a royal palace. The re-building of Buckingham Palace was begun in 1825. Nash's plan was elaborate, but carelessly thought out, and there was constant difficulty with Ministers about expenses. Finally, when George IV died in 1830, Nash was hastily dismissed, and his plans modified. Meanwhile Carlton House was pulled down, and Nash erected one of his most successful creations, Carlton House Terrace. He was also responsible for the lay-out of St. James's Park, which is still largely as he planned it. Altogether no architect in history, not even Wren, has left so large a mark on London, and although he lacked the vision and genius of his great predecessor, he was the only architect in London's history who deserves comparison with him.

By 1830 architecture and painting in England were at a low ebb. Among the architects Henry Holland and James Wyatt were dead, and Nash had only five years of retirement before him. Among the painters Crome, Fuseli, Blake, Romney, Raeburn and Lawrence were dead; Constable lived on until 1837, Wilkie until 1841, Cotman until the following year, and Turner until 1851, but all their best work had been done by 1830. The next age would be that of Charles Barry (the architect of the Houses of Parliament), the Pre-Raphaelites, John Landseer and John Ruskin. It would take us too far out of our way to examine all the reasons for the artistic decline in England, but some might be suggested. First, there was a break-up of the eighteenth-century system of patronage. Many of the aristocracy inherited great houses from the golden age which was past, and those who did not, often could not afford a great programme of building. The newly-rich industrial magnates were less tasteful, less generous, and more concerned with comfort than with beauty. Whereas the aristocracy had required excellence, the middle class were content with a competent mediocrity. There was moreover a ferment of styles, with the age hovering uncertainly between classical and Gothic standards. But above all the mental climate of the age was inimical to a flourishing art, for on the one hand there was the materialism which came with mass production, and on the other the deep trend of piety, or religiosity, which imposed a narrow view of moral standards. Often the artist thought of himself as little more than a book-illustrator, or narrator of anecdotes, illustrating a literary theme, or telling a moral story which would be suitable for family viewing, and reproduction by one or other of the processes of engraving. In fact both painting and architecture suffered from the dominance of literature as the accepted literary form of the time. The very fact that the age was a great age of literature militated against it being also a great age of the visual arts.

There remain to be mentioned two steps towards the formation of a national art collection, and consequently a national taste. The first was the acquisition of the Elgin Marbles, and the second was the foundation of the National Gallery.

In 1799 the seventh Earl of Elgin was appointed Ambassador to the Porte, and he at once decided to take the opportunity to record and collect classical art. When an eighteenth-century nobleman went abroad he often took a draftsman or artist with him, and Elgin was assisted, not only by his loyal secretary, W. R. Hamilton, but also by a number of skilled artists recruited in Italy, the chief of whom were Lusieri, who then had the reputation of being the first painter of Italy, a Russian named Feodar, and two architects, Vincenzo Balestra and Sebastian Ittar. Elgin was inspired, not only by a deep love for Greek art, but also by the fear that the French might seize the Morea, and carry off the art treasures to Paris. He began to make his collection at once. There were many local difficulties to overcome, and the Turkish authorities charged his artists a fee of five guineas a day, but by 1802 a cargo of marbles was being shipped to England. The first ship was wrecked, and was not salvaged until 1804. Lord Elgin himself, returning to England via France in 1803, was arrested by orders of the First Consul, and remained a prisoner of war until 1806, but in his absence his team continued their work, and from time to time shipments got through to England.

When Elgin returned to England, he had his treasures unpacked and displayed in his house in Park Lane in 1807. They created a sensation among artists and connoisseurs. Benjamin Haydon was one of the first to draw from them, and he was followed rapidly by Benjamin West, the President of the Royal Academy and Sir Thomas Lawrence. Haydon was perhaps the most deeply impressed, and has left this account of his first reactions:

The first thing I fixed my eyes on, was the wrist of a figure in one of the female groups, in which were visible, though in a feminine form, the radius and ulna. I was astonished, for I had never seen them hinted at in any female wrist in the antique. I darted my eye to the elbow, and saw the outer condyle visibly affecting the shape as in nature. I saw that the arm was in repose and the soft parts in relaxation. That combination of nature and idea which I had felt was so much wanting for high art was here displayed to midday conviction. My heart beat! But when I turned to the Theseus, and saw that every form was altered by action or repose,—when I saw that the two sides of his back varied, one side stretched from the shoulder blade being pulled forward, and the other side, compressed, from the shoulder blade being pushed close to the spine, as he rested on his elbow, with the belly flat because the bowels fell into the pelvis as he sat,— . . . when I saw, in fact, the most heroic style of art, combined with all the essential detail of actual life, the thing was done at once and for ever . . . Here were principles which the great Greeks in their finest time established, and here was I, the most prominent historical student, perfectly qualified to appreciate all this. . . . I felt the future, I foretold that they would prove themselves the finest things on earth, that they would overturn the false beau-ideal, where nature was nothing, and would establish the true beau-ideal, of which Nature alone is the basis. I shall never forget the horses' heads, the feet in the metopes! I felt as if a divine truth had blazed inwardly upon my mind, and I knew they would at last rouse the art of Europe from its slumber in the darkness.' (*Life of B. R. Haydon*, i, 84.)

Mrs. Siddons saw them in 1809, and a group of the Fates 'so rivetted and agitated her feelings', that she wept. Even fashions were affected, for *The Times* of 8 Jan. 1814 carried an advertisement of 'Ross's newly-invented GRECIAN VOLUTE HEAD-DRESS, formed from the true marble models, brought into this country from the Acropolis of Athens by Lord Elgin', which combined 'elegance of taste and simplicity of nature'.

Negotiations for the national purchase of the Elgin marbles began in 1810, but as Elgin put his expenses at over sixty-two thousand pounds, and Spencer Perceval did not feel that Parliament would contemplate paying more than thirty thousand pounds, they made little progress. Elgin was attacked by some M.P.s for having abused his position as Ambassador. Sir John Newport declared that 'he was afraid that the noble Lord had availed himself of most unwarrantable measures, and had committed the most flagrant acts of spoliation. It seemed to have been reserved for an ambassador of this country to take away what Turks and other barbarians had always held sacred'. Elgin however was able to defend himself by showing that 'the Turkish government attached no importance to them in the world', and that the marbles were deteriorating so rapidly that, but for his intervention, they would soon have been entirely destroyed.

In February 1816 the Commons set up a committee to enquire into the question of purchase. In the previous year Canova had visited England especially to see the collection, and had been overwhelmed by what he saw. He declared to Hamilton: 'Oh that I had but to begin again! to unlearn all that I have learned—I now at last see what ought to form the real school of sculpture!'; while one of his party declared that 'he was quite astonished when he saw the Marbles and they appeared to him executed on a principle of which the World had no notion before'. (Haydon, Letter of 12 Dec. 1815.) Even the Commons' committee were impressed, and reported in favour of a national purchase for thirty-five thousand pounds: 'if it be true, as we learn from history and experience, that free governments afford a soil most suitable to the production of native talent, to the maturing of the powers of the human mind, and to the growth of every species of excellence, by opening to merit the prospect of reward and distinction, no country can be better adapted than our own to afford an honourable asylum to these monuments of the school of Phidias, and of the administration of Pericles'. Accordingly in 1816 the Elgin marbles were transferred to the British Museum.

Another step was taken towards the formation of a national taste with the foundation of the National Gallery. Since 1805 Sir George Beaumont had let it be known that if a National Gallery were established, he would leave his pictures to the nation. The subject was debated and shelved from time to time mainly in the interests of economy, although Constable was convinced that such an institution would be the death of English art. Matters were brought to a head in 1823 by the death of the great banker, John Julius Angerstein, and the risk that his fine art collection might be bought by some foreign monarch. The government gave way, and thus the National Gallery was founded. Beaumont wrote: 'I think the public already begin to feel works of art are not merely toys for connoisseurs, but solid objects of concern to the nation; and those who consider it in the narrowest point of view, will perceive that works of high excellence pay ample interest for the money they cost. My belief is, that the Apollo, the Venus, the Laocoön, etc., are worth thousands a year to the country which possesses them'. Sir George's collection could not equal Angerstein's, but it was impressive enough, with four Claude's, including his favourite 'Hagar and the Angel', a Poussin, a Rembrandt, a Rubens and a Reynolds. The National Gallery, which was finally opened in 1838, owed its foundation more to Sir George Beaumont than to any other individual.

Neither the possession of the Elgin Marbles, nor the foundation of the National Gallery could arrest the decline of the arts in nineteenth-century England; which was the more strange because the Victorians were genuinely interested in both architecture and painting.

NOTES

[1] Constable wrote: 'I have all Cowper's works on my table. . . . He is an author I prefer to almost any other, and when with him I always feel the better for it. . . . He is the poet of religion and nature.'

[2] *English Political Caricature* (C.U.P., 1959).

[3] Canning also employed William Gifford. Cobbett commented: 'The Anti-Jacobin weekly newspaper was set up at the public expense; and Mr. William Gifford, whom they employed to assist them and to edit the paper, had first a patent place of a hundred a year bestowed on him; next he was made a double commissioner of the Lottery, and since, in addition, pay-master of the Gentlemen-Pensioners, making in all about a thousand a year for life at our expense; and, never in his whole life time, though he is a very modest, and, I believe, a very worthy man, has he ever rendered any service to the country.' *Political Register*, 11 April 1807.

[4] See *Reason and Nature*, p. 309. For Burke's theory see *idem* p. 282.

17 : Conclusion: The March of Mind

For an amusing summary of the cross-currents of the thought of the period which is the theme of this book, we cannot do better than turn to the works of Thomas Love Peacock (1785–1866). Peacock moved in the literary circles of the eighteen-twenties, and was a friend of Shelley (who appears as Scythrop in *Nightmare Abbey*), Bentham, James Mill, Edward Strachey and John Cam Hobhouse. He wrote a number of novels, which were incidental to his main occupation, a lucrative post with the East India Company, and in them he poked fun at most of the current intellectual fashions of his time, and included satirical studies of the chief literary figures of his day.

His favourite theme, which he used both in *Headlong Hall* and *Crotchet Castle*, was to gather a number of eccentrics at a country house, and allow them to talk. Mr. Crotchet, for instance, a wealthy business man, gathered a number of experts at his home because he wanted to hear settled once and for all the great controversies of his day, 'The sentimental against the rational, the intuitive against the inductive, the ornamental against the useful, the intense against the tranquil, the romantic against the classical; these are great and interesting controversies, which I should like, before I die, to see satisfactorily settled' (Ch. II).

The Rev. Dr. Folliott, representing earthy common sense, was out of sympathy with most of the new tendencies of his age. 'I am out of all patience with this march of mind. Here has my house been nearly burned down, by my cook taking it into her head to study hydrostatics, in a sixpenny tract, published by the Steam Intellect Society, and written by a learned friend who is for doing all the world's business as well as his own, and is equally well qualified to handle every branch of human knowledge. I have a great abomination of this learned friend; as author, lawyer, and politician, he is *triformis* like Hecate. . . . My cook must read his rubbish in bed; and as might naturally be expected, she dropped suddenly fast asleep, overturned the candle, and set the curtains in a blaze.' (Ch. II.) This was a satire upon Lord Brougham, the brilliant but unstable radical who advocated universal education, and had founded the Society for the Diffusion of Useful Knowledge (1825). Dr. Folliott described it as a creed of 'every thing for every body, science for all, schools for all, rhetoric for all, law for all, physic for all, words for all, and sense for none. I say, law for lawyers, and cookery for cooks; and I wish the learned friend, for all his life, a cook that will pass her time in studying his works; then every dinner he sits down to at home, he will sit on the stool of repentance'.

Adam Smith had argued that there was very little difference in intelligence between one man and another; the apparent differences were merely the result of education. It followed therefore, according to Brougham, and the Scottish economist MacCulloch, that education would be the great equaliser in society. Dr. Folliott on the other hand declared: 'I hold that there is every variety of natural capacity from the idiot to Newton and Shakespeare; the mass of mankind, midway between these extremes, being block-heads of different degrees; education leaving them pretty nearly as it found them, with this single difference, that it gives a fixed direction to their stupidity, a sort of incurable wry neck to the thing they call the understanding. So one nose points always east, and another always west, and each is ready to swear that it points due north.' (Ch. IV.)

Dr. Folliott was equally forthright on the subject of the *Edinburgh Review*, the writers of which he called 'a sort of sugar-plum manufacturers to the Whig aristocracy. . . . These gentlemen have practised as much dishonesty as, in any other department than literature, would have brought the practitioner under the cognisance of the police. In politics, they have run with the hare and hunted with the hounds. In criticism they have, knowingly and unblushingly, given false characters, both for good and for evil: sticking at no art of misrepresentation, to clear out of the field of literature all who stood in the way of the interests of their own clique. They have never allowed their own profound ignorance of any thing (Greek, for instance) to throw even an air of hesitation into their oracular decision on the matter. They set an example of profligate contempt for truth, of which the success was in proportion to the effrontery; and when their prosperity had filled the market with competitors, they cried out against their own reflected sin, as if they had never committed it, or were entitled to a monopoly of it.' (Ch. IV.)

In aesthetic matters Dr. Folliott was shocked at the consequences of the vogue for Greek sculpture which had followed the arrival of the Elgin marbles in England. Mr. Crotchet had determined 'to fill his house with Venuses of all sizes and kinds. . . . There were the Medicean Venus, and the Bathing Venus; the Uranian Venus, and the Pandemanian Venus; the Crouching Venus, and the Sleeping Venus; the Venus rising from the sea, the Venus with the apple of Paris, and the Venus with the armour of Mars'. Dr. Folliott was torn between his admiration for Greek thought, and his doubts about so much nudity. For how could Christians renounce the devil when they were confronted with such invitations to lascivious-ness? Mr. Crotchet replied: 'Sir, ancient sculpture is the true school of modesty. But where the Greeks had modesty, we have cant; where they had poetry, we have cant; where they had patriotism, we have cant; where they had any thing that exalts, delights or adorns humanity, we have nothing but cant, cant, cant. And, sir, to show my contempt for cant in all its shapes, I have adorned my house with the Greek Venus, in all her shapes, and am ready to fight her battle against all the societies that ever were instituted for the suppression of truth and beauty.' (Ch. VII.)

It soon however became apparent, that Dr. Folliott's dislike of female nudes in art was connected with his innate conviction, against which Peacock always protested, that women should remain in a humble and subordinate position in society. The sort of woman Dr. Folliott liked was 'a modest woman, who stays at home and looks after her husband's dinner'. Mr. Crotchet replied that 'that was not the taste of the Athenians. They preferred the society of women who would not have made any scruple about sitting as models to Praxitiles. ... Why do we call the Elgin marbles inestimable? Simply because they are true to nature. And why are they so superior in that point to all modern works, with all our greater knowledge of anatomy? Why, sir, but because the Greeks, having no cant, had better opportunities of studying models?' (ibid.)

The *laissez-faire* school of Scottish economists which stemmed from Adam Smith, came in for further severe drubbing. It was represented in *Crotchet Castle* by Mr. MacQuedy, a portrait of the economist MacCulloch, who, according to Lady Clarinda, 'lays down the law about everything, and therefore may be taken to understand everything. He turns all the affairs of this world into questions of buying and selling. He is the Spirit of the Frozen Ocean to everything like romance and sentiment. He condenses their volume of steam into a drop of cold water in a moment. He has satisfied me that I am a commodity in the market, and that I ought to set myself at a high price' (Ch. V). The Scots, MacQuedy declared, were 'the modern Athenians', capable of teaching the modern world all it needed to know of both the arts and the sciences. But with all his self-assurance, he made little headway against the redoubtable Dr. Folliott:

> *Mr. MacQuedy:* Nothing is so easy as to lay down the out-lines of perfect society. There wants nothing but money to set it going. I will explain myself clearly and fully by reading a paper. (*Producing a large scroll*) ...
>
> *The Rev. Dr. Folliott:* I hate lectures over the bottle. But pray, sir, what is political economy?
>
> *Mr. MacQuedy:* Political economy is to the state what domestic economy is to the family.
>
> *The Rev. Dr. Folliott:* No such thing, sir. In the family there is a *pater-familias,* who regulates the distribution, and takes care that there shall be no such thing in the household as one dying of hunger, while another dies of surfeit. In the state it is all hunger at one end, and all surfeit at the other. (Ch. VI.)

This was an argument which appealed to Mr. Toogood (Robert Owen), who declared that 'It is the distribution that must be looked to: it is the *paterfamilias* that is wanting in the state'.

The beginnings of bureaucracy, so dear to the Benthamites, were satirised in the persons of the Charity Commissioners, who came to hold an enquiry into the state of the public charities of the village. Their enquiries discover a single charity of one pound per year.

> *The Rev. Dr. Folliott:* They have come here in a chaise and four, to make a fuss about a pound per annum, which, after all, they leave as it was. I wonder who pays them for their trouble, and how much.
>
> *Mr. Appletwig:* The public pay for it, sir. It is a job of the learned friend whom you admire so much (i.e. Lord Brougham). It makes away with public money in salaries, and private money in lawsuits, and does no particle of good to any living soul.
>
> *The Rev. Dr. Folliott:* Ay, ay, Mr. Appletwig; that is just the sort of public service to be looked for from the learned friend. Oh, the learned friend! the learned friend! He is the evil genius of everything that falls in his way.' (Ch. VIII.)

If Peacock disliked the materialism and the bureaucracy of the *laissez-faire* school and the Benthamites, he disliked some of the romantic poets almost as much. Wordsworth and Southey appeared as Mr. Wilful Wontsee and Mr. Rumplesack Shantsee, visionaries of Utopia and Pantisocracy who turned their coats for their own advantage. Coleridge he attacked, both for his desertion of his early principles of liberty, and for the obscurity of his German metaphysics. In *Nightmare Abbey* he appears as Mr. Flosky (=a lover of shadows). 'Mystery was his mental element. He lived in the midst of that visionary world in which nothing is but what is not. He dreamed with his eyes open, and saw ghosts dancing round him at noontide. He had been in his youth an enthusiast for liberty, and had hailed the dawn of the French Revolution as the promise of a day that was to banish war and slavery, and every form of vice and misery, from the face of the earth. Because all this was not done, he deduced that nothing was done; and from this deduction, according to his system of logic, he drew a conclusion that worse than nothing was done; that the overthrow of the feudal fortresses of tyranny and superstition was the greatest calamity that had ever befallen mankind; and that their only hope was to rake the rubbish together, and rebuild it without any of those loopholes by which the light had originally crept in. To qualify himself for a coadjutor in this laudable task, he plunged into the central opacity of Kantian metaphysics, and lay *perdu* several years in transcendental darkness, till the common daylight of common sense became intolerable to his eyes.' (Ch. I.) Later Mr. Flosky commented that the 'rage for novelty is the bane of literature. Except my works and those of my particular friends, nothing is good that is not as old as Jeremy Taylor: and, *entre nous*, the best parts of my friends' books were either written or suggested by myself.' (Ch. V.) This was a palpable hit at the great influence which Coleridge had on the works of Wordsworth, Southey and others. In *Crotchet Castle* Coleridge appears again, now in subdued light, as Mr. Skionar, totally opposed to Utilitarianism, and still expounding transcendental philosophy. 'Transcendentalism is the philosophy of intuition, the development of universal convictions; truths which are inherent on the organisation of mind, which cannot be obliterated, though they may be obscured, by superstitious prejudice on the one hand, and by Aristotelian logic on the other. . . . There is only one true logic, which is the transcendental; and this can prove only the one true philosophy, which is also the transcendental. The logic of your modern Athens can prove everything equally, and that is, in my opinion, tantamount to proving nothing at all.' (Ch. II.) Lady Clarinda declares that Skionar 'has got an ill name by keeping bad company. He has two dear friends, Mr. Wilful Wontsee, and Mr. Rumplesack Shantsee, poets of some note, who used to see visions of Utopia, and pure republics beyond the Western deep: but finding that these El Dorados brought them no revenue, they turned their vision-seeing faculty into the more profitable channel of espying all sorts of virtues in the high and mighty, who were able and willing to pay for the discovery'.

CC

The tory squirearchy appear as villains personified by Sir Simon Steeltrap, of Steeltrap Lodge, Member for Crouching-Curtown, Justice of Peace for the county, and Lord of the United Manors of Spring-gun and Treadmill, a great preserver of game and public morals. 'By administering the laws which he assists in making, he disposes, at his pleasure, of the land and its live stock, including all the two-legged varieties, with and without feathers, in a circumference of several miles round Steeltrap Lodge. He has enclosed commons and woodlands; abolished cottage-gardens; taken the village cricket-ground into his own park, out of pure regard to the sanctity of Sunday; shut up footpaths and alehouses, (all but those which belong to his electioneering friend, Mr. Quassia, the brewer;) put down fairs and fiddlers; committed many poachers; shot a few; convicted one third of the peasantry; suspected the rest; and passed nearly the whole of them through a wholesome course of prison discipline, which has finished their education at the expense of the county.' (Ch. V.)

Mr. Chainmail, in fact Sir Edward Strachey, Peacock's friend, represented the romantic return to mediaevalism. 'He is', Lady Clarinda reported, 'fond of old poetry, and is something of a poet himself. He is deep in monkish literature, and holds that the best state of society was that of the twelfth century, when nothing was going forward but fighting, feasting and praying, which he says are the three great purposes for which man was made. He laments bitterly over the inventions of gunpowder, steam, and gas, which he says have ruined the world. He has a large hall, adorned with rusty pikes, shields, helmets, swords, and tattered banners, and furnished with yew-tree chairs, and two long, old, worm-eaten oak tables, where he dines with all his household, after the fashion of his favourite age.' (Ch. V.) To Mr. MacQuedy the twelfth century was a period of 'brutality, ignorance, fanaticism and tyranny'. To Mr. Chainmail it was the age of chivalry, of Richard I, of Magna Carta, 'the first step of liberty', and a sturdy and independent peasantry. For MacQuedy Sir Walter Scott had painted too bright a picture of the middle ages, for Mr. Chainmail not bright enough. Dr. Folliott, as usual, had the last word. Since they differed in this way, it appeared likely that Sir Walter Scott had got the picture correctly. 'My quarrel with him is, that his works contain nothing worth quoting; and a book that furnishes no quotations is, *me judice*, no book.' In any case, historical comparisons were difficult things to make. 'Gentlemen, you will never settle this controversy, till you have first settled what is good for man in this world; the great question *de finibus*, which has puzzled all philosophers.' (Ch. IX.)

Mr. Chainmail argued against Mr. MacQuedy that in some ways the twelfth century was superior to their own age. 'I do not see, in all your boasted improvements, any compensation for the religious charity of the twelfth century. I do not see any compensation for that kindly feeling which, within their own little communities, bound the several classes of society together, while full scope was left for the development of natural character, wherein individuals differed as conspicuously as in costume. Now, we all wear one conventional dress, one conventional face; we have no bond of union, but pecuniary interest; we talk any thing that comes uppermost, for talking's sake, and without expecting to be believed; we have no nature, no simplicity, no picturesqueness: every thing about us is as artificial and as complicated as our steam-machinery.' (Ch. IX.)

He was equally scathing about the achievements of science. 'You have given the name of a science to what is yet an imperfect enquiry; and the upshot of your so-called science is this, that you increase the wealth of a nation by increasing in it the quantity of things which are produced by labour; no matter what they are, no matter how produced, no matter how distributed. The greater the quantity of labour that has gone to the production of the quantity of things in a community, the richer is the community. That is your doctrine. Now, I say, if this be so, riches are not the object for a community to aim at. I say, the nation is best off, in relation to other nations, which has the greatest quantity of the common necessaries of life distributed among the greatest number of persons; which has the greatest number of honest hearts and stout arms united in a common interest, willing to offend no one, but ready to fight in defence of their own community against all the rest of the world, because they have something in it worth fighting for. The moment you admit that one class of things, without any reference to what they respectively cost, is better worth having than another; that a smaller commercial value, with one mode of distribution, is better than a greater commercial value, with another mode of distribution, the whole of that curious fabric of postulates and dogmas which you call the science of political economy, tumbles to pieces.' (Ch. X.)

The final scene of the book was a splendid Christmas Day mediaeval feast at Chainmail Hall, which was however interrupted by an attack by Captain Swing and the agrarian rioters,[1] final proof to Dr. Folliott of 'the march of mind'. 'It has marched into my rick-yard, and set my stacks on fire, with chemical materials most scientifically compounded. It has marched up to the door of my vicarage, a hundred and fifty strong; ordered me to surrender half my tithes; consumed all the provisions I had provided for my audit feast, and drunk up my old October. It has marched in through my back-parlour, in the dead of night. . . . All this comes of education.' (Ch. XVII.) As an accompaniment to the feast, he declared, 'here is a piece of the dark ages we did not bargain for. Here is the Jacquerie. Here is the march of mind with a witness'. On this occasion the rioters were soon dispersed, and with this uncomfortable reminder of the social discontents of the new age, the guests returned to enjoy a wassail-bowl in true mediaeval style.

It is not necessary to attempt to identify Peacock with the views of any one of the characters in *Crotchet Castle*. His main purpose was to poke fun at the many system-makers of his day. He was always hostile to the tories, without being an adherent of the whigs. He had none of Southey's interest in the schemes of Robert Owen, and he was hostile to the radicalism of Lord Brougham. He smiled at the ineffectual radicalism of Shelley and the posturing of Byron. In spite of his close friendship with the Utilitarians, he was hostile to the cold theories of the *laissez-faire* economists. He was more than a little attracted by the mediaevalism of the Romantics, and indeed wrote two stories of mediaeval times,[2] but he detested Coleridge, and thought poorly of the achievements of Sir Walter Scott. The appearance of the agrarian rioters in *Crotchet Castle* reveals the nervousness he experienced at the troubled times of the whig ministry of 1830. Perhaps the most we can say is that he was a warm-hearted individualist with an acute understanding of the controversies of his day. After *Crotchet Castle* he was silent for nearly thirty years, when in 1860 he published *Gryll Grange*, a kindly comment on the Victorian age, in which one comment stands out with especial freshness: 'Science is one thing and wisdom is another. . . . I almost think it is the ultimate destiny of science to exterminate the human race.'

NOTES

[1] A reference to the agrarian riots of 1831.
[2] *Maid Marion* and *The Misfortunes of Elphin*.

The Chief Works of Principal Authors Mentioned

Anti-Jacobin Review (1798–9)
JANE AUSTEN (1775–1817)
  Sense and Sensibility (1811)
  Northanger Abbey (1817)
WILLIAM BLAKE (1757–1827)
  Songs of Innocence (1789)
  The Marriage of Heaven and Hell (1790)
  America (1793)
  Songs of Experience (1794)
  The Book of Urizen (1794)
  Jerusalem (1794)
  The Book of Los (1795)
  Four Zoas (1800)
  Milton (1804)
EDMUND BURKE (1729–1797)
  A Vindication of Natural Society (1756)
  A Philosophical Enquiry into the Sublime and Beautiful (1756)
  Observations on the Present State of the Nation (1769)
  On the Causes of the Present Discontents (1770)
  Speeches and Correspondence
  Reflections on the Revolution in France (1790)
  An Appeal from the New to the Old Whigs (1791)
LORD BYRON (1788–1824)
  Hours of Idleness (1807)
  English Bards and Scotch Reviewers (1809)
  Childe Harold's Pilgrimage (1812–18)
  The Giaour (1813)
  The Bride of Abydos (1813)
  The Corsair (1814)
  Lava (1814)
  The Siege of Corinth (1816)
  The Prisoner of Chillon (1816)

Manfred (1817)
Don Juan (1819–24)
The Vision of Judgment (1822)
WILLIAM COBBETT (1762–1835)
Political Register (1802–35)
Rural Rides (1830)
S. T. COLERIDGE (1772–1834)
Lyrical Ballads (1792)
The Friend (1809–10)
The Statesman's Manual (1816)
Poems (1816–17)
Biographia Literaria (1817)
Philosophical Lectures (1818–19)
On the Constitution of Church and State (1830)
Table Talk (1835)
WILLIAM COWPER (1731–1800)
Olney Hymns (1779)
Table Talk (1782)
The Task (1785)
Letters (1911)
GEORGE CRABBE (1754–1832)
The Library (1781)
The Village (1783)
The Parish Register (1807)
The Borough (1810)
Tales in Verse (1812)
Tales of the Hall (1819)
Edinburgh Review (1802+)
WILLIAM GODWIN (1756–1836)
An Enquiry Concerning Political Justice (1793)
Caleb Williams (1794)
B. R. HAYDON (1786–1846)
Lectures on Painting and Design (1844)
Life (1853)
Correspondence and Table-Talk (1876)
WILLIAM HAZLITT (1778–1830)
Essay on the Principles of Human Action (1805)
Free Thoughts on Public Affairs (1806)
A Reply to . . . The Rev. Malthus (1807)
The Round Table (1817)
Political Essays (1819)
Table Talk (1821–2)
The Spirit of the Age (1825)

JOHN KEATS (1795–1821)
  Poems (1817)
  Endymion (1818)
  Odes (1819)
  Poems (1820)
RICHARD PAYNE KNIGHT (1750–1824)
  Principles of Taste (1805)
WALTER SAVAGE LANDOR (1775–1864)
  Poems (1795)
  Gebir (1798)
  Imaginary Conversations (1824–9)
ROBERT MALTHUS (1766–1834)
  Essay on the Principle of Population (1798)
  Principles of Political Economy (1820)
HANNAH MORE (1745–1833)
  Thoughts on the Importance of the Manners of the Great to General
    Society (1788)
  An Estimate of the Religion of the Fashionable World (1791)
  Village Politics by Will Chip (1793)
  A Cure for Melancholy (1794)
  Tom White, the Post-Boy ⎫
  The Shepherd of Salisbury Plain ⎬ Cheap Repository Tracts 1795–8
  The History of Mr. Fantom ⎭
ROBERT OWEN (1771–1858)
  A New View of Society (1813)
  Address to the Inhabitants of New Lanark (1816)
THOMAS PAINE (1737–1809)
  Common Sense (1776)
  The Rights of Man (1791)
  The Age of Reason (1794)
THOMAS LOVE PEACOCK (1785–1866)
  Headlong Hall (1816)
  Nightmare Abbey (1818)
  Maid Marion (1822)
  The Misfortunes of Elphin (1829)
  Crotchet Castle (1831)
  Gryll Grange (1861)
SIR UVEDALE PRICE (1747–1829)
  Essays on the Picturesque (1794)
AUGUSTUS CHARLES PUGIN (1762–1832)
  Specimens of Gothic Architecture (1821–3)
Quarterly Review (1809+)
MRS. ANN RADCLIFFE (1764–1823)
  The Castle of Athlin and Dunbayne (1789)

The Sicilian Romance (1790)
The Romance of the Forest (1791)
The Mysteries of Udolpho (1794)
The Italian (1797)
SIR JOSHUA REYNOLDS (1723–1792)
  Discourses (1769–90)
DAVID RICARDO (1772–1823)
  Principles of Political Economy and Taxation (1817)
  Notes on Malthus (1820)
SIR WALTER SCOTT (1771–1832)
  The Minstrelsy of the Scottish Border (1802)
  The Lay of the Last Minstrel (1805)
  Marmion (1808)
  Waverley (1814)
  The Heart of Midlothian (1819)
  The Monastery (1820)
  The Abbot (1820)
  Kenilworth (1821)
  The Fortunes of Nigel (1822)
  Redgauntlet (1824)
PERCY BYSSHE SHELLEY (1792–1822)
  Queen Mab (1813)
  Alastor (1816)
  The Revolt of Islam (1818)
  The Cenci (1819)
  Prometheus Unbound (1820)
  Swellfoot the Tyrant (1820)
  Epipsychidion (1821)
  Adonais (1821)
  A Defence of Poetry (1821)
  Hellas (1822)
  Posthumous Poems
SYDNEY SMITH (1771–1845)
  Edinburgh Review Articles
  Letters of Peter Plymley (1807)
ROBERT SOUTHEY (1774–1843)
  Wat Tyler (1794)
  Poems (1794)
  Joan of Arc (1795)
  A Vision of Judgment (1821)
  Prose Works
HORACE WALPOLE (1717–1797)
  Letters
  Some Anecdotes of Painting in England (1762)

Index